T0244320

# Religion, Power, and Illusion

## A Genealogy of Religious Belief

Patrick J. Hurley

Prometheus Books

Essex, Connecticut

 Prometheus Books

An imprint of Globe Pequot, the trade division of
The Rowman & Littlefield Publishing Group, Inc.
4501 Forbes Boulevard, Suite 200, Lanham, Maryland 20706
www.rowman.com

Distributed by NATIONAL BOOK NETWORK

British Library Cataloguing in Publication Information Available

Library of Congress Cataloging-in-Publication Data Available

ISBN 9781633888401 (cloth : alk. paper) | ISBN 9781633888418 (epub)

♾™ The paper used in this publication meets the minimum requirements of
American National Standard for Information Sciences—Permanence of Paper
for Printed Library Materials, ANSI/NISO Z39.48-1992.

# CONTENTS

# PREFACE

The idea for this book was conceived during a trip to Egypt in 2011. Together with my wife, Linda, I visited all the tourist spots including the pyramids at Giza, the Valley of the Kings, and the massive temple complex at Karnak. I immediately came to realize that it is one thing to see images of these wonders in books and on TV and quite another to rest your hands on the huge blocks composing the pyramids, to climb up them (if for only eight or ten feet), to walk hundreds of yards through tunnels cut in solid rock to the tomb at the end where the pharaoh's mummy was interred, and to lean against the great pillars that composed the temples. The power needed to produce these giant structures was almost beyond my imagination. And where did that power come from? I was told that it came from religion. The priests of ancient Egypt, together with the pharaoh, had convinced the people that they were in communion with the gods, and if the people did their bidding, they would, when the time came, ensure a successful transition to the afterlife. Making it to the afterlife meant everything to these people.

While in Egypt, I was lucky to meet up with Kent Weeks, the Egyptologist who discovered the famous lost tomb. During an evening's discussion devoted to the marvels of ancient Egypt, we turned to the topic of religion. When I recalled my understanding of the connection between the pyramids and religion, he expressed his agreement, and he then said, "Don't you see that the same kind of thing is going on in Roman Catholicism?" If Catholics believe what the pope and the priests tell them and live their lives accordingly, they will be rewarded with a heavenly afterlife. Kent's observation was immediately intriguing. Having once been a good Catholic altar boy, I did know something about the Church of Rome and had a long-standing interest in religion, so I began to wonder if Kent's insight might be the key to understanding the nature of religion in general. Also, few people today would consider belief in the Egyptian gods, those entities having the heads of jackals, rams, and falcons, to be anything short of an illusion. Thus, I was led to wonder, could it be the case that all religious beliefs are illusions?

After returning to the United States, this question continued to haunt me. The subjects of religion and the existence of God come up all the time in philosophy, and I was already fairly well versed in that field since I had taught it for many years. Also I knew something about Christian theology. But I would have to know a lot more about a great many other things. That realization led to a ten-year-long inquiry into Egyptology, anthropology, biblical archaeology, Old Testament studies, Egyptian mathematics, the psychology of memory, the biological theory of natural selection, early Christian heresies, ancient Jewish history, and other topics. Could I come up with any genuine evidence to support the idea that all religious beliefs are illusions created by priests to augment their own power—power to build things and power over people's lives? I will let the reader be the judge of that.

For their invaluable assistance, I want to extend my thanks to my wife and colleague in philosophy, Linda Peterson, for her insights, for helping me acquire research materials, and for patiently putting up with me while I wrote this book; to my colleague, Brian Clack, for introducing me to the work of James George Frazer, to Freud's idea of being at home in the *Unheimliche*, and for suggesting a great publisher; to Kent Weeks for his insights about religion; to my friend and neighbor, Larry Behrendt, for calling my attention to the importance of oral traditions in religion and for his many observations about Judaism; and to his wife, Stephanie Barbe Hammer, for triggering my interest in Michel Foucault and for pointers on writing a query letter.

Throughout this book, quotations from the Bible are taken from the New International Version.

# CHAPTER ONE
# OVERVIEW

## Religion and Power

The year was 1077. A young man dressed in sackcloth, the garb of a penitent, was lying chest down with arms outstretched on the floor of a large room in a castle in northern Italy. His body took the shape of a cross, and he was begging forgiveness from a much older man seated on a throne. The older man was not in a forgiving mood because he doubted the younger man's sincerity. To make his point, he had required that the younger man stand barefoot in the snow, outside the castle, for the better part of three days while he decided whether to see him. It was an especially harsh winter that year, and January was the coldest month, but the penitent thought he could prove his sincerity by living up to the test. Happily for him, two prominent figures interceded on his behalf, and his plea was granted. The older man seated on the throne was Pope Gregory VII, and the younger man prostrate on the floor was King Henry IV of Germany. A few months earlier, Gregory had excommunicated Henry and relieved all of his subjects of their duty of loyalty to him. By granting forgiveness on this day, Gregory erased the stain of excommunication and welcomed Henry back into the Church. This, in turn, restored Henry's status in the eyes of his subjects. Henry's sin had been to elevate priests to the office of bishop without the approval of the pope, which outraged Gregory. Gregory thought that he had ultimate authority in these matters, and he reacted in the strongest way possible.

Gregory's action in excommunicating Henry marked the first time in history that a pope had excommunicated and deposed a king. Of course, popes had removed bishops but never a monarch, much less one as important as Henry. Thanks to his reinstatement, in just a few years, Henry would be named Holy Roman emperor, the most powerful man in the Western world. However, by his action in 1077, Pope Gregory had shown that he was even more powerful than King Henry. How is it possible for a religious authority to acquire such power? Doesn't religion deal with spiritual, unworldly matters? Answering these questions relates to the central purpose of this book. And the answer I propose is that religious leaders acquire power by creating and sustaining illusions. Throughout the centuries, these illusions build on themselves, and they generate extraordinary power for their creators. One of those illusions at the time of Henry IV was the belief that excommunication causes such a serious separation from God that if the sinner should die in that state, he would suffer everlasting punishment in hell. By extension, the same threat might attach to any subject who vowed allegiance to an excommunicated king. It is for this reason that excommunication was perilous to Henry's political ambitions.

Religious power over civil authority may have reached a zenith in the eleventh century, but by no means did it fade away in the years to follow. Nor was it connected exclusively with the Church of Rome. Today, in the United States, Protestant evangelicals have amassed enormous power, and their support has elected numerous politicians to higher office. These actions have occurred despite laws and constitutional provisions that mandate separation of church and state. Additional evidence of this power is ubiquitous. "In God we trust" appears on coins and currency; both houses of Congress begin their daily sessions with prayers offered by official chaplains whose salaries are paid by the taxpayers; "One nation under God" is in the pledge of allegiance; Christmas, the birthday of Jesus, is a national holiday; and nativity scenes appear on public property. Outside the United States, religion exerts great influence on the nation of Israel, which was named a specifically Jewish state at the time of its formation in 1948. Both Israel and the Vatican have diplomatic missions that influence political decisions in many countries. The nation of Iran is governed by ayatollahs, who are Islamic clerics. The reigning monarch of Great Britain is also the official head of the Church of England, and Catholic bishops exert power on the leadership of many nations.

Another kind of power is monetary power. Simply put, religion generates massive quantities of money for its promoters. A modern example is offered by the dozens of televangelists who operate in several countries. One of the pioneers of this business in the United States was Oral Roberts, a minister in the Pentecostal Holiness Church, who made a name for himself as a faith healer. At the time of his death in 2009, he is reported to have been worth $117 million. The wealthiest of the group appears to be the charismatic preacher Kenneth Copeland, who runs Kenneth Copeland Ministries in Fort Worth, Texas, and who, in 2018, was said to be worth $717 million. Other examples are provided by organized churches that operate worldwide. The Mormon Church, which has been in existence for less than 200 years, has a net worth of $50 billion to $100 billion. The Vatican, the headquarters of the Roman Catholic Church, is widely thought to have a net worth well in excess of $100 billion. And this is just the small city-state located inside the city of Rome. When the entire Roman Catholic Church is taken into account, which comprises some 220,000 parishes worldwide, the net worth exceeds many trillions of dollars, making it the wealthiest organization on the planet.

A third type of power exercised by every religion is power over human thinking. This is the most important kind of power because it is the source of all the other forms. Central to this control is the belief that religious leaders are in communication with a divine being and that whoever is in touch with the divine speaks the truth. Therefore, when such leaders issue proclamations about the rightness or wrongness of human actions, those commands are thought to be grounded in truth because they originate with God. For the same reason, whatever is stated in certain books (the Quran, the Gospels, and the Torah) is true. This includes the belief that there is only one God, that angels exist, that Jesus is divine, that the mother of Jesus was (and is) a virgin, that sin exists, that sins can be forgiven by priests, that humans will be judged by their actions, that there is a life after death available to persons who have faith and live righteously, and that a place of everlasting suffering is reserved for those who fail to believe the right things or who adopt unapproved lifestyles. In addition, certain states of mind are forbidden by some religious sects. These include sexual lust and coveting the property of another. To ensure that these latter commandments are obeyed, there is the underlying belief that God sees one's innermost thoughts and takes them into account in the final judgment. Religion thus invades the most intimate aspects of human life.

## Sources of Religious Power

How did the religions of the world succeed in amassing such extraordinary power—political power, monetary power, and control over human thought? A conventional answer is that religious leaders and religious organizations are especially close to God and that God has endowed them with power to enable them to carry out his will. This is the supernatural explanation. The explanation developed on the pages that follow is that the power attaching to religion has nothing to do with any independently existing deity but is the natural product of religious promoters milking power from their followers. They do this by creating gods which they then purport to be in communion with. They then reinforce the god idea with many supporting entities, such as sin, prayer, ritual, holy books, and church buildings. These entities amplify the natural and relatively meager power of the promoters of religion to the point where it vastly exceeds what they are capable of producing by their unaided labors. I call these reinforcing entities "constructs," and I will treat them in greater detail shortly. For now, a single example will suffice. Television is a construct, and it reinforces the power of ordinary preachers, allowing them to become televangelists. Without it, these preachers could never generate the kind of wealth that they do with it.

However, merely saying that the promoters of religion armed with prayers, churches, and holy books milk power from their followers provides only half the answer to the power question. The other half concerns how the promoters of religion are able to persuade large numbers of potential followers to go along with the program. How does it happen that the potential followers seem incapable of seeing what the promoters are up to and just fall in line like sheep to the slaughter? The answer, I think, is that the promoters cloak the entire process in illusion, and this keeps the followers in a state of constant confusion. The persistent fog clouds the mind, and it prevents the intended prey from reasoning clearly about claims that obviously violate common sense. In all religions, the central construct is an entity called God that stands as an object of prayer, worship, and sacrifice. The creators of this entity misrepresent their own role in the creation process. Instead of revealing themselves as the source of the God entity, they say that it existed in its own right long before any human beings appeared on the scene. However, they then say that they have the ability to interact with, to bargain with, and to influence the God entity, so they are uniquely situated to secure favors from it. If the potential followers agree to go along, they will share in those favors.

What makes prospective believers especially vulnerable to religious illusion is the fact that modern society is thoroughly saturated with religious constructs, each of which serves to condition the mind of the potential believer to the reasonableness of religious claims. In North America, South America, Europe, and Australia, every small town and village has a church or two, and every big city has dozens or hundreds of them, as well as synagogues, mosques, and impressive cathedrals. Many of them have been around for hundreds of years, and they are as real as the ground that we walk on. If these structures, all of them constructs, are supposed to house a God entity, then ordinary people come to believe that this entity must be as real as the bricks and stone that compose them. Also, every week, thousands of people are seen entering these structures to worship the God entity who metaphorically dwells therein. Can it possibly be the case that they do so to worship an entity that is less than totally real? And practically every home has a book (Bible, Torah, Quran, or Book of Mormon) that is thought to convey information about the God entity. The lineage of these books goes back hundreds or thousands of years. Can it possibly be the case that books that are so old could convey a message that is wrong? Also, the message they express is believed by millions. Can it be the case that all of these people have been duped? And every museum of art contains magnificent paintings that depict important events relating to the lives of religious figures. Surely, the events they depict must have really happened. Finally, most believers have parents who are believers and who have indoctrinated them from an early age. In the face of such massive inducement, it is a wonder that anyone could be an atheist.

## Illusion

Most people are aware of the fact that there are different kinds of illusion. There are optical illusions where a pair of lines drawn on paper seem to converge but in fact do not. There are illusions created by magicians where rabbits appear to come forth from hats but in fact do not. There are neurotic illusions where people spend much of their lives living a hopelessly unrealistic dream. But none of these captures the kind of illusion that the current study sees as underlying religious belief. The latter illusion is what I call "factitious illusion," from the Latin word *facere*, "to make." This is an illusion manufactured, or created, by other people, resulting in the formation of an erroneous belief that alters the victim's perspective on things, worldview, or hopes for the future. For an example of how such an illusion is produced, consider the following scenario.

Suppose a person asks to borrow $10 and promises to pay you back the next day. You take him at his word and lend him the money, but instead of paying you back, the borrower uses the money to buy drugs. The decision to lend the money was an error in judgment. You should have taken some precaution to ensure that the borrower was not a drug user. But the decision did not result in an illusion because you did not expect to gain anything by making the loan, least of all anything important. On the other hand, suppose that this person asks to borrow $10,000 and promises to pay you back $20,000 in three months. You lend him the money, but, again, the borrower uses the money to buy drugs. Here we do have an illusion because you were really hoping to make $10,000 on the deal. Every day, you looked forward to being paid back, and you dwelled on all the possible things you might do with the extra money. Perhaps you would go on a cruise, and you dream of gazing out into the open ocean toward a glowing sunset. Or you might buy a piece of jewelry, and you dream about how it would look on your finger or around your neck. You imagine the admiring comments of those who see you wearing it. In short, you are living an illusion. Factitious illusions always involve matters of relative importance, and the expected payback is usually some distance into the future. Generalizing from the loan example, a factitious illusion is a mistaken belief resulting from an error in judgment. The error in judgment is induced by some other person who plays on the believer's hopes and fears. In this case, the borrower plays on the lender's hope to earn an easy $10,000. But from the start, the borrower never intended to repay the loan.

Extending this example to religion, the present study concludes that religious beliefs are factitious illusions. They are illusions induced by other people who play on the hopes and fears of their victims. These hopes and fears include many things, such as getting a good job, avoiding a life-threatening illness, or being rewarded in the afterlife. The inducers of religious illusion assure their victims that through prayer, worship, and sacrifice, their hopes will be realized and their fears averted. These assurances involve an element of trickery, so they succeed in persuading even highly intelligent individuals. Even the most intelligent person can be tricked into something. Also, like the person who is tricked into extending the loan, the agreement to become a religious believer involves an element of bad judgment. But it is not always the believer himself who exercises the bad judgment; it may be this person's distant ancestors. Many highly intelligent people fall into religion because their parents were religious or they live in a very religious community. But somewhere back in time, some ancestor or early member of that community failed to exercise good judgment in signing on to their beliefs.

The idea that religious beliefs are illusions is hardly a new one. Sigmund Freud said the same thing nearly 100 years ago in *The Future of an Illusion*. According to Freud, religion is grounded in neurosis. All religious people, he claims, are neurotic. Many people grow out of this condition in early adulthood, but if this fails to happen, they can be relieved of their affliction (at least in theory) by a lengthy course of psychoanalysis. The kind of illusion envisioned in the current study is quite different from Freud's. Whereas neurotic illusion is generated by the person who is the subject of the illusion, factitious illusion is generated by other, sometimes unscrupulous human beings who produce it to augment their own power. Thus, according to the theory developed here, religious belief is not the child of neurosis; rather, it is the child of power.

There are multiple sources of factitious illusion. Political figures create illusions to gain an advantage over opponents. Advertisers create illusions to sell products. Securities brokers create illusions to line up investors. Trial lawyers create illusions to mislead jurors. In all of these cases, the subject of the illusion is something detectable by the senses. The subject matter of religious illusion is quite different. It consists of gods of various kinds, angels, demons, sin, grace, heaven, and hell, all of which lie outside the realm of sensory experience. The gods of religion typically have no size, color, shape, or location. They emit no auditory stimuli; they have no fragrance; and they have no warmth, coldness, or any other tactile qualities. As a result, religious illusion is hard to detect, and if a believer is victimized, there is usually no recourse. If a politician makes promises and fails to carry through, voters can recall this person or at least refuse to vote that way in the next election. But if a promoter of religion promises a heavenly reward in exchange for prayers and sacrifice, there is no way in this life for anyone to tell if the promise was fulfilled, and even if there were, there is nothing a believer can do if the promise falls through.

## Priests

I use the general term "priest" to refer to the promoters of religion. They include all the ministers, rabbis, pastors, priests, bishops, televangelists, preachers, mullahs, monks, and ayatollahs, both male and female, operating anywhere in the world. As so defined, the chief function of priests everywhere is to create gods and to sustain them in existence. The kind of gods they create are those that stand as objects of prayer, worship, and sacrifice. In ancient times, sacrifice involved the slaughter of some animal or the burning of grain or something else related to human sustenance; in other words, it involved the giving up of something valued by the believer. Today, it means giving up money or property, and since whatever is sacrificed usually ends up in the hands of priests, offering sacrifice increases priestly power. Worship serves to make the believer subject to the god entity. Through worship, the believer expresses his or her submissive status in relation to the god, and this intensifies and defines the relationship between the believer and that entity. In exchange for worship, the believer expects to receive something from the god entity. Prayer is the means of expressing what that something is—something that benefits either the believer himself or some other person. To improve the chances of receiving the benefit, the believer offers sacrifice.

Given that the promoters of religion send a message that is thoroughly misleading, we might be tempted to accuse them all of blatant dishonesty. The problem with such an accusation is that it conflicts with actual experience. In the experience of most, priests are kind, decent, caring people who would never intentionally engage in any form of deception. They comfort people in times of sorrow, encourage them in despair, and in desperate times even help provide for their material needs. How could such caring individuals ever be complicit in something dishonest? The answer lies in the fact that the dishonesty was created hundreds or thousands of years ago. At least for the most part, it is not today's priests who initiate the misrepresentation; rather, it is their predecessors. The fraud is ingredient in our culture, and the priests of today only help to sustain it. As a result, most of them are as much victims of the illusion as they are perpetrators of it. The vast majority firmly believe that there is a God who listens to human prayers, that this God replies to prayers, and that the process is facilitated by making people more religious. As they see it, in promoting religion, they are acting to bring people closer to God.

However, some of today's priests are highly educated, and some have studied logic and are sensitive to the fact that circular reasoning is rampant in religion. Also, some are naturally blessed with critical minds and can glimpse, however briefly and on rare occasions, that not all is right with religious thinking. Some have flashes of insight that reveal the foundations of religion as shaky at best and nonexistent at worst. But all too often, these gifted individuals respond with silence. They fail to take seriously questions such as how there can be thousands of religions that preach different things when each claims to have the final truth. And they fail to call out the more outrageous among them, the faith healers, for their blatant chicanery. Perhaps their thinking is that if they rock others' boats, they may end up rocking their own; but if this is the case, their silence amounts to an admission of guilt. And they fail to point out that divine intervention never occurs in many cases (such as those suffering from certain diseases), but if God never intervenes in these cases, can we be sure that he intervenes in any? To remain silent on these occasions is to be dishonest.

## Constructs

A construct, as the term is used here, is any arrangement of ideas, beliefs, memories, physical things, or human beings that can be used to achieve some purpose. Several of the more important types of constructs are classified as follows. A physical construct is composed of physical materials, such as wood, stone, metal, paper, cloth, and so on. They include buildings, weapons, works of art, machines, clothing, and books. Power uses constructs to augment its own potency, and this is easy to see in the case of physical constructs. For example, one's physical strength, which is a certain kind of power, is increased in a combat situation by weapons. A warrior with a tomahawk is usually more powerful than a warrior without one. Similarly, a priest with a church, even a modest one, is usually more powerful than a priest without a church. A priest with a prayer book or Bible is more powerful than a priest without any books. Physical constructs are essential to religion, and they include church buildings, cathedrals, synagogues, temples, mosques, religious works of art, musical pieces, holy books, priestly vestments, candles, organs, statues, crosses, scrolls, and other such things. Many of these things are exquisitely beautiful, and the aesthetic feelings they elicit become attached to the religion they represent. Church buildings are taken to be houses of God, and they provide a place for believers to enter and be with God. Also, many of these structures have been around for centuries, and this feature adds importance and credibility to the associated beliefs. But most significantly, physical constructs are real. They are as real as the stone, wood, concrete, and steel used to build them. The best way to make an illusion appear to be real is to dress it up in real clothing.

A social construct is any kind of structure or organization uniting a group of people or their actions. In the secular realm, social constructs include corporations, partnerships, societies, political parties, labor unions, schools, cities, counties, and states. As with physical constructs, social constructs serve to increase the power of individuals or groups of individuals. The bargaining power of a worker is often increased by joining a labor union, the power of a person or group of people wanting to grow their wealth is increased by forming a partnership or corporation, and the power of an environmental activist to effect change is increased by forming or joining an organization. Similarly, the power of an aspiring religious leader is increased by forming a church (a religious sect) or working within an established church. Other social constructs that serve the same purpose are religious societies, schools, student groups, and other organizations. Another kind of social construct consists of rituals, festivals, holidays, pilgrimages, revivals, camp meetings, bar mitzvahs, baptisms, and public prayer sessions. All of these constructs connect religious beliefs with bodily actions, and this serves to ground those beliefs and to incorporate them in the believer's lived world. Also, holidays and festivals are particularly joyful and meaningful times, and by participating in the festivities, the believer links his or her beliefs with good feelings, happy times, and meaningful experiences.

A personal construct is composed of memories of other people. The memories we have of ourselves are constructs, too, but they are of less importance to the matter at hand than the memories of others. Such memories are based on our perceptions, both direct and indirect. For example, the knowledge we have of a next-door neighbor is a personal construct based on our direct interactions with this person and also on conversations we may have had with this person's spouse and friends. We compile the memories of these perceptions into a unit, and this unit is a personal construct. Because the totality of our perceptions relating to this person is inevitably limited and fragmentary, the personal construct that we form in our mind will never exactly reflect the full reality of this person. With people who are more remote from us, the construct that we form of them is usually even less accurate. Such constructs are based on newspaper articles, photographs, sound and video recordings, autobiographical pieces, biographies, and history books. But even these accounts are inevitably sketchy, and they often reveal nothing about the person's hopes, fears, ambitions, goals, likes, dislikes, and private feelings. The person may be a thief or child abuser, and these features might never be mentioned in the sources that come to our attention. If so, they would never enter into the personal construct we form of this individual. With people who have lived in the distant past, the challenge of forming an accurate personal construct is even greater. If the person lived so long ago that there were no newspapers, no electronic media, no trustworthy biographies, and no photographs or painted portraits and the person wrote nothing, it may be nearly impossible to form an accurate construct of this person. Such is the case with Moses, Jesus, and Muhammad. We may think that we know a great deal about these individuals, but what we think we know is a construct, and it may differ in countless ways from what the person was really like.

A belief construct is composed of beliefs knit together in a loose kind of way to form a moderately coherent amalgamation. Like personal constructs, belief constructs exist in our minds, and they relate to things and events in the world outside. They are affected by our values, education, social and economic status, family background, and overall outlook on the world. In the political sphere, belief constructs include liberalism, conservatism, socialism, libertarianism, patriotism, totalitarianism, and so on. In the United States, political conservatism includes beliefs about the importance of property rights, small government, free markets, social stability, and national defense. Political liberalism includes beliefs about the importance of equal opportunity, widespread education, universal suffrage, civil rights, social safety nets, and access to health care. Belief constructs tend to be vague, with the result that it may be impossible to determine who is a true liberal and who is a true conservative. All religions are belief constructs. They include Protestantism, Catholicism, Judaism, Mormonism, Islam, Hinduism, and so on. Catholicism includes belief in a triune God and belief that Jesus is the Son of God, that the mother of Jesus is a virgin, that the pope is the representative of God, that priests have the power to forgive sin, and many others. Protestantism includes the belief that faith in Jesus brings salvation, that every important doctrine is contained in the Bible, that Jesus is the only mediator between God and believers, and that the Bible can be correctly understood through individual interpretation. As is the case with other belief constructs, religious constructs tend to be vague, individuals on the fringe have uncertain status, and multiple factions exist (such as Orthodox Judaism and Reform Judaism) that reject the beliefs of other factions. Nevertheless, belief constructs provide order and meaning to the lives of those who are committed to them, and they often do so with little financial outlay.

A theoretical construct is a network of tightly linked concepts that adheres rigidly to clearly defined rules. Examples include science, philosophy, mathematics, and logic. Theoretical constructs can be confused with belief constructs because both are mental entities; they exist inside our minds. But the similarity ends there. First off, concepts are not beliefs. Concepts include such things as circularity, number, substance, cause, effect, energy, momentum, and so on. But beliefs are mental commitments, and they are expressed in terms of statements—not mere words. For example, "Demons exist," "There is only one God," "Prayers are efficacious," and "Faith is the key to salvation" are statements of belief. Since belief constructs are composed of beliefs, these constructs, as a whole, invite belief. But science, philosophy, and mathematics do not invite belief, at least not properly speaking. Of course, the scientist may believe tentatively that what his or her theory says about the world is true, but this tentative belief is always open to the possibility of refutation or alteration. The person who subscribes to a belief construct is almost never open to this possibility. Furthermore, theoretical constructs provide the basis for inferences that are true of necessity or at least high probability, but belief constructs generally do not. For example, knowing the mass of two heavenly bodies and the distance separating them allows the physicist or astronomer to infer with near certainty the gravitational attraction between them. But knowing the length of a prayer and the fervor of the one who prays does not allow anyone to compute the probability of the prayer's being answered. Theoretical constructs and belief constructs can also be distinguished by their purpose. Belief constructs usually aim at some kind of social change, such as relieving the plight of the poor or ending the practice of abortion, while science and philosophy aim at explaining things, arithmetic and geometry bring order to our intuitions of space and time, and logic brings order to our use of language.

A fictive construct is composed of products of the human imagination. Examples include the characters and situations found in novels. Captain Ahab, Madame Bovary, Jayne Eyre, and Atticus Finch are all fictive constructs assembled piece by piece throughout the course of the novel. The current study concludes that all the central elements of religion are fictive constructs. These include, most importantly, the god entity, together with multiple associated constructs, including angels, demons, sin, salvation, heaven, hell, divine covenants, divine law, and the meaning of rituals.

## Constructs and Illusion

Returning to the question of illusion, it is important to be clear where illusions fit in this account. First off, illusions are not the same thing as constructs. Thus, church buildings are constructs, but there is nothing illusory about them. They are made of wood or stone or some other building material, and these things are fully real. The illusion arises in connection with *beliefs about* constructs. The belief that a church building is a holy place and that it is, in some sense, the dwelling place of God is an illusion. The god entity is a construct, but this construct in itself is not an illusion. The illusion comes with the belief that the god entity really exists and wants to be prayed to, worshipped, and offered sacrifices to. The idea of sin is a religious construct, but the bare idea is not an illusion. The belief that sin actually exists, that it is offensive to God, and that it blocks our access to heaven is an illusion. However, not all beliefs about religious constructs are illusions. For example, the belief that a certain church building has a solid foundation is not an illusion. The belief that sin evokes fear of punishment in the mind of the sinner is not an illusion. Illusory beliefs are distinguished from those that are not illusory in that the illusory ones are always about or depend on the god construct. The belief that sin can land a person in hell depends on the idea that sin offends God, so God will punish the sinner.

## Religion

We are now in a position to provide a tentative definition for the term "religion." Religion is a collection of beliefs that are about or depend on a god construct. The central beliefs are those that are about the god entity. If the god construct consists of a single entity, the religion is monotheistic (such as Judaism, Christianity, or Islam); if it comprises multiple entities, the religion is polytheistic (such as Hinduism, Taoism, or Shinto); and if it consists of a single entity having three persons, the religion is most likely Christianity. The inclusion of additional beliefs about constructs further defines the religion. These include beliefs about holy books (the Torah, the New Testament, or the Quran), holy places (Jerusalem, Mecca, or Bethlehem), personal constructs (memories of Moses, Jesus, Muhammad, or Buddha), prayers (the Lord's Prayer, the Shema, Salah, or various mantras), architectural structures, clothing, rituals, angels, demons, and so on. This procedure allows for an unlimited number of outcomes, which is reflected in the thousands of different religions that have appeared throughout the years. Because any specific religion is an organized group of beliefs, it counts as a construct. Thus, any specific religion is a construct consisting of beliefs that are about or depend on other constructs. The most important of these constructs is the god construct.

## Atheolatrism

The theological stance supported by the arguments in this book is what I call "atheolatrism." I define it to designate the theological position that there are no gods that stand as objects of prayer, worship, and sacrifice—that is, no such gods existing independently of human thought. The term derives from the Greek words *theos*, meaning "god," and *latreia*, meaning "worship." By extension, the definition includes prayer and sacrifice as well. Atheolatrism does not mean the same thing as radical atheism, which holds there is no transcendent being of any kind; it simply means there are no independently existing divinities that are supposed to be prayed to, worshipped, and offered sacrifices to. Atheolatrism is open to the possibility that there are ultimate philosophical first principles that serve various purposes, such as the source of order in the universe or a necessary being that underlies contingent realities. The term does not imply that there are such beings but only that they might possibly exist as a requirement of some philosophical system. However, if such entities are deemed to exist, they cannot serve as objects of prayer, worship, or sacrifice. No philosophical principle could ever properly serve as an object of worship, nor could such a principle ever want to be worshipped, as does the god of religion. The term does not mean the same thing as agnosticism. Agnosticism means that we are incapable of knowing (now or forever) if there is such a thing as a divinity, and atheolatrism leaves open the possibility of such knowledge. And atheolatrism does not have the same meaning as deism, which holds that there is no god susceptible of a personal relation with humans. If there is any entity that serves as a first principle in some philosophical system, it might well qualify as a person and therefore be capable of relating to other persons. Further, atheolatrism does not imply any kind of materialism whereby everything that exists can be reduced to some kind of inert, mindless stuff stretched out in space and time. Such theories, I contend, cannot make sense of consciousness and subjectivity, which, I hold, are part of reality. As a result, atheolatrism does not preclude the persistence of consciousness after death (i.e., an afterlife). It merely says that if there is any such thing, it has nothing to do with any religion or any priests.

A requirement entailed by atheolatrism is that there be a strict line of demarcation drawn between religion and philosophy. Here I use the word "philosophy" broadly to include any kind of reasoned effort, however humble, to make sense of the general content of our experience. Religion and philosophy have totally different objectives and methodologies. If what I say about religion is correct, the objective of religion is to augment the power of priests, whereas the objective of philosophy is to explain things, namely, the content of our lived experience. The methodology of religion is to create constructs that are cloaked in illusion to entice potential believers, whereas the methodology of philosophy is to create theories that can be used to interpret and make sense of things such as the origin of knowledge, the meaning of truth, the relation between thinking and language, and the foundation of morality. The method of philosophy, as I see it, is quite close to the method of science, and this should hardly be surprising since science grew out of philosophy beginning in the seventeenth century. Also, the quality of mind that attends religion is quite different from what we find in philosophy. Religion seeks a kind of total commitment, a full-blown and unswerving belief that what the holy books and the church leaders say is the absolute truth. On the contrary, the kind of belief that attaches to philosophical theories is much more tentative. In science, if the results of experimentation should conflict with theory, the theory must be either modified, abandoned, or at least worked on until the conflict is resolved. Similarly in philosophy, if persistent experience should conflict with the theory, the philosophical attitude of mind requires that we be prepared to abandon or modify the theory.

What complicates matters is that religion and philosophy often talk about the same or similar topics, so the accounts can be muddled together. This occurs in a major way when religious thinkers borrow ideas from philosophical systems in an effort to make sense of what they are saying. Philosophical concepts are always clearer and more precise than the correlative notions in religion, so philosophy is highly useful for that purpose. This practice reached its zenith in the Middle Ages when Augustine and Aquinas, the most prominent Christian theologians of the period, borrowed ideas from Plato and Aristotle, respectively, to clarify and render precise their understanding of God, the human soul, immortality, creation, order in the universe, moral law, justice, goodness, divine providence, and others. During the same period, Moses Maimonides performed a similar service for Judaism, and Avicenna and Averroes did the same for Islam. The results of their efforts were not totally successful because the ideas of Plato and Aristotle were never intended to be used for these purposes. Furthermore, this mixing of philosophy with religion had a corresponding negative influence on philosophy. When philosophy gets mixed up with religion, purely philosophical issues, such as the source of order in the universe and the question of immortality, and ethical issues, such as the morality of abortion, become entangled in religious dogma, and the line of reasoning gets cut short. Religion hijacks the reasoning process and forces it off track. Before reason can proceed to its proper conclusion, religion predetermines the outcome.

## Historical Roots of Religion

Religion is one of the oldest features of human culture. It goes back thousands of years—perhaps more than 10,000—beyond the ancient Egyptian and Mesopotamian civilizations to tribal societies. Many anthropologists hold the view—and I think they are right about this—that religion originated in animism. This is the view that ordinary things, such as mountains, trees, and rocks, embody spirits. In due course, some clever member of a tribe convinced his fellows that he could communicate with these spirits—in particular with the spirits that inhabited the rain, the sun, the storms, and the seeds that produce the crops. In exchange for prayer, worship, and sacrifice, he could bargain with these spirits to yield just the right amount of moisture from the clouds, moderate temperatures, infrequent storms, fertile seeds, and plentiful crops.

If the tribesmen, in their collective wisdom, believed that this compatriot of theirs could indeed bargain with the spirits that controlled the elements, they appointed him priest. (In all societies, a priest is one who bargains with spirits or gods on behalf of the people.) The beginnings of religion came into existence with the creation of the first priest. But, of course, since there were probably hundreds of such tribes and hundreds of such priests, the birth of religion was probably not a singular event. In every case, however, the principal motivating factor was an increase in power for the ambitious priest to be. Thus did power give rise to religion. And if the priest met with success in persuading his fellows that he could indeed control the elements, he was made chief of the tribe. With further success, he was elevated to the status of a god. In time, at the instigation of the priest, the spirits that control the elements became gods themselves. Anyone who can bargain with gods has more power than someone who can bargain with mere spirits.

If we direct our attention to the state of mind of the tribesmen who believe so fervently in the power of their priest, practically no one today would consider their beliefs anything other than illusions. Those who are appointed priests are ordinary people. In fact, they have no power over the elements no matter how impressive their vocalizations or ritual dances. The priests exert their influence over the tribespeople by creating the illusion that they have special powers, but, in fact, they have none. It is the claim of this book that precisely the same illusion that was so common in ancient times has been passed down generation after generation to the present time and that it infects and defines the thinking of religious people to this day. Of course, the response of modern believers is that somewhere along the line there was a divine intervention. The power of some independently existing divinity intervened in the flow of human history and redirected it along the pathway of truth. But there is not a shred of evidence or a single good reason to think such an event ever happened. Furthermore, the divine intervention argument is blatantly circular. The only support for the existence of such a god rests on the product of that intervention, which is today's religion. Religion tells us that there is a god and that this god then intervened in the course of history to produce today's religion.

To counteract this kind of thinking, I offer two principles of explanation: Ockham's razor, created by the fourteenth-century philosopher William of Ockham, and the principle of continuity, originated by the seventeenth-century philosopher Gottfried Wilhelm von Leibniz. According to the first principle, which "shaves off" useless or redundant reasons for things, the simplest explanations are the best explanations. If a phenomenon (in this case the fact of religion) can be explained using a few simple reasons, there is no point in appealing to a large multitude of reasons. Stated otherwise, if a phenomenon can be explained in terms of purely natural causes, there is no point in appealing to a multitude of supernatural causes that are infinitely more complex than the natural ones. The principle of continuity (which reaches the same result in this context) holds that things do not pop into existence out of nowhere. They have a history. Modern religion did not originate from some miraculous occurrence that suddenly appeared unannounced. Rather, today's religion came from yesterday's religion. Yesterday's religion came from some religion before that and so on.

## Layout of This Study

This study takes a historical approach to exposing the character of religious belief. When attention is confined to a single religion over a narrow expanse of time, it becomes nearly impossible to see what is really going on. But when patterns are exposed during a lengthy period covering thousands of years and these patterns reveal the role that power plays in creating religious constructs and how those constructs serve to enhance the power of their creators, the element of illusion becomes easier to detect. Accordingly, I begin as far back as possible, with the Neolithic period, a time beginning around 11,000 years ago. This period witnessed the so-called Neolithic Revolution, which resulted in the shift from a hunter-gatherer lifestyle to one based on agriculture. The agrarian way of living provided the needed free time for people to converse with one another, and since the chief concern was plentiful crops, an important topic of conversation was how to ensure this outcome. My account depends heavily on the work of the Scottish anthropologist James George Frazer and his intellectual predecessor and the founder of cultural anthropology, E. B. Tylor. Tylor developed the concept of the fetish, which is an inanimate object, such as a stone or figurine, that was thought to be imbued with a spirit. It was further thought that the spirit of the fetish could communicate with the spirit of the clouds or the spirit of the grain in the field and that the maker of the fetish could communicate with the spirit of the fetish. Thus, through the fetish, the maker could communicate with the spirits responsible for a good crop. These fetish makers became the first priests, and the spirits inhabiting the clouds and the grain became the first gods. The priests, then, became the experts who could negotiate with the gods for the benefit of the tribespeople. Obviously, the priests came to be highly valued individuals.

From there, the discussion moves to the Egyptians, a society that came to have more than 1,000 gods and tens of thousands of priests. The gods in this society were the fictional product of priestly power. The priests derived their livelihood from conducting rituals in temples, so the more temples there were, the more opportunities there were for priests. But each temple needed a god to inhabit it, so as temples multiplied, so did the gods. The priests ensured that there would be a sufficient supply of gods by creating new ones as circumstances required. As this pattern of operation continued for 3,000 years, the number of gods increased proportionately. The only interruption in Egyptian polytheism occurred during the reign of the pharaoh Akhenaten, who initiated a string of events that led to a strict monotheism. He created a god called the Aten that was represented by the sun disk. This god soon absorbed all the other gods, leaving the Aten itself as the only one. This series of events caused great upheaval throughout Egypt. All the temples except the one dedicated to the Aten were shut down. This put all the priests out of business, and, by eliminating all the gods who managed the afterlife, it destroyed the opportunity for ordinary people to reach the afterlife. Furthermore, since the temple rituals were needed to sustain all order in the universe, Akhenaten's reign was accompanied by a constant fear that the universe would come apart at any moment. By all indications, the priests and citizenry alike despised Akhenaten, and when he died, they restored all the other gods to their former status, and they did their best to obliterate every indication that this pharaoh ever existed.

Judaism appears to have started in Egypt about 100 years after the reign of Akhenaten. Recent scholarship has consigned Abraham, Isaac, and Jacob to the category of myth, and many scholars accord the same treatment to Moses, but the argument that there was some kind of exodus out of Egypt and that a person named Moses led it is persuasive to some (including myself) that Moses really existed. As an Egyptian priest and military leader, Moses learned about Akhenaten and the Aten from memory traces that would have survived in the community of priests. According to the argument developed in chapter 4, Moses took the Aten, changed its name to Yahweh, and sold the newly named god to the Levites who had taken up residence in the eastern Nile Delta. As belief in the new god began to spread, it alarmed the native Egyptians, who feared a return to monotheism with all its attendant horrors. They responded by driving the Levites out of Egypt, an event remembered today as the Exodus. So the Exodus was no massive departure of some 2 million Jews, as the Bible depicts it, but a much smaller affair consisting only of Levites. My guess is that it may have amounted to no more than 400 travelers. Also, the Exodus was not an escape to freedom from the angry grasp of the pharaoh but an expulsion by terrified Egyptians. The incident was so insignificant that the pharaoh may not have even been aware of it. After departing Egypt, the Levites did not wander in the desert for some forty years but for a much shorter period, perhaps only three or four weeks. On nearing their destination, there was no conquest of the cities in the region because there was nothing to conquer. The cities had no fortifications at that time. In particular, the walls of Jericho did not come tumbling down because there were no walls. After arriving in Canaan, the Levites became priests for the resident Hebrews, working to convert those residents from polytheism to belief in Yahweh, a belief that I call the "Yahweh illusion." Hundreds of years later, they wrote most of the documents that became the Hebrew Bible.

The first chapter relating to the Christians deals with Jesus, who died around 30 CE. Given that the earliest Christian writings that speak to what Jesus said and did are the Gospels and that the first Gospel (Mark) was written around 70 CE, there was a period of forty years when the only record of Jesus the person was a group of memories. (The letters of Paul are earlier, but they say practically nothing about the person of Jesus.) So if we are to explore the sayings and actions of Jesus, it is imperative that we be equipped with a theory of memory, in particular a theory of collective memory. With this thought in mind, I develop such a theory based on Darwin's concept of natural selection. I call it the "natural selection model of collective memory." It solidifies the idea that collective memory works to enhance the survival of the community of people who create it. Applying this idea to the Jesus construct that appears in the Gospels, I am led to conclude that all the exceptional features that qualify this construct are the invention of the apostles, their successors, and their assistants—people I take to be the first Christian priests. What this means is that Jesus never rose from the dead, he is not the Son of God, he was not the Messiah, he performed no genuine miracles, he was not born of a virgin, and he did not die for the remission of human sins. I call the collection of beliefs that relate to these exceptional features the "Jesus Illusion." When these features are subtracted from the Jesus construct of the Gospels, we are left with a man who was mistaken in his probable belief that he was the Jewish Messiah but who taught an elevated set of ethical ideals that caused his followers to love him deeply.

Some scholars describe Paul the apostle as being the second founder of Christianity. In chapter 6, I develop the idea that Paul was largely responsible for creating the basic components of the Christian god, consisting of Father, Son, and Holy Spirit. Paul says in his letters that after being converted to the Jesus movement, he went to Arabia. I suggest that "Arabia," for Paul, was the Egyptian city of Alexandria. Egypt, or at least the northern portion, has been a part of Arabia for the past 5,000 years. Assuming that Paul did visit Alexandria, he most likely would have

21

come into contact with a group of cutting-edge thinkers in the Jewish community called Gnostics. Jewish Gnosticism represented a melting pot of ideas drawn from Hellenism, Judaism, and Egyptian Hermeticism. From Hellenism, Paul would have learned about the Platonic idea of the One, which, in the religious context provided by Judaism, became God the Father. From Hermeticism, Paul would have derived the idea that this Father produced a Son in an existential, nonmetaphorical sense. And from a book written in Alexandria about that time, the Wisdom of Solomon, Paul would have learned about the goddess of Wisdom, which, in that document, is otherwise called the Holy Spirit. I argue that Paul synthesized these divine components to create the basic makeup of the God of Christianity.

Refining the concept of the Christian god to the point where it currently stands required an additional 300 years, and this subject is taken up in chapter 7. Since this accomplishment is found to be wrapped up with priestly power, I begin in that chapter by exploring the origins of and early challenges to this power. Priestly power appears to have originated with the belief shared by the Apostles that Jesus had received great authority from the Father and that he had transferred that power to them and to their successors. This made the apostles and their successors a very special group. An early challenge to their lofty status was launched by a Christian theologian named Valentinus. His teaching would have destroyed the power of the bishops, and they responded by declaring it a heresy. This action by the bishops introduced for the first time in Christian teaching the distinction between orthodoxy and heresy. I argue that this distinction is reducible to priestly power. A doctrine is orthodox if it increases priestly power, and it is heretical if it undermines priestly power. The dispute involving Valentinus was the first in a long series of such disputes related to the nature of the Christian god, and the bishops settled all of them by declaring heretical the doctrine that tended to undermine their own power. Each of these declarations was an incremental step in a series of steps that led to the final definition of the triune God. The Christian god is a construct assembled through these many steps. It was created by priests and is a product of their power.

Following the historical account of religion, chapter 8 focuses on the thought of four prominent philosophers who are known for their theories of power: Thomas Hobbes, Friedrich Nietzsche, Michel Foucault, and

Alfred North Whitehead. Hobbes argued that human life is, in essence, a quest for power. He shows how people use constructs to augment their power and how they create illusions for the same purpose. Religious leaders, both current and past, are no less impacted by this quest than everyone else. Life is competition, the important thing is to win, and winning requires power. Thus, power is as important in religion as it is in any other endeavor. Nietzsche argued that the desire for power is intrinsic to human life, if not to life in general. Power is connected to willing, to the exercise of one's will, and all people will things constantly. Power is life enhancing, and this entails replacing false values with healthy ones. The false values that must be replaced are the values of religion, particularly the values of Christianity: holiness, meekness, faith, otherworldliness, self-sacrifice, piety, and unquestioning obedience. Foucault's theory of power envisions every person in society as linked to every other person through a network of power relations. Human subjects are literally constituted by the power relations that link them to others. Foucault sees power as mainly a question of management, of getting other people to do what you want them to do. The panopticon, an architectural design in which a single individual can manage a large group of people with maximum efficiency, illustrates how priests manage their followers. Also, his theory that power produces knowledge sheds light on the origin of both the monotheistic God of Judaism and the triune God of Christianity. Whitehead, the only theist in this group of philosophers, developed a theory involving a "God" having limited knowledge and limited power. It is in a continual state of development, it learns things, and it exerts a continual persuasive influence on the world. The theory is arguably more coherent and more in accord with the facts than the conventional theory, but it leaves no room for miracles.

Chapter 9 explores Freud's theory that religion is grounded in neurosis and then distinguishes that theory from the theory presented in this book. Freud held that religious illusion is reducible to the subject's proclivity for wishful thinking, while my own theory is that religious belief is induced by other people who prey on the hopes and fears of target individuals. These inducers of religious illusion were originally ancient priests, and the results of their efforts have been passed down through countless generations to the present age. What renders potential victims vulnerable to these inducers includes the hope of gaining everlasting life, the fear of death, and the refusal to take seriously even the most basic principles of good reasoning.

In preferring abstractions to concrete experience, religious believers have lost touch with the real, but this touch might be restored by attending to the interactive aspect of experience. Religious illusions are maintained by rituals and festivals. Rituals make illusions appear to be real by engaging the body of the believer, and festivals establish a connection between religious beliefs and enjoyable times and places. The fact that religion has both good and bad effects implies that religious beliefs are caused not by any independently existing deity but by the multiple and disparate *ideas* of such a deity in the minds of religious leaders.

# CHAPTER TWO
# THE EMERGENCE OF RELIGION

Any attempt to pin down when and how religion emerged on the human stage is exceedingly difficult for the simple reason that there is no written record of the event and that the archaeological record is inevitably ambiguous. Such an attempt must therefore include an element of conjecture and will proceed by piecing together bits of evidence from multiple sources, including anthropology, history, and philosophy. From history and anthropology, we have the undisputed facts that ancient civilizations, in particular the civilizations of ancient Egypt and Mesopotamia (Babylon), featured a huge organization of priests. Also, there were massive temples the remains of which still exist (although the temples of Babylon lie chiefly beneath the surface of the Euphrates River today). Any account of the origin of religion must explain how these priests and temples came to exist. From anthropology, we have documentary evidence, such as the Egyptian Book of the Dead. We must explain how this fits into the picture. Also, from anthropology, we are furnished with evidence of tombs and burial practices that are linked to belief in an afterlife. Finally, from philosophy, we have (what I would consider) the well-supported theory that humans (at least humans at the top of the social structure) are heavily motivated by power and the feeling of power. Assuming that this theory is well founded, it is hard to imagine that it is unrelated to the emergence of religion.

Although vestigial traces of religion go back at least 100,000 years to the first ritual burial sites, a good argument can be made that religion in an organized sense emerged in the Neolithic period, which began in the Middle East around 11,000 years ago. This period witnessed the so-called Neolithic Revolution, the central feature of which was the transition from a hunter-gather lifestyle to one based on agriculture. The hunter-gatherer lifestyle was largely nomadic, with people moving from place to place depending on where food could best be found. With the rise of the agrarian lifestyle, people began settling down in small communities. These communities offered a quality of social life never before enjoyed by members of the human race. Leisure time became available in unprecedented amounts, so people had time to engage in conversation. They had time to reflect on topics that concerned them the most, and the most important topic was undoubtedly crop production: how to obtain the best seeds in the greatest number, how to produce the most plentiful yields, and how to avoid the ravages of drought, flood, and inclement weather. Time to reflect led to experiments with crops, which, in turn, produced the first selective breading of cereal plants. Barley, emmer wheat, and einkorn wheat were the earliest results of such experiments. According to the theory developed here, this intense focus on crop production was one of two necessary conditions that led to the emergence of organized religion.

## Animism

The other necessary condition was what might be called the spiritual beliefs of Neolithic peoples. Edward Burnet Tylor, the founder of cultural anthropology, reported these beliefs in great detail in his two-volume work *Primitive Culture*. He uses the word "animism" to refer to the general belief in spirits, and he devotes approximately 450 pages to exploring the nuances of the term. Tylor defines what he takes to be the ancient notion of "spirit," in a culturally comprehensive sense, as follows:

> It is a thin, unsubstantial, human image, in its nature a sort of vapour, film, or shadow; the cause of life and thought in the individual it animates; independently possessing the personal consciousness and volition of its corporeal owner, past or present, capable of leaving the body far behind, to flash swiftly from place to place; mostly impalpable and invisible, yet also manifesting physical power, and especially appearing to men waking or asleep as a phantasm separate from the body of which it

bears the likeness; continuing to exist and appear to men after the death of that body; able to enter into, possess, and act in the bodies of other men, of animals, and even of things.[1]

The belief in spirits was no trivial or insignificant part of the world-view of ancient people. It invaded practically every part of their lives and explained a broad cross section of phenomena, including the difference between a living person and a corpse, the fact of disease, and the occurrence of visions and dreams. A corpse is a person who has lost its spirit on a more or less permanent basis; disease is explained by being possessed by evil spirits,[2] restoration of health by the driving out of evil spirits, dreams of other people by those people's spirits visiting the spirit of the dreamer when asleep, and visions by spirits visiting someone's spirit while awake.

Ancient people saw spirits as occupying many naturally occurring things and substances. Trees, forests, and groves had spirits, as did rivers, lakes, wells, and springs. Water, in general, and fire had spirits. Mountains, volcanos, rocks, and whirlpools had spirits. The ancient Nicaraguans offered sacrifices to their volcano spirits by throwing human bodies into the craters.[3] To this day, volcanos are common in that region. In West Africa, the natives made oblations to lakes, ponds, and rivers, and in the East, they venerated streams as personal deities.[4] In India, the Ganges, of course, has been considered sacred for centuries. In many regions, the inhabitants have considered individual trees and groves as having a conscious personal life, and they have offered them adoration and sacrifice.[5]

An important consequence of the description of spirits as disembodied souls is the fact that spirits are things capable of communication. One of the most important features of human social life is the fact of communication between living people. But since a person's spirit is responsible for all thinking and volition (as Tylor observes), there is no reason why disembodied spirits should not be able to communicate directly with other disembodied spirits as well as with live humans. Through such communication, one spirit could influence the actions of another spirit as well as the actions of a living person, and, conversely, a living person could influence the actions of a disembodied spirit. And since spirits can manifest physical power over things, by communicating with a spirit, a living human could, with the right technique, influence physical occurrences, such as rainfall, storms, droughts, and the fertility of plants.

27

When we combine this account of spirit with the earlier description of the concern with crop production, we have the description of a nearly perfect power vacuum. Humans living in the Neolithic era were assuredly as hungry for power as humans living today. They wanted prestige and recognition within the tribe; they wanted wealth, they wanted mastership over their fellows, they wanted to be the recipient of life-enhancing services, and they wanted the best mating opportunities and the best living accommodations. All of these could be had by any enterprising member who could convince his fellows that he could communicate with the spirits controlling the elements and persuade them to cooperate. Such communication would guarantee (in their minds) or at least improve the chances for good weather and fertile crops. But any such enterprising soul would need help in accomplishing such a daunting task. In accord with the maxim introduced in chapter 1 of this book, that physical constructs enhance the acquisition of power, the needed help is available through what Tylor calls fetishes.

## The Fetish

"Any object whatsoever may be a fetish," Tylor writes.[6] To convert such an object (which may be a stone, a tooth, a claw, a shell, or a figurine) into a fetish, what is required is the action by a human being that assigns a spirit to the object. "To class an object as a fetish, demands [an] explicit statement that a spirit is considered as embodied in it or acting through it or communicating by it."[7] Once an object has been converted into a fetish, it has a power to accomplish things, such as alter the weather, drive out evil spirits, or protect women in childbirth. The "logic" behind the power of the fetish appears to be this: the spirit of the person who creates and controls the fetish communicates with the spirit in the fetish, and the latter spirit then communicates with the spirit in the clouds or the trees or the person afflicted with disease.

Tylor collected dozens of cases of fetish cures. For example, among the Dayaks of Borneo, a priest waving or jingling a fetish charm over a diseased patient is said to be able to cure the patient by drawing evil spirits from the patient's stomach.[8] "In our time," Tylor continues, "West Africa is still a world of fetishes. The traveler finds them on every path, at every ford, on every house door, they hang as amulets around every man's neck, they guard against sickness or inflict it if neglected, they bring rain, they fill the sea with fishes willing to swim into the fisherman's net, they catch and punish thieves, they give their owner a bold heart and confound his enemies, there is nothing that the fetish cannot do or undo if it be but the right fetish."[9] Any creative soul from ancient times who had the skill to create the right fetish and use it in the right way was richly rewarded.

James George Frazer, an anthropologist who can be seen as following in the footsteps of Tylor, explored the idea of the fetish as it related to grain growing. In relatively recent times, he writes, cultures in various parts of the world celebrated a spirit called a corn mother, an oat mother, a barley mother, a rye mother, or a flax mother that was supposed to nurture and fertilize the respective crops and ensure a bountiful harvest. In the spring, people would speak of the corn mother, for example, as blowing through the fields and making the plants grow. In some parts, people would say, "It will be a good year for flax; the Flax-mother has been seen."[10] To ensure favorable treatment from these spirits, at harvest time, sheaves of grain, whether corn, oats, or whatever grew in the area, would be gathered up and shaped in the form of a female puppet dressed in a woman's clothing. This puppet would then be made the center of an elaborate celebration. Alternately, sheaves of grain would be shaped in the form of a wreath and twined with flowers. These puppets and wreathes are fetishes that were thought to embody or communicate with the maternal spirit of the grain. In the language of this book, they are physical constructs that were supposed to augment the power of the grain growers.

Even though these celebrations featuring maternal puppets and wreathes are figures of relatively recent vintage, they are undoubtedly vestiges of similar celebrations that trace their roots back thousands of years. Tylor would say they are cases of "survival," where a practice that was originated centuries earlier persists into modern times because of its relevance to current happenings. Assuming that these anthropologists are correct, one can imagine, thousands of years earlier, a figure with face heavily painted, draped in animal skins, and gyrating wildly to the rhythm of beating drums. One hand holds a female puppet composed of sheathes of grain, while the other gestures intently toward a recently sown field. The performance is embellished with loud chanting, pierced with intermittent shrieks. If, with the arrival of harvest, the yield is bountiful, the figure with the painted face offers it as proof that the attempted communication with the corn mother was successful.

With the shift to an agrarian way of living, which defined the Neolithic period, adequate rainfall became a central concern. For hunter-gatherers, the personal need for water could usually be satisfied by setting up camp on the banks of a stream or river. But an agrarian-based community needs rain. Without rain, the crops will die. So once again, we have a power vacuum: a need that must be fulfilled (rain) and a promising way to fulfill it (communicate with the rain spirit), which draws forth any member of the tribe with the right communication skills. Frazer describes several rain-making techniques from various parts of the world. In a village in Russia, three members would cooperate to make rain. One would climb to the top of a sacred tree and strike a kettle or small cask with a hammer to evoke thunder. The kettle and cask were fetishes that were presumably imbued with the thunder spirit (or at least with a spirit that could communicate with the thunder spirit). Another member would rub two firebrands (fetishes) together to produce sparks, which in turn would entice lightning from the sky. The third sprinkled water on a handful of branches (more fetishes) and then shook them, which was intended to persuade the rain spirit to let forth a deluge.[11] For another example, in North America, members of the Natchez tribe would fill their mouths with water, then, while dancing, they would insert perforated pipes into their mouths and blow the water into the air. The resulting shower was intended to persuade the rain spirits to follow suit.[12]

## Priests

By definition, a priest is one who mediates between the people and the spirits or the gods. He bargains with the spirits or gods to secure some benefit for the people. The tribal officials who conducted the ceremonies involving the corn-sheaf puppets and the rain fetishes were priests. They must be distinguished from other practitioners—call them medicine men or witch doctors—who performed services on a private basis, such as effecting a cure or casting a spell. As public bargainers, the first priests arranged something that the people could give in exchange for the sought benefit: possibly a sheep or a goat or several pieces of fruit. Thus were offered the first sacrifices. And ceremonies that the first priests organized to impress the spirits became the setting for chants and songs, which were the first prayers. All of this was conducted, of course, to secure prestige and power for the priests. And to enhance this prestige and power even further, the priests elevated the spirits to gods, at which time the fetishes became idols. The appropriate response of the people to the gods and idols was, of course, worship. This brought to a close the first stage in the formation of religion, which culminated in the control of the priests over the public lives of the tribesmen. The second stage, which extended priestly control over the private lives of the tribesmen, will be discussed shortly.

In this scenario depicting the creation of the first gods, the priests who created these gods were almost certainly not the ones who used the first fetishes. They were separated from the fetish users by hundreds of years or longer. Also, it was almost certainly not a case of spirits being replaced by gods. It was more a case of spirits evolving into gods. These gods began as very powerful spirits, and their emergence reflected the growing power of the priests over a lengthy period of time. Also, the transition from spirits to gods was probably not confined to any specific geographic region. The use of fetishes was extremely widespread.[13] Practically every place humans could be found, there were fetishes. When the spirits of the fetishes evolved into gods, belief in gods was equally widespread.

Did the first priests realize that their social construct was really based on an illusion? Did they really think that their antics with fetishes were modes of communication with the corn mother and the rain spirits? Or was it all a ruse to enhance their own power and prestige within the tribe? Of course, no certain answer is possible, but Frazer offers some interesting thoughts on the subject:

> The development of such a class of [public] functionaries [i.e., priests, in my account] is of great importance for the political as well as the religious evolution of society. For when the welfare of the tribe is supposed to depend on the performance of these magical rites, the magician [i.e., the priest] rises into the position of much influence and repute, and may readily acquire the rank and authority of a chief or king. The profession accordingly draws into its ranks some of the ablest and most ambitious men of the tribe, because it holds out to them a prospect of honour, wealth, and power such as hardly any other career could offer. The acuter minds see how easily it is to dupe their weaker brother and

to play on his superstition for their own advantage. Not that the sorcerer [priest] is always a knave and imposter, he is often sincerely convinced that he really possesses those wonderful powers which the credulity of his fellows ascribes to him. But the more sagacious he is, the more likely he is to see through the fallacies which impose on duller wits. Thus the ablest members of the profession must tend to be more or less conscious deceivers; and it is just these men who in virtue of their superior ability will generally come to the top and win for themselves positions of the highest dignity and the most commanding authority.[14]

Frazer goes on to discuss the potential pitfalls that threaten the life of a priest who promises fertile fields and adequate rain when those promises fail to materialize. The honest priest, who sincerely believes in his own pretensions, will stammer and act befuddled, and this will lead to his downfall. Only a priest of "coolest head and sharpest wit" will be able to furnish plausible excuses in the limited time allowed. So the priests who survive in their profession for any length of time are the dishonest ones:

The general result is that . . . the supreme power tends to fall into the hands of men of the keenest intelligence and the most unscrupulous character. If we could balance the harm they do by their knavery against the benefits they confer by their superior sagacity, it might well be found that the good greatly outweighed the evil. For more mischief has probably been wrought in the world by honest fools in high places than by intelligent rascals.[15]

Frazer's comments (which have a distinctly Machiavellian flavor) may be as applicable to religious and political leaders of today as they are to the very same kind of leaders in ancient times.

## Belief in the Afterlife

At this point in our account, the priests have succeeded in establishing control over the public lives of the tribespeople as displayed in public rituals to ensure fertile crops, temperate weather, and adequate rainfall. Such goals are public goods shared by the tribe as a whole. Priestly control was rendered complete through its extension to the private lives of the people. Control over the private lives of the people was accomplished in connection with belief in the afterlife. The development of this belief is fairly well evidenced in burial practices that go back further than 100,000 years. When ancient humans began the practice of intentionally burying their dead comrades, as opposed to simply leaving the bodies out in the field for animals to devour, they signaled that there was something special about these bodies. While living, these bodies were inhabited by a spirit, and after death, the spirit may return. If so, the body (or at least the bones) should be preserved in some way. But if the spirit may return, this implies that the spirit continues to live beyond the death of the body. In other words, there is an afterlife.

One unambiguous indication of intentional burial was the use of red ocher to cover the body prior to refilling the grave. Ocher is a pigment composed of iron oxide that occurs naturally in the earth, and it comes in multiple colors including yellow, orange, brown, and red. It is generally agreed that ancient peoples associated red ocher with life since it is similar to the color of human blood. According to anthropologist E. O. James,

> This widespread custom of coating the corpse with red ochre clearly had a ritual significance. Red is the color of living health. Therefore, as professor Macalister has pointed out, if the dead man was to live again in his own body, of which the bones were the framework, to paint them with the ruddy coloring of life was "the nearest thing to mummification that the Paleolithic people knew; it was an attempt to make the body again serviceable for its owner's use."[16]

Red ocher was used by ancient peoples for, among other things, preserving animal skins and tanning leather, and this is what E. O. James undoubtedly has in mind when he says that coating a corpse with red ocher was an early form of mummification. The ancient Egyptians mummified the bodies of their dead pharaohs to preserve them, and the purpose of such preservation was to ensure that the spirit of the pharaoh would have a home to return to after death. If the spirit of the pharaoh could not return to its body, there could be no afterlife.

Admittedly, it is not known for certain what the ancients had in mind by sprinkling red ocher on corpses in the grave. There are possibilities other than preservation of the corpse. One is that it served to alert those who might dig in that area years later that a human body was buried there and that therefore the area should not be disturbed. If the grave were destroyed, the returning spirit would have no body to reanimate. Another possibility is that marking a grave with this substance would alert the returning spirit as to the location of its body. Red ocher retains its color indefinitely into the future. Finally, red ocher symbolized life, so it served as a kind of invitation or inducement to the departed spirit to reenter its body. All three of these purposes were tied to belief in an afterlife. The use of red ocher in grave sites persisted for tens of thousands of years.

Relating to this very early practice, human corpses have also been discovered wearing jewelry or ornaments made of such materials as bone, teeth, shell, or ivory and also accompanied with tools of various kinds and food. These accoutrements were found in addition to copious quantities of red ocher. The tools may have been the same ones or of the same sort used by the deceased prior to death. The apparent implication is that if the spirit should return to its body, it would have food to sustain it and the implements needed for continued living. The practice of burying corpses with tools and jewelry reached its pinnacle expression many years later in ancient Egypt where the mummy of the pharaoh was buried together with food, eating utensils, furniture, weapons, chariots, and other things he had used in life. When the spirit of the pharaoh returned to his mummy he could use these things in the afterlife.

Assuming that the priestly profession arose during the Neolithic period, belief in an afterlife took root long before there were any priests. But according to the theory developed here, once the priests discovered that people had a desire for an afterlife, they were presented an opportunity that promised a vast expansion of their own power. By this time, the priests had already invented gods to control the weather and ensure the fertility of crops. So why not invent more gods and put them in charge of the afterlife? These new gods would decide who was admitted and who was not and, among those who were admitted, who was rewarded with the best quality of life. But because the priests had invented these gods in the first place, it was really the priests who would be in charge of the afterlife. This marked a significant expansion of priestly power. The innovation did not occur overnight but probably required hundreds of years to accomplish, and it probably occurred in some parts of the world earlier than it occurred in others. But when the people finally came to believe that the gods were in charge of the afterlife, the priests had come a long way toward controlling the private lives of ordinary people.

As with mummification, envisioning the afterlife as conducted by priests achieved full-blown expression in ancient Egypt. The gates of the underworld, through which the ka (or spirit/personality) of the deceased must pass, were guarded by a great number of gods and goddesses. The god Osiris served as lord of the underworld and as the chief judge of spirits seeking entry. The spirit's eligibility would first be judged by forty-two gods, after which the god Anubis would lead the spirit to a two-pan balance scale that would weigh the applicant's worthiness. The goddess Maat would supply the standard of worthiness, and Thoth, the god of scribes, would record the result. The god Ammut would dispatch the spirits of those who were judged unworthy. Presiding over the entire procedure was the god Horus. If the spirit passed muster, it would be led into the afterlife, where it could continue worshipping the same gods it had worshipped in its prior life. The Egyptian concept of the afterlife and its admission procedure was extremely complex involving hundreds of deities, all of them invented by priests.

## The Continuity of Religion

Religion emerged on the world stage through a coalescence of human power, human constructs, and the creation of illusions. In very early times, the most prominent construct was the fetish, an inanimate object thought to be infused with a spirit. Such fetishes included everything from rattles and drums to pieces of wood or stone to puppets and wreaths made from stalks of grain. The spirit of the fetish was thought to be able to communicate with the spirits inhabiting the weather, the rain, the grain in the field, and human beings inflicted with disease. Certain members of the tribe who were more hungry for power than the others convinced their fellows that they could communicate with the spirit of the fetish, and these individuals became the first priests. Before long, these priests hit on the idea of elevating the spirits to the status of gods, and thus emerged the second great construct leading to religion: the god entity. To persuade their fellows that they actually could influence the weather and the crops, the priests effectively enshrouded the entire process in illusion. The earliest religious illusions were the beliefs that the fetish really contained a spirit, that this spirit could communicate with the spirits in the rain and crops, and that the priest could communicate with the spirit of the fetish. The next great set of illusions included the belief that it was really the gods who controlled the rain and the fertility of the crops and that the priests were influential with the gods. Finally, there was the illusion that gods were in charge of the afterlife and that they were offended by something called sin.

Religion, as it was formed in the Neolithic period and perfected during the time of the ancient Egyptians, has persisted largely unchanged all the way to the present day. Certainly, the essential features of today's religions have remained largely identical to the correlative features in the religions of ancient times. Religious people today still have their fetishes. Objects such as crosses, Bibles, Torahs, Qurans, consecrated bread and wine, water blessed by a priest, rosary beads, medals hung around the neck, and Russian icons—all of these things to the extent that they are thought of as imbued with powers or as holy—are modern-day fetishes. People still pray to their gods for favors, they believe that their priests can influence the gods, and they offer sacrifices in the form of money contributed to churches and religious organizations. People still believe in sin, they cling to belief in an afterlife run by gods, and they believe that sin blocks access to the afterlife. They believe that the word of the priest is the word of God (and therefore true) because priests are in constant communication with God. Just as the ancients considered favorable weather or a good crop as a blessing from some god, people today consider any good fortune, such as recovery from a disease or narrowly avoiding a horrific car accident, as a similar blessing. Religion is still viewed as the great exchange mechanism where believers offer prayer, worship, and sacrifice to their gods for some perceived benefit either in this life or in the next, while most of the payback ends up in the hands of the priests.

Assuming that religion today is linked by a continuous thread to Neolithic religion, the question remains as to how it is possible for a set of beliefs and practices to continue in existence through literally thousands of years. By what feature of nature or human society has this happened? Much of the answer can be found in the constructs religious leaders employ to augment their power. Especially important are the social constructs and the physical constructs. Religion started out with individual priests engaging with the gods to bring clement weather and sufficient rain for an abundant harvest. Priests who were especially successful soon found themselves with more business than they could handle on their own. They employed associates to address the growing need, and soon there arose organizations of priests, each having a distinct specialty and headed up by a chief priest. These organizations became solidly rooted in the larger society as more people were employed for auxiliary purposes. Tradespeople were hired to provide sacrificial plants and animals, builders to construct temples, garment workers to make vestments for the priests, laborers to maintain the temples and grounds, and accountants to keep track of everything. Priestly organizations functioned like ancient corporations, and just as modern corporations outlive their directors and employees, these priestly organizations outlived the individual priests who composed them at any particular time. They could last for centuries until something happened to precipitate their collapse. Other social constructs that worked to perpetuate religious beliefs were rituals and festivals. A ritual, consisting of a pattern of practices, can easily outlive the priests who practice it, and the same holds true of festivals. People love festivals, and they look forward to them. This anticipation sustains a festival and the beliefs associated with it indefinitely into the future.

Among the physical constructs responsible for the survival of religious beliefs, two principal ones are documents and architectural structures. Documents, whether written on stone, wood, paper, or some other medium, can capture the essential kernel of a religious belief, and they tend to be permanent, long outliving the life of the author. Of course, documents depend on the existence of a written language, so they were not available to religion in its earliest years. But prior to documents, there were figurines and other artifacts made of pottery that expressed religious motifs, and these helped sustain the beliefs associated with them. As religious belief gradually matured, priests came to see that it was useful to have a place to situate their gods, and thus arose the temple, which was seen as the house of some god or other. These architectural structures can last for centuries, thus sustaining the life of the deity they house. Imagine, if you will, a man in his later years strolling past one of these structures. He gazes at the impressive facade and remembers as a youth having passed by there and been overwhelmed by the awesome sight. From his perspective, the building has been there forever. Dozens of people he has known have come and gone, but the building remains the same, a permanent

37

fixture in his life. The god that dwells therein and the religion the building represents are taken to be as permanent as the building itself. Physical constructs can last for an indefinitely long time, and they carry their associated beliefs along with them.

## Tylor and Frazer

This chapter closes with a few words about the British anthropologists Edward Burnet Tylor (1832–1917) and James George Frazer (1854–1941), who are the source of much of the information on which this chapter is based. Both were highly prominent figures in their day. Tylor is considered to be the founder of cultural anthropology, and he held the chair in that field at Oxford University, the first such position in the English-speaking world. Frazer's magnum opus, *The Golden Bough*, is a massive study that, in its unabridged form, comprises thirteen volumes. Frazer is recognized as one of the founders of modern anthropology, and he, along with Tylor, was knighted for his work in that field. In spite of their illustrious credentials, however, these two figures have largely disappeared from the current literature. The reason for this neglect is that anthropologists in the early part of the twentieth century were engaged in a struggle to have their field recognized as a full-fledged science in the academic world, and this required that it rest on a well-defined methodology of data collection. And this, in turn, required that anthropologists conduct their own field work. But neither Tylor nor Frazer did this. Both relied on reports furnished by missionaries, travelers, and responses to questionnaires. Nonetheless, both figures succeeded in compiling a huge trove of data and information that, I contend, remains of interest to philosophers, much in the way that Sigmund Freud, who has been largely abandoned by contemporary psychiatry and psychology, retains the interest of researchers outside those fields.

Tylor's work in anthropology was influenced by Darwin's theory of natural selection, and he interpreted human culture as evolving through three periods that began with savagery, proceeded through a stage of barbarism, and ended with civilization. Frazer was heavily influenced by Tylor, and he, too, saw the human species as progressing through three stages. Beginning with magic, it passed through a stage of religion and ended with science. Frazer developed his theory of magic by largely abandoning Tylor's theory of animism and by replacing his fetishes with mere artifacts made of wood, beeswax, plant products, and curiously shaped stones. By manipulating these artifacts in various ways and uttering certain incantations, Frazer saw ancient people as engaging in magic. A typical example is the voodoo doll, an image made of wood or other materials, which is then pierced with needles or arrows to cause injury or death to the person the image resembles.

I take this move by Frazer to be a mistake. His concept of magic is both excessively ethnocentric and unenlightening in comparison with Tylor's theory of the fetish. I propose deleting it entirely and replacing its underpinnings with a principle I call the "primacy of communication." Where Frazer sees ancient people manipulating crude artifacts and uttering incantations, I see an effort to communicate. Before almost anything else, people are communicators and have been for thousands of years. Increased opportunity for communication was one of the chief by-products of the Neolithic Revolution. Communication between people is what eventually led to the invention of writing. When Frazer's theory is amended in this way and when animism and the fetish are brought to center stage, Frazer's work in anthropology becomes a seamless whole with Tylor's.[17] Also, Frazer's magicians and sorcerers become priests because they are now seen as communicating with the spirits and the gods. Finally, Frazier's idea that religion arose from magic disappears, and the pathway is cleared for what I take to be a better theory: religion was not the product of magic; it was the product of power. But once religion got a foothold in civilized society, it sensitized an already gullible public to countless modes of magical thinking.

# CHAPTER THREE
# THE EGYPTIANS

## The Importance of Egypt

The religion of ancient Egypt serves as the linchpin between the religion of the Neolithic period and the modern religions of the West, Judaism, Christianity, and Islam. Egypt came into existence as the world's first nation-state around 3100 BCE when Upper Egypt (the southern part, which is upriver) was united with Lower Egypt (the northern part) under the rule of King Narmer (otherwise called King Menes). Narmer came to be known as the first king of the First Dynasty, and he was succeeded by approximately 170 kings and queens stretching through thirty-one dynasties and ending with Cleopatra, who died in 30 BCE. Each dynasty consisted roughly of rulers connected by blood relationships. Prior to unification, the upper and lower parts of Egypt consisted of autonomous villages each having a totem-god (usually cows or bulls) and ruled by a local chieftain. During the reign of the pharaohs, with the help of the priests, those simple gods would grow into a huge pantheon that would unify the people into a collective unit and make Egypt the most powerful nation on earth.

What makes Egypt unique among ancient civilizations is its geographical isolation from the rest of the world. It is bordered on the east and west by deserts, which are nearly uninhabitable; on the north by the Nile Delta, which in ancient times was mostly marshland; and on the south by a series of cataracts (rapids or waterfalls) on the river, which impeded boat travel to the south. This relative isolation, added to the fact that the Neolithic Revolution did not occur there until around 5000 BCE, renders ancient Egypt a historical microcosm unto itself, a virtual laboratory exhibit for studying the connection between the culture of the Neolithic period and that of the common era. Such a study is blessed with an abundance of written evidence consisting of hieroglyphics and bas-relief images on temples and painted images and written messages on the walls of tombs. Given the near absence of rainfall in Egypt, what is left of the temples is remarkably well preserved, and the writing and imagery on the walls of the tombs appear as though they were painted only yesterday. Additionally, there are hundreds of scrolls and sheets of papyrus, stelae, and tablets containing images and writing that still exist and have provided an abundance of information about everything, from the ordinary lives of ancient Egyptians to their mathematics, astronomy, and theology.

Unfortunately, the written evidence extends back in time only to the First Dynasty, so that leaves a span of about 2,000 years from the Neolithic Revolution, for which there is nothing in writing. But the archaeological evidence shows that the Egyptians living in the years following the revolution had the same concerns as similarly situated people in other locations. Throughout that period, people were burying their dead in graves and tombs, the tombs became ever more elaborate with the passing of years, and they contained ever-increasing amounts of worldly goods to ensure the welfare of the spirits of the dead. This shows beyond doubt that pre-dynastic people had an abiding conviction in the existence of the afterlife. Also, as with agrarian people in other lands, the people inhabiting the land that would become Egypt were concerned about their crops. Of course, the crops depended on the annual flood of the Nile, but the ancient people had no idea as to what caused the flood. Most of the time, it was regular, but in some years, there was too little and in other years too much. Perhaps next year, the flood would not occur at all. And the sunshine seemed to be regular too, but whether that would continue was another unknown. For these reasons, those ancient people were sympathetic to the idea that the regularity of these natural events was upheld by divine entities.

## The Afterlife

The great pyramid of Cheops at Giza is the most massive structure ever assembled by human hands. At its base, each side measures 756 feet, and it consists of approximately 2,300,000 stone blocks each weighing around two and a half tons. The Greek historian Herodotus, who visited Egypt in the fifth century BCE and who chronicled many of her achievements, wrote that it took 100,000 men working twenty years to build it. And even though the historian wrote this more than 2,000 years after its completion, his figures seem plausible to historians today given that most of the workers labored only during the summer months when they were not taken up with agriculture. Hollywood filmmakers depict the construction of the great pyramid as having been accomplished by slaves working under the lash of cruel Egyptian taskmasters. But since there were relatively few slaves in Egypt during the Fourth Dynasty, when the great pyramid was built, the vast majority of the workers could not have been slaves. So who were they? The answer can only be that they were ordinary Egyptian citizens who worked on the project of their own free choice.

What could have persuaded 100,000 men to work for twenty years beneath a blazing summer sun that is practically never interrupted by a single cloud, to say nothing of a refreshing shower? For the answer, one must understand that the pyramid was intended to serve as the tomb of Cheops (Khufu), the Fourth Dynasty pharaoh, whose afterlife would last as long as his tomb. The priests of the day had convinced the Egyptian populace that their own afterlife was inextricably linked to the afterlife of their king, so if the king succeeded in making it into the afterlife, so would they. Exactly how this was supposed to work remains a bit of a mystery. But they believed beyond any doubt that it was true. They also believed that stone would last for eternity, and if the tomb were large enough (so that no one could ever dismantle it) and if it were made of solid stone, then it, too, would last for eternity. This would guarantee an eternal afterlife for the pharaoh and also for every Egyptian. In persuading the citizenry of the entire Egyptian nation of the absolute truth of this proposition, the priests of ancient Egypt effected the greatest illusion that had ever been perpetrated on so many people up until that time. And with only a few modifications, the illusion lasted for 3,000 years.

The great pyramid was the pinnacle expression of the practice that had begun thousands of years earlier when ancient peoples would sprinkle the graves of their dead companions with red ocher to express the belief that those loved ones would live once again. The ocher marked the spot where the body was buried so that the returning spirit could not miss finding it. The pyramids of Egypt served the same purpose for the spirit of the returning pharaoh. They were so large that the spirit of the pharaoh could not fail to find it. Throughout the stretch of time leading from the ancient graves marked with ocher to the pyramids of Egypt, everything related to the afterlife was the province of priests. Indeed, the highest of high priests in ancient Egypt was none other than the pharaoh himself, who specified the design and location of his own tomb. And the various illusions associated with the afterlife, which were the products of priestly ingenuity, grew in proportion to the size and grandeur of the tombs. During the Second Dynasty (ca. 2890–2686 BCE), the priests made the observation that if the spirit (called the "ka") of the dead pharaoh were to make a successful return, it would have to have a body to return to. Without a body, there would be no afterlife. They had noticed that bodies that had been buried in the dry, hot sand uphill from the banks of the Nile tended to be well preserved years later. This observation led to the practice of mummification.

Mummification was a procedure aimed at preserving every detail of the body of the deceased. This procedure led to the emergence of an entire science and industry devoted to the preservation of corpses. The process of creating a mummy took two and a half months. First, it was crucial that the head remain attached to the torso, so whatever was needed to accomplish this was done. The internal organs, including the brain, were removed and stored in jars (canopic jars) that were placed alongside the coffin in the tomb. The body cavities that remained after the organs were removed were stuffed with linen wads. At intermittent points in the ceremony, the embalmers would don masks and headdresses depicting Anubis, the god of the dead, and a priest would appear to recite the prayer "You live again, you live again for ever, you are young once more forever." Finally, the body would be impregnated with natron, a kind of naturally occurring soda ash, which would dry up the fats in the body, artificial eyes would be placed in the sockets, cosmeticians would go to work to make the body appear as similar as possible to the once-living pharaoh, and the whole body would then be wrapped in linen bandages to preserve the shape. All of this was done to implement the illusion that the afterlife required a restored body, and the ka (spirit/personality) of the pharaoh would return to that body.

As a result of being mummified, a dead pharaoh was enabled to relive the events of his or her life, or so it was thought. The first pharaohs were buried not in pyramids but in mastabas, which were tombs that resembled houses down to the last detail. These eventually gave way to multiroom mansions. The mastabas and mansion tombs were furnished in the most elegant way with tables, chairs, lounges, beds, garments worn by the pharaoh, wardrobes, weapons used by the pharaoh, vases, gold decorations of all sorts, dinnerware, implements for hunting game, chariots, and, of course, food. The food was replenished on a regular basis. The mastaba was intended to be the literal home of the mummified pharaoh, and it was built to be as comfortable as possible. It was intended to assist the pharaoh in reliving the life he or she lived prior to death. In response to the obvious question as to how a mummified individual could possibly eat anything, the response was that the pharaoh's ka would consume the food by gazing at it. Whatever was left over could be consumed by the servants. By extended reasoning, the ka could lounge on the sofa by gazing at it, could ride a chariot by gazing at it, could engage in a hunting expedition by gazing at the arrows and spears, and so on. Clearly, this was all an elaborate illusion created by priests to support the story of the afterlife.

Unfortunately, the mastabas and mansions were open invitations to tomb robbers, a threat that plagued Egypt throughout its entire history. To alleviate this threat, beginning with the Third Dynasty (2686–2613 BCE), the pharaohs came up with the idea of interring their own mummified bodies in pyramids. All together, there are more than seventy-five pyramids scattered about Egypt, most of them located on the west bank of the Nile, where the view of the setting sun symbolized death. The coffin containing the pharaoh's mummy would be located deep inside the pyramid, sometimes at the end of a long tunnel. The chamber housing the coffin would be large enough to contain the various articles that were formerly put into mastabas, but the entrance would be blocked with stones or bricks to deter even the most stalwart robber. Sometimes, ingenious architectural tricks, such as entrances in ceilings and false doors, were used to conceal the location of the coffin. However, even this did not work. In due course, every tomb located inside a pyramid was ransacked, netting the thieves a king's ransom in gold and jewels.

Commencing with the Eleventh Dynasty, some of the pharaohs decided to carve out caverns in solid stone for their sarcophagi. King

Mentuhotpe II was the first pharaoh to do so, and he selected Deir el-Bahari, on the west bank of the Nile, for the excavation. But his tomb, too, was soon invaded and defiled. Eventually, beginning with the Eighteenth Dynasty (1567–1320 BCE), the pharaohs moved a short distance to the southwest to what is now called the Valley of the Kings. The valley is situated just across the Nile from Thebes (modern-day Luxor), and originally it had a very narrow entrance, which facilitated enhanced security. The extremely rugged terrain also served as a deterrent to prospective tomb robbers. There, during a period of nearly 500 years, hundreds of thousands of workers, equipped only with copper tools, dug shafts hundreds of yards long (some are a mile or longer) into solid rock and excavated hundreds of chambers to serve as the final resting place of pharaohs and Egyptian royalty. The amount of labor required for this vast project is nearly impossible to imagine, and all of it was expended to fulfill an illusion created by ancient priests.

Merely having a well-preserved body and a secure tomb was never considered to be an absolute guarantee of an afterlife. After the ka had departed from the deceased pharaoh, it descended to the underworld, where it was expected to follow a set of instructions, created by priests, before it was allowed to proceed to the next stage. In the early dynasties, the instructions and information about what to expect in the netherworld were written in hieroglyphics on the walls of the chambers and passageways inside the pyramids, and they were later copied onto sheets of papyrus, at which time they came to be called the Pyramid Texts. All together, the texts are quite long, with the English translation running about 300 pages. They first instruct the pharaoh's ka to rise up out of the tomb. The texts were usually personalized to fit a certain pharaoh; in the case at hand, it was the pharaoh Teti:

> Oho! Oho! Rise up, O Teti!
> Take your head, collect your bones,
> Gather your limbs, shake the earth from your flesh!
> Take your bread that rots not, your beer that sours not,
> Stand at the gates that bar the common people!

Later instructions inform the ka about various ways to proceed: by climbing a ladder or by taking a boat and what to do if the boatman refuses to cooperate. The final destination is for the deceased pharaoh to take his or her place as a full-fledged god among the Egyptian pantheon. The Pyramid Texts, together with similar documents that came later, have been described as "crib notes" that the ka of the pharaoh could consult along the way lest he or she forget the instructions that were undoubtedly taught to him or her earlier.

Commencing around the Seventh Dynasty (ca. 2184 BCE), the concept of the afterlife started to become democratized, and the view came to be accepted that direct access to the afterlife was open not only to the pharaoh but to the aristocracy as well. The aristocrats and the social elite were the only people who could afford mummification and an expensive tomb. Riding on the coattails of the pharaoh was no longer thought to be the only way of getting to the afterlife, but still, it could not hurt to stay close to the pharaoh in death. Thus, at that time, tombs of aristocrats started to pop up in close vicinity to the tomb of the pharaoh. Also, it became important for these people to obtain a set of personalized instructions on how best to gain admission to the heavenly realm. For a price, the priests were only too happy to comply. The instructions were written in hieroglyphics inside their coffins, and once they were transcribed onto papyrus sheets, they were known as the Coffin Texts. They are significantly longer than the Pyramid Texts, with the English translation running 800 pages. These texts envision the pathway to the afterlife as strewn with treacherous pitfalls, and they instruct the traveler on how to avoid them. Being thoroughly versed in their arcane details was thought to be essential to reaching the afterlife.

## Book of the Dead

Finally, by the time of the New Kingdom, which began with the Eighteenth Dynasty (ca. 1507 BCE), the attitude toward the afterlife had become thoroughly democratized, and every Egyptian citizen was thought to be individually eligible for it. Gradually, the Coffin Texts had been replaced by the Book of the Dead, a set of texts that included much of the earlier Coffin Texts and a copy of which was placed inside the coffin of the deceased. The Book of the Dead remained the standard funerary text for 1,500 years. One of its more famous sections, Chapter 125, describes the so-called weighing of the heart, where "heart" refers to a person's center of consciousness and power of choice (will). In today's language, it would mean about the same thing as "soul." The text usually includes a painted scene that shows the deceased approaching a large balance scale tended by the jackal-headed god Anubis. The "heart" of the deceased is placed on one pan of the scale, and a feather, which represents *maat* (goodness and order), is placed on the other. The god of scribes, Thoth, records the result. If it turns out that the heart weighs less than the feather, which means that it is not burdened down with sin, then the deceased is presented to Osiris, the god of the underworld, who will lead him or her to the afterlife. On the other hand, if the verdict is negative, then the deceased will be turned over to a hungry crocodile-headed monster. This idea of a final judgment for every individual person was a powerful instrument of control by the priests, and it had a profound influence on all Western religions.

In the same chapter of the Book of the Dead, there is another famous passage that lists the forty-two principles of Maat that have come to be called the Negative Confession. The applicant for the afterlife is supposed to recite them to the gods in attendance, and if the gods find that the applicant has spoken the truth, they are expected to respond favorably. The principles resemble pleadings by the defendant in a modern criminal trial. The first fifteen are as follows:

1. I have not committed sin.

2. I have not committed robbery with violence.

3. I have not stolen.

4. I have not slain men or women.

5. I have not stolen food.

6. I have not swindled offerings.

7. I have not stolen from God/Goddesses.

8. I have not told lies.

9. I have not carried away food.

10. I have not cursed.

11. I have not closed my ears to truth.

12. I have not committed adultery.

13. I have not made anyone cry.

14. I have not felt sorrow without reason.

15. I have not assaulted anyone.

This reference to sin and the particular instances of it may be the first such reference in Western literature. If so, it launched a career for the priests of Egypt and their modern successors that so far has lasted more than 3,500 years. Sin, for the Egyptians, was closely tied to the concept of Maat, which was the absolute expression of truth, harmony, order, justice, and morality. Every Egyptian was expected to live his or her life according to Maat and treat everyone with honor and respect. If a person were to sin, such a person would be thought of as having violated the principles of Maat. The pharaoh was both the interpreter and the dispenser of Maat. Therefore, since the pharaoh was considered to be a living god, sin amounted to a violation of the will of a god. This is the meaning that sin has for most people today.

The Book of the Dead was intended for the general population. Artistic renditions depicting the weighing of the heart (soul) were reproduced throughout Egypt for the edification of everyone, and they undoubtedly struck fear in whoever saw them. The crocodile-headed monster waiting to devour anyone who failed to measure up would have been particularly frightening, especially for children. Of course, the ordeal that was depicted would not occur until the next life, but the implications of that ordeal extended to every moment of premortem existence. Anyone whose soul was so weighed down by sin that it was heavier than a feather would be turned over, after death, to the monster. And these were sins that accumulated day by day throughout one's entire life. The actions that were considered sinful were determined by the priests. Obviously, the priests in the later dynasties became very important to ordinary people every day, and this greatly increased their power and prestige. Also, a sizable number, perhaps the vast majority, of ordinary people purchased copies of the Book of the Dead for their own coffins, thus yielding considerable income for the priests. In Egypt, the afterlife was an obsession for everyone from the pharaoh down to the lowliest farmworker. Everyone did everything he or she could possibly do to ensure a successful passage.

## Priests and Gods

The Great Harris Papyrus (named after the man who purchased it in modern times) provides information about the number of personnel in the service of the great god Amun during the reign of the Twentieth Dynasty king Rameses III (ca. 1186–1155 BCE). For the city of Thebes, which included the huge temple complex at Karnak, it reports 81,322 people.[1] This number includes everyone in Amun's service: priests, peasants, boatmen, administrators, construction workers, artisans, cooks, scribes, and so on. Exactly how many of them were priests is hard to say because no separate figure is given for the priests, and any one person might serve, perhaps at different times, in more than one capacity, such as priest and scribe or priest and administrator. But the number of priests for the entire city, including priests in the service of other gods, probably ran in the thousands. This growth in the number of priests from the time of the First Dynasty is nothing short of astonishing when one considers that a single village in earlier times might have had one or two priests. The priesthood grew like a cluster of viruses in a host organism. The Harris Papyrus also gives figures for the number of animals, 421,362, and the number of fields (in acres), 591,320, all property of the temple of Amun. The animals (which included oxen, cows, geese, and ducks) and the fields under cultivation were all under the control of the priests. This made the priesthood at this temple alone (granted, it was the largest in Egypt), enormously wealthy and powerful, rivaling the wealth and power of the pharaoh himself.

The span of time that witnessed the remarkable growth in the number of priests also saw a substantial growth in the number of gods. As would be expected with a society emerging from the Neolithic period, the earliest gods addressed concerns related to the growth of crops and the afterlife. The crops needed adequate sunlight and sufficient water. Accordingly, the oldest and originally the most powerful god was Re, the sun god. This god was later supplemented by three gods: Khepri (morning sun), Herakhte (midday sun), and Atum (evening sun). Re remained as additional security for the midday sun. To ensure an adequate supply of water, Egyptians prayed to the god Hapy, who was thought to control the annual flood of the Nile. They also prayed to the Apis bull, the god responsible for fecundity of the land; Maat, the goddess of order in the world; and Nepri, the god of grain. If the annual flood was late, they would pray to Sothis, the harbinger of the inundation. For the afterlife, Egyptians would pray to Osiris, the god of the underworld and the ruler of the dead; Hathor, the goddess of the dead; Salkis, the goddess who protects the deceased; and Anubis, the god of embalming and the lord of the necropolis.

As Egyptian society became more diversified and roles became more defined, additional gods appeared for specialized jobs and personal concerns. There were Ptah and Sokar, the gods of craftsmanship; Heqet and Thoeris, the goddesses who protect women in childbirth; Bess, the goddess who repels evil at childbirth; Khededu, the god of fishing (even though consuming fish was off limits for many Egyptians); Sakhmet, the goddess who cures disease; Onuris, the god of hunting; Shezmu, the god of the winepress; and Thoth and Seshat, gods of learning and the art of writing. Also, there were Mont and Neith, whom military leaders would beseech for success with weapons and war. In addition to these, there were several gods, some of them very ancient, whom Egyptians would pray to for almost any cause: Amun, "the hidden one," a primeval deity who was the creator and sustainer of the world; Aten, the sun disk, considered by the pharaoh Akhenaten to be the one and only god; Atum, "the undifferentiated one," the creator of the world; Horus, "the distant one," often depicted as a falcon who was linked to the ancient sun god Re; and Isis, "the multiform one," who was the sister and wife of Osiris and the mother of Horus.

The ancient priests embellished the account of the gods with various stories aimed at satisfying human curiosity. Some of these stories related to the creation of both the world and the gods. According to one such story, the creation of the gods came first. The great god Atum (who was presumably eternal) produced the twin gods Shu and Tefnut by masturbating in what would become the city of Heliopolis: "He took his phallus in his grasp that he might create orgasm by means of it, and so were born the twins Shu and Tefnut." Shu, as the god of air and sunlight, then mated with his sister, Tefnut, the goddess of moisture, to produce Geb, god of earth, and Nut, goddess of the sky. This procedure is often represented pictorially where Shu, arms raised upward, separates Nut (sky) from Geb (earth), who is resting below. The human quest for the afterlife is depicted in the story of Osiris, the offspring of Geb and Nut. According to the story, Osiris was drowned in the Nile by his wicked brother Seth, who proceeded to chop the dead body into many pieces. Osiris's wife, Isis, together with her sister, Nepthys, then reassembled the body and brought it back to life. The resurrection of Osiris nurtured the hope of all Egyptians for a personal resurrection. Yet another story related to the journey of the sun god Re through the heavens. Re was said to sail in a boat from dawn until dusk, then to expire, only to be resurrected the next morning. Re's steady, incremental motion was accounted for by appealing to the scarab beetle god Khepri, who pushed the sun along much in the way that scarab beetles push small balls of mud and dung over the ground.

Richard Wilkinson, an archaeologist specializing in Egyptology, reports in his "complete" account that the ancient Egyptians had more than 1,400 gods and goddesses.[2] This profusion of gods leads to the question, where did they all come from, and why are there so many? The related question is, how does one explain the explosive growth in the number of priests? The answer to both questions, which to me is fairly obvious, is that the priests created the gods, and the gods, once they had become established, expanded the power of the priests and thereby increased their numbers. The system of gods was a construct, a belief construct, and as with all constructs, it was produced for the purpose of augmenting the power of the person or people who created it. And as the power of the priests increased, so did their numbers. This follows from the fact that every god that became popular would have its own temple,[3] and every temple needed priests.[4] Some gods, such as the sun god Re, had dozens of temples, each with its coterie of priests. Before long, there were thousands of priests. And this led to the emergence of a priestly hierarchy (a social construct), which expanded even further the power of the priests, especially those on top. The hierarchy led to the emergence of priests who specialized in theology, and these were the ones who created the gods. So the causal chain went like this: the more gods, the more temples; the more temples, the more priests; the more priests, the more theologians; and the more theologians, the more gods.

No priest, of course, ever claimed to have created any god. The most that might have been said is that after intense study, prayer, and meditation, such and such entity has been "discovered" to be a god, or such and such entity has chosen at this time to "reveal" himself. Yet there is one practice that the priests undoubtedly were responsible for that resulted in the existence of a new god.[5] This practice, which Egyptologists call "syncretism," is the combining of two or more gods to produce a new, more powerful god having the attributes of both of the original deities. Thus, if the theologians thought that it was useful to increase the power of a minor deity, such as Sobek, they would link it with a powerful god, such as Re, to produce Sobek-Re. If they had need of a god that represented the greatest visible and invisible powers of the world, they combined Amun with Re to produce Amun-Re. Sometimes, the process would result in several gods being joined together, such as Ptah-Sokar-Osiris or Harmachis-Khepri-Re-Atum. At other times, it was useful to increase the power of a local god, and this would be done by linking it to the all-powerful god Re. The procedure of syncretism may provide the best direct evidence of priests creating gods.

The priestly hierarchy was divided into a higher and a lower clergy. At the very top, of course, was the pharaoh, but the highest individual in a temple context, such as the temple of Amun in Karnak, was the first prophet, otherwise called the high priest. Beneath the first prophet was the second prophet, who stepped in for the first prophet when he was away on business. He was also in charge of the temple's secular administration, supervised workshops and agricultural production, and oversaw deliveries of foreign gifts to the god. Beneath the second prophet were a large number of talented people who have come to be called "specialists." They included a wide assortment: lector priests, stolists, sem priests, hour-priests, horoscope priests, and sacred musicians and singers. The lector priests were the scholars and intellectuals of the kingdom. As keepers of the sacred writings, some of them would have been theologians. The lector priests also recorded the history of the ancient kings, practiced medicine, and officiated at private funerals. The stolists attended daily to bathing and clothing the statue of the god and bedecking it with jewelry. They also cared for those jewels as well as the divine clothing. Sem priests were funerary priests who officiated at the Opening of the Mouth ceremony, which was considered essential to bringing the deceased back to life. An open mouth was thought to be the key for breathing, eating, drinking, and speaking. Hour-priests were astronomers who specialized in determining the exact hour in which a cultic act was supposed to begin in the temple. The astrologer priests, as their name implies, determined which days were lucky and which unlucky for engaging in any activity, how the day on which a person was born determined that person's destiny in life, and how the person would die. The sacred musicians and singers, who were often women, served an important role in the liturgy by chanting, singing, or playing a harp at designated intervals during the service. They also awakened the god of the temple in the morning and delighted it during the day with musical performances. Subsidiary to all of these individuals were the lower clergy, who performed menial tasks, such as carrying the sacred barque in processions; cleaning the temples; supervising artisans, painters, and draftsmen; and even crafting sacred objects, such as sandals, for the god of the temple.

Egyptian priests could easily be recognized as important persons through their outward appearance, by the clothing they wore, and, in the case of higher-level priests, by their wealth and power. The priests had to shave their bodies every other day to remove every strand of hair, including eyebrows and eyelashes. Any priest who was found to shirk this obligation was subject to a fine of 1,000 drachmas. The priests were known as the "pure ones," and, as Herodotus observed, the removal of hair was thought to "guard against the presence of lice or anything else equally unpleasant, while they are about their religious duties." To preserve purity, it was also required that every priest be circumcised. According to Herodotus, "They circumcise themselves for cleanliness' sake, preferring to be clean rather than comely." (The ancient Greeks considered the appearance of a circumcised phallus to be abhorrent.) For their clothing, anything made of wool was forbidden since wool came from animals that were thought to be a source of contamination. Instead, most priests had to be clothed in an outfit made of fine white linen that was always cut in the same way, together with white sandals. The lector priests wore a sash across their chests, sem priests wore a specially tailored garment made of panther skin (apparently panthers were considered clean), the priests of Heliopolis wore a garment spangled with stars, and the high priest of Memphis donned a specially shaped collar and a sidelock. The shaven heads of the priests and their distinctive dress were a constant and ever-present reminder to the people that the gods were real and were to be taken seriously and that the priests, as mediators between the gods and the people, were the most important component of society.

The high priest, generally appointed directly by the pharaoh, was often rewarded with generous amounts of silver and gold for work the pharaoh found pleasing. These rewards were usually shared with priests lower down in the hierarchy. It was also typical for priests on the upper end to hold high positions in the government, which further increased their power and prestige. According to an inscription in the temple of Karnak, when a priest named Nebwenenef was raised to the position of high priest of Amun,

> His majesty [gave Nebwenenef] his two golden rings and his staff of electrum, he being named first prophet of Amun, overseer of the double house of silver and gold, overseer of the double granary, overseer of works, and overseer of all the crafts in Thebes. A royal messenger was sent [to let all Egypt know that] the temple of Amun [was turned over] to him, along with all its property and all its people.[6]

The two golden rings symbolized political and religious authority. In being named high priest of Amun, Nebwenenef became one of the most powerful and wealthy people in the entire country.

The exact protocol for creating a god or for linking two or more gods together via syncretism is a matter of speculation. It was probably accomplished in private by a relatively small number of theologian priests, who were the ultimate insiders in the hierarchy. The lector priests, the larger group that would have included the theologians, were known to be experts in practical magic, and they spent hours entertaining the pharaoh and royalty with conjured tricks. In view of this expertise, magic may have played a role in convincing the priestly rank and file that such and such entity was now taken to be a god.[7] In any event, once a god had taken root in the mind of the average priest and the public at large, it became necessary to *sustain* the god's existence. This was accomplished through a highly elaborate ritual in which the god is said to have been "cultivated." The presumed meaning is that *belief* in the god is cultivated in the minds of the believers—first in the minds of the priests in general and then in the minds of the public. "Cultivated" serves as the basis for the word "cult." The believers associated with any temple are said to compose a cult, which is a religion based on ritual.

## Rituals, Processions, and Festivals

Every day of the year, just as the sun crept above the horizon, the chief officiant of the temple (a priest of the highest rank) broke the clay seal barring entry to the sanctuary, slid the bolt on the double doors, and entered the holy of holies. The priest had already bathed in the sacred lake, put on special white garments selected for the service, and washed out his mouth with a bit of natron, which the Egyptians used for soap. As he (or she—some officiants were women) approached the altar, he sang, "Awake (oh great god) in peace, wake peacefully." The huge choir then took up the song, "Wake peacefully, wake beautifully, in peace! Wake to life oh (god of this city)." With variations, this invocation was repeated forty-five times. Then the officiant broke the clay seal locking the tabernacle and exposed the statue of the god (the cult statue). As he did so, the spirit of the god, which is omnipresent throughout the universe, entered the statue, and the statue became a living being.[8] After uttering the words, "I adore your great majesty with choice expressions and prayers that magnify your prestige," the priest presented the god with the offerings that had been placed there earlier: cuts of meat, vegetables, loaves of bread, cakes, fruits, and beer or wine. The god proceeded to consume the offerings by gazing at them. After he was satiated, what was left of the meal (all of it, of course) was given to the priests for their breakfast. Then the statue was bathed, the clothing from the previous day was removed and replaced with fresh clothing, and it was adorned with the finest jewelry (at least this was done on festival days). Finally, the statue was anointed with perfumed oil, sprinkled with holy water, and placed back in its tabernacle, and the doors were shut and sealed. On departing, the officiant fumigated the sanctuary with incense and used a broom to sweep away any footprints that might have been left in the sand as he stepped backward from the tabernacle. The entire service took perhaps three hours from start to finish.[9]

A shorter ritual was performed at midday and in the evening, and essentially identical rituals (morning, noon, and evening) were performed simultaneously in every temple in Egypt. Only the chief officiant was allowed to view the statue of the god, and only priests were allowed in the temple, which means that the services were intended chiefly for the priests. The rule for each service had to be obeyed down to the letter, which was intended to impress on the priests the overall importance of the services and the importance of the god that was being cultivated. Given the frequency of the services, the gods were constantly in the forefront of every priest's mind. Although the rituals were intended primarily to strengthen the faith of the priests, since the priests influenced the public in its quest for the afterlife, the rituals strengthened the faith of the public as well. The religious functions that were directed specifically toward the public were the many processions and festivals held during the year.

At any given temple, a procession usually occurred every four or five days. The statue of the god was placed in a kind of portable wooden tabernacle with doors closed, and this was mounted on a small boat, called the sacred barque. It was a smaller version of the barque that, from time to time, carried the god on journeys up or down the Nile. Long poles were attached to either side of the boat to allow it to be carried on the shoulders of several priests and transported in a forward direction. The procession was led by a priest with a censor and followed up by a long line of priests dressed in white linen and chanting prayers and hymns. Along the way, the procession would stop at designated stations where sacred rites were performed that included incense, readings from sacred books, and various kinds of offerings. Throngs of people, anxious to catch a glimpse of their deity (or at least the box that contained it), would line the way as the procession snaked through the town. Processions of this sort were usually included as a part of the many festivals that took place throughout Egypt during the year: the Festival of the Nile celebrating the arrival of the inundation, the harvest festivals, the Festival of Drunkenness, and festivals devoted to the various gods. The festivities would often go on for days, and vast quantities of food, beer, and wine would be consumed, with the end result being the establishment of a favorable association between the lives of the people and the gods. All of the processions were under the direction of the priests, and so, probably, were most of the festivals.

## The Fictitious Nature of the Gods

If the gods were created by theologian priests; if the priests used rituals, processions, and festivals to sustain belief in the gods by rank-and-file priests and the public at large; and if, without those rituals and festivals, the gods would have quickly ceased to exist, then the gods were fictitious entities, every single one of them. The gods did not really exist. They existed only in the minds of the believers, and in so believing, both the rank-and-file priests and the people at large bought into an illusion. This, of course, should come as no surprise to any of us living today. After all, the sun is not a god, with thoughts, feelings, and desires, nor does it sail in a boat across the heavens, only to be extinguished at the end of the day and resurrected at the beginning of the next, nor is it pushed through the heavens by a beetle god. No god modeled after humans (as were all of the Egyptian gods) could consume food by merely gazing at it. The earth that we stand on, the air that we breathe, and the sky, replete with planets and stars, are not gods. No resurrected pharaoh (who became a god in the afterlife) could ride a chariot or engage in a hunt by merely gazing at the vehicle or at a spear, bow, and arrow. No god (Osiris) could be resurrected by reassembling the parts of his cut-up body and breathing new life into the composite. No god modeled after humans could produce offspring gods by merely masturbating without the help of a female partner. Anyone today who would believe any of these things would be considered deluded or insane.

Even the process of syncretism, by which one god could be fused with another to produce a single composite god, serves to undermine the idea that the gods were real. Imagine an apple and an orange sitting next to each other. Could these two fruits be somehow fused together to produce a single fruit? Of course not. The result would be a destruction of both fruits. If it should be argued that the gods were not like fruits, that they were more nebulous or abstract, then I would invite you to consider two abstractions, such as circularity and triangularity. Could these two entities, whether they are considered real (as for Plato) or mental, be melded to produce a composite called circular triangularity? Again, the answer is, of course not. The composite is self-contradictory. The only kind of entities that allow for the kind of fusion envisioned by syncretism are imaginary beings like Donald Duck and Bugs Bunny. It is indeed possible to imagine some kind of composite entity that shares features of both of these imaginary beings. So the conclusion is that the gods of ancient Egypt simply did not exist, not as real entities such as one's parents, spouse, or friend.

But some will be quick to reply that the Egyptian gods may not exist for people living today, but they did exist for the Egyptians. Isn't it possible that what does not exist for one group of people does exist for another?

First off, when we speak of something existing *for* someone, we are talking about a *belief* about what may or may not exist—not about existence per se. Existence as such, I contend, is an absolute. Assuming that there is a mind-independent reality (in other words, a reality that ordinary people cannot create to suit their own purposes), something either exists or it does not. It makes no difference whether someone may happen to believe that it does or does not or when and where that person may happen to live. But *beliefs* about existence may indeed be relative to time, place, and culture. An example may help to clarify this issue.

In the seventeenth century, most chemists believed that an invisible substance called phlogiston existed and that it accounted for the phenomenon of burning. When a combustible material, such as wood, caught fire and continued to burn, the process was explained by saying that the wood was giving up its phlogiston. Phlogiston might be loosely defined as "fire stuff," and when it was released from something, such as wood, it manifested itself as flame. The theory was supported by the fact that ash and charcoal, which were left over after the wood had burned, weighed less than the wood, which suggested that something had been given up. However, the theory ran into trouble when it was found that certain metals, when burned, gained weight. After the discovery of oxygen in the nineteenth century, burning was explained in terms of oxidation, and the metals in question weighed more after they were burned because they had gained oxygen. After that, the phlogiston theory lived on for a while, but it was gradually abandoned. So when we say that phlogiston existed for chemists in the seventeenth century but not for chemists in the nineteenth century, do we mean that phlogiston actually existed in the earlier period but not in the later? No. Rather, we mean that chemists in the earlier period *believed* that phlogiston existed, but they did not believe it in the later period. Further, we would observe that chemists today, in the twenty-first century, have excellent reasons for saying that phlogiston never existed and that the seventeenth-century chemists who believed that it did were simply wrong. However, we must qualify this last statement just a bit. No matter of fact can be 100 percent certain. It is conceivable (not self-contradictory) that something might happen in the future to reawaken the phlogiston theory. But this is extremely unlikely. So we can say with something like 99.99 percent certainty that phlogiston never existed and never will exist and that whoever believed that it did was wrong.

The Egyptian gods, being invisible "beings," were similar in some ways to phlogiston. And just as we know with virtual certainty that phlogiston never existed, so we know with equal certainty that the Egyptian gods never existed. Hopefully, this will not be received as a pompous statement of ethnocentric superiority: we in the twenty-first century are smarter and better informed than the ancient Egyptians, so we know that their gods, whom they believed in with such fervor, did not exist. Rather, the point I am trying to make is that beginning mainly with Galileo in the seventeenth century, we have discovered certain regularities in nature that are, for our purposes, independent of time. These regularities we call "laws of nature," and they hold true for the world today just as they did for the world 5,000 years ago. They govern phenomena such as the apparent motion of the sun, moon, and planets; the heat and light emitted by the sun; the conditions needed for the growth of plant and animal life; the physiological conditions needed for the support of human life; the function of the organs in an animal body; the conditions that cause rivers to rise and fall; and countless others. As a result of our knowledge of these laws, we know with virtual certainty that a mummified body cannot be restored to life, that no god pushes the sun through the heavens, that no god is responsible for the rise and fall of the Nile, that no god is responsible for the germination and growth of plants, and so on.

Furthermore, in saying these things, I am mindful of the proscription by anthropologists to the effect that cross-cultural judgments like this one are generally to be avoided. I would agree with the social scientists that cross-cultural judgments that relate to mores (e.g., it is permissible to go naked in public) and possibly some that relate to morals (e.g., it is permissible to kill defective infants) are relative to culture. I am also mindful of the rule, often attributed to Wittgenstein, that forms of life are epistemically self-contained, so that one cannot form judgments grounded in one form of life that apply to another form of life. But I would not agree that such proscriptions apply to judgments that rest on time-invariant laws of nature. And when the existence of something depends on such laws, I would hold that it is quite permissible to form judgments within one form of life that apply to another form of life.

If, in believing in the existence of their gods, the ancient Egyptians bought into an illusion, then at some point, they must have made some serious errors in judgment. All illusions are grounded in erroneous judgments. I believe that this was indeed the case. The Egyptians were thoroughly versed in the operation of boats. Boat travel was the most common mode of transportation. There were thousands of boats that floated up and down the Nile every day, and everyone had seen them and practically everyone ridden in one. The lesson is that boats float in water, not in air. So how could the Egyptians have been persuaded that the sun god (Re and others) sailed in a boat that floated in the air? Such an occurrence would have been considered to be impossible. Also, the Egyptians were thoroughly versed in the science and art of medicine. They knew the details of anatomy and physiology better than any other ancient people. So how could they have been coaxed into thinking that a dismembered body (Osiris's) could be reassembled and brought back to life? Or how could they believe that a mummified body with its internal organs removed could be revivified? Such occurrences were ordinarily unimaginable. And how could they possibly have been led to think that mere masturbation could generate a living, thinking entity, albeit a god? No such phenomenon had ever occurred to the best of their knowledge. The answer to these questions rests in their hopes and fears. Every Egyptian yearned desperately for the afterlife, and everyone feared the "second death of the soul"—being gobbled up by the crocodile-headed monster that sat beside the scale that would weigh their hearts. The only route to the afterlife and the only way of avoiding the second death was through the priests. They must believe what the priests said, down to the last detail, and they must follow every word of the Book of the Dead. This required that they believe in the gods and conform their lives to priestly norms.

## A Theistic Objection

At this point, I will address an objection that is likely to be raised by certain theists to the effect that a transcendent and eternal god exists who creates (or has created) the world and in so doing discloses himself in his creative activity or work product. According to this view, the multiple gods of the Egyptians were simply manifestations of the creating deity, and as such, they really did exist in a supernatural sense. Even certain Egyptologists seem to have succumbed to this view, which explains their reluctance to come out and admit forthrightly that belief in the gods was an illusion and that the gods did not really exist. The Egyptologist Erik Hornung recalls that many early Egyptologists, French, English, and German, saw a single god (apparently identical with the God of Christianity) lying behind the multiple gods of the Egyptians. He also notes the influence of the German idealist philosopher F. W. von Schelling, whose dynamic pantheism envisioned manifestations of the divine emerging everywhere in created reality. The view that a single creating god is responsible for the many gods of the Egyptians has a seductive simplicity to it. After all, if there is a god who created the world, wouldn't he have wanted to disclose himself in his creation? And if this god is all-powerful, can't he do anything?

My response to this view is two pronged. First, if it results from personal religious beliefs, as it seems to have in some cases, then it has no business forming the substance of a scientific account. Egyptology is supposed to be a science. Second, if the view is philosophical, then it is nowhere near as simple as it might first appear. Initially, there is the problem as to why a god who is the essence of simplicity would choose to manifest himself as a multiplicity. Isn't this a case of misrepresentation? Also, does this god act freely, or is he compelled? If compelled, what compels him? If freely, what motivates him to manifest himself? What does he hope to gain by doing so? Also, if this god is all-powerful, why does the manifestation process take so long? Why drag it out for thousands of years when it could be done instantly? Furthermore, if this god acts in the temporal dimension, does not this imply that he changes? At least he would be aware of the passage of time, which is a kind of change. If he changes (which involves acquiring a perfection), how can he be infinitely perfect? Attempting to answer questions such as these has occupied the attention of hundreds of philosophers and required thousands of pages of extremely complex theorizing. Why not simply say that the Egyptian gods were created by the priests and that the priests did this for the purpose of augmenting their own power?

The attempt to explain the emergence of the Egyptian gods through an appeal to a single god who manifests himself through a multiplicity of gods cries out for a serious application of Ockham's razor. This principle, named after the fourteenth-century Franciscan friar William of Ockham, says, in effect, that in the case of competing explanations, the simpler one is the preferred one. For example, suppose you are trying to explain why helium balloons tend to rise. You could say that helium is less dense than air, so a balloon filled with helium is buoyed upward by a force equal to the weight of the displaced air. Or you could say that the balloon tends to rise because it is pushed upward by pixies who love rarefied air. Now the pixie explanation seems simple enough because it involves only one element: pixies. But it is nowhere near as simple as it seems. Exactly what are pixies, and why do they like rarefied air? Are they visible entities? If so, why does no one see them? If not, how do we know they exist? And how do pixies fly? Do they have wings, and, if so, are they strong enough to push a balloon upward? How many of them would it take? Dozens more questions could be added to these, and none of them has a plausible answer. So the explanation based on the density of air is far simpler than the pixie explanation, and it rests on well-established scientific laws. This does not mean that the pixie explanation is irrefutably false, but it does mean that no reasonable person would accept it. Thus, as concerns the Egyptian gods, attributing the existence of these gods to the creative activity of priests is preferred over the competing explanation that they are manifestations of some transcendent deity.

## Were the Egyptians Actually Monotheists?

One would think that the mere fact that ancient Egypt managed to assemble a pantheon consisting of more than 1,000 deities would ipso facto establish its religion as polytheistic beyond any doubt. But such was not the case among early Egyptologists, where the prevailing view was that beneath the surface, behind the countless images of deities bearing heads of falcons, jackals, rams, and bulls, the religion of ancient Egypt was solidly and unquestionably monotheistic. Thus, in a lecture in 1869, the French Egyptologist Emmanuel de Rougé urged,

> I said *God*, not *the gods*. The first characteristic of [Egyptian] religion is the Unity [of God] most energetically expressed: God, One, Sole, and Only; no others with Him.—He is the Only Being—living in truth.—Thou art One, and millions of beings proceed from thee.—He has made everything, and he alone has not been made. . . .
> One idea predominates, that of a single and primeval God; everywhere it is One Substance, self-existent and an unapproachable God.[10]

The use of capital letters and the general tone of this passage suggest that de Rougé's personal religious and/or philosophical commitments have leaked into his Egyptology. Also, the claim that all finite beings, including those many gods having the heads of jackals, rams, and so on, "proceed from" this one God suggests a kind of emanation theory in which the multitude of creatures pour forth from the one true God and in doing so retain an imprint from their divine source.

Among German Egyptologists, Heinrich Brugsch, one of the two leading figures of his day, maintained much the same view, holding that from the earliest times, the Egyptians worshipped "the one, nameless, incomprehensible, eternal God in his highest purity."[11] After the turn of the century, the monotheistic view was challenged by the American Egyptologist James Henry Breasted, who argued that the Egyptians were genuine polytheists tinged with a kind of pantheism, but then the monotheistic interpretation returned in the work of Egyptologists such as E. A. Wallace Budge, Etienne Drioton, Eberhard Otto, and Hermann Junker. The possibility that the ancient Egyptians were henotheists (belief in one chief god among many lesser deities—the term was coined by Schelling) was added to the mix in those years.

While it may be true that personal religious and/or philosophical commitments may have influenced these early Egyptologists, we may still ask whether there were any objective features of Egyptian religion that suggested a monotheist interpretation. To that question, we answer cautiously in the affirmative. For example, there is a hymn to Amun-Re that reads in part,

> Thou art the sole one who made all there is,
> The solitary one, who made what exists,
> From whose eyes mankind came forth,
> And upon whose mouth the gods came into being . . .
> Hail to thee who did this!
> Solitary sole one, with many hands.[12]

Taken literally, this passage has a clear monotheistic bent. But the object of such praise was not always Amun-Re. In the Berlin Hymn to Ptah, the god Ptah, patron of craftsmen, is addressed:

He who has made all gods, men and animals; he who has created all lands and shores and the ocean in his name "fashioner of the earth."[13]

From very early times, the god Atum, said to be the creator of the world, was called "the greatest one";[14] in the Pyramid Texts, the sun god Re is called the "greatest god"; and in the underworld books of the New Kingdom, the epithet "greatest god" is assigned to Osiris, Atum, Anubis, Horus, and Mekhentienirti.[15] From these conflicting descriptions, we might conclude that expressions of the form "sole one," "only one," "creator of all things," and "greatest god" are intended chiefly as phrases of worship or endearment, much as a spouse might say to his or her partner, "I only have eyes for you."

Another possible candidate for chief god is none other than the pharaoh or, better, the office of pharaoh. From his titles, the pharaoh is considered to be a god in the full sense of the term. He is called "perfect god," "greatest god," and even "greater than the gods."[16] These are titles that he acquires at the moment of his accession to the throne. He is also identified in some way, perhaps as an incarnation, with the gods Horus, Mont, Khnum, Sakhmet, Re, and others.[17] Yet on other occasions, the pharaoh is called the "son of Re," a designation that implies inferiority to Re, and if the pharaoh were to serve as the chief officiant in a ritual that cultivated one of the gods, he would prostrate himself before the cult image, which again suggests a status inferior to the gods.[18] And then there are countless images on papyrus and elsewhere showing one pharaoh or another presenting offerings to the gods. Furthermore, one teaching going back to the Old Kingdom held that on coronation, the pharaoh entered the world of the divine but did not become wholly divine until after death. Thus, any appeal to pharaonic divinity in support of the claim that the religion of ancient Egypt was monotheistic is ambiguous at best.

Syncretism, the process by which one god can enter into another god to produce unitary beings, such as Amun-Re and Re-Osiris, has also been cited as evidence supporting monotheism. If one god can enter another to increase its power, why not a single god entering into every individual god to give power and existence to those gods?[19] Another possibility is all of the gods uniting in one grand synthesis to form a single god. In opposition to these imaginative extensions of the idea of syncretism, which was originally intended as a solution to the problem of how to increase the power of local gods, both Morenz and Hornung point out that syncretism is a temporary arrangement in which a more powerful god takes up short-term residence in a less powerful one.[20] It cannot be used to explain the permanent synthesis of multiple gods. Furthermore, if the account of syncretism offered in this book is correct, that syncretism is the product of priestly action, then, if the priests wanted a single god to underpin the multitude of gods, they would have created one for that purpose. But they did nothing of the sort. Thus, we can conclude that syncretism cannot support the view that the ancient Egyptians were monotheists.

## Akhenaten

According to most accounts, the only unambiguous and uncontested instance of genuine monotheism ever to emerge in the 3,000-year history of ancient Egyptian religion was introduced by the Eighteenth Dynasty pharaoh Amenophis IV, who switched from being a polytheist to a monotheist beginning around 1350 BCE. As was usual with Egyptian pharaohs, the name "Amenophis" was connected to a deity, in this case Amun; it meant "Amun is pleased." About four years after his coronation, Amenophis decided to replace Amun with the Aten, which is an aspect or manifestation of the sun god Re. It refers specifically to the disk of the sun. At about the same time he changed his name to Akhenaten, which means "Servant of the Aten," he proceeded to initiate a high-speed religious revolution throughout Egypt by declaring that the Aten was the only god that Egyptians were permitted to worship. Akhenaten had thus reduced the original polytheism to henotheism because even though the Aten had become the sole object of veneration, the other gods continued to exist. But within a short period of time, all the other gods were absorbed into the Aten, the result being that the Aten was the only god that remained. Henotheism was thus converted into a strict monotheism.[21]

Soon after converting to Aten worship, Akhenaten shut down all the temples devoted to the other gods. This action infuriated the priests because it put them out of a job. They could no longer conduct the temple rituals that were their chief function. One of the best ways of generating hostility among an established group of people is to threaten their livelihood. Closing the temples also struck terror in the mind of every Egyptian because the temple rituals were believed to be necessary for cosmic order.

Without them, everyone thought that the entire cosmos could disintegrate at any moment. Akhenaten then sent his stonemasons throughout Egypt, hammer and chisel in hand, to deface the images of the other gods, particularly Amun, on statues, bas-reliefs, and inscriptions everywhere. This destruction produced great heartache in the mind of the average Egyptian because the people loved their gods and were horrified to see the images of their dearest friends mutilated and disfigured. The reaction by the establishment to Akhenaten's measures was so intense that it made governing difficult, and this may have been the reason why Akhenaten moved the capital of the nation from Thebes to a newly created city several miles to the north that he named Akhetaten ("Horizon of the Aten"). The city is today called Amarna, and it served as the new home for Akhenaten and his famous wife, Queen Nefertiti, for fifteen years.

Another and underappreciated effect of Akhenaten's shift to monotheism is that it virtually destroyed any possibility of an afterlife as the Egyptians had come to understand it. A strict monotheism implied that there was no Anubis, god and protector of the dead and lord of the underworld; no Osiris to lead the deceased individual, following a successful weighing of the heart, to a heavenly reward; no Maat, goddess of truth and justice, to maintain standards by which the righteous attained their desired goal; no jury of gods to sit in judgment over the deceased and to grant passage to the underworld; and no Thoth, god of scribes, to record the verdict of the divine jury. Furthermore, it is unlikely that the Aten could replace all of these gods in their service to the deceased. The proper location of the Aten was in the heavens, while the proper location of the deceased was in the lower regions. Given that the afterlife was the universal obsession of the Egyptian people, it should come as no surprise that Akhenaten was thoroughly reviled during his lifetime.

As a replacement for the afterlife, it appears that Akhenaten proposed a thoroughly this-worldly reward. A famous depiction of Akhenaten shows the pharaoh together with his wife, Nefertiti, and their daughters sitting beneath a huge image of the Aten. The rays emanating from the solar disk terminate in human hands that appear to offer support and sustenance to the royal family in this life. There is no hint in this bas-relief of any afterlife. However, a this-worldly award would never satisfy the average Egyptian who had come to expect an afterlife in the company of the gods. All the average Egyptian could look forward to in this life was another day of toiling in the fields, shaping stone blocks for temples and pyramids, or carving tombs in mountainsides for dead pharaohs and their offspring. Any suggestion of such a postmortem reward would have come as an insult to these people, so it was hardly surprising that they hated this pharaoh. In fact, Akhenaten may have been the most hated and despised king in the 3,000-year history of Egypt.

When Akhenaten died (possibly he was murdered) after a seventeen-year reign, his son, Tutankhamun (King Tut), lost no time in restoring the old gods (particularly Amun) to their former glory, reopening the temples, giving the priests back their jobs, returning the capital to Thebes, and restoring belief in the afterlife. This in itself stands as evidence that the Egyptians were genuine polytheists and not crypto-monotheists. The Egyptians wanted their many gods restored, and they wanted nothing to do with any single god. Akhenaten was branded a heretic and a "blasphemer," his images in stone were effaced, his monuments were buried, his name was removed from the list of kings, and the brief episode of Egyptian monotheism came to an abrupt end. The effort to remove any trace of Akhenaten from the Egyptian memory explains why historians and Egyptologists were utterly unaware of his existence until the nineteenth century CE, when the ruins of the city of Amarna were unearthed by archaeologists.

How do we explain the motivation behind the Amarna experiment? I suggest that the most salient clues are to be found in a before-and-after look at the lives and religious practices of the Egyptian people. Prior to the revolution, the people would pray to their gods through various intermediaries: sacred animals, statues, and deceased friends and relatives who had become deified. Following the revolution, nothing was sacred except the Aten. The Aten was far removed from the people, an inscrutable god, and the only intermediary was Akhenaten. Every home in Amarna had an altar with an image of Akhenaten, and the people would pray to the distant god through entreaties directed to the image. As Hornung has put it, "There is no god but Aten, and Akhenaten is his prophet."[22] The famous Hymn to the Aten, probably written by Akhenaten, concludes with these words:

> Everything is made to flourish for the King . . . since thou didst found the earth and raise everything up for thy son, who came forth from thy

body, the King of Upper and Lower Egypt . . . Akhenaten . . . and the
Chief Wife of the King . . . Nefertiti, living and youthful forever and
ever.[23]

Everything is made to flourish for the king. This makes the king the center of the universe. Prior to Akhenaten, every pharaoh was considered to
be the son of a god, but with the Aten as the only god and Akhenaten as
the only son, this son occupies a very special place indeed. Amarna (the
horizon of the Aten) was built specifically for the purpose of recognizing
this special relationship between the king and the one god. It was a kingdom within a kingdom, a "theater of the absurd," as Johnson put it, where
Akhenaten could rule as its sole lord and master. Even the inscriptions
on the tombs were directed first and foremost not to the deceased but to
Akhenaten, the king.

Akhenaten is widely considered to be an egomaniac beyond all re-
straints. In light of this fact and the foregoing observations, is not the conclusion warranted that Akhenaten created the Aten for the sole purpose
of increasing his own power and glory? Of course, the king did not create
the Aten from scratch. Re, the sun god whose manifestation is the Aten,
had been around for centuries. But in raising the Aten to the status of one
and only god, whose only son was none other than Akhenaten himself, in
a very real sense, Akhenaten did create the Aten, at least as this god came
be recognized during the Amarna period. One of the overriding themes
of this book is that the primary function of priests everywhere is to create
gods and sustain them in existence. Akhenaten was the highest among
all the high priests of Egypt. Hence, if our interpretation of his actions
is correct, it serves as a confirming instance for our thesis about priests.

Most (if not all) Egyptologists, scholars, and researchers have expressed views or theories about the Amarna period that either reinforce
or that are at least consistent with the view expressed here. Certainly, I
am not aware of anyone who holds that Akhenaten acted out of anything
approaching love for his people or that he sought to render their lives
happier and more fulfilled. By all indications, the Egyptian people had a
dim view of their pharaoh, which is suggested by the fact that whenever
he rode his chariot outside the confines of Amarna, he was accompanied
by a contingent of guards running on foot alongside the vehicle. Without
them, the people might rise up and assault or kill the driver. Also, to

maintain civil order, Akhenaten had the surrounding countryside constantly patrolled by armed soldiers.[24] The reign of terror caused general paranoia throughout the region. Far from acting out of benevolent feelings for his subjects, Akhenaten was almost certainly motivated by the desire to promote himself. In the view of Eric Hornung, Akhenaten was a "methodical rationalist" who implemented a carefully thought out, well-defined plan using a step-by-step method.[25] The decision to change his name, to move the nation's capital, to hijack the high priest of Amun by sending him into the wilderness while the plan was being implemented, to carefully replace Amun with the Aten by constructing a series of temples in Karnak devoted to the new state god, by carefully absorbing all the other gods into the being of the Aten—all of this was well thought out ahead of time, says Hornung. But this interpretation is perfectly consistent with the idea that Akhenaten did it all to increase his own power.

A different approach to the Amarna phenomenon begins with the visual images that depict the pharaoh. These images are bizarre, to say the least. Akhenaten is shown having thick thighs, spindly lower legs, wide hips, sunken chest, enlarged breasts, drooping belly, and elongated head, neck, face, and nose.[26] For years, Egyptologists have asked whether Akhenaten really looked like this or whether he was depicted in this way to fulfill a theological purpose. In regard to the latter, the Aten was said to be both the mother and the father of the human race. Given that Akhenaten was supposed to be the only son of the Aten and the only intermediary, is it plausible that he directed his painters and stonecutters to depict him as having both male and female features? Many Egyptologists have answered in the affirmative. However, having a grossly elongated head is hardly a female attribute. So on the assumption that the visual representations are accurate, several theorists have raised the question of whether Akhenaten suffered from some kind of genetic defect. One of the more intriguing possibilities is that he had temporal lobe epilepsy.[27] This form of epilepsy alters the release of sex hormones, which could account for the pharaoh's apparently feminine features. Also, since the disease is hereditary, it would account for Tutankhamun's feminine physique and his premature death. But most important, people who suffer from this form of epilepsy are known to experience hallucinations and religious visions, especially after exposure to sunlight. An episode of this sort could easily have led Akhenaten to attribute special religious significance to the sun. However, even if temporal lobe epilepsy did lead Akhenaten to select the Aten as the one and only god, this in no way undermines the idea that in carrying out a religious revolution based on the Aten, he was motivated by the desire to enhance his own power. The epileptic vision simply gave him insight into the direction the revolution would take.

Why was Akhenaten's attempt to convert the nation of Egypt to monotheism such a resounding failure? The immediate reason, of course, is that it is nearly impossible in the span of a few short years to change the ingrained habits, viewpoints, and manner of living of an entire nation. Belief in the gods had social momentum. The constant yearning for the afterlife and the sheer hope for survival in this life rested on prayer and worship directed toward a plethora of gods. No pharaoh could simply replace all of them with a single god and expect that everyone would go along without putting up a fight. And then there were the priests. The priests despised what Akhenaten tried to accomplish for reasons already stated. But the subtler issue remains as to whether there may have been something more deeply ingrained in the Egyptian psyche that favored the multiple and the concrete over the simple and the abstract. If so, this would provide further evidence that the ancient Egyptians were thoroughly polytheistic despite the assertions by certain Egyptologists and historians of religion to the contrary. For an affirmative response to this question, I would suggest that such evidence may be found in the Egyptians' written language, their mathematics, and their funerary documents.

## Evidence for Genuine Polytheism: A Love for Multiplicity

As everyone knows, the language of the Egyptians consisted of hieroglyphs. The hieroglyphs ("glyphs" for short) served three basic functions. Some were phonograms, which are signs that represent a specific sound. The phonograms included the alphabet, which comprised twenty-four glyphs that represented the sounds of consonants. There were no genuine vowels, and this, as might be expected, invited ambiguity. To assist in eliminating the ambiguity, other glyphs served as determinatives, which were symbols inserted at the end of words, to pin down the meaning. A third group of glyphs served as ideograms, which represented ideas. The ideograms included images for the ideas of such things as the sun, a god, a mountain, a tree, or a bird. In any hieroglyphic expression, the majority of components were usually phonograms, which means that the written language of the ancient Egyptians was essentially phonetic. It represented language as it was spoken.

To illustrate the ambiguity that arose from an alphabet that included no vowels, suppose that we eliminate the vowels from the English alphabet, and with that limited alphabet, suppose we attempt to write out the word for the spoken word "bud," meaning a flower bud. We would write it "bd." But this written word would also represent the spoken words "bid," "bad," "bed," and "bead." To specify which spoken word was intended, we would introduce a determinative at the end of the written word, which might consist of the image of a plant. To pin down the meaning even further, we might insert an ideogram, perhaps the image of a budding flower. The ideograms (as well as many of the alphabetic signs and determinatives) served to enhance the visual beauty of the written language, which was a major objective of the scribes who wrote it. Any written expression that was not considered beautiful would not pass muster.

As the language of hieroglyphs developed throughout the years, the number of determinatives increased to more than 700,[28] and the number of glyphs combined exceeded 3,000. A scribe was expected to master the use of all of them, and this required years of concentrated study. All in all, the hieroglyphic language was enormously complex, but much of the complexity could have been avoided had the scribes developed their alphabet by including glyphs for vowels. But this they adamantly refused to do. It was as if complexity and multiplicity were values unto themselves, and perhaps they were. Indeed, the word "hieroglyph" is Greek for "sacred writing." Each glyph was thought to have religious value, so once a glyph was introduced, even though it had fallen out of use, it was never discarded. Similarly for the gods, if a god should fall out of popularity, no priest would ever think of abolishing it. This preference for multiplicity and complexity, in opposition to the abstract and the simple, suggests that polytheism meant more to the ancient Egyptians than mere social convention, and when Akhenaten attempted to abolish polytheism in favor of a single god, the resistance ran deeper that what he had anticipated.

A similar preference for the multiple and the complex can be found in Egyptian mathematics. This preference extends to both arithmetic and geometric procedures. The Rhind Mathematical Papyrus, currently in the British Museum, contains the famous Table of Two, which addresses a certain problem the Egyptians had with numerical fractions. The Egyptians were able to *conceive* fractions such as 2 divided by 13 and 2 divided by 73, but they were not able to write them in hieroglyphs. The only fractions they could write were ½, ⅔, and, rarely, ¾. To address this problem, they produced a table that reduced all fractions of the form 2/n, where n is odd and ranges from 3 to 101, to unitary fractions (fractions having numerator 1), which they *could* write. For example, 2 divided by 11 was expressed as ⅙ + 1/66, and 2 divided by 13 was expressed as ⅛ + 1/52 + 1/104. In some cases, producing these strings of unitary fractions was very complicated, and the Egyptians left no general rule for accomplishing the task. The far simpler solution would have been to develop their writing system so as to allow them to write the fractions 2/11, 2/13, and so on for all fractions generally. But instead, they favored the far more complex solution of writing all fractions as sums of unitary fractions.

In geometry, the Egyptians had no abstract concept of any geometrical figure, such as the circle, square, triangle, rectangle, trapezoid, and so on. This antipathy for abstraction of any kind meant that the Egyptians had to work with physical manifestations of these figures having a certain size and configuration. Thus, for example, they could compute the area of a triangle having a base of 5 units and a height of 10 units or a base of 8 units and a height of 11 units, but they lacked the general formula for the area of a triangle: $A = \frac{1}{2} b \times h$, where $b$ is the base and $h$ is the height. This shortcoming results from the fact that the Egyptians had no concept of a mathematical variable, a symbol that could range over any number that one chooses. As a result, they were confined to working on the level of the particular, which introduced extraordinary multiplicity and complexity into their work. So perhaps it is no wonder that they favored a multiplicity of gods. Or perhaps the multiplicity of gods, which were created by the priests, is what led them to favor the particular over the abstract in mathematics. Whatever the case, in practically every area of life, the ancient Egyptians had a penchant for multiplicity.

Even the use of hieroglyphs to represent numbers illustrated this fondness for multiplicity. The numerals 1, 10, 100, and so on were represented by glyphs as follows. Single capitalized English letters represent the glyphs:

| 1 | Vertical Stroke (S) |
| 10 | Hobble for Cattle (H) |
| 100 | Coil of Rope (C) |
| 1,000 | Lotus Flower (L) |
| 10,000 | Finger (F) |
| 100,000 | Tadpole (T) |
| 1,000,000 | God with Raised Hands (G) |

The Egyptian number system was obviously a base-10 system, but it lacked the simplicity of the Arabic system in that a number could not be multiplied by 10 simply by adding a zero at the end. But any number could be represented by determining the number of 1s, the number of 10s, the number of 100s, and so on that the number in question contains and by then writing them out in a string. For example, the number 724 contains 7 100s, 2 10s, and 4 1s, so it would be written as follows:

CCCCCCCHHSSSS

Addition and subtraction could be accomplished without too much trouble, but the problem came with multiplication and division. The Egyptians had no true multiplication or division, and the needed operations were accomplished through rather cumbersome algorithms. Multiplication involved the doubling of the multiplier to build up the product through a series of steps, and division involved doubling the divisor and eliminating the remainder through a series of steps. Given the obvious sophistication of the ancient Egyptians in working with numbers, this system could probably have been simplified by some gifted scribe who wanted to do so, but nobody in ancient Egypt wanted to simplify anything.

What appears to be a sheer love for multiplicity is also evident in funerary documents. One of the earliest, the Pyramid Texts, provides evidence of this wordy redundancy in practically every passage or set of passages. For example, in the version customized for the Fifth Dynasty pharaoh Unas, in the antechamber of his sarcophagus, south wall, we find this:

Your smell comes to Unas, O gods!
The smell of Unas comes to you, O gods!
May Unas be with you, O gods!

May you be with Unas, O gods!
May Unas live with you, O gods!
May you live with Unas, O gods![29]

In the antechamber, north wall, we find this:

Hail to you, Bull of Re, you with the four horns!
Your horn is in the West,
Your horn is in the East,
Your horn is in the South,
Your horn is in the North!
Bow that Western horn of yours for Unas, that Unas may pass.[30]

In the sarcophagus chamber, north wall, second register, we find this:

O Unas, the arm of your Ka is before you.
O Unas, the arm of your Ka is behind you.
O Unas, the leg of your Ka is before you.
O Unas, the leg of your Ka is behind you.
Osiris Unas, I give you the Eye of Horus, that your face may be adorned with it.[31]

In the sarcophagus chamber, north wall, first register, we find this:

You purify (yourself), Horus purifies (himself),
you purify (yourself), Seth purifies (himself),
You purify yourself . . .
Thoth purifies (himself), you purify (yourself),
The god purifies (himself)
You purify yourself, your Ka purifies (himself),
You purify (yourself), purify, you purify (yourself).
This your own self purifies you among your brothers.[32]

If any one of these selections were a single stand-alone prayer or chant, the repetition might be understandable. But this material runs on for hundreds of pages. It suggests that the longer and more repetitious the selections are, the more pleasing they will be to the gods. In other words, multiplicity is divine. The same sort of redundancy appears in the gods themselves, where multiple gods could be conceived to serve any single purpose.

Of course, it is quite possible that the priests who wrote the Pyramid Texts and the other funerary documents indulged in such effusive redundancy simply to create the impression in the mind of the pharaoh and other important parties that the texts were of immense importance and that therefore their authors were to be accorded great respect. Such a conclusion would be thoroughly consistent with the idea that the priests created the gods to enhance their own power, and the more gods, the greater the power. But certainly, this conclusion about the texts in no way supports the view that the ancient priests were crypto-monotheists. Any kind of monotheism or even henotheism involves a movement in the direction of abstraction, and if the scribes had any interest in abstraction, we would find it full blown in that great monument to abstract reasoning: mathematics. But Egyptian mathematics is practically devoid of any abstraction. It involves no variables and no abstract concepts of geometrical figures. The closest the Egyptians ever got to abstract reasoning was to work out certain problems based on selected constants with the intent that other scribes faced with similar tasks could follow the same procedure with a different set of constants. So the conclusion we draw about the Egyptians is that (with the exception of Akhenaten) they were thoroughgoing polytheists who exhibited a few hints at monotheism. Those hints were a single divine pharaoh who could become any god or all of them, depending on the needs of the moment, and the theory of syncretism that allowed two or more gods to coalesce into one for a limited amount of time. Apart from those slight indications, the gods constituted a multiplicity.

## Conclusion and a Final Comment

The ancient Egyptians really were full-fledged polytheists, as opposed to being henotheists or crypto-monotheists, and their many gods were created by priests for the purpose of augmenting priestly power. These gods were either created from scratch or syncretic unions of already existing gods, but in both cases, they were constructs that served the interests of the priests. Every new god needed a temple, and every temple needed a priest to conduct the necessary rituals, so as the number of gods increased, so did the number of priests. The priests sustained belief in the gods by conducting temple rituals, and the rituals were reinforced by processions and festivals. As ever more priests were added to the priestly ranks, the priesthood became ever more powerful, much like a growing bureaucracy in any modern government. Finally, the whole process was supported by a veritable cornucopia of illusions. The afterlife of the pharaoh depended on the longevity of his or her tomb, so it was important that the tomb last forever; to be admitted to the afterlife the pharaoh needed a body (a mummy), and mummification was a job reserved for the priests; the pharaoh, once having attained the afterlife, controlled access to it by ordinary Egyptians; ordinary Egyptians could gain access to the afterlife if they did things in this life that were pleasing to the pharaoh; the gods really existed, and they entered into their cult statue during temple rituals; a god would consume the offerings placed before its statue by simply gazing at them; and a dead god (such as Osiris) could be brought back to life by correctly reassembling its dismembered parts. Further, the sun moves through the heavens because a god pushes it in the way that a scarab beetle pushes balls of dung; gods can sail in boats through the air much as people sail in boats on the Nile; a dead pharaoh could be brought back to life if its body were properly mummified; the revivified pharaoh could engage in the activities it enjoyed in its former life by gazing at the food, drink, weapons, and chariots placed in its tomb; to reach the afterlife, it was necessary to follow a set of instructions compiled by the priests; and only the priests were qualified to provide these instructions.

As a final comment about polytheism, I never fail to react with amusement when I hear some religious commentator or historian state in effect that human civilization wallowed in the error of polytheism for millennia until it finally hit on the truth of monotheism. In fact, there is nothing erroneous or false about polytheism as such, just as there is nothing true or superior about monotheism as such. Religions are constructs, and a construct can be assembled any way the designer likes. For the same reason, there is nothing true about a bridge or highway or false about a house or piece of machinery. However, monotheism might be said to enjoy certain advantages over polytheism and vice versa. To the unsophisticated believer, polytheism might be more charming, more colorful, more interesting, or more comforting than monotheism. The idea of a multiplicity of gods interacting with one another in entertaining ways has an intrinsic interest that is impossible with monotheism, while for those with a philosophic bent, the simplicity of monotheism has a certain elegance that is lacking in polytheism. We can also say that polytheism might be more successful than monotheism and vice versa. Given that the purpose of religion is to augment the power of priests, one religious form might be more effective or less so than another in accomplishing this goal. But this is an empirical question that can be answered only by conducting studies or experiments; it is not a question that can be answered a priori.

# CHAPTER FOUR
# THE JEWS

Accccording to the theory developed in this book, the general practice of priests everywhere is to create gods, conceal their role in the creation process, and then attribute marvelous occurrences to the agency of these gods. In the Neolithic period, the first priests created gods from the spirits of the clouds and the seeds, they attributed clement weather and abundant crops to the agency of these gods, and then, as interlocutors with these gods, they took credit for the results. In ancient Egypt, the priests, enlightened by their forerunners, created more than 1,000 gods, which they credited with everything from victory in battle to the birth of healthy children to successful transit to the afterlife, and they then took credit for it all in virtue of their having pleased the gods through daily rituals in countless temples. In this chapter, I attempt to show that Moses, an Egyptian priest and founder of the Jewish religion, created Yahweh out of materials he derived from the course of his earlier employment, and he then credited Yahweh with extending an offer to the Jewish people that provided land and protection in exchange for their recognizing him as sole divinity. The famous episode atop Mount Sinai, far from being a revelation from an actually existing divinity, was in fact a period of intense creativity by the master architect. The secluded setting offered Moses the needed privacy to put the finishing touches on his principal creation and the needed time to come up with the terms of the soon-to-be-disclosed covenant. It also enabled him to keep the goings-on a secret from the assembled crowd of Hebrews.

## Moses

The main problem with Moses is that apart from the Bible, there is not a shred of evidence of a contemporaneous nature that any such man ever existed. Not a single stele refers to any such person. No inscription on a temple pylon or column makes any such reference. No relief cut into stone depicts any such person. No writing on any tomb or sheet of papyrus yet discovered mentions this Moses. According to Exodus, Moses led a large group of Hebrews, estimated to be about 2 million, out of Egypt and into the desert, where they wandered for forty years. Given the size of this group, one would think there would be some record in Egypt making reference to this departure. After all, the Egyptians wrote down everything. But again, there is no such reference. Furthermore, while in the desert, one would think that such a large group of people during such a long period of time would have left some trace of their having been there. But no such trace has ever been found—not a single pottery shard, not a piece of brick from a dwelling place, nothing. By widespread agreement, the patriarchs Abraham, Isaac, and Jacob have been consigned to the class of fictitious individuals who were invented by the Pentateuch writers to give age and pedigree to the ancient Israelites. One is tempted to assign Moses to the same category of fictitious persons. But isn't Moses the person who wrote the Pentateuch, the so-called Books of Moses? If these books exist, as they do, is it not certain that Moses existed? It was indeed the case that at one time, Moses was credited with having written these books. But today, virtually all scholars agree that the Pentateuch was written hundreds of years after the period when Moses was thought to have lived. Yet in spite of all this negative evidence, the biblical scholar Richard Friedman argues that based on certain textual evidence and after making certain adjustments in the biblical account, a strong case can be made that Moses did indeed exist. I happen to find Friedman's argument persuasive, and so I conclude that it is probably the case that Moses was a real person. I will consider Friedman's argument presently.

Assuming that Moses did in fact exist, additional problems arise in connection with the details of his life. Scholars generally agree that the name "Moses" is Egyptian. The famous Egyptologist Henry Breasted observed that "Moses" is the same Egyptian word as "mose," which means "child."[1] The final "s" was added to "mose" in the Greek translation of the Old Testament to produce "moses." Following this line of thought, several Egyptian pharaohs had the name "Mose." Thus, we have "Dedumose" in the Sixteenth Dynasty, "Kamose" in the Seventeenth Dynasty, and "Ahmose" (Child of Ah) and "Thutmose" (Child of Thoth) in the Eighteenth Dynasty. Even the abbreviated name "Mose," adds Breasted, is common on Egyptian monuments. So how did someone who, according to tradition, was Hebrew end up with an Egyptian name? The story is told in Exodus 3:15 that a Hebrew woman named Jochebed placed her child in a basket and set it afloat on the Nile to prevent the child's being killed by Pharaoh. One of Pharaoh's daughters then found the basket and named the child "Mosche," a name that, in Hebrew, is related to the verb "to draw out." The idea is that the Egyptian princess named the child Moshe because she drew him out of the water. However, as Freud points out, it is hardly credible that an Egyptian princess would be cognizant of Hebrew etymologies. Furthermore, even if the princess were fluent in Hebrew, the name Mosche could at best mean "the drawer out."[2] And I find it even less credible that a mother would set her baby afloat on a river that, at the time, was infested with crocodiles.[3] For these reasons, I am persuaded that the biblical account is apocryphal.

Just as most people with Hispanic names are Hispanic and most people with Irish names are Irish or at least partly Irish, so most people with Egyptian names are (or were) Egyptian, especially 3,000 years ago. Thus, I find it plausible that Moses was indeed Egyptian. This is the conclusion that Freud, who was Jewish, reached in his last work, *Moses and Monotheism*, a book that he says he worked on most of his life and published shortly before his death. And Jan Assmann, the widely respected Egyptologist and biblical scholar, draws the same conclusion: "Moses, if there ever existed a historical figure of that name, was indeed an Egyptian."[4] Interpreting Moses as an Egyptian makes sense of several beliefs associated with the man. In Acts 7:22, we read, "Moses was trained in all the wisdom of the Egyptians." It is, of course, possible that a Hebrew should be trained in Egyptian wisdom, but this idea makes more sense if the person so trained was himself Egyptian—and not only Egyptian but an Egyptian priest. Freud thought Moses was a distinguished individual, "perhaps a prince, priest, or high official."[5] He also thought that Moses may have been a governor of the Goshen region in the eastern Nile Delta, which would have put him in contact with Hebrew leaders living there.[6]

Also, many writers living after the time of Moses referred to Moses as an Egyptian priest. Manetho (ca. 250 BCE), an Egyptian priest himself, spoke of Moses as a priest of the Egyptian city of Heliopolis, whom he identified with a figure named Osarsiph.[7] Apion (ca. 30 BCE–48 CE), a Hellenized Egyptian grammarian, also wrote that Moses was an Egyptian priest from Heliopolis.[8] And Strabo (64 BCE–24 CE), a Greek geographer, historian, and philosopher, claimed that Moses was an Egyptian priest who was dissatisfied with Egyptian religion and who founded a new religion.[9] If Moses were a priest, he would have had extensive knowledge of Egyptian divinities, which would have prepared him to be the religious leader of the Hebrews. Also, as a priest, he would have been circumcised. All Egyptian priests were circumcised. And this explains in part the motivation to promote this practice among the Hebrews and make it a signal identifier in Judaism. It was also thought that Moses was a military figure, an Egyptian field marshal, who led a victorious campaign in Ethiopia.[10] As a military leader, he would have had the skills to lead large numbers of men, which would have prepared him to lead a group of Hebrews out of Egypt and into Canaan.

## Yahweh and the Aten

Freud was the first scholar to argue for a connection between the Aten, the singular god invented by the pharaoh Akhenaten, and Yahweh, the god of Moses. Why it took so long for this connection to be recognized is explained in large measure by what happened in Egypt following the death of Akhenaten. Subsequent pharaohs, probably beginning with King Tut and with the enthusiastic support of the priesthood, launched a systematic effort to abolish every trace of Akhenaten's existence. For 3,000 years, no one had even an inkling that such a person had ever lived. Then, in 1887, an Egyptian woman digging up material for fertilizer unearthed some 300 tablets that came to be known as the Amarna letters. This discovery triggered further excavations at the site, and these led to the discovery that a pharaoh named Akhenaten (originally Amenophis IV) lived in Amarna—actually, he created the city and named it Akhetaten—and promoted what is widely recognized as the first genuinely monotheistic religion. Freud was around forty-two years old when the existence of Akhenaten was announced to the public, at which time he may have already been thinking about Moses and the origins of monotheism. In any event, once the discovery of Akhenaten became public, Freud noticed how similar Judaism was to the religion of Akhenaten, and after further study, he concluded that the original religion of Moses was identical to the religion of Akhenaten.[11] This, of course, implied that the Aten, the sun disk god, was identical to Yahweh, the god of Moses. The two gods, who began as one and the same deity, slowly drifted apart during the span of hundreds of years, and they became clearly distinct only after the concept of Yahweh reached final form following the Exile some 800 years later.

One possible response to Freud's conclusion is that Yahweh is eternal. Yahweh revealed himself to Moses on Mount Sinai through a miraculous communication. However, this response is not rationally satisfying. It says practically nothing about Yahweh. According to the Sinai story, Yahweh simply pops into existence from nowhere. The writers of Exodus were obviously sensitive to this deficiency, for they have Yahweh introduce himself as none other than "your fathers' God, Abraham's God, Isaac's God, and Jacob's God."[12] The writers thereby attempted to rationalize Yahweh by establishing a connection to these historical figures. But we have already seen that according to the considered judgment of archaeologists and biblical scholars alike, it is highly improbable that these quasi-historical figures ever existed. So Yahweh becomes a god without a history. His introduction in the Bible reminds me of the famous painting *Birth of Venus* by Botticelli. The painting depicts a gorgeous woman emerging from an open clamshell. She is fully developed; has beautifully flowing blond hair, a perfectly shaped body, and unblemished skin; and probably speaks flawless Greek. Who coiffed that perfect hair? Where did she get such an exquisite body? Had she no childhood or adolescence? Or parents? The canvas is silent. It depicts the ultimate irrationality.[13]

Another possible response to Freud's conclusion is that Freud may be on to something, and that Yahweh may indeed be linked to the Aten. In drawing his conclusion, Freud was obviously guided by the principle that "everything new must have its roots in what was before."[14] This principle expresses the essential insight present in Leibniz's principle of temporal continuity, according to which every particle of reality (Leibniz called these particles monads) reflected the past features of other such particles. In characterizing Moses as an Egyptian priest and in linking Yahweh to the Aten and the religion of Moses to that of Akhenaten, Freud laid bare the roots of what was new in Judaism, and in so doing, he shed light on many of its essential features. First off, why is Judaism monotheistic? Because the religion of Akhenaten is monotheistic. (I will argue shortly that there is another important reason.) Why does Judaism forbid graven images of Yahweh? Because Akhenaten rejected graven images in depicting the Aten.[15] It is true, of course, that he did represent the Aten as a disk in the sky, the solar disk, but he did not represent it using animals or the heads of animals, which marked a break with Egyptian polytheism. Why is there no reference to the afterlife in the five Books of Moses when the afterlife had been the overriding obsession of the Egyptian people for more than a millennium? Because there is no afterlife for Akhenaten, at least not in the traditional sense of ancient Egypt. In eliminating all of the traditional gods, Akhenaten abolished the divine machinery needed for the afterlife. As a result, the Aten is viewed as the source of blessings in this life, as is Yahweh.

These similarities extend to various incidental features of Judaism. Why does Judaism forbid the eating of pork? Because the priests of Egypt did not eat pork and Moses was an Egyptian priest (at least according to the view presented here). Pigs, for the ancient Egyptians, were considered unclean, and even though many ordinary Egyptians ate pork, the priests, who were obsessed with cleanliness, avoided it. Why are Jewish males circumcised? Because Moses, as an Egyptian priest, was circumcised. Again, the reason for this (as Herodotus observed) was purity. In foisting this practice on the Israelites, Moses ensured that his followers would be at least as pure as the purest Egyptians. The fact that the Jews inherited male circumcision from the Egyptians and not from any other people is supported by the fact that Egypt was the only major nation that practiced it—not the Semites, not the Babylonians, not the Sumerians, not the Canaanites.[16] Returning to the issue at hand, why did Moses, when confronted with the prospect of addressing the Hebrews, refer to himself as being "slow of speech" (Exodus 4:10)? Because (possibly) he spoke Egyptian while the Hebrews spoke Hebrew.[17] If he spoke Egyptian, he was probably Egyptian. Why did the Ark of the Covenant, which consisted of a decorated box having rings on the side through which poles could be inserted for transportation, have this particular design? Because it was modeled after the Egyptian barks used in processions to carry the pharaoh.[18] Why did the tabernacle, the dwelling place of Yahweh, have the elaborate design that it had? Because it was copied in detail from the battle tent of the Nineteenth Dynasty pharaoh Ramesses II.[19] Why was ancient Judaism run by priests, and why did their garb set them apart from the general public? Because the religion of ancient Egypt was run by priests whose clothing made them easily identifiable as special people.

## Consequences of the Yahweh–Aten Hypothesis

Admittedly, this Yahweh–Aten hypothesis is not without its difficulties, but if we set them aside for the moment, we can explore some of the consequences that it implies. The most important consequence is that Yahweh is clearly a fictional entity, as much of a fiction as the Aten. If Freud is correct, and I think he is on this point, then Yahweh, as he was characterized at the time of Moses, and the Aten are identically the same being. But if the Aten is a fiction and Yahweh is identical to it, then Yahweh, too, is a fiction. In thinking about this conclusion, it might be useful to consider for a moment the kind of "reality" that a fiction can be said to have. One kind of reality consists of the many representations—pictures, statues, images of all kinds, and words—used to depict the fiction. The other kind of reality—and this is the kind we are chiefly concerned with—consists of memories in the minds of the people who think about the fiction. In the case of the Aten, the first memories were probably in the mind of Akhenaten, the pharaoh who invented the Aten. Until the first physical images were produced, these memory traces were the only reality that the Aten had. So the Aten on Monday was identical to the Aten on Tuesday only because certain memory traces on Monday were identical to certain memory traces on Tuesday. Gradually, Akhenaten conveyed his belief in the Aten to others, and at that point, the Aten came to exist as a set of traces in the collective memory of Egyptian society. When Moses happened on the scene some years later, he came to share in the collective memory of the Aten. The experience of sharing in this collective memory was undoubtedly what led Moses to consider the possibility of a monotheistic deity. When Moses decided to call this deity Yahweh, the only way it differed from the Aten was in name. Moses reinforced the Yahweh fiction when he converted the god into a party to a covenant with the Hebrews. An immediate consequence of our conclusion that Yahweh is a fiction is that all of Moses' followers who came to believe in the genuine reality of

Yahweh bought into an illusion. With the passage of time, the illusion became widespread, and it continues to this day.

The concept of Yahweh did not reach its final form until several hundred years after the death of Moses, when Yahweh was conceived of as a transcendent deity—that is, as a deity separate from and independent of the material world. Such a deity is beyond space and time and not detectable by any of the senses. It has no size, shape, spatial location, color, tactile qualities, age, or temporal location. None of the Egyptian gods were transcendent because they all had bodies or at least were represented as having bodies: a human body often attached to the head of a nonhuman animal. When Yahweh became transcendent, he could not be represented by any image, graven or otherwise. Also, at that point, Yahweh took on a distinct kind of oneness. Yahweh was always conceived as one in the sense of being an *only* god, at least among the Hebrews. But in his final form, Yahweh became one in the sense of having no parts. Any being that has no parts is nonmaterial in a radical sense, the ultimate abstraction. Obviously, this Yahweh would never have been acceptable to the Egyptians, who could not tolerate anything abstract, either in mathematics or in theology. A deity conceived in this way anticipated the work of Plato, Aristotle, and the philosopher-theologians of the Middle Ages. So we have now reached a kind of meeting ground between religion and philosophy. Is the new Yahweh still a fiction, as was the Yahweh of Moses? To this question, I think we must answer in the affirmative if Yahweh is still the same entity that was created by Akhenaten and Moses and is still an object of prayer, worship, and sacrifice. The belief construct that is Judaism remains a belief construct; it has not transitioned into a theoretical (philosophical) construct. What happened to Yahweh in becoming transcendent is that a fiction became dressed up in philosophical clothing. But a dressed-up fiction is still a fiction, and belief in the genuine reality of that fiction is still an illusion.

## Difficulties with Moses and Yahweh

We can now address some of the difficulties attending our Moses–Yahweh hypothesis. One has to do with time and memory. Most scholars who think an exodus actually occurred seem to agree that it happened around the time of Ramesses II, who died in 1213 BCE.[20] And Akhenaten died in 1335 BCE, give or take a year. Assuming the accuracy of these dates, more than 100 years may have elapsed between the Exodus and the death of Akhenaten. So the question arises as to how Moses could have learned about Akhenaten and his singular god the Aten when the Egyptians did everything they could, following Akhenaten's death, to erase every trace of his existence. The Egyptologist Jan Assmann has a highly plausible answer. He points out that "trauma can act as a stabilizer of memory."[21] Anyone who has ever been in a serious car crash or suffered any other life-threatening experience knows what Assmann is talking about. The experience becomes burned into the memory with such intensity that it is impossible to forget. Years after the incident, the victim can recall with special vividness the onrushing vehicle, the drawn and threatening gun of the assailant, or the engulfing flames of the wind-driven inferno. Not only is the event not forgotten, but it is remembered with special intensity; also, the recollection tends to be highly accurate in its details. Assmann argues that Akhenaten's abolition of the traditional gods of Egypt was precisely such an event.[22] The very order of the universe and the stability of the kingdom, both of which were thought to depend on the continuous performance of temple rituals, were threatened when the temples were closed. And, of course, the universal obsession of the Egyptian people, pursuit of the afterlife, was upended when the gods needed for its continued availability and sustenance were abolished. Akhenaten's monotheistic revolution must have been received by all Egyptians as a catastrophe beyond any other, and the people who were most heavily affected and whose collective memory would have been most vivid were the priests. As an Egyptian priest, Moses would certainly have been swept up in this tide of collective memory, and the god whom he named Yahweh must have been a virtual replica of the Aten. Another difficulty, a minor one, concerns the name Yahweh and how Moses learned of it. The earliest known reference to a god bearing this name appears, about 100 years before the time of Moses, in a temple dedicated to the Egyptian god Amun.[23] The temple was built by the pharaoh Amenophis III (d. 1350 BCE), and a copy of the inscription in this temple appears in a temple built by Ramesses II (d. 1213 BCE). In these inscriptions, the name Yahweh is linked to a group of nomads called the Shasu, who lived south of today's nation of Israel and who included, among others, the Kenites, Midianites, and Levites.[24] According to the biblical story, Moses traveled to the land of the Midianites, married a Midian woman, and had two children by her.

The woman's father, Jethro (also called Reuel), was a Midianite priest who probably worshipped Yahweh, and this priest (assuming the historicity of the Midian story) probably familiarized Moses with that god. According to the story in the Bible, however, as everyone knows, the name Yahweh was revealed miraculously to Moses on a nearby mountain by the god himself. An alternate explanation, which seems plausible to me, enlists the services of Moses' parents, who were Levites (Exodus 2:1–10). Some of the Levites worshipped Yahweh along with the Midianites, so it seems not inconceivable that Moses was first introduced to Yahweh by his own parents. After all, that's what parents typically do with their children. In any event, the important part for the theory at hand is that Moses took the name Yahweh and attached it to the collective memory of the Aten, thereby creating a new god, a monotheistic god, that he proceeded to introduce to the Hebrews. In so doing, Moses acted in the tradition of countless priests going back millennia whose chief function has been to create gods and sustain them in existence. The next difficulty relates to the likely reaction of today's believers for whom it would be nothing short of blasphemous even to think that Moses would be influenced by an urge so profane as the desire for power. Moses was a holy man, they will observe, perhaps the holiest man in the entire Jewish tradition. He was selected personally by Yahweh to lead the chosen people to a life of service to the one true god. Such a man could never succumb to the vain quest for power or any other worldly motive. In response, I suggest that the aura of holiness surrounding Moses is simply an illusion that arises as a consequence of monotheism. This does not imply that Moses was a nefarious individual or a deceiver. It simply means that, like all men, he was subject to the same hopes, desires, aspirations, foibles, and ambitions that affect every man. Nor does it mean that Moses tricked his followers into believing in the existence of a replica of the Aten, who allegedly entered into a covenant with them. Moses may have sincerely believed that the Aten was the one true god, but to convince the Hebrews to accept it, he had to change its name. In doing so, he chose the name Yahweh. Furthermore, in creating the covenant, Moses probably believed that he was acting in the best interest of the Hebrews living in the delta who, he may have thought, were not living up to their true potential. To realize this potential, Moses had to find a way to convert them into a unified force with a clearly defined, singular vision, and that would be accomplished through the covenant. I will argue for these points in the next section of this chapter by drawing on the work of Jan Assmann and, in particular, on his concept of the Mosaic distinction.

The final difficulty I will consider is the existential one. I have already alluded to the fact that there is not a shred of archaeological evidence that there ever was a Moses or that any exodus from Egypt ever occurred. I will explore these facts in greater detail momentarily. I will also look into the textual basis for thinking that there was a Moses and that some kind of exodus did occur. One possible explanation for the lack of any archaeological evidence for Moses is the alleged possibility that Moses was murdered by his followers and the crime was covered up. If the cover-up in any way resembled what happened to Moses' predecessor Akhenaten, then there may be good reason why archaeologists have failed to find any trace of his existence. The idea that Moses was murdered goes back to Freud, who cites the work of the distinguished Old Testament scholar and archaeologist Ernst Sellin in support of it.[25] There are several reasons that lend plausibility to the murder theory. Freud's own reason is that Moses forced his religion on the Hebrews, and they were unable to meet its stringent requirements.[26] Other possibilities include a frustrated desire for an afterlife: as acculturated Egyptians, the Hebrews may have looked forward to an afterlife just as much as any other Egyptian did, but monotheism dashed those hopes, just as it did for Egyptians living during the time of Akhenaten. Or perhaps, after wandering in the desert for some time without anything to show for it, the Hebrews concluded that Moses had duped them, and they rose up in revolt. There are even passages in the Bible that suggest as much: "And Moses cried unto the Lord, saying, What shall I do unto this people? They be almost ready to stone me" (Exodus 17:4). And in Numbers 14:10, we read, "But all the congregation bade stone them [Moses and Aaron] with stones." Yet another reason supporting the homicide theory is that Moses' followers were known to be an insubordinate lot with a reputation for violence.[27] So the theory that Moses was murdered by his followers may not be all that far-fetched.

## The Exodus

With the patriarchs being demoted to creatures of the imagination, perhaps collective imagination, there comes the temptation to see Moses as an imaginary character as well. But Moses stands out from his ancestors, at least according to the Bible, in one major respect. He is credited with having led a very large group of people, said to be slaves, to freedom in a new land. Moses is so closely tied to this singular event that his existential status stands or falls with the historicity of the Exodus. Accordingly, it will be useful to recall what the Bible has to say about the Exodus, focusing on times, places, and events that are susceptible to archaeological confirmation. First, as to the time of the Exodus, the Bible says that it occurred 480 years before work began on the temple, which occurred in the fourth year of Solomon's reign. Solomon reigned forty years and died in 930 BCE. Thus, his reign began in 970, and the fourth year of his reign would have been 966. Hence, according to the Bible, the Exodus occurred in 1446 BCE, which is the result of adding 966 to 480. However, all archaeologists agree that this date cannot be correct. The crisis that supposedly precipitated the Exodus was Pharaoh's enslavement of the Hebrews living in the eastern Nile Delta, and the purpose of the enslavement was to build the store-cities of Pithom and Ramses (Exodus 1:11). But these cities were built by Ramesses II, who lived 200 years after the biblical date of the Exodus. The correct date of the Exodus, if indeed it occurred at all, is the mid- to late thirteenth century BCE, with 1225 BCE being a reasonable estimate.

The next question, again assuming that the Exodus actually happened, is how many people participated in the venture. The Bible tells us that the number included 600,000 fighting men (Exodus 12:37), so scholars have estimated the total number to be around 2.5 million, which included women, children, elderly folks, and others incapable of fighting.[28] Obviously, the challenge of moving such a large number of migrants across a blazing-hot desert would have been formidable. If one assumes that each ate around a half pound of food per day and required a gallon of water per day for drinking and washing, the horde would have required the equivalent of 250 modern eighteen-wheel tanker trucks for the water and forty eighteen-wheel vans for the food *every day*. And one can only imagine the size and capacity of the latrines. To this, we must add the difficulty of communicating with such a large crowd. Moses could not simply have climbed up on a high rock and shouted "forward march" to get them going in the morning and "halt" to get them all to stop at the end of the day as he might have with a company of troops.

The Bible does not tell us what route Moses took from the eastern delta up to Canaan, but it does say that he crossed the Reed Sea (*yam sûf* in Hebrew; *yam* means sea and *sûf* means reed; hence sea of reeds— the term occurs twenty-three times in the *Tanakh*). Certain Hollywood producers and a few others have translated this term to mean Red Sea, the large and deep natural channel where Moses miraculously parted the waters; however, biblical scholars have argued that it was a marshy region, a string of lakes, north of the Gulf of Suez, where reeds are known to flourish. The exact location of this region is unknown, which makes Moses' itinerary a matter of conjecture. The most direct route for Moses would have been the so-called Way of Horus, which was the coastal road between the eastern delta and Canaan that was heavily traveled by military units and commercial traders. And this would also have been the easiest route because it was well trodden and offered a dependable supply of food and water along the way (although not for 2.5 million). But the Way of Horus was also well defended by a series of Egyptian forts separated from one another by a one-day march along the entire route, and the officers in charge of the garrisons would surely have made records of any sizable band of individuals making the trek. However, there is not a single record anywhere of any person named Moses leading any group of Jews out of Egypt.

One spot along the way that the Bible does mention is Kadesh-barnea, which is an oasis in the northeastern Sinai Peninsula, where Moses and his entourage were said to have camped for thirty-eight of their forty years in the desert (Numbers 32:8). Imagine what such a location would have required to sustain 2.5 million travelers: an extensive system of aqueducts for distributing water to the people, an equally extensive food distribution system, pots and kettles for cooking the food, and cooking implements and eating utensils. There would also have been thousands of domiciles to shield the inhabitants from sandstorms and the relentless sun and, of course, large and permanent latrine facilities. Thirty-eight years is a long time. Tens of thousands of children would have been born; many of them would have grown into adulthood, married, and had children of their own; the adults would have had countless knives, spears for hunting, and other tools that would have broken with use and the pieces tossed out; and tens of thousands of sick and elderly would have died, leaving bones and graves with burial accoutrements. However, archaeologists have gone

91

over the area around Kadesh-barnea with a fine-tooth comb during a period of many years, and not a single trace has been found of people living there in the thirteenth to the twelfth century BCE—not a single potsherd or eating utensil, not a broken tool, not a discarded toy, not a single religious artifact.[29] Even if the domiciles were made of mud brick, arguably the ruins of many would have survived in the dry desert sand, but none have been found. Furthermore, no trace of Moses and his entourage has been found anywhere else in Sinai.

## Friedman's Argument

Despite the results of these numerous archaeological investigations, which would appear to disprove the claims for an exodus, the highly respected biblical scholar Richard Elliot Friedman insists that the Exodus did indeed occur. The kernel of his argument is that the Exodus was not large. The conventional view is that the entire nation of Israel left Egypt under the leadership of Moses, wandered through the Sinai for forty years, made numerous conquests, and finally occupied Canaan. Friedman argues that it was not the entire nation of Israel that made the trip but only the Levites who were living in the eastern Nile Delta. In support of his belief that there was an exodus and that it consisted exclusively of Levites, he cites a good number of facts, discussed in the following paragraphs.

Many of the Levites living in Israel have Egyptian names, and, among the Israelites, only Levites have Egyptian names. This strongly suggests that the Levites came from Egypt (so there was an exodus), but it consisted exclusively of Levites (otherwise, there would be others in Israel with Egyptian names).

The Song of the Sea is a poem that goes back to the earliest period in Israel's history, and it celebrates the victory of Yahweh over Pharaoh's chariots at the Red Sea (or Reed Sea). It may have been composed close to the time of the actual event. Assuming this to be so, it serves as evidence that Hebrews were traveling across northern Sinai at that time. But the poem makes no reference to the entire nation of Israel; it refers only to a "people" leaving Egypt. That these people were Levites is suggested by the lines that describe Yahweh as leading them to his "holy abode," his "sanctuary"—a reference to the Temple. As the priests of Israel, the proper place of the Levites was the Temple.

The Bible says that both of Moses' parents were Levites. Assuming this to be so, Moses would have felt most comfortable among the Levites, and if he were to lead anybody out of Egypt, it most likely would have been the people he was most comfortable with.

The Levite priests' description of their Tabernacle shows that it was modeled after the battle tent of Rameses II. This fact demonstrates a connection between the Levites in Egypt and the priests of Israel.

The Levite description of the Ark of the Covenant reveals a similarity between the ark and the Egyptian barks used to carry the pharaoh. Again, this demonstrates the same connection just mentioned.

The practice of circumcision, which originated in Egypt, was conveyed to the Israelites in Canaan by the Levites. This practice is featured very prominently in the Levite documents that compose the Hebrew Bible, but it is not mentioned in the non-Levite document.

Other connections between Egypt and Israel that are found in the Levite sources of the Bible display a broad familiarity with Egyptian traditions and beliefs, including turning an inanimate object into a reptile, converting water to blood, the death of the firstborn, and techniques of making mud bricks.

## An Exodus Reduced in Size and Duration

In arguing that the Exodus consisted of Levites, Friedman never attaches a specific number to the group of Levites who departed from the eastern delta. He says simply that it was a much smaller group than tradition envisions it as being. If one were to attach a number to this group, it would have to be small enough to be manageable and large enough to excite the imagination of an ambitious and power-hungry military leader (Moses). With these parameters in mind, I would suggest a number of around 400. Of course, the number of Levites living in the delta may have ranged in the thousands. The claim is not that *every* Levite left but only that those who chose to leave were Levites. Yet reducing the number of these emigrants to 400 will not, it seems to me, solve the problem posed by Kadesh-barnea. Even a group of 400, during a period of thirty-eight years, would very probably have left some trace of its visit that archaeologists would by now have uncovered. Friedman does not address this problem. The closest that he comes to it is to recall that an archaeologist had once told him that a vehicle lost in Sinai in 1973 was found forty years later under sixteen meters of sand.[30] I am not an archaeologist, but I suspect that this incident bears little relevance to Kadesh-barnea. The only way to solve the problem with any degree of probability, I think, is to shorten the time that the Hebrews were thought to be traveling in Sinai. So let us recall the background behind those alleged forty years of wandering.

The Bible reports that Moses, while he was in the wilderness, dispatched twelve chieftains to Canaan as scouts to investigate the kind of obstacles that the Hebrews were likely to face when they entered their future home (Numbers 13:1–33). The twelve scouts reported back that they saw fortified cities and resident giants, and ten of the twelve concluded that it would be impossible for the Hebrews to penetrate the area. The larger group believed the report of the ten, and by so doing, it was thought that they had disbelieved the word of Yahweh about the land being promised to them. Because of their lack of faith, the Hebrews were forced to wander in the desert for forty years until most of them had died. Today, we know that the alleged report of fortified cities was simply false. Archaeology has proven to a virtual certainty that none of the cities had fortifications at that time. And, of course, the report about the giants is preposterous. If any such beings ever existed in the area, their bones would have been unearthed by archaeologists. This whole line of reasoning was made up by the biblical redactors hundreds of years after the incident was supposed to have happened. The conclusion is that there is no good reason to think that Moses and his followers actually wandered in the desert for forty years. As a replacement number, I would suggest four weeks. This figure is reasonable in view of the fact that the distance between the eastern delta and Gaza in Canaan is about 250 kilometers (about 155 miles) and that Pharaoh Tutmose III marched his troops the entire distance along the Way of Horus in ten days.[31] If the pharaoh could do it in ten days, Moses could probably have done it in thirty days or less, even though the route he took was longer and less well traveled.

If Moses and his contingent of Levites anticipated a journey lasting four weeks, they could have taken enough food to get them the whole distance and enough water to last until they reached Kadesh-barnea, which is about half the distance, assuming they traveled through Transjordan, east of the Dead Sea. At the Kadesh-barnea oasis, they could have replenished their supply of water, stayed a few days to rest, and then continued on their journey. A group of travelers numbering only 400 could almost certainly have stayed a few days at Kadesh-barnea without leaving evidence of their visit that could be unearthed by archaeologists some 3,000 years later. Reducing the number of travelers to 400 and shortening the trip to four weeks results in a set of conditions that makes the Exodus entirely possible in the light of recent archaeological discoveries. Furthermore, something is needed to explain the transmission of Yahweh worship from Egypt to Canaan, and the Exodus fills this need. Of course, there are other possible explanations. Possibly, the Yahweh-worshipping residents of Canaan brought Yahweh with them when they emigrated from Asia. But there are not many facts to support this theory, and the hypothesis that Moses brought Yahweh to Canaan is simple, it gets the job done, and it explains where Yahweh came from in the first place. Thus, I think it reasonable to conclude that a modified exodus, an exodus reduced in size and duration and consisting of Levites who worshipped Yahweh, probably did occur. The result is that Moses, as its leader, was probably a real person.

## Additional Facts That Bear on an Exodus

Given the absence of any contemporaneous extrabiblical evidence of a textual nature relating to a man called Moses and the absence of any archaeological evidence that supports the claim that any such person ever existed, any explanation as to the origins of Jewish monotheism is inevitably conjectural. But one thing that we can be certain of is that Jewish monotheism did arise at some point, and it did so against the backdrop of Egyptian polytheism. Also, there is abundant archaeological evidence that the eastern delta of the Nile was populated by people who had come down from the Canaan region.[32] We also know that many of these people were Levites who bore Egyptian names. Such names included Hophni, Hur, Phinehas, Merari, Mushi, Pashur, and Moses.[33] When, to these facts, we include the additional facts that the Levites were the priests among the Israelites and that the business of priests consists of divinities, the further conclusion seems warranted that Jewish monotheism got its start in the eastern Nile Delta. The eastern delta is the only place where Levites were known to live at that time, and the Levites were the only Israelites who had Egyptian names.

Once the new monotheism had reached the attention of the public, it likely created fear in the minds of local Egyptians who happened to recall, through a chain of vague collective memories, Akhenaten's rule in Amarna. I have already noted Assmann's theory (which is undoubtedly correct) that trauma has a way of stabilizing memory, and the Amarna experience was certainly traumatic. Akhenaten's elimination of the traditional gods destroyed the hope for and possibility of an afterlife as the Egyptians understood it. Further, if Amun, Re, Ptah, and the other gods did not exist, the daily temple rituals would come to a halt, and this would threaten not only the national order but also the very harmony of the cosmos. And if the temples were closed (as they were under Akhenaten), thousands of priests would be left without a job. Undoubtedly, as word of a new monotheism began to spread, both priests and rank-and-file Egyptians reacted with horror. The Amarna catastrophe, they must have thought, is starting up all over again. An event that undoubtedly added to the horror was the fact that immediately following Akhenaton's reign, a plague of epidemic proportions ravaged the Middle East for twenty years.[34] The temporal contiguity of the two occurrences probably led the Egyptians to conclude that Amarna caused the plague. Surely, they thought, the monotheistic theology of Amarna angered the gods, and this led them to take revenge. The occurrence of this plague was probably instrumental in creating an association in the minds of the Egyptians between monotheism and disease, for when monotheism arose in the eastern delta region, the proponents were thought to be infected with a terrible disease. In particular, the Egyptians took the Jewish monotheists to be lepers, which probably made sense to them given that leprosy was the most feared disease in all of Egypt.

Identifying Jews with lepers dominated the Egyptian collective memory of the Jews for hundreds of years. Some details of what that collective memory consisted of are revealed in a story told by an Egyptian priest-historian named Manetho, who lived around 300 BCE. According to Manetho, an Egyptian priest called Osarsiph assumed leadership of a group of lepers whom the pharaoh Amenophis III had imprisoned in the stone quarries in the eastern desert. Amenophis III was the father of Akhenaten, which places the time of the story around the Amarna period. According to a prediction, Egypt would be punished for this cruel treatment of the sick when the lepers rose up, took over the country, and reigned for thirteen years. This thirteen years corresponds roughly to the reign of Akhenaten, so Osarsiph is now the alter ego of Akhenaten. According to the story, Osarsiph would make laws commanding that the lepers cease worshipping the gods and that they discontinue slaughtering the sacred animals. But this is also what Akhenaten had commanded of the Egyptians. At the end of the story, Osarsiph is revealed to have an alternate name: Moses. So Akhenaten, Osarsiph, and Moses are all the same person. The upshot of Manetho's story is that without ever mentioning the name Akhenaten (which apparently was forbidden), he has identified Akhenaten with Moses and the monotheists in Akhenaten's court with the Jewish monotheists. So did Jewish monotheism actually come from Amarna? Is Moses simply the resurrected memory of Akhenaten? If one believes Manetho's story, it appears the answer is yes.

A philosopher, priest, and historian named Chaeremon, who lived in Alexandria (in the western Nile Delta) in the first century CE and who wrote a history of Egypt, reported a story in which the goddess Isis appeared to the pharaoh Amenophis in a dream.[35] In this dream, Isis was angry about the destruction of her temple, and the pharaoh was advised to assuage her anger by purging Egypt of its lepers. The pharaoh responded by gathering together 250,000 lepers (Jews) and driving them into the desert. The lepers were said to be led by two individuals: Moses and Joseph. Obviously, this story differs from the biblical account in that the Jews were not slaves who were released against the will of the pharaoh (as per the Bible) but were considered to be diseased individuals who were contaminating the country and who were driven out to protect the population.

The Roman senator and historian Tacitus, who lived in the first century CE, reported a story in which the pharaoh Bocchoris (ca. 720 BCE) was faced with the eruption in Egypt of a bodily disfiguring disease. An oracle advised the pharaoh to respond to the crisis by expelling the lepers (Jews) because they are hateful to the gods. The pharaoh followed this advice and drove the lepers into the desert. The lepers then chose a person named Moses to lead them to Canaan, at which point they founded the city of Jerusalem.[36]

Lysimachos, an Egyptian grammarian who lived in Alexandria in the first century BCE, relates an incident in which the pharaoh Bocchoris is forced to deal with a famine in his country. He decides to follow the advice of an oracle who tells him to cleanse the temples of impure ones who had taken up residence there to escape from leprosy and other diseases. The pharaoh gives orders to drown the lepers and expel the others into the desert. Once again, "lepers" refers to the Jewish monotheists. The outcasts were said to have gathered around a person named Moses who led them out of the country.[37]

The connection between Jews and lepers was apparently so well rooted in certain avenues of collective memory that it reemerged more than 2,000 years after it had first appeared. In southern France in 1321 CE, a rumor rose up to the effect that Jews had conspired with lepers to poison the wells and fountains from which Christians drew their drinking water.[38] The alleged intention was to wipe out Christianity throughout Europe. Apparently, several barrels of moldy bread had been found in a leper colony, and it was thought that the lepers had intended to use the bread to prepare poisonous powders that would then be dumped into the water supply.

## The Exodus as an Expulsion

Given that the Egyptians were so terrified of monotheism that they saw the Jews as lepers, the most reasonable action they could have taken would have been to expel them from the country before the disease could spread. The most reasonable conclusion is that the people who followed Moses into the desert were driven out by the Egyptians. It was not an escape, contrary to the wishes of the pharaoh, but rather an expulsion. This conclusion is reinforced by Friedman's thesis that the Exodus consisted of Levites. As the People of Yahweh, the Levites were first and foremost monotheists. Therefore, in the eyes of the Egyptians, they were the worst of a bad lot, and they posed the greatest danger to Egyptian society. More than any of the other Hebrews, the Egyptians would have wanted to expel the Levites as quickly as possible. From this, it follows that if the Egyptians sent out chariots in pursuit of the Levites crossing the Reed Sea, this was not an effort to bring the Levites back to Egypt, but it was a harassment operation intended ensure that the Levites never returned. The contingent of soldiers may have originated from one of the garrisons along the Way of Horus, and, of course, some of the charioteers may have intended to rob the fleeing Hebrews. When they reached the

Sea of Reeds, one or more of the chariots got bogged down in the mud (or deep water), while the Hebrews, who were on foot, were able to make the crossing more or less unimpeded. The idea that the pursuing soldiers were out to rob the fleeing Hebrews is suggested by the lines from the Song of the Sea that read, "The enemy boasted, I will pursue, I will overtake them. I will divide the spoils; I will gorge myself on them." Further, there is no hint in the poem that the pursuing Egyptians intended to bring the Hebrews back to Egypt. They simply wanted to be rid of them as quickly as possible.

When the Exodus is seen as an expulsion, it becomes immediately clear that there is no need whatever for the alleged ten plagues that Moses is said to have brought down on the pharaoh—no need for turning the water of the Nile to blood; no need for the frogs, lice, flies, and locusts; and no need for any firstborn child to die. If Pharaoh was even aware of the departure of the Jews, he would have given his complete blessing to it. Also, with an exodus reduced in size and duration to a few hundred travelers during a span of a few weeks, there is no need for Yahweh to supply food and water. No need for any manna from heaven and no need for any water produced from a rock. Further, when it is realized that the route of the Exodus was through a marsh, there is no need for the parting of any waters. None of these miracles or plagues ever occurred. What Moses and the authors of the Torah accomplished was to create a god, attribute marvelous occurrences to him, and then take credit for having persuaded Yahweh to produce them. Once Yahweh's intercession is seen to be pointless, his status as a fiction should be apparent. The final stage of Yahweh's alleged involvement occurred during the last part of the Exodus conventionally called the Conquest.

## The Historical Conquest

After leaving Kadesh-barnea, apparently to avoid any further contact with hostile Egyptians, Moses and his followers embarked on an inland route east of the Dead Sea. The Bible mentions numerous interruptions and battles that occurred along the way, but archaeological research indicates that none of these incidents ever happened. For example, the Bible (Numbers 20:14–21) says that the king of Edom refused to allow the group passage through his country, but Edom did not exist as a state until

500 years later, so there was no such king to refuse passage.[39] The Bible (Numbers 21:1–3) says that the Israelites laid waste to the town of Arad, but Arad was deserted at the time of the Exodus. The Bible (Numbers 21:21–32) says that the Israelites destroyed the town of Heshbon, but this town was not founded until long after the Exodus. The Bible says that the Israelites won victories at Jahaz and Dibon, but there is no indication that these towns existed at the time of the Exodus.[40] The likely conclusion is that Moses and his followers had smooth sailing all the way from Kadesh-barnea to the Jordan River—which is fortunate because if the group was as small as I have suggested, it was not enough of a threat to defeat a company of camping boy scouts.

On crossing the Jordan, the group encountered a region that was completely under the iron grip of Egypt. All of the city-states, including Jerusalem, Shechem, Megiddo, Hazor, and Lachish, were vassals of Egypt, and they consisted of little more than administrative strongholds. They included a palace, a temple compound, and a few other public buildings that housed the king and a few bureaucrats, with the peasants living out in the countryside.[41] None of these cities had walls or fortifications of any kind. Obviously, the biblical account that depicts the massive walls of Jericho coming down through divine intervention or the conquest of Ai through the military genius of Joshua is a fiction. Jericho had no walls at the time of the Exodus probably because it was under the total protection of Egypt and therefore had no need for any walls. Furthermore, if any group of traveling emigrants had so much as laid a finger on any of the Canaanite cities, the Egyptian garrisons defending the region would have come down on it like a ton of bricks. Today, no scholar of any repute acknowledges any conquest of Canaan. Richard Friedman, who, as a biblicist, goes to any reasonable extent to defend the Bible, puts it very succinctly: "The archeologists are right: there was no conquest."[42] It is true, however, that during the first half of the twentieth century, a group of archaeologists including William Foxwell Albright thought that they had found evidence of an Israeli conquest in the burned ruins of many structures throughout Canaan, but today, these ruins are attributed to a wide-ranging attack by a mysterious group called the Sea People that occurred a few years after the time of the Exodus.[43]

After Moses' group of Levites passed through eastern Canaan, they settled in with the inhabitants of Judah and Israel, and they became their priests and teachers.[44] That these communities already existed prior to the Exodus is clear from the Merneptah stele, which describes a well-developed country called Israel that was large enough to have caught the attention of Pharaoh Merneptah, who in turn had erected a stele mentioning it around 1207 BCE. This country did not develop overnight but was certainly thriving at the time of the Exodus a few years earlier. In exchange for their services as priests and teachers, the Levites were well compensated: they received 10 percent of the produce of all of Israel.[45] As teachers, the Levites educated the people of Israel about the commandments of Yahweh and about Yahweh's promise that if the people obeyed those commandments, they would enjoy the personal protection of Yahweh, and the land they occupied would be theirs forever. As priests, the Levites became the sole intermediary between the people and their god. They had the exclusive right to occupy the temple, and only they could offer sacrifices in the temple. Since sacrifices are always offered in exchange for favors from the divinity, the Levites became the clearinghouse for such favors. This arrangement gave the Levites an extraordinary amount of power—much more power than they ever could have amassed in Egypt.

## Summary of the Exodus

An Egyptian priest and military leader named Moses was afforded a once-in-a-lifetime opportunity to lead a group of Hebrews out of their home in the eastern Nile Delta to a new life in Canaan, some distance to the northeast. As a priest, he was vaguely familiar with an obscure pharaoh from the past who had set up a new religion based on a god whom he called the Aten. This new god was a singular figure who had replaced all the other gods, and instead of an afterlife, he promised his adherents unlimited riches in this life. As a military leader, this Moses was driven by the same motivation that had driven every other great leader from time immemorial: power—power greater than anything he could expect in his current capacity. As a priest, Moses was familiar with the loose contractual arrangement that all Egyptians had with their gods: in exchange for obedience to their pharaoh, they would be rewarded with an afterlife. Moses hit on the idea of recasting this loose arrangement as an explicit covenant by which his followers would be rewarded with untold riches in this life in exchange for their obedience to the commandments of a singular god whom he named Yahweh.

Moses proceeded to draw up the terms of this covenant, and he made it as detailed as possible, replete with a great many laws. He was a good enough student of human behavior to realize that if these laws governed practically every aspect of daily life, they would be highly effective in uniting his followers into a tight-knit group who would remain united day after day and year after year. Also, if he could convince his followers that not he but Yahweh himself was the one who had drawn up this covenant and had explicitly chosen this group of Hebrews to be its beneficiary, these Hebrews would see themselves as very special persons indeed, distinct from and better than all the other Egyptians. Furthermore, since the divine signatory was a single god who alone could be held to the terms of the deal, the covenant was more clear-cut and less ambiguous than it could ever be if that signatory had been some nebulous collection of Egyptian deities. So Moses presented this proposal to the Hebrews, most (or all) of whom were Levites, and he told them that on arriving at Canaan, they would serve as priests and teachers for the Hebrews already living there and be given great wealth and power on a scale proportional with the priests of Amun in Karnack and other temples in Egypt.[46] The Levites saw this as a deal they couldn't pass up.

As word began to spread that Moses was promoting a singular deity among the Levites living in the eastern Nile Delta, the Egyptians became alarmed that the horrors that had attended the reign of Akhenaten 100 years earlier were about to re-erupt. Yahweh appeared to be none other than the resurrection of the Aten, and if Yahweh worship were allowed to set in, all of the other gods would be destroyed. This would mean no more afterlife, and when the temple rituals were halted, the very order of the cosmos would be threatened. The Jews came to be seen as lepers who threatened the nation with a terrible disease. The most judicious response would have been to drive the Levites, together with Moses, their leader, out of Egypt. This is exactly what they did, an occurrence that came to be called the Exodus. Hundreds of years later, when the Levites sat down to write the account of this event, they recast it as a great struggle with a wicked pharaoh. To persuade the pharaoh to release the Jews (who were said to number in the millions), they invented several punishing plagues that tormented the pharaoh and his people. The plagues were completely fictional, and they were invented purely to demonstrate the power of Yahweh and his love for the Jewish people.

## After the Exodus

When Joshua and his Levite followers (Moses had been left behind) crossed the Jordan River, they encountered a group of settlers living in the hill country of Canaan. The hill country was a region running north and south along a line parallel to the Jordan River and centered about twenty miles east of the Mediterranean Sea, and it was divided into two territories named Israel and Judah. According to the Bible, these two territories were originally a single kingdom that had split up, but archaeological research has established that the so-called original monarchy never in fact existed.[47] Israel and Judah were always separate. Also, according to the Bible, Judah, the land to the south, was the larger and more important of the two, but again, archaeology has shown the exact opposite was the case, with about 90 percent of the inhabitants living in Israel.[48] Israel was blessed with a better climate, regular rainfall, and more fertile soil than Judah, the result being that Israel developed a burgeoning trade in wine and olive oil at a time when most of the inhabitants of Judah were still tending flocks out in the field.[49] The capital of Judah was Jerusalem, a city depicted in the Bible as having a large population, impressive fortifications, and a splendid palace and temple, but archaeology has shown that at that particular time, it was a mere highland village with a tiny population.[50]

After crossing the Jordan, the Levites took up residence in both Israel and Judah, and they introduced Yahweh and the covenant to both territories.[51] It is highly unlikely that these Levites met with instantaneous success in this endeavor. Converting the settlers from belief in Elohim to belief in Yahweh undoubtedly took time, even though the promise offered by the covenant was an attractive inducement. In exchange for worshipping Yahweh, the settlers got what they thought was an absolute right to the land and the promise of protection from invading forces—even though both beliefs were illusions. But the multiple additional gods that the settlers had worshipped for years were a different matter.[52] In addition to Yahweh, the people of Israel and Judah worshipped the sun, moon, planets, and stars (the heavenly host); Baal (a collection of gods); Tammuz of Mesopotamia; and, according to the Bible, Milcom of Ammon,

Chemosh of Moab, and Astoreth of Sidon (Kings 11:5, 2 Kings 23:13).[53] In addition, the Bible says that the number of deities worshipped in Judah equaled the number of its cities and that the number of altars to Baal in Jerusalem equaled the number of stalls in the city's bazaar (Jeremiah 11:13).

All of these gods were present in the land before the Levites arrived. But there is one deity the Levites can take credit for themselves. At some point after introducing Yahweh to the people of Israel and Judah, the Levites came up with the idea of giving Yahweh a wife. In doing so, they addressed a big problem with Yahweh. Yahweh was too isolated, too alone, and too singular for ordinary people to relate to. Giving him a wife made him much more approachable and more like ordinary people. Also, the people of both countries needed a fertility goddess. So to satisfy these needs, the Levites invented Asherah.[54] The word is generic for "goddess," but it might also be used to name a specific goddess.[55] The phrase "Yahweh and his Asherah" appears in archaeological findings,[56] and references to Asherah as the Queen of the Heavens also appear in the Bible.[57] When the Levites came up with the idea of giving Yahweh a wife, not only did they fulfill one of the chief functions of priests, namely to create gods (in this case a goddess), but they also gave us yet another reason for considering Yahweh to be a fictional being. If one should happen to write a biographical account of a real human being, it is hardly possible or appropriate simply to invent a spouse for that person out of whole cloth. The subject of the biography either has a spouse or does not have a spouse. It is not possible to treat the subject cavalierly. But such a treatment is quite possible and appropriate with fictional characters. Thus, when Walt Disney created the character of Donald Duck in 1934, the fictional bird was alone. But when, six years later, Disney created Daisy to be Donald's girlfriend, the addition was considered both appropriate and charming. And in introducing Daisy, the cartoonist effected a change in Donald. The male duck changed from being unrelated to a female to a duck being in a relationship with Daisy. Similarly, when the Levites created a spouse for Yahweh, they effected an analogous change in Yahweh. Yahweh went from being a single god to a married one. So the Levites could do anything they wanted to do with Yahweh. After all, they were the ones who created him in the first place.

If those Levites were here today to defend themselves, they probably would say that they simply "discovered" that Yahweh had a wife. Yahweh always had a wife, but it took a long time to discover it. But then, after many years had passed, the Levites saw fit to abolish Asherah. After the time of King Josiah, there is no more Asherah. What happened? Did Asherah die? Did Yahweh get a divorce? No one knows. Perhaps the Levites would say that after many years had passed, they "discovered" that Yahweh did not have a wife after all. But this stretches the limits of credulity beyond the breaking point. If one wants to argue (as the Bible does) that the worship of Asherah resulted from sinfulness, the argument begs the question: how do we know that Yahweh is an independently existing being that is capable of actually having or not having a wife? Claiming that belief in Asherah is a sin implies that Yahweh in fact had no wife and that the idolaters sinned by creating one. But if Yahweh is a fictional being, whether he had a wife is not a matter of fact: it is simply a matter of choice. Do the Levites choose to give him a wife or not?

## The Fall of Israel and the Rise of Judah

After the days of the Exodus, the land of Israel grew in power and wealth, reaching a peak in the years following 884 BCE when King Omri took control. Under the four kings of the Omride dynasty (which lasted forty-two years), Israel developed one of the most powerful armies in the region, and it conquered all the lands east of the Jordan River from the vicinity of Damascus in the north all the way to the territory of Moab in the south. However, during most of the next 120 years, the strength of Israel declined. Sometime between 835 and 800 BCE, King Hazael of Damascus took much of the territory that Israel had conquered east of the Jordan River, and then in 738 BCE, Tiglath-Pileser III, king of Assyria, began a major expansion campaign and conquered or destroyed most of the cities of Israel outside its capital: Samaria. The final catastrophe occurred in 722 BCE when a new Assyrian king, Shalmaneser V (followed by Sargon II), laid siege to Samaria, conquered it, and carted off its wealth. The invader also resettled much of Israel's urban populace in various Assyrian cities, but it allowed most of the rural population to stay in place. In the meantime, the kingdom of Judah, Israel's neighbor to the south, was left largely untouched. Judah, the land that produced David and Solomon and that is described in the Bible as a great kingdom with opulent courts and palaces, was in fact so undeveloped and impoverished that no one was interested in conquering it. All that was about to change with the fall of Israel.

During the years of the Assyrian invasion, thousands of refugees poured out of Israel into Judah, causing its population to explode. The area of Jerusalem, Judah's capital, expanded from ten or fifteen acres to 150 acres, its population increased from around 1,000 to 15,000, and the nation of Judah increased from just a few villages to more than 300. The refugees entering Judah brought wealth, skills, and business acumen into the country, the result being that in just a few decades, Judah grew into a major trading partner with Assyria, and its economy flourished for the first time in history. Judah was now a nation to be dealt with on the international stage, and this brought with it a need for a new central government. This new government would rule over not only the people of Judah but also the Israelites living to the north who were left there following the Assyrian invasion. Obviously, a theme was needed to effect a unification of these peoples. This need was addressed by a movement that had emerged about this time among the Levite priests that has come to be called the "Yahweh alone" movement.[58] Whether this movement started in the north and entered Judah along with the refugees or whether it was a homegrown phenomenon is uncertain,[59] but the thrust of it was that worshipping Yahweh along with all these other gods—Asherah, Baal, the heavenly host, and so on—is sinful and that, in the future, Yahweh must be worshipped all by himself as a solitary god. The priests presented this idea to Hezekiah, who had ascended to the throne of Judah in 727 BCE.

Hezekiah bought into the idea, and he proceeded to smash all the idols, eliminate the Asherah, cleanse the temple of its idolatrous rites, and destroy the altars on the "high places." The high places were open areas or hilltops located throughout the country where the people could come to offer sacrifices to the gods of their choice. In place of these local altars, Hezekiah required that all sacrifices be offered on one central altar in the Temple in Jerusalem. These changes effected a major centralization of religion throughout the region and focused the national attention on Yahweh as the one god of the Jewish people. The renowned biblical scholar Baruch Halpern contends that these changes marked the true beginning of monotheism in the Jewish nation.[60] The argument can be made that without the fortuitous union of Hezekiah and the Yahweh-alone movement, Yahweh might have ended up 1,000 years later as just one among a welter of other minor deities. He never would have risen in status to the one god of Israel. Hezekiah was indeed a second Moses, as the Bible suggests, and this fact offers further reason for saying that Yahweh is the product of power. For Moses, it was largely personal power; it benefited him personally. But for Hezekiah, it was political power; it benefited not only him but also the people as a whole. Hezekiah wanted to unify the people of Israel and Judah for political reasons, and he used Yahweh as the chief instrument to accomplish it.

## The Yahweh Illusion

Sargon II, the Assyrian king who supervised the final destruction of Israel in 722 BCE, died in 705 BCE, and he was superseded by his son Sennacherib. In the meantime, the Assyrian oppression of Judah continued unabated, and this, together with Sennacherib's relative inexperience, induced Hezekiah to enter into a coalition with other regional powers to rebel against the oppressor. The coalition was backed by Assyria's long-time enemy Egypt, but what probably led Hezekiah to take the final step was his conviction that Yahweh would intervene to protect the nation of Judah should the rebellion lead to war. Hezekiah was a true believer who trusted in the promise of the Covenant. If Judah was faithful to Yahweh, Yahweh would defend it against all invaders. Unfortunately, things did not work out that way. In 701 BCE, the enraged Sennacherib invaded Judah, and he proceeded to destroy all its cities along the Mediterranean coast, which prevented Egypt from coming to the rescue. Sennacherib then moved against Jerusalem, but after a long siege, he failed to penetrate its walls. Jerusalem was able to hold out because Hezekiah had the foresight to ensure a dependable water supply. In the end, Hezekiah bought off the invader with a hefty amount of gold, silver, ivory, and other precious items. But the second most important city in the nation, Lachish, did not fare as well. After a long siege, Sennacherib overwhelmed the defenders and destroyed the city. On returning to Nineveh, the Assyrian capital, he created a large relief to memorialize the conquest of Lachish.

The relief depicts a battle of epic proportions. The Assyrians construct a siege ramp to launch their battering rams against the fortification wall. The Lachish defenders fight back desperately with torches and arrows, while the Assyrians pour water on their war machines to extinguish the fires. In the end, the defensive actions are all in vain. The Assyrians invade the city, take captives, and remove all the sacred objects from the Temple, while the bodies of dead defenders are hoisted on spears. In the meantime, Sennacherib, seated in splendor on a throne before the royal tent, observes the procession of captives and plunder.[61] Lachish was a tragic victim of what I call the "Yahweh illusion." This is the erroneous belief perpetrated by Levite priests that a deity actually exists who made a promise of land and protection to obedient Israelites. But Lachish was just the largest and most important of these victims. Dozens of smaller towns were burned to the ground, the result being that practically the entire nation of Judah was destroyed. Jerusalem escaped only by the skin of its teeth.

After Hezekiah died in 698 BCE, he was succeeded by his son Manasseh. The new king was obviously a rational pragmatist who could see that exclusive trust in Yahweh was a foolish error. Hence, he lost no time in restoring all the old gods to what he thought was their rightful position. Asherah came back to life. Yahweh must have been happy to get his wife back. Baal was revived, along with the heavenly host. And altars were restored to the high places so the people could worship their favorite gods in places much closer to home. It was the end of religious centralization and national unification. But, of course, at this point, there was nothing left to unify. The task for Manasseh was somehow to resurrect his ruined country from the ashes of war, and in this, he succeeded rather well. He was able to reintegrate the economy of Judah into the larger Assyrian economy, he created numerous cities and settlements throughout the countryside devoted to agriculture, and he expanded agricultural output in the arid regions (which had never been done before). The population of both Jerusalem and the rural areas increased, and his fifty-five-year reign was marked by peaceful relations with Judah's neighbors. For this success, Manasseh should be ranked as one of Judah's best kings. But the Levite writers of the Bible consign him to the position of absolute worst and most sinful (2 Kings 21:3–7)—because he refused to succumb to the Yahweh illusion.

Manasseh died in 642 BCE, and he was succeeded by his son Amon, who followed in his father's idolatrous footsteps. However, after only two years on the throne, he was assassinated in a coup attempt. Whether the

Levite priests had anything to do with it is unknown. Amon was succeeded by his eight-year-old son Josiah, and since eight-year-old boys
are hardly capable of running a kingdom, he was almost certainly assisted
by a regent. There is good reason to believe that the regent was the high
priest or some other priestly official.[62] Assuming this to be the case, the
need for a regent offered an excellent opportunity for the Levites to mold
the young Josiah as they saw fit and to instill in him the goals and values
of the Yahweh-alone movement. As Josiah got older, he discovered that
he could use this movement in the same way that Hezekiah had used
it to unify the nation of Judah with the lands of the former Israel. The
time seemed ripe given that Assyria was now on the decline and Egypt,
although it was undergoing a revival, was more interested in the coastal
regions than it was in the highlands. What was needed was a grand program of religious reform focused on Yahweh. Thus, Josiah proceeded in
the same way that his great grandfather had many years earlier. The Bible
puts it this way:

> And the king commanded Hilkiah, the high priest, and the priests of
> the second order, and the keepers of the threshold, to bring out of the
> temple of the Lord all the vessels made for Baal, for Asherah, and for
> all the host of heaven; he burned them outside Jerusalem in the fields
> of the Kidron and carried their ashes to Bethel. And he deposed the
> idolatrous priests whom the kings of Judah had ordained to burn incense
> in the high places at the cities of Judah and round about Jerusalem;
> and those also who burned incense to Baal, to the sun, and the moon,
> and the constellations, and all the host of the heavens. And he brought
> out the Asherah from the house of the Lord, outside Jerusalem, to the
> brook Kidron, and burned it at the brook Kidron, and beat it to dust
> and cast the dust of it upon the graves of the common people. And he
> broke down the houses of the male cult prostitutes, which were in the
> house of the Lord, where women wove hangings for the Asherah. (2
> Kings 23:4–7)

So Yahweh was once again without a wife, and all the minor deities,
who must have enjoyed the attention they had received under Manasseh,
were now abolished. Josiah did everything that Hezekiah had done to
bring Israel together under one god. He smashed the idols, cleansed the
temple, and expanded his authority to include the former Kingdom of

Israel. He destroyed the local high places, commanded the people to bring their sacrifices to the central altar in the Temple, and brought the priests from the high places to Jerusalem, where they worked as minions of the Temple priests.[63] Thus, Josiah represents the second case where Yahweh is rescued for posterity by political power, the power of a king. Josiah does not give reasons for why Yahweh is the one true god of Israel. Rather, he says this: "I am king. I have power. I will use that power to establish Yahweh as the one god of Israel. Therefore, henceforth Yahweh will be recognized as Israel's singular god." Thus, once again, the god of Israel has been shown to be the product of power. First, it was the power of Moses, next the power of Hezekiah, and, finally, the power of Josiah. And behind it all was the power of priests.

Twelve years after the death of Josiah, Nebuchadnezzar, king of Babylon, laid siege to Jerusalem and forced the surrender of King Jehoiachin. According to the Bible, the invader hauled away practically everything of value to Babylon, including the king's relatives, servants, palace officials, all the gold in the king's residence and in the temple, and all the warriors, craftsmen, and smiths.[64] Also taken captive were all the priests and aristocrats.[65] Nebuchadnezzar then installed the puppet king Zedekiah on the throne in Jerusalem. When Zedekiah rebelled ten years later, in 587, Nebuchadnezzar returned in a rage, laid siege to Jerusalem once again, breached its walls, and burned the entire city to the ground, including the temple, palace, and all the private houses. He captured Zedekiah (who had tried to escape), slew his sons right in front of him, put out his eyes, and dragged him in fetters off to Babylon. Just prior to that, Nebuchadnezzar's army had rampaged across the countryside, burning all the cities, towns, and villages until nothing remained. All of this happened just a few years after Josiah had assured the people of Judah that Yahweh would protect them if only they would accept him as their one and only god. Clearly, this posed a huge problem for the priests, who were now living in exile in Babylon. How could they possibly retain any credibility in the face of such a catastrophe? The solution was to issue a new version of Deuteronomy that blamed the whole disaster on the good king Manasseh and the people of Judah who had followed him into apostasy:

> Manasseh instigated them to do wrong. . . . And Yahweh said by the
> hand of his servants the prophets, "Because Manasseh King of Judah

has done these abominations . . . he has caused Judah to sin by his idols. Therefore I am bringing such evil on Jerusalem and Judah that the ears of whoever hears about it will tingle." (2 Kings 21:8–15)

But Yahweh did not turn back from his great fury which burned against Judah over all the things in which Manasseh had angered him. (2 Kings 23:26)

The exile lasted about fifty years. Most of the Hebrew Bible was written in the years following the exile, and since one of the chief objectives of the Bible was to bring power to the Levite priests (who had written it), the priests became one of the most powerful components in Israelite society. That power was achieved through centralization of religion and the worship of Yahweh alone, and it was during that period that monotheism became a permanent fixture in the religion of Judah. The perpetual swings from idol worship to the worship of Yahweh alone and back to idol worship at last came to an end. Yahweh, as sole god of Israel, was a construct created and sustained by the priests, and, as is the case with all such constructs, its chief purpose was to augment the power of those who created it.

## The Effect of Monotheism

The adoption of monotheism by the Jews had an effect on the Jewish mentality that ran parallel in some ways to the effect it had on the Egyptian mentality, but it was backed by a different logic. When the Jews selected Yahweh as their god, this was not at all similar to the Egyptians adding a new god to their pantheon. In the latter case, all the other gods would simply move over and make room for the new god. But when Yahweh entered the picture, all the other gods were destroyed. Yahweh was the only one that existed. Yahweh became the only true god, and all the others became false gods. And with this demarcation, truth itself and falsity itself entered the realm of religion. From that time forward, believers began identifying their religion as the true religion and all the others as false religions. Thus, for the Jews, Judaism was the true religion, and Egyptian polytheism was the false religion. This cognitive separation, which I call the "monotheistic demarcation," carried over into future religions. For the Christians, Christianity was the true religion, and all the others were false religions. For the Protestants, Protestantism became the true religion, and Catholicism became the false religion. No such discourse was possible or conceivable in ancient Egypt. No believer in Amun would ever character-ize belief in Isis as false; no believer in Ptah would ever characterize belief in Re as false. All beliefs were equal, more or less, and no one of them could ever displace any of the others. But that is exactly the effect that the introduction of monotheism had on religious belief at the time it arose in ancient Egypt. For the Jews, belief in Yahweh became the true religion, and paganism entered the picture for the first time as the false religion of the Egyptians.

When truth and falsity made its entry into religion, so did the notions of good and bad. This result follows by combining monotheism with the notion that every believer has had of deities since the Neolithic period—namely, as a source of various kinds of benefits. When the monotheistic shift occurred, believers put all their eggs into one basket, so to speak. If the benefits were to come at all, they would come from the one god, which made that god good and all the other gods neutral at best. But when believers recalled that the one god is very much an anthropomorphic entity, with human desires and feelings, especially jealousy, and the one god gets angry when it has to share worship, prayers, and sacrifices with other gods, then all the other gods become very bad indeed. Directing prayer, worship, and sacrifices to the other gods would work to cut off the flow of benefits. Thus, monotheism had the effect of erecting a bar-rier in the mind of every Jew, and on one side of that barrier, everything was good and pure and virtuous and holy, and on the other side, all was bad and corrupt and evil and infected with vice. The ultimate sin became idolatry, and this fact was reflected in the first two (and most important) of their commandments: "I am the lord your god" and "You shall have no other gods before me." Moses, who was on the good side of that barrier, became the holiest, most humble man ever to have existed, and anyone who opposed Moses was thought of as bad. The biblical story of the Exodus reflects this dichotomy. The actions of Moses in freeing the in-nocent Hebrew slaves and leading them out of Egypt (bad) and into the promised land (good) are presented as especially good and accompanied with miracles, while the actions of the pharaoh in raising up obstacles to what Moses was trying to do are seen as very bad and accompanied with negative miracles (plagues). Just as the link between Jews and lepers came to dominate the collective memory of the Egyptians, so the link between Moses and holiness came to dominate the collective memory of the Jews, and that is the memory that has been passed down to most Europeans and Americans living today. Also, that is the reason why today's westerners find it so difficult even to imagine Moses (good) as an Egyptian (bad) or to think of him as an ordinary man influenced by concerns so mundane as the pursuit of power.[66]

Jewish monotheism implied immediate logical consequences for both Egyptians and Jews. For Egyptians, Jewish monotheism threatened both the nation and the cosmos because it led to the termination of temple rituals on which national and cosmic order depended, and it destroyed the possibility of an afterlife for every Egyptian. This in turn led to the conclusion that the Jews were contaminated and diseased; specifically, they were lepers. The original leper was Akhenaten, and Moses was simply the extended memory of the leprous pharaoh. To the Jews, Jewish monotheism logically implied that Yahweh was the only true god; that all other gods were false because, among other things, they did not even exist; that everything related to Judaism was good and holy; and that everything related to Egyptian polytheism was evil and corrupt. Once these implications had settled in the minds of Egyptians and Jews, the dynamics of collective memory worked to guide future actions.

## Collective Memory

The originator of the theory of collective memory was a French philosopher and sociologist named Maurice Halbwachs (1877–1945). I treat his theory in greater depth in the next chapter, but at this point, it will be useful to present a few ideas related to it. The central idea behind the theory is that memory is not a process in which the past is preserved but rather a process in which the past is reconstructed.[67] The reconstruction is guided by the needs of the present moment, and the greatest need in any moment is survival. This means that collective memory is a survival-enhancing mechanism (or process). As a result of its operation, people remember their past in a way that enhances their chances for survival. If, to these observations, we add the principle that people act in accord with the way they remember things, collective memory works to determine (to some extent) the way people act.

Let us now apply these ideas to the Egyptians and the Jews. The Egyptians remembered the monotheism of Akhenaten as a disease. As a result, when the Levites in the eastern delta began preaching monotheism, the Egyptians saw them as having a disease, and since the worst, most threatening of all diseases was leprosy, they saw them as lepers. Further, since these leprous Jews lived in Egypt and since the Egyptians could manage their own country as they chose, the most reasonable action they could take at that time would be to drive the Jews out of the country. This action was undoubtedly seen as necessary for the preservation of the nation. The further conclusion follows that an actual exodus probably did occur. Also, it is very possible that some (or many) of the Jews who departed had been slaves before they left. But these Jews did not depart against the wishes of their masters. Also, if the pharaoh even knew about it, the departure would have met with his total approval. Further, it is quite possible, even likely, that the Jews had a leader either before or following their departure. According to at least some traces of Egyptian collective memory, this leader was named Moses.

As for the Jews, the collective memory they developed about themselves had a long time to evolve. Assuming that there was an actual Moses, he would have lived around 1225 BCE, and the earliest parts of the Bible were written perhaps around 800 BCE give or take 100 years or so.[68] That leaves around 400 years of oral (or largely oral) tradition, during which time memories congealed, separated, and underwent modifications of all sorts. Given that collective memory is a survival-enhancing mechanism, the Levites at work writing the Bible began to remember themselves in ways that that would ensure the survival of Judaism and the Jewish people. One way of doing this was to see Moses as closely connected with Yahweh. They depicted Moses as meeting with Yahweh on top of a mountain to receive the Law and by receiving directions from him on multiple occasions. Also, they did it by depicting Yahweh as a loving god who showered multiple blessings on his people by freeing them from slavery, by leading them out of Egypt, by bringing down the walls of Jericho, by ensuring victory in battle, and by granting them a land of their own.

Through another likely operation of collective memory, the Levites remembered many important events in their own history in ways that were highly flattering and therefore survival enhancing. They remembered an ignominious expulsion as a daring escape. They remembered a

114

journey involving a mere handful of people as a grand departure involving millions. They remembered an uneventful sojourn as a military venture strewn with victories. And they remembered an expedition lasting three or four weeks as a massive excursion lasting forty years. If the account in this book is correct, none of these occurrences actually happened. Thus, we would be tempted to accuse the Levites of telling lies or engaging in some fundamental dishonesty. But if the stories are the result of shifting collective memory, the Levites simply reported the events as they remembered them. There is nothing dishonest about that. In the next chapter, I show that the same operation of collective memory is most likely responsible for the depiction of Jesus as Son of God.

## The Textual Evidence

The historicity of events related to ancient Israel depends on two kinds of evidence: textual evidence and the findings of archaeology. The most important piece of textual evidence is the Bible, but there are two other candidates that are not without interest. These are the Merneptah stele and the Amarna letters. The Merneptah stele is an engraved stone slab found at Thebes on which the pharaoh Merneptah brags about his military victories in Libya and Canaan. In connection with Canaan, we read, "Israel is laid waste and his seed is not"—obviously an empty boast. Merneptah was the son of Ramesses II, and his victory stele is dated 1207 BCE. It contains the first known mention of Israel in any text of any kind, so we know that Israel existed as of that date, and it was large enough and important enough to attract the attention of an Egyptian pharaoh. But it is important to note that the stele makes no mention whatsoever of any Jews living in Egypt, and the Jews that the stele refers to could have been in Canaan for a very long time. So the stele does not necessarily imply anything at all about any Jewish exodus from Egypt. The other piece of textual evidence is the Amarna letters, which consist of nearly 400 pieces of diplomatic correspondence written on clay tablets and found in the ruins of Amarna (Akhetaten). Most of the letters were written by administrative assistants of pharaohs Akhenaten and Amenophis III (Akhenaten's father) and their correspondents, and they span a period of about thirty years. They are important because they say a great deal about the language, culture, people, and events in countries to the northeast of

Egypt, including Canaan, and some may relate to Jews living in Canaan. But they tell us nothing about any Jews living in Egypt.

By far the most important piece of textual evidence relating to ancient Israel is the Bible. For centuries, the vast majority of Jews and Christians took the Bible as absolutely true in every respect. The Jews saw it as the revealed word of the Jewish god, the Christians saw it as the revealed word of the Christian god, and both saw this revelation as mediated by the mind and hand of Moses, who was universally understood to be the author of the Five Books. Thus, it came as quite a shock when careful readers began to express doubts as to the authorship of those books.[69] Among the earliest of these skeptics was Isaac Ibn Yushush, a Jewish physician in a Spanish court in the eleventh century. He pointed out that a list of Edomite kings that appears in Genesis contained names of people who lived long after Moses had died. Thus, Moses cannot have written this list.

In the twelfth century, a Spanish rabbi named Abraham Ibn Ezra, who inexplicably argued that Ibn Yashush's book "deserves to be burned," made several damaging observations of his own. Passages that refer to Moses in the third person, passages that use terms that Moses would not have known, passages that describe places that Moses had never visited, and passages that use language that reflect a time and place other than the one in which Moses had lived all suggest an authorship other than Moses. Yet Ibn Ezra declined to draw the obvious conclusion that Moses was not the author. In the fourteenth century in Damascus, the Jewish scholar Joseph Bonfils went ahead and drew the conclusion that Ibn Ezra had shirked from drawing, that the passages in question were not written by Moses but rather were written later. Moving from Jews to Christians, in the fifteenth century, the Bishop of Avila, Alonso Tostado, observed that biblical passages that describe Moses' death could obviously not have been written by Moses. The traditional response had been that Joshua, Moses' successor, had written those passages. But then in the sixteenth century, Andreas Karlstadt noted that the passages supposedly written by Joshua had the same style as other, preceding passages, so they could not have been written by someone else. Then, in the same century, a Flemish Catholic named Andreas van Maes and two Jesuit scholars, Benedict Pereira and Jacques Bonfrere, suggested that Moses had written only the basic text of the Five Books and that later editors had embellished it as they saw fit. Van Maes's book was placed on the Index.

Skipping to the seventeenth century, the British philosopher Thomas Hobbes, who was for all practical purposes an atheist, concluded outright that Moses did not write the majority of the Pentateuch. Hobbes was joined four years later by the French Calvinist Isaac de la Peyrère, whose book was banned and burned. At about the same time, the Dutch philosopher Baruch Spinoza published an extensive analysis showing that the alleged Mosaic authorship of the five Books was rife with contradictions and other problems. As a result, he wrote, "It is . . . clearer than the sun at noon that the Pentateuch was not written by Moses, but by someone who lived long after Moses." At this point, Richard Simon, a Catholic priest in France, criticized Spinoza's argument, but when Simon agreed that a tiny part of what Spinoza had said might be correct, his books were burned, and he was expelled from the priesthood. Gradually, however, the voice of reason prevailed, and the work of these authors came to be the accepted view. This turn of events marked the beginning of the end of biblical historicity as a general rule.

## The Bible and Archaeology

Of course, the religious power structure reacted with alarm to what had happened with the authorship of the Pentateuch. It clearly threatened their claim to have the final truth about related matters. So, when archaeology came to be recognized as a science in the nineteenth century, a small army of religious individuals took it as a clarion call to launch a counterattack and to use the new science for the purpose of validating the historicity of the Bible. One of the early biblical archaeologists was Edward Robinson, an American Congregationalist minister. In 1838 and 1852, Robinson launched two explorations through Palestine in an effort to identify prominent geographical sites that were mentioned in the Bible but whose location had long been lost. These explorations and later ones succeeded in disclosing the likely location of dozens of lost towns, including Gibeon, Bethel, Shiloah, Megiddo, Hazor, and Lachish, thus proving that the biblical mention of these places was not fictional. A later study by the British Royal Engineers produced detailed topographical maps that identified many regions and landscapes having attributes that closely

matched the descriptions given in the Bible. Additional excavations farther north, in Mesopotamia, disclosed a wealth of information related
to Assyria and Babylonia, places that had previously been known chiefly
through the Bible. Ancient archives were discovered that mentioned the
Israelite kings Omri, Ahab, and Jehu and the Judahite kings Hezekiah
and Manasseh, and these discoveries led to an integrated understanding of the role these figures played in relation to other national leaders
and important historical times and events. Furthermore, biblical stories
relating to the measurement of wealth in terms of sheep and goats (Genesis 30:30–43), the method of settling clan conflicts over watering wells
(Genesis 21:25–33), and disputes over grazing lands (Genesis 13:5–12)
seemed to ring true in light of the way such activities were conducted in
recent times.[70] The totality of all these discoveries prompted the famous
American archaeologist William Foxwell Albright to remark that, "as a
whole, the picture in Genesis is historical, and there is no reason to doubt
the general accuracy of the biographical details."[71]

However, Albright's optimism was not to last. By the 1970s, biblical
archaeology had begun to change its focus. Instead of examining artifacts
from Israel and nearby regions for the purpose of linking them to the Bible,
archaeologists examined them with an eye to revealing something about
the people who made and used them, their economy, religious practices,
population density, politics, and social structure. The range of items in
which archaeologists took an interest broadened to include animal bones,
seeds, the chemical composition of soils, human settlement patterns, and
anthropological models developed for other cultures. Even the Bible itself
came to be treated as an artifact that could show something about the
literary sophistication of the society that produced it. The picture that
emerged conflicted in many ways with stories found in the Bible, and it
also revealed many gaping holes where one would expect to find archaeological evidence for biblical stories but where no such evidence exists. It
also disclosed holes in the biblical text where it was expected that certain
things would have been mentioned but were not. The contradictions and
deficiencies appeared so extreme to biblical scholar Thomas L. Thompson
that they led him to deny that the Bible was historical at all: "Today we
no longer have a history of Israel. Not only have Adam and Eve and the
flood story passed over into mythology, but we can no longer talk about
a time of the patriarchs . . . the Bible is not a history of anyone's past."[72]

Some of these contradictions and deficiencies are evident in the search for evidence supporting the existence of the patriarchs. Narrowly defined, the patriarchs include Abraham, his son Isaac, and Isaac's son Jacob (also named Israel). Each of the twelve sons of Jacob became the father of one of the twelve tribes of Israel. If we rely on the dates and time spans given in the Bible, Abraham traveled with his herds of sheep from Ur in Mesopotamia to Canaan around 2100 BCE. Once in Canaan, he is described as wandering with his flocks around Shechem, Bethel, and Hebron. However, archaeological findings related to this area have revealed that it was highly urbanized at that time and therefore inappropriate for grazing sheep. To "save" the biblical account, William Albright came up with a theory he called the "Amorite migration," according to which large groups of Bedouins were thought to have suddenly left Mesopotamia for Canaan around 2000 BCE, and Abraham and his family were thought to have been a part of this migration. However, subsequent archaeological investigations completely disproved the Amorite migration. Then, in a renewed effort to save the Abraham story, biblical scholars tried to change the time frame in which Abraham was thought to have lived: first to the Middle Bronze Age (2000–1550 BCE), then to the Late Bronze Age (1550–1150 BCE), and finally to the Early Iron Age (1150–900 BCE). For different reasons, none of these periods worked, either.

Then there is the issue of camels. The patriarch stories are replete with mentions of camels, usually herds of them, as beasts of burden. But archaeological research has proved that camels were not used at all as beasts of burden until the late second millennium, and they were not common in that capacity in the Near East until well after 1000 BCE. According to the Bible, the patriarchs were said to have traveled by camel more than 1,000 years before that time.

Next, there is the problem regarding the Philistines. According to the Bible, Isaac is said to have had an encounter with Abimelech, king of the Philistines (Genesis 26:1). But the Philistines, who were migrants from the eastern Mediterranean region, had not become established in Canaan until after 1200 BCE, nearly 1,000 years after the time when Isaac was said to have met up with them. After the Philistines had entered Canaan, they built large cities that dominated the area for several hundred years.

Yet another problem involves the city of Gerar. Isaac is said to have met the king of the Philistines in Gerar (Genesis 26:1), and Abraham is also mentioned in connection with Gerar (Genesis 20:1). The references to this city suggest that it was an important location known to everyone in the area. But at the time when Abraham and Isaac were supposed to have visited the place, Gerar was a small, insignificant village, hardly a place for kings. However, by around 700 BCE, it had grown into a heavily fortified stronghold that was known to everyone. Clearly, it sounds like the Bible writers were referring to this later period in their references to Gerar. Furthermore, at the time when Abraham and Isaac were supposed to have lived, Hazor, Magiddo, and Gezer were heavily fortified cities with massive gates, yet the Bible makes no mention of these places at all.

Finally, in the story about Joseph, one of the sons of the patriarch Jacob, the Bible refers to a camel caravan carrying gum, balm, and myrrh. These were products that featured prominently in the Arabian trade that flourished during the eighth and seventh centuries BCE but not during the time when the patriarchs were supposed to have lived. These four anachronisms involving camels, Philistines, Gerar, and Arabian trade goods suggest that the Bible writers put these features into their story about the patriarchs to give it a sense of realism, but they described these features in the only way they knew how to describe them, namely, as they existed when the stories were written: in the eighth and late seventh centuries BCE. But this strongly suggests that the entire story about the patriarchs is a fictional account featuring characters cast in a setting that did not exist at the time when the characters were supposed to have existed.

For an instance of a contradiction that occurs in connection with the patriarchs, one phrased in empirical terms, consider this one involving Moses, Aaron, and Joshua. Moses and his brother Aaron were said to be fourth-generation descendants of Jacob's son Levi. But Joshua, who was contemporary with Moses and Aaron, was said to be a *twelfth*-generation descendent of Jacob's son Joseph. The only way this could happen is if the birth of Jacob's sons extended during a period of several hundred years. In fiction, the existence of contradictions serves to add an element of interest, but in stories that are supposed to be nonfictional, they cause serious problems. Today, in the considered opinion of the vast majority of archaeologists, the patriarchs are little better than fictional characters. In the words of archaeologist William Dever, "After a century of exhaustive investigation, all respectable archaeologists have given up hope of recovering any context that would make Abraham, Isaac, or Jacob credible 'historical figures.'"[73] Given Dever's antirevisionist (antiminimalist) stance in biblical archaeology, I suspect that if any archaeological evidence should turn up that supports the existence of the patriarchs, Dever would be among the first to announce it. So, coming from him, this judgment about the reality of the patriarchs is especially credible.

## The Levites

Since the Hebrew Bible was written largely by Levites, we should pause for a moment and ask, who, exactly, were these Levites? What were they like? Tradition has it that the Levites were descended from Levi, the supposed founder of one of the original twelve tribes. But recent genetic testing has shown that this is not the case.[74] The Levites are not all related genetically. As for what the Levites were like, the best way of answering this question may be to turn to the passages in the Bible that mention these folks. Following the episode involving the golden calf, Moses summoned all the people who believed in Yahweh to come forth, and those who responded were Levites. Then he instructed the Levites to take their swords and go out among the people who had not come forth and kill all of those most closely related to them. In other words, he instructed the Levites to kill their own brothers, sisters, parents, children, and friends, all of whom were presumably idolaters. The Levites followed Moses' order, and those who were killed numbered 3,000 (Exodus 32:26–29). In another story, a Levite named Phinehas discovered two non-Levites, a man and a woman, in the Temple, a place reserved only for Levites. Phinehas noticed that the two were close enough to each other that he could pierce them both with a single thrust of his spear. The spear went through the man and into the woman, killing them both. Phinehas was later made high priest of Israel.[75] Of course, it is possible that nothing related to either of these stories ever occurred. The 3,000 figure would be impossible given my own estimate of the size of the Exodus. But the message these stories convey is that the Levites at the time of Moses were natural born killers. The second story suggests that they even made a sport of killing. If there is any truth at all in these stories, making the Levites the priests of Israel was like hiring Al Capone to teach a course in ethics.

I mentioned early in this chapter that several years ago, the biblical scholar Ernest Sellin theorized that Moses was murdered. Given what we know about the Levites, it is certainly conceivable that they killed him before crossing the Jordan River and then claimed he had died of natural causes on the top of a mountain. Perhaps they thought that Moses had, at that point, served out his usefulness. He had created Yahweh and the covenant, and the Levites no longer needed his assistance in selling these ideas to the people of Israel and Judah. The theory that the Levites murdered Moses and then covered up the crime solves another mystery. Why is it that the Song of the Sea, one of the oldest components in the Bible, makes no mention of Moses? If Moses was the one who led the Israelites through the sea, he should have a prominent place in the poem. But if the Levites killed him and covered up the crime, they would have removed any mention of him in the final version of the poem, which, as redactors of the Bible, they were responsible for.

When the Levites arrived in Israel and Judah, the inhabitants were worshipping multiple gods, but they had a favorite one named Elohim (or El). So the first challenge for the Levites was to replace Elohim with Yahweh. Friedman argues that the Levites fused the two gods together.[76] Such a procedure was probably familiar to them since that is exactly what the Egyptians had been doing for centuries when they created composite gods such as Amun-Re, Sobek-Re, and Ptah-Sokar. The fusion of Yahweh and Elohim was not named Yahweh-Elohim or Yahweh-El but just Yahweh—which admittedly sounds more like a replacement than a fusion. In either event, the emergence of Yahweh as the principal god of Israel and Judah marks the beginning of monotheism in those countries, and it was accomplished through the work of the Levites. Yet it looks like those Levites were interested more in maintaining their own power than in securing Yahweh worship, for, after a few years, Israel and Judah lapsed back into full-fledged polytheism. The Levites had apparently discovered that, once they had gained a foothold as the official priests, they could retain power regardless of what god was being worshipped. Several hundred years would elapse before Israel became fully monotheistic.

If Levite power was born through the sword, the Levites learned in due course that the pathway to real power was through the pen. Scholars widely agree that the sources of the Hebrew Bible can be traced to four documents, and three of these documents were written largely or completely by Levites. Furthermore, the book of Deuteronomy ("Second Law") was written almost entirely by Levites, and that book gives exceptional power to this group. One of these laws is the so-called Law of the King, which requires that the king be chosen by Yahweh.[77] Since Yahweh was a mere puppet in the hands of the Levites (having been created years earlier by Moses the Levite), this law entails in effect that the king be chosen by the Levites. Also, Deuteronomy requires that the people provide for the Levites through tithes and offerings, it prohibits laypeople from offering their own sacrifices (which restricts the offering of sacrifices to the priests), and it requires that the Levites be the rightful priestly tribe (Deuteronomy 12–26). The Levites also made themselves indispensable in countless ways. Suppose you wanted to serve lamb for dinner on a certain night or perhaps goat or mutton. You could not simply go out and slaughter the animal. You had to take the live animal to the Levite priest, who would then slaughter it on an altar (for a fee—a tithe), and only then could you prepare your meal.[78]

The single commandment of Deuteronomy that gives the most power to the Levites is the so-called Great one that reads, "Love Yahweh your God with all your heart and with all your soul and with all your might" (Deuteronomy 6:5). We should reflect for a moment on what this commandment entails. Suppose that a person should love someone in this way, with such great intensity. The beloved becomes a constant haunting presence in the mind of the one who loves. The beloved colors every thought and feeling, and pleasing the beloved is the most important thing in this person's life. Through this commandment to love, the Levites invaded the most personal, the most private, region of the believer's mind and set up a command and control center. The Egyptian priests, with their concept of sin, approximated this kind of control over the Egyptians, but through the commandment to love, the Levite priests went much further. They secured total control. They achieved near absolute power. If any believer should question exactly what Yahweh wants or what Yahweh finds pleasing, the believer must consult the priest, and the believer is obligated to follow the priest's instruction (Deuteronomy 17:8–13). If a believer wants to know what he or she should do in any situation, the believer must turn to the priest. We have seen that the chief function of priests everywhere is to create gods and to sustain them in existence. Commanding the people to love Yahweh was surely the most effective way of ensuring the continued existence of Yahweh.

## Historicity of the Bible

Finally, a few words on the historicity of the Bible. How can the Hebrew Bible be so wrong about so many details relating to Moses, the Exodus, and the two kingdoms of Israel and Judah? By now, much of the answer should be apparent. Most of the material in the Hebrew Bible was written in the sixth to seventh centuries BCE, while many of the events and places reported therein happened hundreds of years earlier. The biblical writers had no idea what these events and places were like at the earlier time, so they tailored them to appear as if they had happened at the time the reports were written. The writers may have thought that in doing so, they were standing on solid ground because nobody would ever come along to prove them wrong. They had no idea that 2,500 years later, a science called archaeology would turn up that would unearth the untainted facts. Thus, the camels that we mentioned earlier that were linked to the time of the patriarchs did not exist because camels were not used as beasts of burden until hundreds of years later. The accounts of the city of Gerar and the territory of Edom do not fit the period given to them in the Bible, but they do fit a much later period. The Exodus could not have happened at the time and in the manner described in the Bible because such an event would have left at least some tiny trace that would have been found later, but there is no such trace. The description of Joshua bringing down the walls of Jericho is completely wrong because Jericho had no walls at that time. And the temple, gate, and palace said to have been built by Solomon did not exist because the place in question was at that time a mere hillside populated by sheep and shepherds. The structures, if they were built at all, were built hundreds of years later.

The other chief source of error arises from the fact that the Bible is heavily laden with religious propaganda. A good example is offered in 2 Kings, where the author explains why the Kingdom of Israel fell to the Assyrians:

> All this took place because the Israelites had sinned against the Lord their God, who had brought them up out of Egypt from under the power of Pharaoh king of Egypt. They worshipped other gods and followed the practices of the nations the Lord had driven out before them, as well as the practices that the kings of Israel had introduced. The Israelites secretly did things against the Lord their God that were not right.

From watchtower to fortified city they built themselves high places in all their towns. They set up sacred stones and Asherah poles on every high hill and under every spreading tree. At every high place they burned incense, as the nations whom the Lord had driven out before them had done. They did wicked things that aroused the Lord's anger. They worshipped idols, though the Lord had said, "You shall not do this." . . . So the Lord was very angry with Israel and removed them from his presence. Only the tribe of Judah was left, and even Judah did not keep the commandments of the lord their God. They followed the practices that Israel had introduced. Therefore the Lord rejected all the people of Israel; he afflicted them and gave them into the hands of plunderers, until he thrust them from his presence. (2 Kings 17:13–20)

The message is that Israel fell to the Assyrians because it had sinned. The sin caused the fall. And what was the sin? Idolatry. The Israelites had worshipped Baal, Asherah, and other gods in the place of Yahweh. And why was that so bad? Because the priests (after they turned to Yahweh alone) had hooked their fortune to Yahweh. If Yahweh went down, so did they. As long as Yahweh alone was worshipped, the priests had power. So it was essential to shape the worldview of the leaders of Judah and the people of Judah that turning away from Yahweh meant trouble. As long as they worship Yahweh alone, they will be protected.

Of course, the single biggest piece of propaganda was the story of the Exodus. The Bible writers fulfilled their agenda, possibly with the aid of collective memory, by miscasting history. They took an occurrence involving a handful of people who were expelled from their home by neighbors who hated and feared them, and they recast it as an escape by millions of enslaved Hebrews from the clutches of a wicked ruler. The whole purpose of this fiction was to convince the people that there was a god who loved and cared for them, and this fiction was easy to create because the handful of expelled people was none other than the writers themselves. Since only they were involved, they could tell the story in any way they chose.

The propaganda continued with the literary treatment accorded Israel and Judah. The Bible writers went to great lengths to show how Judah was continually being rewarded for its faithfulness to Yahweh in contrast to sinful Israel. It was reported to be richer, more populous, and more successful than the nation to the north. Actually, it was not. And it was reported as having magnificent palaces, courts, gates, and temples when in fact it had none of these things. Also, numbers were constantly exaggerated to favor anything associated with Yahweh.

Thus, what we have here is a case of priests (Levites) producing a construct (the Bible) to sustain a god (Yahweh) for the purpose of augmenting their own power. Those in the community who took the construct at face value bought into an illusion. Belief that Moses was chosen by Yahweh was an illusion, belief that Yahweh delivered a group of Jewish slaves out of Egypt was an illusion, and belief that Yahweh promised land and protection in exchange for worship was also an illusion.

## CHAPTER FIVE

# THE CHRISTIANS
## Memories of Jesus

I
n his massive study on the life of Jesus, James D. G. Dunn observes that every generation or so, some religious writer comes along to argue that Jesus, the central figure in Christianity, never really existed as an actual person and that the entire Jesus tradition is a wholesale invention.[1] Dunn himself does not subscribe to this view (and neither do I), but the mere fact that these writers should pop up so regularly suggests that the evidence for the actual existence of Jesus is less than rock solid. Arguably, there is more credible evidence that Socrates, for example, really existed—and that was some 400 years before the time of Jesus—than that Jesus actually existed. Like Jesus, Socrates wrote nothing (or at least nothing that survives), but unlike Jesus, Socrates had a younger contemporary (Plato) who followed him around and wrote down what he said. Two problems with the evidence for Jesus are that most of it is found in the four Gospels, and the authors of these documents lived many years after Jesus and never laid eyes on him. The other problem is that the writers of the Gospels had an agenda. As evangelists, their undisputed goal was to win converts to Christianity, not to compile an objective record of events in the life of its central figure.

## Documentary Sources

The only nonbiblical literature that ostensibly makes reference to Jesus comes from the hand of the Roman Jewish historian Flavius Josephus and the Roman historian Tacitus. In his *Jewish Antiquities*, written in the last decade of the first century, Josephus refers to Jesus in two brief passages. The first passage (*Antiquities* 18.63–64) says only that Jesus had a wide following among both Jews and Gentiles, that he was condemned by Pilate to be crucified, and that after his death, those who had loved him continued to remember him. The second passage (*Antiquities* 20.200), which is briefer still, says only that Jesus was called Messiah and that he had a brother named James. The single reference by Tacitus, who wrote early in the second century, speaks of a "Christus" who was executed by the procurator Pontius Pilate and who had followers who were called Christians (*Annals* 15.44). However, since Josephus wrote some sixty years after the death of Jesus and Tacitus more than eighty years after, it is not inconceivable that their sources were tainted by religious belief or were unreliable for some other reason. Thus, even these secular references to Jesus are not completely immune to criticism.

The fact that the four evangelists had an agenda is not the only problem with the Gospels as sources of evidence for a historical Jesus. Two additional problems surround the identity of their authors and the time of their composition. As everyone knows, the authors of the Gospels go by the names Matthew, Mark, Luke, and John. Also, there was a tax collector and presumed follower of Jesus named Matthew, the apostle Peter supposedly had a secretary named Mark, there was a physician and traveling companion of Paul named Luke, and there was a man known as the beloved disciple who was named John. But scholars are virtually unanimous in their understanding that the latter characters are not the people who wrote the Gospels. The authors of the Gospels are anonymous, and the names we know them by today were not attached until around 180 CE.[2] Furthermore, the authors very probably never knew or even laid eyes on Jesus. They were not eyewitnesses. They arose from a different culture, hailed from a different geographical region, and spoke a different language than that spoken by Jesus and his followers (Greek as opposed to Aramaic).[3] E. P. Sanders points out that the fact that the authors are anonymous did not undermine the authority of their writings for ancient readers because anonymous writings at that time carried the same level of authority as anonymous encyclopedia articles do for readers today.[4] Nevertheless, knowing the actual names and identities of the Gospel writers might well provide useful information for interpreting their work. As it is, we are left largely in the dark in this regard.

The other problem relates to the dating of the Gospels. Scholars are largely in agreement that the Gospel according to Mark came first, and it was written around 70 CE. That was followed by Matthew and Luke, written around 80–85, and finally came John, written around 90–100. Given that forty years elapsed between the death of Jesus and the writing of the first Gospel and more than fifty years for the other Gospels, the big problem is how do we bridge the time gap? How did it happen that the Gospel writers came to be informed about events in the life of Jesus and the sayings attributed to him when they were separated by such a large time span? Jesus himself wrote nothing, and there was no stenographer who followed him around to take notes. Also, his disciples were convinced, following their teacher's death, that Jesus would soon return to take charge of the kingdom they would all be a part of, so there was no point for them to write anything down. In addition, the vast majority, including the apostles, were not literate, so they could not have written anything even if they had wanted to. After many years had passed and Jesus still had not returned, an effort, probably sporadic, was eventually begun to memorialize some of his words and actions. The few people who could write would have recorded what they understood of these things on papyrus, a relatively expensive (and therefore scarce) medium for record keeping. These bits and pieces of papyrus were then collected together by the writers of the Gospels to construct a more or less coherent account. But how do we know that these scraps of material, written decades after the actual events and creatively stitched together, accurately report what Jesus said and did? Answering this question has been a central concern of New Testament scholars for more than 100 years.

Vestiges of this early history of the Gospels appear to be evident in the finished documents. Many years ago, scholars noticed that the Gospels, especially the first three (Mark, Matthew, and Luke) were composed of movable units of text called pericopes (pronounced "pera-cupees"). The term derives from two Greek words that mean "cut out" or "cut around." The word conveys the idea that the Gospels appear to be made up of self-contained units that were cut out of some other text so that they could be moved around from one location to another. Each pericope consists of a group of verses that express a complete thought, and it often happens that the same pericope appears in two or all three of these Gospels. For example, the following verses from Matthew (18:1–5), which relate to who is greatest in the kingdom of heaven, is a pericope:

> At that time the disciples came to Jesus, saying, "Who is the greatest in the kingdom of heaven?" And calling to him a child, he put them in the midst of them, and said, "Truly, I say to you, unless you turn and become like children, you will never enter the kingdom of heaven. Whoever humbles himself like this child, he is the greatest in the kingdom of heaven. Whoever receives one such child in my name receives me."[5]

The same pericope appears in Mark (9:33–37) and Luke (9:66–48), but the phrasing is somewhat different, as is the context. Nearly all the material in the first three Gospels can be separated into distinct pericopes like this one, and they can be compared with one another—which is the reason these Gospels are called "synoptic," which means "seen together" ("syn" + "optic"). The pericopes from the three Gospels can be arranged in three vertical columns on sheets of paper where they can be *seen together* and compared with one another. Some pericopes appear in all three Gospels, some only in Matthew and Mark, some only in Mark and Luke, some only in Matthew and Luke, and some only in the Gospels individually. This rather loose arrangement of the pericopes in the synoptic Gospels led the New Testament scholar Karl Ludwig Schmidt, in 1919, to compare the synoptic Gospels with strings of pearls.[6] The pericopes were the pearls, and the strings consisted of the interconnecting phraseology and the contexts, both of which were supplied by the evangelists. Each evangelist can be seen as arranging the pearls in the order that seemed best to him and as supplying the most appropriate context for those pearls.

The fact that one and the same pericope usually occurs in more than one Gospel strongly implies that one was copied from another or that they were copied from a third source. Virtually every New Testament scholar agrees with this conclusion, and it has led to the invention of what is called the two-source hypothesis. This is the idea that Matthew and Luke copied material from Mark and from an independent writing called Q (from the German word *Quelle*, which means "spring" or "source").[7] The Q writing, which has never been discovered, was supposed to be a compilation of sayings by Jesus assembled by some unknown author. The

Gospel of Mark, on the other hand, was supposed to depend not on Q but rather on an undiscovered additional source sometimes called M. Yet the two-source hypothesis (the sources being Mark and Q) is not without difficulties. In a lengthy and carefully constructed argument, E. P. Sanders has concluded that in its simple formulation, it cannot be maintained at all, and he notes that the Q writing, being a mere explanatory convention, may never have existed.[8] The work of this scholar is sometimes considered the wave of the future, and I suspect that he may be correct. In his later book *The Historical Figure of Jesus*, instead of appealing to any two-source hypothesis or Q writing, Sanders speaks of "bits and pieces" of papyrus.[9] These bits and pieces, containing written references by unknown authors to the words and actions of Jesus, are thought to be the sources of the synoptic Gospels. Among these scraps of papyrus, the shortest of them may have provided the material for a single pericope. The longer ones may have been cut up to form several pericopes.

It is not difficult to imagine the original sources of these small pieces of papyrus. One source would likely have been letters. Literate folks have written letters back and forth from the time of the ancient Egyptians. They wrote about all sorts of things, from the most trivial to the most profound, but one topic that held the attention of the early Christians was the return of Jesus and the coming of the kingdom. Surely, they would have written letters about what they understood of these matters, and many recipients of such letters would have preserved them, just as people often do today. Some of these preserved letters may have ended up in the hands of the evangelists. Also, many of the successors to the apostles were probably literate, and some may have written letters to their congregations, just as St. Paul did. These, too, could have found their way to the evangelists. Another probable source was personal notes. The successors to the apostles would have given sermons, and they likely would have taken notes to organize their thoughts and to preserve them for future occasions. Also, instructional lessons were probably offered to those who were interested in becoming Christians, just as they are today in certain denominations. The instructors would likely have written notes relating to what they considered the essential beliefs of Christianity, just as college instructors today write lecture notes for their classes, and the catechumens, the students, may have taken notes for themselves as reminders of those beliefs. Notes also would have come in handy in the inevitable verbal confrontations that would have occurred between the early Christians and the Jews of the day. Christian leaders may have created sets of notes to serve as guides in negotiating the pitfalls of such confrontations. Finally, the early Christians may have made notes that recorded the content of dreams and visions they experienced. Everyone knows that unless they are written down, the contents of a dream are quickly forgotten. It is thought that many of these written materials eventually ended up in the hands of the evangelists. They became the pearls that the evangelists strung together to form the Gospels.

## The Oral Tradition

Let us now move backward in time to a period before the appearance of many of these written materials. What we find is a vibrant oral tradition that went back to the very beginning of Jesus' ministry. Jesus' followers certainly talked to one another, and they shared with one another what they understood to be his message. This was the great conversation. It took place among those who assembled to hear Jesus' sermons and those who followed him on the pathways of Galilee. It occurred on street corners, in the public market, and in the gatherings that followed religious services. It arose spontaneously in people's homes following meals and during social visits. Religious festivals and celebrations attracted crowds that provided a natural setting for discussions about what Jesus was thought to have said and done. I contend that this oral tradition was the occasion for the formation of many of the most important Christian beliefs.[10] And it did not end with the first expression of these beliefs in written form. It continued right alongside the gradual emergence of the written record and well past the appearance of the first iteration of the Gospels.

Now the lifeblood of any oral tradition is human memory. Furthermore, in the oral tradition that constituted early Christianity, it was *only* memory. There were no newspapers or magazines to correct for errors in memory. There were no history books or encyclopedias to set wayward memories straight. There were no photographs, no sound recordings, and no videos to show that something didn't really happen that way. If errors occurred, they were integrated into the seamless stream of what was firmly accepted as the past. More specifically, the kind of memory we are talking about here is collective memory. Collective memory is the fluctuating, shifting, constantly dividing and reuniting memory shared by the community. It is the sum total of all the memories of individuals in the community knit together, where the stitching is provided by the constant intercommunication that occurs among the members. The treatment of collective memory is the centerpiece of this chapter relating to the memory of Jesus, and we now commence a brief digression into that topic.

## Collective Memory

Maurice Halbwachs (1877–1945), the inventor of the theory of collective memory, in the preface to his seminal work, recalls having read a story in a magazine about a nine- or ten-year-old girl who was found in the woods near Châlons, France, in 1731. No one could determine who she was or where she came from because she had no recollections of her childhood. After further inquiry, it was thought that she was born in the far north, probably among the Eskimos, and that she had been transported to France through the Antilles, a group of islands in the Caribbean. When she was shown pictures of seals and huts from Eskimo country and pictures of sugarcane, she appeared to recognize them, but apart from that, she seemed to have few other memories. Reading this account led Halbwachs to reflect on what it would be like for a child to be abruptly separated from his or her family, to be transported to a country where a different language was spoken, where the people and places were unfamiliar and the customs were totally different. This child would likely remember nothing about his or her society of origin because those memories are no longer connected to anything in the new society. We use those connections to retrieve the memories. To retrieve those memories, the child would have to be shown images that reconstructed, at least for a moment, the milieu from which the child had been torn.

Pursuing this idea further, people normally acquire their memories in a social context, and it is also in society that they recall those memories. The greatest number of memories come back to us when parents, friends, and others ask us to recall events from the past that were experienced together. "Do you remember the time when . . . ? And do you remember what happened after that?" Without being prompted in these ways, we might never recall the memories. These observations about memory imply an essential feature of Halbwachs's theory, namely, that *memory is selective.*

We remember many things only insofar as they are connected to things in the present. Events in the present perform a selective function in regard to what we recall from the past. We drive along a mountain road, and that leads us to recall the last time we took that drive. We prepare a meal, and recalling the last time we prepared it leads us to alter the recipe in some way. We go to open the hood of a car, and when we can't find the latch, we try to recall where we found it the last time. We attempt to fill out an IRS form, and when we run into trouble, we try to recall how we filled it out a year earlier. Concerns in the present lead us to draw forth recollections about the past. These present-day concerns are what keep the past alive. If we stopped wrestling with problems in the present and stopped engaging in reveries about the past (which is itself an activity in the present), our recollections of the past would certainly shrink, and many of them would vanish completely.

At this point, we must ask, exactly what is collective memory? The initial answer is that collective memory is the sum total of all the memories of the members of any society that are considered to be important. Unfortunately, this definition is unenlightening because of its generality. We can narrow it down by asking about the collective memory of some widely known event, such as the outbreak of some conflict that widely impacts the members of the society. The collective memory of this event will be the totality of all the memories of the event entertained by the members of the society in question. These memories are likely to be different for each member, and they are likely to change with the passage of time. Let us simplify things further by assuming that the society is preliterate and that all the communication among the members is oral. Now suppose two members of this society, Alice and Tom, strike up a conversation about the event. Alice recalls what she knows of the event and relates it to Tom. Merely by attaching words to her memories, Alice makes a selection, but Alice's selection is further specified by her perspective on the event. Alice may have a friend who is involved in the conflict in question, and this leads her to see it in a unique way. In joining the conversation, Tom, too, attaches words to his memories, memories rooted in his own perspective. As each conversant hears the other's account, he or she will form a mental synthesis of the two accounts. As the conversation continues, there will be additional selections from the personal storehouse of memories followed by additional syntheses. Now, depending on the size of the society, imagine this conversation occurring many times, perhaps hundreds or thousands of times. Eventually, a more or less common memory of the big event will take shape in the public mind, and this will be the collective memory of the event. But this collective memory will very likely lack much uniformity at any moment in time, and it will be constantly changing and developing according to the rule of selection followed by synthesis followed by selection followed by synthesis and so on. Collective memory is thus a constantly evolving social construct.

Collective memory is rendered even more fluid by the fact that every time a memory is recalled, every time it is brought to mind, it changes slightly. With each act of recollection, what is recalled gets integrated with new information from the present. Then, with the next recollection, the product of the prior recollection is recalled, and it gets integrated with even more new information, so the memory in question gradually drifts ever farther from the original. The definitive work leading to this conclusion was done by a team of researchers at the Northwestern University School of Medicine. The research shows that memory rewrites the past with current information, updating our recollections with new experiences.[11] According to team leader Donna Jo Bridge, memory is *survival enhancing*. "To help us survive, our memories adapt to an ever-changing environment and help us deal with what's important now. . . . Our memory is not like a video camera. Your memory reframes and edits events to create a story to fit your current world. It's built to be current." As explained by coresearcher and senior author Joel Voss, "Everyone likes to think of memory as this thing that that lets us vividly remember our childhoods or what we did last week. But memory is designed to help us make good decisions in the moment and, therefore, memory has to stay up-to-date. The information that is relevant right now can overwrite what was there to begin with." These findings reinforce Halbwachs's conclusion that memory addresses the needs of the present, which is just another way of saying that memory helps us survive.

## Collective Memory and Natural Selection

Collective memory operates through selection, and it enhances survival. These facts give rise to the thought that collective memory is governed by the same law of natural selection that governs biological evolution. Let us explore this idea further. As everyone knows, Charles Darwin invented natural selection to account for the origin of species. One species that he was keenly interested in were the finches that populated the Galapagos Islands, and he noted that these birds were differentiated largely by the size and shape of their beaks. The beaks, in turn, appeared to be adapted to the kind of food they ate. Those that ate seeds had beaks suited for crushing, those that ate insects had beaks suited for grasping, those that fed on cactuses had pointed beaks suited for penetrating the surface of the plants, and those that ate fruit had beaks similar to the beaks of parrots, which ate fruit. Darwin theorized that the different kinds of beaks arose naturally, through a selection process, as the birds interacted with their environment (in this case the food supply). Natural selection works similarly to artificial selection (selective breeding), but where artificial selection depends on human intentionality, natural selection does not.

As typically explained, natural selection depends on three requirements:

1.  There must be a variation in traits. In the case of the finches, going back in time some 2 million years, slight variations appeared in the shape of their beaks. These variations became more pronounced with the passage of time.

2.  There must be differential reproduction. In reference to the finches, if the food supply on a certain island consisted mostly of seeds, the finches with beaks suited for crushing would fare better than those with beaks less suited for that purpose. These finches would then reproduce in greater numbers than the other finches. Given that the food supply was limited mainly to seeds, the other finches would tend to die out.

3.  The trait in question must be heritable. In finches, beak size and shape is heritable.

The result is that finches having beaks suitable for crushing come to dominate the population on islands where the food consists of seeds.

Now these very same requirements needed for natural selection in biology exist also in collective memory. The variation in traits is obvious. Memories differ from one another. The memory of your mother as a lovable person is different from the memory of her as, say, a shoplifter. One might be reinforced while the other is suppressed. Differential reproduction is also present. Every time a memory arises in conscious awareness, every time it is called to mind, it is reproduced. Furthermore, memories that are relevant to contemporary concerns are called to mind more often than those that are not. Memories that have no relevance at all to such concerns are liable to be permanently forgotten (like the traits of finches that die out). This differential reproduction also exists when a memory is conveyed from one person to another. For example, if a certain item of gossip should be recalled by one person and described to another, the recipient is likely to remember it for a few minutes and then convey it right away to a third person. In this way, gossip spreads like wildfire. Memories that have no common interest are not spread at all. The third requirement, that of heritability, is implied by the second. When a memory is called to mind in one moment in time, it is inherited from an earlier moment, and when the item of gossip is received by a listener, it is inherited from the speaker.

In biology, evolution results from the interaction of individuals with their environment. In collective memory, the role of the environment is supplied by the social milieu—whatever the society considers to be important at the moment. For the finches, the environment, in particular, the food supply, determined which finches would thrive and live to reproduce. The physical environment accomplished the selective function. In the context of memory, the social environment serves the same purpose. It determines which memories will survive and which will lapse or be forgotten. It does this by defining what the public finds interesting. And what the public finds interesting is what answers to the needs of the moment. So just as the physical environment determines which traits will thrive and become dominant in the biological group, so the social milieu determines which memories will thrive and become dominant in the public mind.

I call the interpretation of collective memory introduced here the "natural selection model of collective memory." The essential markers of this theory are that the collective memory in question results from a selection process, that it serves to enhance the survival of the pertinent group, and that the selection is indeed natural (i.e., not artificial). The last marker is all-important. In regard to Darwin's theory, one of the finches did not think to itself, "If only I had a more robust beak, I could crunch these seeds more easily, so I think I will evolve one." This is not the way it happened. Rather, minute changes emerged naturally in the structure of the beaks, some of the changes facilitated survival and reproduction, and so these changes naturally became dominant in the group. Similarly, in the natural selection model of collective memory, the selection is made automatically, so to speak, and without conscious deliberation. Suppose, for example, that you want to remove a walnut from its shell and you lack a mechanical nutcracker. But then you notice a nice rock nearby, and you immediately grab it and use it to crack the shell. What led to this action was an immediate insight, not a conscious process of deliberation followed by a decision. The insight consists in seeing that something is useful for a certain purpose. Addressing the needs of the present in collective memory involves the same kind of insight. It consists in seeing that some memory will satisfy a need. It happens automatically and spontaneously. This is the kind of process, I contend, that underlies the selection of adaptive memories. It is grounded in insight, and there is a kind of necessity to it. At the end of this chapter, I will use the natural selection model to account for the collective memory of Jesus in the first several decades of the Christian era. I will argue that this interpretation accounts for all the exceptional beliefs surrounding the figure of Jesus—the belief that he rose from the dead, the belief that he is the son of God, and four others—through the inexorable operation of a scientific law. This is the same law of natural selection that governs biological evolution. In other words, the argument is that these beliefs can be explained through purely naturalistic reasons without the appeal to any miracles. But first we must complete the analogy between collective memory and biological evolution.

## Mutant Memories

In the population of Galapagos finches, novel elements, such as increased beak size, were introduced thousands of years ago through genetic accidents called mutations. Each mutation, if it was adaptive (i.e., if it enhanced survival), resulted in some tiny change in the finches. As these mutations multiplied and built on one another, the appearance and behavior of the finches changed in noticeable ways. An analogous kind of mutation occurs in the context of memory. I call these mutations mutant memories. Mutant memories are novel memories that differ from other memories in the collective memory. Many (if not most) mutant memories begin as suggestions, proposals, inferences, guesses, hopes, and desires. Once these mental states are expressed in words and the words are recalled minutes or days later, they become memories. And when the words are conveyed to others through conversation, they become memories in the mind of the listener. These memories then enter what I call the "memory pool" (analogous to the gene pool). This is the sum of all the memories of all the members of the society in question. Once a memory is in the memory pool, natural selection goes to work and either selects the memory as adaptive or rejects it. The selected memories then go on to color the collective memory, and the rejected ones lapse into forgetfulness. Selected memories that are especially important can cause the collective memory about some person or thing to veer off in an entirely new direction. I have said that the natural selection of memories operates according to an empirically necessary law. So, I contend, does the generation of mutant memories. Mutant memories will continue to arise as long as the human imagination continues to function, and imagination will function as long as humans populate the planet.

Another source of mutant memories is the mere passage of time. Everyone is aware of the fact that memory degrades with time, and this fact is well established in the psychological literature. If we should listen to a lecture, for example, we may recall many of the details an hour later, including the appearance of the lecturer. But the accuracy of recall will seriously trail off a few weeks later, and we may recall practically nothing a year later. With the passage of time, gaps will develop in the original memory; for example, you may not recall exactly what the lecturer looked like. She may have had brown hair, but a month after having heard the lecture, you may have heard another lecture in which the speaker had blond hair. You could easily mix up the two lecturers and conclude that the original lecturer had blond hair. This error, which is extremely common, is sometimes called "confabulation," and it is a kind of mutant memory.

Yet another source of mutant memories is post-encoding experiences, where "encoding" refers to the initial storage of information in memory. After we first experience something, we often engage in discussions about that thing with other people. These discussions may focus our attention on certain aspects of the initial experience, and, as a result, our memory of those aspects is strengthened, often at the expense of other aspects. For example, suppose we should see a movie about a climbing expedition on Mount Everest and later we discuss the film with some friends who also saw it. If the discussion should focus on how some climbers died because their oxygen ran out, recollection of this fact will be strengthened. As a result, when we recall the film at a later time, this fact about the oxygen may be one of the few that we remember.

An especially important type of post-encoding experience includes the implantation of suggestions by other people. Harvard psychologist Daniel Schacter notes how a suggestion implanted by Dutch psychologists seriously impacted the recollection of an airline accident that happened earlier.[12] In 1992, a cargo plane operated by El Al Airlines crashed into an eleven-story apartment building in Amsterdam, killing thirty-nine residents and all of the crew. Members of the Dutch university where the psychologists worked were asked a series of questions relating to the crash. First, they were asked whether they had seen the television clip of the plane hitting the apartment building. Fifty-five percent of those responding said they had. In a follow-up study, two-thirds responded in the affirmative. Then those who said they had seen the video clip were asked about details of the collision. In response, they recalled the apparent speed of the plane. They recalled the angle of the plane as it hit the building. And they recalled whether the plane had been on fire the moment before the collision. But, in fact, there was no video clip of the plane hitting the building. No such video had ever been taken. The clip didn't exist. It thus becomes apparent that all of the details about the plane crash that the so-called witnesses said they had recalled were in fact made up. Yet these people were certain that they had indeed remembered them as they had reported them. These memories count as mutant memories.

The plane crash example shows how people can claim to remember things that they never in fact experienced. How people can claim to remember things that never really *existed* is shown by the distinguished psychologist Elizabeth Loftus, who pioneered much of the recent research on memory. Loftus describes how a group of her students conducted an experiment in a busy train station.[13] Two female students entered the station, one of them placed her large bag on a bench, and then both walked away to check the train schedules. While they were away, a male student sneaked over to the bag and pretended to remove an article from it. He then appeared to place the article under his coat and quickly walked away.

When the women returned, the one who had left the bag on the bench noticed that it had been tampered with and cried out, "Oh my God, my tape recorder is missing!" She then said within earshot of everyone around that the tape recorder, which was very expensive, had been loaned to her by her boss for a special reason. Those who had seen and heard all of this were sympathetic and offered to help. The woman with the bag then asked them for their phone numbers in case she should need their statements for insurance purposes. A week later, someone called the witnesses and asked them questions about the incident. They were asked whether they had seen the tape recorder. More than half answered yes. Then those who had answered in the affirmative offered details about the recorder. Some said that it was gray, others that it was black; some said it was in a case, others that it was not; some said it had an antenna, others that it did not. In fact, there was no tape recorder, the apparent thief had taken nothing, and all the witnesses who claimed to have seen it had in fact seen nothing. Yet these witnesses were all quite certain about their recollections of the incident and the device. Their apparent memories, mutant memories, were prompted by the highly suggestive actions of the students.

These two examples show how easy it is to introduce a suggestive thought into someone's mind that entirely alters that person's memory about something. A mere question (did you see the video?) or an otherwise innocent sequence of actions (appearing to open a travel bag and reaching under one's outer clothing) can accomplish the trick. Granted, these two examples involved psychological experiments, and the thought that was suggested was done so intentionally. But the same result could happen if the question was entirely innocent and the sequence of actions had no intended result. The lesson is that an ordinary sequence of gestures or words can send a memory of something off in a new direction.

Another type of mutant memory occurs when one person attempts to reproduce some phrase or statement uttered by another person. What happens is that the words get mixed up in the process, and new words, sometimes similar in meaning, get substituted in place of the original words. Loftus reports the results of experiments that address this subject.[14] When a speaker uttered the words "several large firms," the hearer, in trying to reproduce the phrase, said "the last three firms." When the speaker said "a vague impulse," the hearer said "a vague urge," and when the speaker talked about "the geography lesson on Australia" and "the recollection of his grandmother," the hearer said "the grandmother in Australia." This same kind of error in perception and recollection is dramatically illustrated in a game played by both children and adults. The game goes by the name "telephone" and also "Chinese whispers." It is played by lining up ten or fifteen players in a row close enough to each other that one person can whisper something in the ear of an adjacent person but far enough apart so that others cannot hear what is whispered. The first player in the line will whisper some expression in the ear of the person next to him, that person then will then attempt to whisper the expression just heard in the ear of the next person, and so on. In the end, the final iteration of the expression will be compared with the first. Usually, there is a drastic difference between the two. For example, if the original expression is "a guppy in the shark tank," the final expression might be "the shark ate the guppy" or "a groupie in a dark tank top." When mutant memories such as these enter the sphere of collective memory, the whole drift of the original memory can be altered.

Egocentric bias is yet another source of mutant memories. People remember things in ways that benefit them. Loftus reports an incident from a lawsuit in which a woman's daughter was injured by being struck by an oncoming car.[15] The daughter was crossing the street, and the woman saw the car strike her daughter. Shortly after the accident, the woman said the car seemed to be going "a mite fast." But later, at trial, she said the car was going "like a bat out of hell." Of course, if the car was speeding, the woman would stand a greater chance of recovering damages. Did the woman actually remember the car going like a bat out of hell, or did she lie about it? Loftus thinks that the woman's own "internal thoughts, wishes, and desires" influenced how she remembered the accident. Other reasons can be cited to support that interpretation. Schacter observes, for example, that people often remember getting higher grades in school than they actually got because it makes them look better in their own eyes.[16] Also, when a marriage ends in divorce, the husband often attributes the failure to his wife, and the wife does the same to her husband. It appears that the self influences the way we remember things because we want to feel good about ourselves, so we remember things accordingly. This reasoning would seem to extend to things in general. If it makes us feel good, we tend to remember it. However, whether these egocentric factors influence how we remember things or whether they cause us to lie about them, from the standpoint of collective memory, the result is the same. When people report such memories to others and these reports enter the memory pool, it makes no difference whether the reports reflect a true or a false state of mind.

Loftus sums up many of the points I have made in the preceding pages of this chapter:

> During the time between an event and a witness's recollection of that event—a period often called the "retention interval"—the bits and pieces of information that were acquired through perception do not passively reside in memory waiting to be pulled out like fish from water. Rather, they are subject to numerous influences. External information provided from the outside can intrude into the witness's memory, as can his own thoughts, and both can cause dramatic changes in his recollection.
>
> People's memories are fragile things. It is important to realize how easily information can be introduced into memory, to understand why this happens, and to avoid it when it is undesirable.[17]

The most important word in this passage is "fragile." Memory is fragile, and this is what most distinguishes changes in collective memory from the evolution of biological species. Biological species tend to be permanent, an attribute they derive from genes. Genes are atomic units of information that tend to stay the same year after year, and, as a result, biological evolution takes a long time. In the context of memory, the correlative of the gene is the neuron. But neurons are nowhere near as stable as genes. Many neurons, such as those that are involved in sensory perception, are in a state of perpetual flux for long periods of time. However, this does not mean that every memory is fragile. After all, everyone knows that you never forget how to ride a bicycle, and many of us have memorized entire poems and lines of prose and can recall them without a single error years later. So it is important that we distinguish different kinds of memory, some of which are more stable and permanent than others.

Remembering how to ride a bike, how to ski down a mountain, how to eat a bowl of soup, and how to tie our shoes are called cases of implicit memory. The underlying activities are done unconsciously, and performing them does not require that we recall anything from the past. The memories are similar to habits, and once they are instilled, they tend to stay with us. Another kind of remembering relates to our general knowledge of nonpersonal facts. For example, remembering basic pieces of information (e.g., that Boston is in Massachusetts), the National Anthem, that squirrels are mammals, and a poem that we have memorized is called semantic memory. These basic items of knowledge also tend to remain as relatively permanent features of our brains. But a third type of memory, what is called episodic memory, is far less permanent or reliable. Examples include the memory of a dinner conversation, a football game that we may have seen on TV, what the inside of a friend's house looked like the last time we paid a visit, and what happened on a picnic we attended. These memories involve traveling back in time to revisit a certain episode in our lives. The episode always involves our own past experience, and it is limited to relatively brief periods of time. The memories of the airplane crashing into the building and the apparent theft of the tape recorder from the travel bag are episodic memories, and they tend to be highly vulnerable to suggestions of all sorts and to egocentric biases.

Yet, even though episodic memories tend to be fragile, the circumstances can make a difference. The memory of the face of a person we have met for the first time is an episodic memory, and it may not last for long, but as we encounter that person over and over again, the memory tends to become permanent. The same can be said about the memory of our own face. Every time we look at ourselves in a mirror, the memory is refreshed. And the memory of the inside of our own bedroom is an episodic memory that is refreshed every time we enter the room. The permanence of these memories is shored up by the relative permanence of things in the physical world (faces, rooms, houses, natural scenes, and so on). A similar observation can be made about words in print. After we read a poem for the first time, the memory of it is probably a bit hazy, but if we memorize it by reading it over and over again, the memory takes on a kind of permanence. If the memory becomes a bit shaky later on, we can refresh it by rereading the poem. Such memories are shored up by the relative permanence of the printed word. Another group of episodic memories that tends to be permanent includes those that are accompanied by serious personal trauma. The memory of a car accident in which we could have been killed—the recall of a car coming toward us at a high rate of speed when we can't do anything to get out of the way—will likely never be forgotten. And the memory of being robbed at gunpoint—the recollection of the robber pointing a gun at our head while demanding money—is equally unforgettable. It makes sense that such memories be lasting because they are crucial to our survival. If we remember them, we will be more likely to avoid similar ones in the future. But these kinds of episodic memories—those that are continually refreshed and those accompanied by emotional trauma—constitute a special class. Apart from them (and perhaps a few others), episodic memories tend to be fleeting and malleable.

## Memories of Masada

We now turn to two classic cases involving collective memory that serve to illustrate and confirm the natural selection interpretation of this subject. The first involves a battle that took place at Masada, in today's Israel, nearly 2,000 years ago, and the second relates to the shifting memory of Abraham Lincoln in the first two decades of the twentieth century. Let us first consider the battle, which was first researched by Yael Zerubavel in her groundbreaking work *Recovered Roots*.[18] It was the final battle in the first war between the Jews and the Romans, it occurred between the years 73 and 74 CE, and it happened at Masada, a kind of natural fortress located near the eastern border of today's Israel close to the southern end of the Dead Sea. The place is described as a table mountain; it looks like a mountain with its top sliced off, leaving a plateau 1,300 feet above the base with steep cliffs on all sides. At the end of the war, the Jewish rebels (the Sicarii) who had started the war took refuge there, occupying what was left of a palace built by King Herod about 100 years earlier. They hoped they could hold out against the Romans because the only access to their location was a narrow pathway, called the Snake Path, along one side of the cliff. But the Romans were determined to hold the rebels to account. They surrounded the foot of the mountain with a wall to prevent escape or the transport of supplies, and then they constructed a large siege ramp extending from the base of the mountain to the plateau at the top.[19] By the end of the battle, the only survivors, as the story goes, were two women and five children, who had hidden themselves in a cistern. They allegedly told their story to the Romans, who eventually relayed it to the Roman Jewish historian Flavius Josephus, who in turn preserved it in his *Wars of the Jews*. The report by Josephus is our only detailed account of the battle.

In the years following the Masada incident, the story of the rebels' last stand quickly disappeared from the collective memory of the Jewish people. This probably occurred for two reasons. Josephus himself was considered a traitor to the Jewish cause. Prior to Masada, he was commander of the Jewish army in Galilee, where he became a leader in the Great Revolt against the Romans. When the Romans overran his garrison at Jotapata, he suggested a response of mass suicide rather than surrender to the Romans. After all but one of his companions followed his suggestion and killed themselves, Josephus chose to surrender. The other probable reason is because the rebels who died there were viewed by most Jews to be religious fanatics who refused to compromise on anything. They were also thieves, terrorists, and murderers who spent their time killing other Jews (*Wars of the Jews*, 7.8.1). However, today, the defenders of Masada are seen in an entirely different light. Instead of thieves and murderers, they are regarded as heroes who defended a noble cause. The question for us is, what caused this drastic shift in public opinion, and what caused an event that was all but forgotten to be resurrected and projected into the forefront of public attention? Today, every citizen of Israel, practically every visitor, and thousands of people who have never set foot in Israel are aware of the Masada incident.

Part of the answer lies in the fact that elsewhere in his history, Josephus told a different story. By the time the Romans had completed their siege ramp and were about to penetrate the rebels' defenses, the defenders realized that there was no hope for them, so rather than a life of slavery (or worse) under the hated Romans, they decided on mass suicide. Josephus recalls the decision made by the leader of the rebels to kill their wives and children and then kill themselves. By so doing, they would die as freemen:

> Husbands tenderly embraced their wives and took their children in their arms, and gave the longest parting kisses to them with tears in their eyes. . . . Miserable men indeed were they, whose distress forced them to slay their own wives and children with their own hands, as the lightest of those evils that were before them. (*Wars of the Jews* 7.9.1)

After the soldiers had finished their grisly task, they drew lots to select ten among them who would kill the others. Those ten then killed one another, and the last one fell on his sword. When the Romans entered the place the next day, they found, according to Josephus's account, 960 bodies. The only survivors were the aforementioned two women and five children.

What really happened at Masada is, in all likelihood, drastically different from this account by Josephus. Practically anyone familiar with Roman military practices knows that once the soldiers on a siege ramp, any siege ramp, succeed in punching through the opposing defenses with their battering ram, they rush immediately in to slaughter the defenders. This is surely what happened at Masada. The Romans would not have taken the rest of the day (or night) off, allowing the defenders to return to their homes and to kiss their wives and children good-bye. Nor would there have been time for their leader to deliver a lengthy speech to those under his command about the immortality of the soul and life in the world to come (*Wars of the Jews* 7.8.6–7.8.7). Up until the last moment, the defenders would have been desperately trying to reinforce the barricade at the entrance and shower arrows down on the attackers. Also, for the same reason, there was no organized mass suicide. These events never happened at Masada.[20] Where they may have happened was at Jotapata, where Josephus witnessed them firsthand before he turned traitor and surrendered to the Romans. For dramatic effect, Josephus transferred the touching last moments of Jotapata to Masada.

The second part of the explanation for the changed image of the Masada incident and its elevation into the limelight of Jewish memory is the cotemporaneous occurrence of two events. The first was the rise of the Zionist movement in the first part of the twentieth century, and the second was the appearance, in Palestine, of a Hebrew translation of Josephus's *Wars of the Jews*. During the first two decades of that century, the vast majority of Jews knew nothing of Masada. The only surviving version of Josephus's *Wars of the Jews* was in Greek, so it was inaccessible to most speakers of Hebrew. Masada is not mentioned at all in the Talmud, which often makes reference to historical events, and the few people who had heard of Josephus regarded him as a traitorous renegade not worth reading. But then, in 1923, J. N. Simchoni produced a modern Hebrew translation of *Wars of the Jews*. When the Zionists read Josephus's account of the Jewish defense of Masada, how the defenders fought for freedom until the bitter end, how they opted for suicide in place of slavery under the Romans, and how they tenderly kissed their wives and children good-bye, they were electrified. This was exactly what was needed to promote the cause of a Jewish state.

The relatively small number of Jews living in Palestine at the time, surrounded as they were by a far larger number of hostile Arabs, resembled the small number of Jewish fighters at Masada surrounded by some 9,000 hostile Romans. By popularizing the Masada story, the Jews defending Masada would be seen as the common ancestors of the Jews of the twentieth century. They loved freedom so much that they would rather die than give it up, and this bravery was their legacy to future generations. They had the determination to fight to the bitter end against insurmountable odds. Establishing a connection between the defenders of Masada and the modern Jews living in Palestine would help bring about the conditions needed for statehood. These conditions included a set of common values and ideals. They included a feeling of pride in being a member of the group. They included instilling a common national identity. They included correcting the image of Jews in the international community so it depicted them as heroic fighters. They included creating a bond between the Jewish identity and the land of Palestine. These needs of the present were addressed by a selective reading of Josephus's account of the Masada incident.

So the occurrence given for us to explain is how something virtually unknown that happened nearly 2,000 years ago should in a matter of a few years become known to millions and how a group of thieves and murderers should become revered as valiant heroes during the same period of time. The clear answer is that the Zionists selected certain passages from Josephus's *Wars of the Jews* that assisted their cause of Jewish statehood, and they ignored the inconvenient passages. In so doing, they altered the character of the Jewish collective memory in a significant way. Thus, collective memory is selective. Next, the selection that was made addressed the needs of the present moment. The most pressing need of the day was the formation of a Jewish state, and the newly shaped collective memory certainly helped achieve this goal. In so doing, it enhanced the survival of the Jewish people in Palestine. Finally, the selection was natural. When the Zionists read the pertinent passages in Josephus, they immediately saw them as the solution to their problem, as the way to crack the walnut. If discursive reasoning had entered the picture, the Zionists would have wrestled with those other passages that depicted the Masada defenders as criminals who murdered other Jews. But they completely ignored those other passages as if they did not even exist. Through a flash of insight, they hit on the selected passages as the way to go. If the action had been taken by a group of robots, the same result would have been reached. It all happened with a kind of necessity, according to the operation of a scientific law. And it made no difference that the reshaped collective memory was littered with falsehoods. The important thing was that it addressed the needs of the present moment.

## Memories of Lincoln

A second illustration of collective memory that serves to confirm the natural selection model involves the memory of Abraham Lincoln and how it changed in the twenty-year span between 1901 and 1921.[21] Abraham Lincoln was shot and killed in April 1865, and news of his death unleashed a massive outpouring of condolences and grief from most of the nation. After the official day of mourning, his body was loaded onto a train and transported from Washington, D.C., to Oak Ridge Cemetery in Springfield, Illinois. The trip took two weeks, and along the way, tens of thousands showed up to pay their respects. Some people thought that Lincoln had become a god. Soon, however, the picture began to change. Hints of this change were apparent even on the day of his funeral. In their eulogies, many clergymen did not hesitate to dwell on his flaws, and they saw them as the defining feature of his presidency. Lincoln was too kind and forgiving to be effective. He was so compassionate that he pardoned army deserters who had been sentenced to death. He was too forgiving toward the southern traitors, men who had been responsible for so many northern deaths. People began to question whether Lincoln's assassin had caused the nation any great loss. Perhaps Lincoln was better off dead. And these negative feelings continued to deepen. Six months later, on the occasion of his birthday, the nation's most influential historian, George Bancroft, complained that Lincoln was no great leader, and he compared him to a child led along by the hand of its father on a dark and threatening night. Bancroft continued to argue that Lincoln's apparent slowness to act was the result of simple indecisiveness, and it did not come "from humility or tenderness of feeling." His stature as a national figure was clearly on the decline.

Lincoln's trajectory shifted in the opposite direction with the turn of the century, and by the end of the second decade, Lincoln had eclipsed Washington as the most loved, most respected, most famous, most revered, most quoted man in America. In Barry Schwartz's words, "He had become the principal occupant of the American pantheon." Undoubtedly, the single year that showed the greatest flurry of Lincoln worship was 1909, the centennial of his birth. In the vast majority of cities, Chicago being a prime example, practically every religious, ethnic, trade, and neighborhood organization held celebrations. The most famous men in the country gave speeches honoring Lincoln: William Jennings Bryan spoke in Springfield, Booker T. Washington spoke in New York, President-elect William Howard Taft spoke in New Orleans, and President Theodore Roosevelt spoke in Lincoln's birthplace in Kentucky. Lincoln's stature in the collective memory was rendered greater by every celebration and by every famous person who gave him homage. Lincoln portraits were everywhere, as were vignettes of his life and memorabilia of all kinds. In that same year, Congress appropriated the unprecedented sum of $2 million for the Lincoln Memorial, which stands today as possibly the most impressive of all national monuments. All of these acts of homage provided stimulus to the general public to learn more about this man who had died half a century earlier, and it solidified his memory in the public mind.

How do we account for this great surge in popularity that Lincoln (or his memory) enjoyed in the first two decades of the twentieth century? According to Halbwachs (and also the theory of collective memory presented here), what is remembered is what answers to the needs of the present. And what were those needs in the first two decades of that century? Barry Schwartz, the author of the Lincoln study, observes that this time frame is generally called the Progressive Era. It was that special time in American history that saw a revitalization of democracy. There was a new concern for the rights and well-being of ordinary people. This period ushered in a multitude of reforms to address the abuses of the industrial revolution. Child and sweatshop labor laws were passed, federal workmen's compensation was introduced, and labor unions came to balance the power of corporations. It was an age of populism. Universal suffrage became the law through the Nineteenth Amendment, the Seventeenth Amendment provided for the popular election of U.S. senators (who were formerly elected by the state legislatures), and the initiative, referendum, and recall gave voters a direct hand in the operation of their government. Antitrust legislation was passed, ensuring fair competition that would benefit ordinary people, and the Federal Corrupt Practices Act controlled the influence of the wealthy and powerful on political campaigns. The Pure Food and Drug Act became law, which improved the lives and health of ordinary people; the progressive income tax provided that poorer people would pay less in taxes; and primary elections came into use, which took political power out of the hands of party bosses and returned it to the people.

But why was Lincoln selected as the representative of the progressives? The nation needed a hero to get all these measures passed, and it was generally thought that Lincoln would have supported all of them. Lincoln was conceived as the original labor leader who espoused the essential rights of the workingman. He also favored universal suffrage. His words backing this cause, "I go for all sharing the privilege of government . . . by no means excluding women," appeared on suffragette billboards along with his portrait. The expression "What would Lincoln do?" became a mantra for the progressive voice. His physical homeliness, informality of dress, awkwardness of demeanor, and penchant for storytelling made Lincoln appear as an ordinary person who identified with the struggle of other ordinary people. Being born in a log cabin in Kentucky only solidified the bond between him and the common man. But Lincoln's influence on the Progressive Era went deeper than political reform. The nation was experiencing a fundamental transition in values and morality, and it needed an icon to ground the new national identity. Lincoln's life and character came into focus and dominated the interest of the public. His kindness, merciful attitude toward condemned soldiers, and sympathy for casualties of the war became ethical models of behavior. Also, his simplicity and unpretentiousness became social ideals. Articles in magazines bore titles such as "Lincoln as I Knew Him," "A Boy at Lincoln's Feet," and "Impressions of Lincoln." In all of these ways, the person and character of Lincoln addressed the needs of the present in early twentieth-century America, and the relationship between his character and those needs determined the precise way that Lincoln would be pictured in the collective memory of that period.

The theory of collective memory presented here depends first of all on a selection, and this requirement was fulfilled by the selection of Lincoln as opposed to, say, Jefferson or Hamilton. Following this first selection, a second one focused on the features of Lincoln. Some features would be brought to the forefront, while others would be allowed to slip away. What was selected and amplified was his commonness and simplicity, and what was deemphasized was, for example, his political astuteness, his ability to control his emotions, his inquisitiveness, his inventiveness, his oratorical ability, his capacity to listen to different points of view, and his leadership skills. All of these are excellent qualities, but they were useless for accomplishing the goals of the Progressive Era. Only the qualities that answered to the needs of the day were selected. The result was a Lincoln shaped and polished so that it addressed a set of requirements, not a replica of the Lincoln that actually existed half a century earlier. It was a social construct that enhanced the survival of the Progressive movement. It gave vitality to the movement and sufficient momentum to keep it going for twenty years.

## The Collective Memory of Jesus

We can now apply the natural selection model of collective memory, as illustrated in the memory of Lincoln and Masada, to the collective memory of Jesus in the years before and shortly after the writing of the Gospels. What makes both Lincoln and Masada different from Jesus is that for both, there was a contemporaneous written record, whereas for Jesus, there was not. For Lincoln, there were countless newspaper and magazine articles and even biographies of the man, and for Masada, there was the historical account written by Josephus, and these documents had an anchoring effect on the respective collective memories. The collective memories were prevented from drifting very far from the written record. The collective memory of Lincoln was composed of certain features of the man that appeared in the newspapers, and Masada focused on certain passages selected from Josephus, so neither collective memory strayed very far from what was written. But in the case of Jesus, there was nothing that prevented the collective memory from drifting miles away, figuratively speaking, from the original memories of him. As a result, given the needs of the day, the collective memory of Jesus eventually came to reflect a man that never in fact existed. Just as dinosaurs eventually came to differ very greatly from the bird-like creatures from which they evolved, so the collective memory of Jesus, which, like the dinosaurs, evolved through natural selection, eventually differed greatly from the original memory.

Another fact that allowed for such a result was that the memories that the disciples had of Jesus were episodic memories, and they were not the kind of episodic memories that could be refreshed in any way. There was no returning to any book containing records of his sermons or descriptions of his actions. There were no photographs to jog the memory. There was no way that his words could have been memorized, as some scholars have proposed, because there was nothing in print that could serve as a basis for such memorizing. The recollections of Jesus were more like the memories of what happened at a picnic where no photographs, videos, or sound recordings were made. They were one-time episodes with no physical backup. Once the events had passed, there was no bringing them back. Furthermore, these episodic memories were not accompanied by any kind of emotional trauma, so this feature, which would have ensured permanence and stability, was also lacking. After Jesus had died, the only way that prospective converts to Christianity could learn about him was through the memories of others. A person who may have heard a sermon of Jesus passed his recollection of it on to a friend, and that person passed what he or she remembered on to a spouse, and the spouse passed it on to a nephew or niece, and so on (as in the telephone game). Given the manifold opportunities for mutant memories, the final memory probably bore little resemblance to the original one. But one thing we can be reasonably certain of: everyone was anticipating the arrival of the Kingdom of God, so this bias must have colored the final message in a major way. The purpose of every memory of Jesus was to facilitate the arrival of the kingdom and with it the king.

To get an idea of what went into the Jesus construct that ended up in the Gospels, we can begin by examining the socioreligious environment of the day. This environment dictated how Jesus would be remembered from year to year. It determined which memories of Jesus would be selected for emphasis and which would lapse into forgetfulness. Also, it determined which mutant memories would be retained and adjusted to fit the ever-developing construct and which would be rejected. One of the most salient aspects of this environment was Jewish salvation history.

According to this history, the Jewish people count as very special in the eyes of God. It begins when God promised Abraham that he would be the father of a great people if Abraham did as God ordered. The law was laid out hundreds of years later through Moses, centuries after that God established Israel as a kingdom ruled by Saul and David, and when the Jewish people disobeyed, God saw to it that they were sent into exile in Babylon. But in due course, God allowed them to return to Judah, where they lived for a short time in relative freedom. However, the long-awaited freedom was not to last, and at the time of Jesus, they were held captive by the Romans. Yet God promised a Messiah who would set up a new kingdom not only for the Jews but for many Gentiles as well. The Messiah would be a descendent of David and would be born in Bethlehem, the city of David.

At the time of Jesus' ministry and for several decades following, the Jewish community in Palestine was enraptured by the thought that the new kingdom was right around the corner. The excitement appears to have been triggered by the preaching of John the Baptist. Scholars are in near universal agreement that John the Baptist really did exist and that he preached a message that led to his death. One part of his message was that Herod Antipas, ruler of Galilee, had broken the law by marrying Herodias, his half niece, and the other part was that the day of judgment was at hand and everyone should repent. If John had attracted only a handful of followers, Antipas would have ignored all of this, so the fact that he took it seriously implies that John's message was both profoundly felt and widespread. In fact, the people were so excited about the prospect of a new kingdom, and the freedom from Roman rule it implied, that Antipas feared insurrection. He reacted by having John arrested and executed, but this only intensified Jewish expectations. And these expectations did not die out after John's death. In his Letter to the Romans, written some twenty-five years later, Paul the apostle wrote, "The hour has already come for you to wake up from your slumber, because our salvation is nearer now than when we first believed. The night is nearly over; the day is almost here" (Romans 13:11–12). And in his First Letter to the Corinthians, he wrote, "What I mean, brothers and sisters, is that the time is short. . . . For this world in its present form is passing away" (1 Corinthians 7:29–31). Also, all three synoptic Gospels, written many years after Paul's epistles, express the same anticipation. The evangelists report Jesus as saying, "Truly I tell you, some who are standing here will not taste death before they see the Son of Man coming in his kingdom" (Matthew 16:28; also Mark 9:1 and Luke 9:27). This anticipation of the imminent arrival of the Kingdom of God constituted an overwhelming egocentric bias that colored and conditioned every memory of Jesus.

## The Resurrection of Jesus

Let us now see how the natural selection model of collective memory accounts for all the exceptional or extraordinary features of the Jesus construct that we find in the Gospels. Such features include the idea that Jesus rose from the dead, that he is the Son of God, that he is the Messiah, that he performed numerous miracles, that he was born of a virgin, and that he died for the remission of human sins. We can begin with the resurrection. No one would doubt that belief in the resurrection is widespread among Christians and has been for nearly two millennia. The question is, what is responsible for this widespread belief? The answer is that today's Christians believe in the resurrection because the earliest Christians believed in it, and this led to its being reported in the New Testament. But why did the earliest Christians believe in the resurrection? The explanation I propose is that a number of mutant memories arose in the months and years following Jesus' death that altered the flow of collective memory, and this led people to believe that Jesus rose from the dead when in fact he did not—just as mutant memories led Zionist Jews to believe that the defenders of Masada were heroes to be emulated when in fact they most likely were not. Let us first consider the traditional Christian view.

One problem with the traditional view of the resurrection is that it rests on a miracle, and miraculous explanations fail to be intellectually satisfying. For example, suppose that a rainbow should occur after a storm, and someone asks why there are rainbows. If the response is that rainbows occur because God wants them to happen, this does not tell us very much. The same explanation could be given for countless other phenomena: why flowers bloom, why birds build nests, why iron rusts, and why copper conducts electricity. Miraculous explanations raise more questions than they answer: you mean to tell me that rainbows occur for the same reason that copper conducts electricity? In contrast, scientific explanations are intellectually satisfying because they link the occurrence of the phenomenon to be explained to countless other phenomena. In other words, they place the phenomenon in question in a network of relationships, and that is precisely what it means for something to be intellectually satisfying. Something is rational precisely because it is related to other things. A *ratio* is a relationship. Thus, when we explain the rainbow in terms of light waves that are reflected and refracted by drops of water in the atmosphere, we link the rainbow to water drops, to rain, to light rays, to prisms that resolve light rays into different wavelengths, to the phenomenon of color, to mirrors that reflect light waves, and to numerous other phenomena. When placed in this network of relationships, the occurrence of rainbows makes sense.

Another problem with the traditional Christian view of the resurrection is that it flies in the face of responsible historical research. According to the traditional view, Jesus was crucified by the Romans, he remained on the cross for a few hours, he died, his body was then taken down, it was placed in a tomb, and three days later, the tomb was found empty. But under normal circumstances, the Romans would never have allowed any such sequence of events for the simple reason that they would never have allowed the body to be removed from the cross. The New Testament scholar John Dominic Crossan argues persuasively that ancient Rome was in large measure a terrorist regime that ruled by instilling a constant state of fear in the minds of the people subject to its rule.[22] Executing political criminals through crucifixion was one of the means of accomplishing this goal. Those with politically subversive intentions who threatened either the local rule or the empire at large could see for themselves what lay in store for them. Crucifixion was the most horrible fate that the regime could dream up. The convict would be flogged and then nailed to a wooden cross and put on display for everyone to see. He would be kept alive for as long as possible so the greatest number of onlookers could witness the agony, and after he died, the decomposing body would be kept there for days to increase the effect. Gradually, the body would be eaten by crows and scavenger dogs, and when nothing was left resembling a human body, the remains would be thrown into a common grave. The sight of animals eating the body and the ignominy of a common grave was part of the intended effect.[23]

The idea that Jesus would have been treated differently from any other political criminal is little more than a pipe dream. The argument is usually made that the body of a crucified Jew had to be taken down from the cross by sunset on Friday because the following day was the Sabbath and it was against Jewish law to allow the body of a Jew to remain on the cross during the Sabbath. But this argument fails to persuade because Jesus was crucified by the Romans, and the Romans had no interest whatever in conforming to Jewish law. The important thing was to keep the Jews in line by subjecting them to constant terror. The further argument is then made that a certain Jew named Joseph of Arimathea made a special appeal to Pontius Pilate, the governor of Judea, to allow Jesus' body to be removed from the cross, and Pilate granted the request. This argument, too, fails because Pilate was, in the words of Philo of Alexandria, noted for "his veniality, his violence, his thefts, his assaults, his abusive behavior, his frequent executions of untried prisoners, and his endless savage ferocity"(*Embassy to Gaius*, 302). After serving ten years as governor, Pilate was dismissed in 36 CE because of large-scale and ill-judged executions (*Antiquities* 18.88f). The thought that such a man would accede to the humanitarian request of a Jew is almost ludicrous.[24] On top of that, there is good reason to doubt that any such Joseph of Arimathea ever existed or, if he did exist, that he made any such request of Pilate.[25] Then yet another argument is made, based on a comment by Philo, that exceptions were occasionally made on the eve of a holiday to allow the body of a crucified individual to be taken down and delivered to his kinfolk. But a more careful reading of the passage by Philo shows that the exceptions occurred when a Roman governor chose to honor a Roman emperor's birthday. In other words, the holiday in question was the emperor's birthday, not the Jewish Sabbath, and the kinfolk who received the body were members of the Roman aristocracy, not ordinary Jews.[26]

The highly probable conclusion is that the body of Jesus was left on the cross for days to be eaten by scavenging animals and was not taken down and put into any tomb. As a result, it should come as no surprise that when certain women were said to have visited a tomb that was thought to be the resting place of Jesus, the tomb was found to be empty. Of course it was empty when no corpse had been put there in the first place. Still, it would have been possible, three days after Jesus had been affixed to the cross, for God to duplicate the Jesus whose body was still hanging on the cross and make that new body available for visions and appearances. After all, God can do anything. But this would not have been a resurrection. For a genuine resurrection, there must be some kind of material continuity between the original Jesus and the resurrected Jesus. This is the chief implication of the empty tomb story: the body that was placed in the tomb was, in some sense, the same body that was later resurrected. Granted, the body of the resurrected Jesus was not identical to the body Jesus had prior to the crucifixion—in the words of St. Paul, it was a glorified body—but there must have been something of a material nature that carried over from the earlier to the later Jesus. Since this could not have happened if Jesus' body remained on the cross for many days and was later cast into a common grave, the conventional Christian view of the resurrection cannot be correct. Another possibility, one that does maintain material continuity between pre- and post-resurrection, is that God resurrected Jesus from the droppings of crows and the intestinal content of carrion dogs. Assuming the occurrence of miracles, God could have done this, but this kind of resurrection would not have appealed to the imagination as much as the version involving the empty tomb. To win converts, it is essential that the story appeal to the imagination.

An alternate explanation, one that does not depend on miracles and does not conflict with historical findings, is that the collective memory of the emergent Christian community evolved to produce in the end the memory of a resurrected Jesus. The logic of the process runs like this. Following the preaching of John the Baptist, the hope for and expectation of the imminent arrival of the Kingdom of God was running at a feverish pitch. Every kingdom needs a king, and the general feeling was that Jesus was the king designate. But then Jesus was arrested and crucified, and dozens of people saw him die. Yet only a living person can serve as king in a real kingdom. So, if Jesus was to serve as king in the Kingdom of God and if Jesus died, then it was necessary that somehow he come back to life. But, as we have just shown, he did not come back to life as an actual flesh-and-blood human being. Rather, he came back to life as a memory, as a component in the collective memory of the newly emergent Christian community. According to the natural selection model of collective memory, the needs of the present dictate the content of collective memory, and the most pressing need in the days and months following the crucifixion was a living Jesus. Given the intensity of the feeling surrounding the arrival of the kingdom, even the slightest suggestion that Jesus was alive would have altered the collective memory of Jesus to produce a living Jesus in the end.

Since there is no "fossil record" of the evolving collective memory of Jesus in the earliest days of Christianity, it is not possible to identify today the precise stages of this development. It is not possible to pinpoint the mutations in memory that natural selection retained to yield the resurrected Jesus. Still, we can suggest some ways that this might have happened. The story of the empty tomb may contain a grain of truth in this regard. It is not likely that any women actually visited any tomb thought to be the resting place of Jesus because everyone would have been familiar with the Roman practice of dealing with political criminals, and everyone would have known that there was virtually no chance of finding the body of Jesus in a tomb. But such a story could have developed in the collective memory of the community according to a scenario such as this. Imagine an early Christian convert saying to another, "My uncle died last week, and he was a follower of Jesus. After his death, his body was placed in a tomb." The listener could easily interpret "his body" as referring to Jesus' body. Then this listener might pose a question to another convert: "Did you know that Jesus' body was placed in a tomb?" The listener might then reply, "No, I didn't know that. But I was told that all the tombs in this area are empty." The listener could then conflate the two pieces of information and ask another convert, "Did you hear that Jesus' tomb was empty? His body was placed in a tomb, and the tomb was later found to be empty." This is exactly the kind of suggestive question that produces mutant memories. It closely resembles the question that the researchers asked the witnesses in Amsterdam: "Did you see the video of the plane striking the building?" The question implies that there was such a video, and it led to all sorts of mutant memories of what happened just before the crash. Similarly, the question "Did you hear that Jesus' tomb was found to be empty?" implies that there was a tomb, and it could easily have produced mutant memories leading to the belief that Jesus was resurrected.

Another possible route to mutant memories is mistaken identification. The Gospels contain three incidents in which the resurrected Jesus appears to his disciples and they fail to recognize him. In one story, two disciples were walking on the road to Emmaus, a village about seven miles from Jerusalem. A man whom they did not recognize joined them on the walk, and they talked among themselves for quite some time. Only after they joined this man in a meal did the disciples recognize the man as Jesus (Luke 24:13–31). In another story, Mary Magdalene is standing in the empty tomb when she sees a man who she thinks is the gardener. She asks him if he knows the whereabouts of Jesus. Not until he replies does she see that the man is Jesus (John 20:14–16). In the third story, some disciples are in a boat on the Sea of Galilee when they see a man standing on the shore. They had fished for some time without catching anything, but then the man tells them to put out their net one more time. They do so, and soon the net is filled with fish. At that point, they recognize that the man is Jesus (John 21:4–8). These passages are puzzling in that it is not clear what the failure of the disciples to recognize Jesus is supposed to mean. I would suggest that the grain of truth in these passages is that after the death of Jesus, the disciples saw people who looked a little like Jesus, and when they reported these sightings to others and the stories were repeated yet again to others, perhaps four or five times, the message became twisted to the point where the disciples were reported as having seen Jesus himself—much as occurs in the telephone game. In this way, the sightings generated mutant memories of a resurrected Jesus. People tend to remember things they wish for.

The previous two paragraphs have shown how mutant memories of the resurrection might have arisen. They are not intended to show how they actually arose. Just because something possibly happened in a certain way does not mean that it actually happened that way. But one thing we can be reasonably certain of is that the collective memory of Jesus following the crucifixion did evolve so as to enhance the survival of the early Christian movement. If the natural selection model is correct, it is not a case of *may* have evolved or *could* have evolved but rather *did* evolve. Collective memory has no choice in the matter, just as Darwin's finches had no choice in whether to develop more robust beaks. Collective memory *must* adapt to the needs of the social environment. This is essential for survival. The early Christians needed the memory of a resurrected Jesus, and they got one. Furthermore, if the natural selection model is correct, we can be reasonably certain that the collective memory of the resurrected Jesus arose spontaneously through a necessary process of memory mutation. It was not something that was consciously fabricated (at least for the most part) by the evangelists any more than the description of the finches was fabricated by Darwin. The evangelists wrote down what they received in the form of bits and pieces of papyrus, and these bits and pieces reflected the mutated memories of the early Christians. Additionally, just as the finches did not think to themselves, "It would be really nice if I had a more robust beak to crunch these seeds, so I think I'll evolve one," the early Christians did not contemplate the utility of a resurrected Jesus as a step in the evolution of such a memory. The memory arose spontaneously through memory mutations and was then selected to satisfy a need. The outcome was not the product of conscious choice any more than the biological process that led to the more robust beaks was the product of conscious choice.

## Jesus as Son of God

Let us now turn to the belief that Jesus is the Son of God.[27] Could it be that people came to believe this because Jesus himself told his followers that he was the Son of God? When addressing this question, scholars often point to certain passages from the Gospel of John where Jesus can be interpreted as claiming to be divine.[28] These alleged assertions occur only in John, and if Jesus actually made them, they surely would have appeared in the synoptic Gospels. Bart Ehrman argues, I think correctly, that the attribution of these claims to Jesus is not historically defensible.[29] Also, if Jesus had literally come out and claimed to be the Son of God, his opponents would have accused him of blasphemy and stoned him to death.[30] The conclusion is therefore warranted that the early Christians did not come to believe that Jesus was the Son of God because he claimed to be such.

A more reasonable answer, I think, can be reached by appealing to collective memory. But this requires that we take another look at the social environment that directed the evolution of collective memory. All nation-states at that time were ruled by kings. Exactly how kings were envisioned by ordinary people is not known with any great certainty, but they must have been thought of as very special individuals, perhaps as superhumans. In this respect, the situation today is quite different from what it was then. In every democratic society today, high-level governmental authorities—presidents and prime ministers—come from the ranks of ordinary citizens, and they return to those ranks at the end of their terms in office. As a result, everyone living in such a country today knows that there is nothing superhuman about their leaders. But in ancient times, most ordinary people had never seen a king. All they knew about them is what they had heard through rumor. One of those rumors was that many kings were sons of gods. In particular, they would have heard that the former emperor, Augustus, was the son of the god Apollo. Also, they would have heard that Romulus, the founder of Rome, was the son of a god, as were all the early Roman kings. Even today, in some isolated countries, the citizens assign divine status to their ruler, North Korea being a prime example.

If the operation of collective memory accounts for the emergence of the belief that Jesus is the Son of God, then there must have been some suggestion or insight that led to the needed mutant memory. In the next chapter, I argue that the letters and sermons of Paul the apostle were largely responsible for this shift in the collective memory. Paul constantly refers to Jesus as the Son of God, and his letters first began to appear about twenty years after the death of Jesus. Once the message of these letters became widely known, everyone would have become conditioned to thinking of Jesus as the Son of God. But murmurs about the divinity of Jesus may have sprung up even before that. The apostles surely preached the message of the coming kingdom and the return of Jesus as king. As the supreme ruler of God's kingdom, Jesus would have been conceived as superior to every ruler on earth, in particular the kings of Rome. Since the kings of Rome, especially Augustus, who had died only a few years earlier, were generally considered to be sons of some god or *the* son of God (as with Augustus), the apostles may have drawn the inference that Jesus was the Son of God. This inference would then have given rise to the corresponding mutant memory, the mutant memory would have been selected as adaptive, and the collective memory would have shifted accordingly. This idea that Jesus was the Son of God would have been reinforced by the belief that God had caused Jesus to rise from the dead. How natural that God should have extended this favor to his own Son.

If we compare these two assertions, that Jesus rose from the dead and that Jesus is the Son of God, we can see how very different they are in relation to historical fact. History is relevant to the first claim but not to the second. If it should be the case that the body of Jesus did indeed remain on the cross for many days and was eventually thrown into a common grave and if resurrection requires some kind of material continuity between pre- and post-resurrection, then it becomes nearly impossible to conceive how Jesus could have risen from the dead within three days of being affixed to the cross. But no historical event can cast doubt on the claim that Jesus is the Son of God. Historical fact is simply not relevant to this claim. What is relevant is conceptual analysis. If we adopt the view that God is a nonmaterial being without parts, then it becomes extremely difficult (if not impossible) to understand how God could produce a son. First off, a son is normally the same kind of being as the father, but in this case, the father would be nonmaterial and invisible, while the son would be made of matter and visible. On the face of it, any such thing is impossible. Further, if we say that God produced a son in time, then we have a time when God was not a father and a time when he became a father, which implies twoness, in violation of our hypothesis that God has no parts. If we say that God produced a son from all eternity, then we must explain how something essentially temporal (a producing activity) could happen outside of time. It appears that we are faced with a contradiction. We could, however, adopt a different view of God entirely, but then we must explain precisely what that view is before we can even begin talking about any son. In the meantime, we run the risk of talking nonsense when we speak of a Son of God. But beliefs are quite another matter. There is no absolute requirement that beliefs conform to logic, and in the preceding paragraphs, we have shown how the widespread belief that Jesus is the Son of God could have arisen through purely natural causes, and it probably did arise that way. Also, this belief could have arisen regardless of whether Jesus really is the Son of God or whether there is any God at all. In effect, the discussion has shifted from the realm of religion (or metaphysics) to the realm of experimental psychology.

## Jesus as Messiah

Turning now to the belief that Jesus is the Messiah, we must inquire first into the meaning of the language. The word "messiah" is Hebrew for "one who is anointed." It is equivalent in meaning to the Greek *Christos* and the Latin *Christus*. In Judaism, those who were anointed were prophets, priests, and kings, but among these, the people who were known first and foremost as being anointed were the Jewish kings. Saul was known as a messiah, as were David and Solomon. Thus, if Jesus was said to be a messiah or *the* Messiah, it was because he was thought to be some kind of king. But there was no grand, public anointment ceremony for Jesus as there always is for earthly kings. So how did this anointment happen? Supposedly, God himself anointed Jesus directly without any public ceremony. But if that is so, how did it happen that others knew about it? And it appears highly likely that they did know about it, and they called him Messiah. In every one of his letters, which are the earliest Christian writings, the apostle Paul either refers to himself as an apostle of Christ Jesus or a servant of Jesus Christ or makes some other reference to Jesus Christ. If "Christ" is just another word for "Messiah," these references are indirect evidence that the writer took Jesus to be the Messiah. In the Gospel of Mark, Jesus is reported to have asked his disciples who they thought he was, and Peter replied, "you are the Messiah" (Mark 8.27–30). And about twenty years after the writing of that Gospel, Josephus observes that Jesus was called Messiah (*Antiquities* 20.200). So the question remains, how did all these people find out about Jesus being the Messiah when there was no public ceremony?

One possible answer is that Jesus told his disciples that he was the Messiah. Several passages from the Gospels relate to this possibility. In the passage from Mark where Jesus asks his disciples who they think he is and Peter answers, "you are the Messiah," Jesus replies by telling his disciples not to tell anyone about him. Does this mean that he rejects the descriptive title Messiah or that he accepts it but wants it kept quiet? There is no clear answer. When Jesus rides into Jerusalem on a donkey a week before his death, is he sending the message that he is the Messiah by fulfilling the prophesy of Zechariah? The prophet Zechariah had written "your king comes to you . . . riding on a donkey" (Zechariah 9:9). If so, the people lining the road may have been aware of the prophesy because they hailed Jesus as king—in other words, as Messiah (Luke 19:38; also Matthew 21:4–9 and Mark 11:9–10). A week later when Jesus was brought before the Sanhedrin, the high priest asked him if he was the Messiah. According to Mark, Jesus answered, "I am" (Mark 14:62), but Matthew has him saying, "You have said so" (Matthew 27:11), and according to Luke, he replied, "If I tell you, you will not believe me, and if I asked you, you would not answer" (Luke 22:67–68). So, on that occasion, the message is mixed. Shortly after that, Jesus was brought before Pilate. When Pilate asked him, "Are you the king of the Jews?," all three synoptics report Jesus as answering, "You have said so" (Mark 15:2, Matthew 27:11, Luke 23:3). Here, Jesus' answer is ambiguous. Pilate had the last word when he ordered that a placard bearing the sarcastic message "Jesus of Nazareth, King of the Jews" be affixed to the top of the cross.

In the face of these mixed messages and ambiguities, E. P. Sanders concludes that Jesus did not call himself Messiah but that it was left for his followers to attach this appellation after his death.[31] If Sanders is right, then Jesus did not tell others that he was the Messiah. Yet it appears that word was swirling around during Jesus' ministry that he was the Messiah. Both the Jewish high priest and Pilate, the governor, seemed to be aware of the rumor. Otherwise, they would not have questioned Jesus about it. The story about Jesus' entrance into Jerusalem on the donkey suggests that the belief was widespread, but in fact, the number of onlookers shouting "Hosanna" on that day may have been exaggerated. The emotional atmosphere in the days surrounding Passover was so volatile that the Romans would likely never have allowed any such incident to happen.[32] They were so afraid of an insurrection that if anyone claiming to be the king of the Jews were to enter Jerusalem with great pomp and hullabaloo, they would have stepped in immediately to shut the demonstration down. Jesus would have been arrested on the spot. Such a response by the Romans can be avoided by proposing that the entrance into Jerusalem was nowhere near as grand as the Gospels describe it and that only a small handful of people hailed Jesus as king. That way, the Roman guards would not have noticed it. If that be the case, then belief that Jesus was the Messiah, while held by a few, may not have been widespread.

I suggest that the natural selection model of collective memory can be used to make sense of the conflicting facts related to the Messiah. During Jesus' ministry, there was great excitement that the Kingdom of God was on the way and that it would arrive in no time. It was natural that many people saw Jesus as the man designated by God to sit on the throne. But before the kingdom arrived, Jesus was executed. News of this fact must have been terribly disappointing to his followers. The collective memory of the emergent Christian community was just starting to consolidate when suddenly Jesus died, and the memory of him shifted in a different direction. But belief that Jesus was the Messiah was renewed as word got around that Jesus had been raised from the dead. This renewal was driven by the expectation that the Kingdom of God was imminent. It was the chief component in the socioreligious environment, and it dictated the evolutionary development of collective memory. Any mutant memory that was seen as adaptive was incorporated into the collective memory, and the memory of Jesus as risen would have qualified as such a memory. The shifting state of collective memory probably generated bits and pieces of papyrus that bore inconsistent messages, and when these messages reached the attention of the evangelists, they probably responded by putting ambiguous language in the mouth of Jesus. When asked whether he was the Messiah, he replied, "You have said so." By the time the apostle Paul started writing his letters, about twenty years after Jesus' death, the majority of those in the movement believed that Jesus was indeed the Messiah, so Paul picked up on this and called himself an apostle of Christ Jesus. This self-description served to firm up the belief that Jesus was indeed the Messiah. When the Gospels were written several years later, the belief was well established.

As an aside, I would suggest that a mutant memory relating to Jesus as Messiah is what probably led to the birth narratives in Matthew and Luke. Matthew introduces his account by saying, "This is how the birth of Jesus the Messiah came about" (Matthew 1:18), and Luke writes, "Today in the town of David a Savior has been born to you; he is the Messiah, the Lord" (Luke 2:11). Both specifically identify Jesus as the Messiah. They link Jesus' being the Messiah with the story of his birth. What probably happened is that after the collective memory of Jesus had settled on Jesus being the Messiah, people began wondering how the Messiah came into the world. Imaginations started running at a fast clip, and many stories began to circulate. Eventually, the charming story involving angels, shepherds, and a manger caught the attention of Luke, and he, in turn, featured it in his Gospel.[33] Without a doubt, his birth narrative is one of the most touching accounts in all of the Gospels, and it has done much to promote the survival and spread of Christianity. All mutant memories that are adaptive have this effect.

## Jesus as Miracle Worker

One of the more prominent features of Jesus and one that often comes to mind first is that he worked miracles. The Gospels report that he walked on water; calmed the sea; multiplied loaves and fishes; changed water into wine; made the blind to see, the deaf to hear, and the paralyzed to walk; cured lepers; exorcised demons; and raised the dead. Those who count these things say that Jesus performed thirty-four miracles, others say thirty-seven. In regard to these miracles, E. P. Sanders makes an important observation. When people witnessed them, they were not immediately disposed to drop what they were doing and become followers.[34] How can this possibly be? Jesus cures a leper or raises somebody from the dead, and those who see it are not totally overwhelmed? The subdued reaction is explained through the fact that "miracles" in that culture were common, so that when Jesus performed one, it was not considered to be something totally out of the ordinary. The reason why miracles were thought to be ordinary occurrences is because many others were performing them. This is not to say that miracles were *actually* being performed, only that the people of the day *believed* that they were. People believed that the cosmos was saturated with spirits and demons and that some individuals had the power to engage these spiritual entities for either beneficial or detrimental results. The widespread belief in miracles was sustained by numerous practitioners of the art who attracted an extensive following in the years surrounding the lifetime of Jesus. Some of the more prominent ones were the Greek god Asclepius, the Pythagorean philosopher Apollonius of Tyana, the Jewish scholar Hanina ben Dosa, and the rabbi Honi. I will say a few words about each of these.

Asclepius was considered to be a god of healing, and there were shrines dedicated to him throughout the Mediterranean region. According to one of many stories celebrating his powers, a woman who was unable to conceive spent the night in one of his shrines. She dreamed that one of the god's sacred snakes entered her while she slept. The next day, she returned home and soon thereafter became pregnant. Asclepius also had a reputation for bringing dead people back to life, a power that he exercised on more than five occasions. Thus, the belief that healers had the power to resurrect the dead preceded the miracles of Jesus by hundreds of years.

Apollonius of Tyana, a later contemporary of Jesus, had a reputation for being an exorcist as well as a healer. According to an account related by his biographer, the philosopher Philostratus, a young woman had died just before she was to be married. Apollonius happened to encounter the funeral procession as it made its way through the streets of Rome, and he instructed those carrying the bier to put it down because he was about to end the great display of lamentation. He then stretched out his hand and touched the body of the woman. After uttering some secret words, the intended bride woke up, started speaking, and then returned to her father's house. On another occasion, Apollonius was delivering a lecture on libations poured out to gods when a young man ridiculed him with loud and coarse laughter. The man's behavior was so erratic and irrational and he had such an evil reputation that Apollonius recognized a case of diabolical possession. At that point, he addressed the demon and demanded that it depart from the man's body but should demonstrate its departure by some kind of sign. The demon agreed to do so and said that on leaving the man's body, it would topple over a statue some distance away. After the statue had fallen down, the young man rubbed his eyes as if he had just woken up, his behavior changed completely, and he began living an exemplary life.

Hanina ben Dosa lived in Galilee a generation after Jesus, and his fame as a healer was widely recognized. His most famous cure involved the son of the renowned Pharisee teacher Rabban Gamaliel, who was sick with a fever. The rabban sent two of his followers from Jerusalem to Galilee to ask Hanina to come and heal the boy. Instead, Hanina went upstairs and prayed. Soon, he came back down and told the messengers to return to Gamaliel and say to him that his son had been healed. The messengers wrote down the day and hour of Hanina's prayer, and on returning to Jerusalem, they discovered that the boy's health returned at that very hour. Hanina was able to tell that his prayers were efficacious by the way they sounded to him. If a prayer was fluent in his mouth, then he knew that the sick person would be cured; if not, then he would die.

Rabbi Honi, known as the circle-drawer, lived in the century before Jesus in Galilee, where he achieved fame as a rainmaker. During a particularly harsh drought, the townsfolk appealed to him to pray for rain. In response to their request, Honi began to pray, but when rain failed to materialize, he drew a circle on the ground, stood in the middle of it, and said to God that that he would not step outside of that circle until God took pity on his children and brought them rain. When a few drops started to fall, Honi told God that this was not what he had in mind. Then it started to rain buckets, and Honi told God that it had gone from too little to too much. Finally, the rain settled down to a moderate downpour, but even with that, the people had to flee from Jerusalem up to the Temple Mount to keep from being inundated.

In addition to these miracle workers, there were numerous magicians who compounded potions from substances such as roots of plants, goat's urine, garlic, and grass and applied them together with incantations for miraculous results. Josephus reports that a certain man named Eleazar exorcised a demon by drawing it forth from the nostrils of the possessed person. This was done by inserting a certain root beneath the seal of a ring and placing the ring beneath the nose of the person possessed so that the person could smell it. The root that was used was one that had been prescribed by Solomon, thus providing further evidence of Solomon's wisdom. In fact, Solomon had (according to Josephus) left behind a list of incantations and techniques, and this list was partly responsible for the rise of magic in the Jewish community. Magicians were so numerous in the ancient world, both Jewish and Gentile, that they formed a virtual guild of practitioners whose members were regularly hired out for both good and bad purposes ("white" magic and "black" magic). The work of magicians differed from that of the typical miracle worker in that magicians did not appeal to God in doing their work, whereas miracle workers did. But the effect on ancient society was the same: it conditioned people to think that there were individuals out there with wondrous powers who could accomplish feats to be marveled at.

Another powerful influence at the time of Jesus was Jewish scripture, which recognized the occurrence of miracles. A great number of miracles are attributed to Moses, including turning a rod into a serpent, the plague of frogs that tormented the Egyptians, the plague of locusts, boils on the bodies of the Egyptians, the punishing hailstorm, the deaths of the Egyptian firstborn, parting the Red (Reed) Sea, and producing water from a rock. Eight miracles are attributed to the prophet Elijah, including multiplying flour and oil for a widow, raising the widow's son from the dead, bringing rain to end a drought, and parting the waters of the Jordan River. The prophet Elisha is said to have worked sixteen miracles, including raising a child from the dead, healing a leper, purifying water, making an iron ax head float in water, multiplying loaves of bread to feed a large crowd, and striking the Arameans blind. Jonah survived being swallowed by a great fish, Daniel avoided being eaten by lions, and, under Joshua's command, the sun and moon stood still in the heavens for a full day and the walls of Jericho came down. The prophet Isaiah predicted that the God of Israel would return to work miracles: the blind would see, the deaf would hear, the lame would walk, and the mute would talk. In short, Jewish scripture is awash in miracles, and it had a major influence on all religious thinking.

Returning to the miracles of Jesus, these miracles are reported in the Gospels, and the message of the Gospels reflected the beliefs of the early Christians. So how did it happen that the early Christians came to believe that Jesus performed miracles? The answer is to be found in the sociore-ligious environment of the time, and this environment was characterized by the events just described. Many of the healers of the day were thought to be able to perform miracles, so if Jesus was a healer, it was natural to remember him as a miracle performer. Even the magicians were believed able to perform miracles, so if Jesus failed to perform them, he would be inferior to the magicians. Perhaps most important, Jewish scripture was saturated with miracles. Important religious figures had performed dozens of them, all of them through divine agency. Also, Isaiah had predicted that the returning God of Israel would perform numerous miracles, and Jesus was thought to be associated with this return. Given this atmo-sphere, it is easy to imagine the formation of a mutant memory that de-picted Jesus as a miracle worker. When this mutant memory entered into the collective memory, it was reported in the Gospels. In this way, even if Jesus had never performed a single miracle, he would be remembered today as having performed many of them.

## The Virgin Birth

Another feature of the Jesus construct that appears in the Gospels is that Jesus was born to a virgin. This occurrence is otherwise called the virgin birth. The logic behind this idea may have run something like this. Jesus was believed to be the Son of God. "Son" can imply either an adopted son or a begotten son. But an adopted son is something less than a begotten son, so Jesus is the begotten son of God. If Jesus is the begotten son of God, then his father cannot have been an ordinary man. But if Mary had engaged in sexual relations prior to the birth of Jesus, then Jesus could have been fathered by an ordinary man (Joseph being the likely one). Therefore, Mary did not engage in sexual relations prior to the birth of

Jesus, and the best way of ensuring this is to say that Mary was a virgin prior to giving birth. Mary would not have lost her virginity by having been made pregnant by God because this was effected through divine power. Luke reports the announcing angel as saying that "the power of the Most High will over shadow you" (Luke 1:35). Her being made pregnant was supposed to have occurred through nonmaterial causation.

Admittedly, this argument has a few weak spots. For Jesus not to have been fathered by Joseph or any other man, it is only necessary that Mary not have had sexual relations nine months or so prior to Jesus' birth. It is not necessary to say that she was a virgin during this time. Another weak spot is the part about adoptive sons being less than begotten sons. This is not necessarily the case. Augustus, the first emperor of Rome, was the adopted son of Julius Caesar, and he was not thought to have been in any way deficient as a result of his adopted status. So if Jesus was the adopted son of God, an interpretation that Paul the apostle seems to have held, then there is nothing that prevents his father from being Joseph or any other man. However, if our theory about collective memory is correct, then the source of the virgin birth story was the collective memory of the Jesus community that formed during the forty or more years following Jesus' death. Collective memory has never been sensitive to logical niceties, so it is easy to see how its loose workings may have produced the virgin birth story.

Mutant memories are selected according to whether they fit in with the social environment, and two chief elements of this environment, in this case the socioreligious environment, were Jewish scripture and the mystique surrounding the emperor. The part of Jewish scripture that undoubtedly played a role was Isaiah 7:14, which is often translated, "The virgin will conceive and give birth to a son, and they will call him Immanuel." Matthew cites this very verse in his account (Matthew 1:23). What probably happened was that someone in the nascent Christian community was familiar with the verse, and he or she tossed it out as a possible justification for Mary's virginity. It made little difference to this individual that the Hebrew word *almah*, which, in this verse, is translated as "virgin," simply means a young woman of childbearing age. It really implies nothing about the woman's being a virgin. But when the suggestion entered the flow of collective memory, this semantic technicality was conveniently ignored. Of course Mary had to be a virgin because this was predicted by the prophet Isaiah. Soon it was seen that the scriptural suggestion enhanced the survival of the movement. It supported the idea that Jesus, having no earthly father, was born as the begotten son of God, and this clearly made the Jesus movement more attractive to potential converts.

The other part of the socioreligious environment that was consistent with the virgin birth idea was the belief that many of the ancient rulers were sons of virgins. Romulus, the first king of Rome, was said to be the son of a vestal virgin; Alexander the Great was the offspring of the virgin Olympias and Zeus; Augustus, who was emperor when Jesus was born, was said to be the son of a virgin; and even the later Caesars were said to be born of virgins. Being born of a virgin was surely seen, at least by some, as a birth befitting kings. But if Jesus was chosen by God to be king in the divine kingdom, then surely he, more than anyone else, must have been born of a virgin. So it probably did not take long for this line of thinking to be reflected in a mutant memory, for that memory to enter the memory pool and then be selected as adaptive. It would serve to make Christianity attractive to those thinking of joining up with the movement. Given that the story of the virgin birth of Jesus occurs in only two gospels, Matthew and Luke, and that the two accounts are quite different, it probably happened that two separate traditions relating to the virgin birth arose in collective memory and that they took separate routes in reaching the attention of the respective evangelists.

## The Reason Jesus Died

One of the most dramatic shifts in the collective memory of Jesus relates to the reason for his death. In the days and weeks following the crucifixion, the reason for Jesus' death gradually solidified. This opinion, of course, depends on my earlier conclusion that there was no physical resurrection. When people began to reflect on why Jesus was executed, the realization almost certainly set in that he got on the wrong side of the Jewish high priest and the Roman authorities and that they had him executed to rid themselves of a nuisance. This was the treatment accorded everyone judged to be a common criminal, and the official view of Jesus was that he was little better than that. But then, when we move forward some twenty-five years or so, we see a great shift in the collective memory.

Jesus is remembered no longer as someone who died because he irritated the authorities but as someone who died to bring salvation to sinful humanity. Moving forward a few more years, Jesus died because he loved sinful humanity, and this was the underlying rationale for his salvific act. So we see the emergence of redemption through love. How do we account for this change? It was not something subtle like the gradual change in a person's appearance as he ages. It was a sea change. How do we account for it?

We can begin by reviewing the two most important perceived infractions that got Jesus in trouble with the authorities. The first was the so-called cleansing of the temple. The operation of the temple had a commercial aspect to it, and it involved the sale of sacrificial animals and the conversion of Roman and Greek coins into Tyrian shekels to purchase those animals and to pay the temple tax. When Jesus entered the temple in the week prior to Passover, all four Gospels report that he overturned the tables of the money changers and those who sold pigeons (or doves), claiming that they had converted a house of prayer into a den of robbers. This incident may have actually happened as described, but there is good reason to think that it was purely a symbolic gesture. Jesus may have been saying, in effect, that the days of the temple system were coming to an end and it would soon be replaced by the Kingdom of God. However, when the high priest received word of the incident, it is unlikely that he saw it as a symbolic gesture. He would have seen it as an attack on the temple itself. Since the activities of the temple provided the sustenance for the entire priesthood, including himself, he would have taken it very seriously. Better to nip this problem in the bud before it gets any worse.

The other perceived grievance that put Jesus in bad stead with the authorities, in this case Pilate, was the rumor that he claimed to be king of the Jews. Only the emperor could appoint someone king of the Jews, so if Jesus actually made this claim, he would be usurping the authority of the emperor. I think it likely that Jesus thought of himself as king of the Jews, and he probably told a few others about this on the quiet. Eventually, word leaked out, and when Pilate and Caiaphas heard rumors to this effect, they probably suspected that Jesus was plotting a revolution. They had no idea that Jesus had in mind an entirely different kind of king and a different kind of kingdom. When Jesus came to Jerusalem prior to Passover, he probably thought that the kingdom would arrive within days or even hours. During his last meal with the apostles, when he shared with them the cup, he said, "I shall not drink again of the fruit of the vine until that day when I drink it new in the kingdom of God" (Mark 14:25, Matthew 26:29; also Luke 22:18). Jesus hoped until the end that God would step in and rescue him, but it didn't happen. The incredible feeling of abandonment may have led him to utter his final words (reiterating Psalms 22:1), "My God, my God, why have you forsaken me?" (Mark 15:34, Matthew 27:46). It was a miscalculation with catastrophic consequences.

In the years after Jesus' death, the people undoubtedly held out hope for the coming of the kingdom. They had been anticipating it for some time. Such an expectation would not die overnight. Perhaps Jesus would return as king, perhaps not. His death was obviously a disappointment. Many of them had thought that he was the king designate. After his death, they probably began to wonder. Why did he die? He made too many enemies, they trumped up charges against him, and they conspired to have him executed. The last thing in the world they would have thought was that he freely accepted crucifixion to save them from their sins. The first hint in the literature that this is what motivated Jesus comes from the hand of St. Paul. Writing perhaps twenty-five years after Jesus' death, he says, "For what I received I passed on to you as of first importance: that Christ died for our sins according to the Scriptures" (1 Corinthians 15:3). Paul says that he heard this from someone else. Did he? From whom could he have heard it? This is a highly sophisticated idea, not the sort of thing that you would expect from the minds of simple, uneducated people like the apostles. Still, there is no hint in the authentic letters of Paul that in giving his life, Jesus was motivated by love for sinful humanity.

Moving to the Gospels, there is nothing in the Gospel of Mark, written about 70 CE, about Jesus dying to save people from their sins. The first we hear of any such thing is in Matthew, in the birth narrative, where the angel says to Joseph, "you are to give him the name Jesus, because he will save his people from their sins" (Matthew 1:21). This was written around 80–85 CE. Later, in the same Gospel, we read that the Son of Man came "to give his life as a ransom for many" (Matthew 20:28). But still there is no talk about Jesus being motivated by love for humanity. We must wait until the Gospel of John, written around 90–100 CE, for the love theme to appear full blown. There, we find the famous statement

"For God so loved the world that he gave his one and only Son" (John 3:16). Also, there is the parable of the good shepherd, where Jesus says, "I am the good shepherd. The good shepherd lays down his life for the sheep" (John 10:11). The clear idea is that the good shepherd lays down his life out of love for the sheep. This theme in John is anticipated in Paul's Epistle to the Ephesians, which was written not by Paul but by one of his followers around 90 CE, probably just a few years before the Gospel of John. It may have been an inspiration for that Gospel. The author urges Christians to "walk in the way of love, just as Christ loved us and gave himself up for us" (Ephesians 5:2). So it was not until sixty years or so after the death of Jesus that his followers began to remember him as someone who died out of love for them. It took sixty years for the collective memory of Jesus to complete this evolutionary development.

We can now ask what may have given rise to these two all-important mutant memories—that Jesus died to redeem sinners and that he did so out of love for them. By the time the memory of Jesus as having risen from the dead had become settled in the collective memory, which probably happened within ten years after his death, people undoubtedly began to ask what was the point of his having suffered and died. He had experienced a horrible death, one of the worst that the Romans could dream up, and all for what? Only so that God could raise him up three days later? This makes little sense. There must be something more to the story. Supplying an answer to this question was the pressing need of the moment. Imaginations went to work. Jesus had died during Passover week. This was a time for sacrificial offerings. Could it be that Jesus gave himself up as a sacrificial offering? And, if so, for what? Many offerings were made at that time to accomplish a reconciliation with God, to bring people closer to God. The idea that Jesus had given himself up as a reconciliation offering for sinful humans was clearly adaptive; it was the missing piece in the puzzle. When Christians would contemplate the person of the remodeled Jesus, the thought that he had suffered such agony to set them right with God would raise up feelings of guilt about their own sinfulness. This, in turn, would make them feel indebted to him for the sacrifice that he had made. And the thought that he did this because he loved them as a good shepherd loves his sheep would generate reciprocal feelings of love and a yearning to be joined with him. Best of all, Jesus had risen from the dead. He was the fully living Son of God who died to redeem sinful humans and who did so out of love. This new Jesus construct was virtually guaranteed to attract converts, and it would shore up the faith of those who were already members of the flock. The rapid growth of the early church indicates just how successful the construct really was.

## The Jesus Illusion

The extraordinary features in the Jesus construct are that Jesus rose from the dead, that he is the Son of God, that he is the Messiah, that he performed numerous miracles, that he was born of a virgin, and that he died for the remission of human sins. The belief that the actual Jesus truly had these features is what I call the Jesus Illusion. In terms introduced earlier in this book, the Jesus Illusion is a factitious illusion, which implies that it was induced in target individuals by other human beings acting as agents. The target individuals, of course, were candidates for conversion to the Jesus movement, and the inducing agents were, in the years surrounding the death of Jesus, the apostles, their assistants (whom we may call proto-priests), and earlier converts. Factitious illusion also implies that the inducing agent would appeal to hopes and fears lurking in the mind of the target individual. In the early years, the chief hope was to become a participant in the Kingdom of God, which, it was thought, would appear at any moment, and the chief fear was the prospect of being left out of the kingdom. The last element in a factitious illusion is an error in judgment on the part of the convert to be. The most significant error was allowing oneself to become convinced that a dead man (Jesus) was still alive. While it is logically possible (not self-contradictory) that a dead man could come back to life, it is extremely improbable—shall we say less than one chance in a billion? Thus, convincing a reasonable person that such a thing had happened should require extremely good evidence. As it was, the only evidence that Jesus had risen from the dead consisted of rumors of certain sightings. Rumors fall short of solid evidence.

Moving forward in time to the end of the first century CE, the hope for a Kingdom of God on this earth had begun to fade. Seventy years had passed and still no kingdom. It was supposed to have happened years earlier. But the successors to the apostles and their assistants kept the hope alive by shifting what many thought was to be a kingdom on this earth to a kingdom in heaven. It was a kingdom that followers of Jesus would participate in after they had died. This is the kind of kingdom that most Christians hope for today. Also, by the end of the century, all four canonical Gospels had appeared, as had the letters of St. Paul. These documents could be cited as evidence that Jesus had risen from the dead, that he was the Son of God, and that he had the other extraordinary features attributed to him. However, to believe something extremely unlikely simply because it says so in a document is to commit an error in judgment. After all, many books and other writings contain assertions that are false. To address this possibility, that the Gospels and other New Testament writings contained inaccuracies, the successors to the apostles put forth the argument that these documents must be accurate because they report the revealed word of God. However, what we have attempted to show in the foregoing pages is that the Jesus construct found in the Gospels has its exceptional attributes because of the operation of collective memory and not because of any divine revelation.

Collective memory is malleable. It responds to the needs of the present. Its purpose is to promote the survival of the community that does the remembering. If the foregoing account is correct, and I think it is, collective memory operates according to the same law of natural selection that governs biological evolution. Mutant memories appear spontaneously from various sources, they enter the memory pool, and natural selection then works to select out the ones that are adaptive. Those that are adaptive (i.e., promote survival) then enter the collective memory. Whether a mutant memory is adaptive is determined by the socioreligious environment. During the time of Jesus, the socioreligious environment was dominated by the anticipated arrival of the Kingdom of God. Jesus came to be thought of as the designated king, and because such a king had to be alive, the collective memory of him was that of a man who rose from the dead. Before long, the socioreligious environment required that he be remembered as the Son of God, the Messiah, and so on, and so, many years later, those are the features that were given to him in the Gospels. But that does not mean that the real Jesus, the man who walked the pathways of Galilee, really had those features. It merely means that this is the way he came to be remembered. Hence, to assign those features to the real Jesus is to commit an error in judgment. Errors in judgment open the door to illusion.

## Mutant Memories of Jesus

Next, we inquire about the source of the mutant memories that shifted the collective memory of Jesus to that of a man possessing extraordinary attributes. In any organization, the people who are responsible for directing the organization are its leaders, and there is no reason to think that the early Jesus movement differed from the norm. The leaders of this movement were the apostles, their successors, and their assistants. So these are the ones who most likely came up with the ideas, inferences, suggestions, and insights that became the mutant memories, which in turn shifted the direction of the collective memory of Jesus.

The next question is, what motivated these individuals to commit themselves to the Jesus movement? A passage from Matthew suggests an answer. After devoting considerable time and effort to the movement, Peter, speaking for the apostles, asks Jesus, "We have left everything to follow you! What then will there be for us?" Jesus said to them, "Truly I tell you, at the renewal of all things, when the Son of Man sits on his glorious throne, you who have followed me will also sit on twelve thrones, judging the twelve tribes of Israel. And everyone who has left houses or brothers or sisters or fathers or mothers or wife or children or fields for my sake will receive a hundred times as much and will inherit eternal life" (Matthew 19:27–29).

This exchange sounds very much like a business transaction. Peter says to Jesus, "Okay, we have done everything for you, so what do we get out of the deal?" Jesus does not dispute what Peter says, but he then replies that in the end, each of them will be rewarded with a throne on which they will judge the twelve tribes of Israel. And why is this so great? The obvious answer is that they will have power—power beyond anything they could have dreamed of as mere members of the peasant class in Palestine. So we here see a repeat of what had been happening since the Neolithic period. Power—and the quest for power—creates constructs, and the constructs then serve to augment the power. In this case, the constructs are first of all the Jesus construct that appears in the Gospels. It was formed by molding the collective memory of Jesus to the point where he exhibited extraordinary features—features that would attract converts in droves. In addition, there was the social construct that became the early church, and this was followed by various physical constructs, including the letters of Paul, the Gospels, religious artifacts, church buildings, and so on. However, this is not to say that the apostles and their successors were motivated exclusively by power. Surely they were also attracted to the ethical ideals embodied in the teachings of Jesus, and they were driven to promote them. But the quest for power was likely a factor that lurked in the back of their minds and worked as a necessary condition to secure their commitment to the movement.

## What Motivated Jesus?

Finally, there is the question of what motivated Jesus to embark on the journey that he chose and to pursue it to its tragic conclusion. The passage just quoted from Matthew may also shed some light on this question. And, incidentally, a similar pericope occurs in Luke (18:28–29), so there is additional reason to think that this exchange between Peter and Jesus actually happened. In the quoted passage, Jesus anticipates the day when he, the Son of Man, will sit on his "glorious throne," presumably ruling over all the nations of the earth in the Kingdom of God. Do we not see here at least a hint about the power he expected to receive? After all, a throne means power. Further, there is good reason to believe that Jesus thought that he was the Messiah. At least a few of his followers seem to have believed it, and they may have come to believe it because Jesus told them that he was the Messiah. Also, in one (but only one) of the Gospels, Jesus is reported as having told the high priest that he was the Messiah (Mark 14:62). The most common meaning of the word "messiah" is "king," and kings have power, so Jesus may have anticipated the day that he would have great power, and this may have motivated some of his actions. Granted, Jesus may have been an exception to the rule that leaders of men are motivated at least in part by power. He may have seen his role as purely a servant of God, and the thought of power may have never entered his mind, but I find this unlikely. In any event, for a person to *believe* that he is the Messiah and for him to *be* the Messiah are two very different things. If Jesus believed he was the Messiah, that belief, I contend, was an illusion.

While Jesus may have thought of himself as the Messiah, it is extremely unlikely that he took himself to be a god or the Son of God. For Jesus, as a good Jew, the only god was Yahweh. If Jesus understood himself to be a god, this would have been a god independent of Yahweh or a god identical to Yahweh. For Jesus to claim to be identical to Yahweh would have been clearly blasphemous (or insane), and for him to claim to be an independent divinity would have violated Jewish monotheism. The only recognized meaning of "Son of God" was metaphorical, according to which all Jews were understood to be sons of God. It appears that "Son of God" as a special designator did not come into use until several years after Jesus' death, and it took on the meaning it has today only after the development of the theory of the triune God, according to which God incorporates three persons: Father, Son, and Holy Spirit. This did not happen until the fourth century CE. Remembering Jesus as the Son of God occurred through the alteration of the collective memory of Jesus accomplished by the apostles, including St. Paul, and their successors.

If we take the Jesus construct of the Gospels and peel off the exceptional features, we are left with an ambitious young man who hoped to initiate a reform movement within Judaism. He may have thought he was the Jewish Messiah, and if he did, he was mistaken. He died hoping that Yahweh would rescue him at the last minute, but that didn't happen. Nevertheless, his efforts were supremely successful, and his movement developed into one of the most powerful organizations on the planet. His success, I think, resulted from the fact that his followers loved him. Josephus, the historian, attests to this fact. And why did they love him? At least in part because he valued them as human beings. To count for something, it was not required that a person be an emperor or a governor, a high priest, a rich man, or famous for some other reason. All that was needed was that he or she be a human being. This message was guaranteed to strike a chord with millions. Jesus gathered about him a group of select followers, and he charged them with the task of spreading the message to all nations. They complied with his wishes, and the message spread throughout the world. In the end, those followers, who were the original priests of Christianity, converted Jesus into a god. If Jesus could have foreseen this, he probably would have been horrified. He didn't realize that this is what priests always do, so this was his destiny.

## CHAPTER SIX
# THE CHRISTIANS
## Paul

## Questions about God

Many Christians, when asked about the god that they worship, will reply that they worship the same god that the Jews worship. After all, both Christianity and Judaism are ostensibly monotheistic religions, and if the Jewish god is the only god that exists and if the Christian god is the only god that exists, then these two gods must be one and the same. The conclusion appears to follow with necessity. Yet this reasoning cannot be correct. The Christian god is triune. It consists of God the Father, God the Son, and God the Holy Spirit. God the Son is identical with Jesus Christ. When Christians worship their god, they worship Jesus Christ. But no Jew who worships Yahweh would acknowledge that in so doing, he or she worships Jesus Christ. The problem with the first line of reasoning is that Jewish monotheism and Christian monotheism are not identical. The word "monotheism" as it occurs in Judaism does not mean the same thing as it does in Christianity. One sense of the word entails exactly one person, while the other entails three. A god consisting of one person is not identical to a god consisting of three persons. Hence, Christians and Jews do not worship the same god. But if that is so, then the question immediately arises, where did the Christian god come from? The answer is a bit of a mystery and not at all obvious.

One promising approach to solving the problem would be to explore early Christian writings keeping an eye out for the words "Father," "Son," and "Holy Spirit." Most people would probably start with the four

181

Gospels, where they would find several occurrences of "Father in heaven," "God's Son," and a few cases of "Spirit of God" and "Holy Spirit." But the Gospels would not give us the earliest occurrences of these words. The Epistles of Paul contain many more references to God our Father, Son of God, and Holy Spirit than do the Gospels, and the last one was written at least ten years before the earliest Gospel. As we have seen, the first Gospel to be written was that of Mark, composed around 70 CE, with the others being written in the interval from 80 to 110 CE, while the Epistles of Paul are thought to have been written from 50 to 60 CE.

An initial obstacle to this approach is raised by scholars who think that Paul did not actually write the letters he is traditionally thought to have written. When the New Testament was compiled at the end of the fourth century, it contained thirteen letters that the apostle Paul was thought to have written to his congregations spread out around the eastern Mediterranean. This number remained largely unquestioned until the early nineteenth century when the German theologian Ferdinand Christian Baur, founder of the Tübingen School of New Testament criticism, argued that only four of the epistles ascribed to Paul were actually written by him. The rest were written much later by other authors. Baur's work caused a huge ruckus in the field of New Testament studies. A few years later, another theologian, Willem C. van Manen of the University of Leiden, made a full sweep by arguing that none of Paul's letters were authentic but that all were written by others after Paul's lifetime. More recently, the American scholar Robert Price has rekindled the same arguments. However, today, the majority of scholars have coalesced in the view that seven of Paul's letters are, for the most part, authentic. These include, in the order they are thought to have been written, 1 Thessalonians, Galatians, 1 and 2 Corinthians, Romans, Philippians, and Philemon. The present study confines its attention to this list.

So, if the apostle Paul was indeed responsible for the first use of the words "Father," "Son," and "Holy Spirit" in the sense in which they are used in the Christian religion, can we give him credit for inventing the Christian god? It would be nice if it were so simple. First off, if the triune God of Christianity does indeed originate with Paul, we should be able to explain how he came up with the idea. Surely, he did not simply create it out of nothing. Why a God having three components? Why not four or five? And why are two of the components related to each other as father to son? The second reason for not giving Paul full credit for the Trinity is that Paul never uses the terms "Father," "Son," and "Holy Spirit" with sufficient precision to allow for the formulation of a theory about the Trinity. It took 300 years of heated debate by countless theologians to address the perplexing questions that arose from Paul's message, and even then, many of the questions were never really answered. This subject occupies the next chapter of this book.

## Paul the Man

According to most estimates, Paul was born in 4 or 5 BCE, about the same time as Jesus. He says that he was born a Jew, of the tribe of Benjamin, and was circumcised on the eighth day according to the Jewish law. At least for a time, he was a pharisee, and as he got older, he advanced beyond his companions in the study of his religion. He was clearly very zealous in the practice of his faith, and he welcomed the opportunity to persecute members of the newly emergent Jesus movement, which he did with great enthusiasm. Around 37 CE, he had a visionary experience in which he claimed to have seen the risen Jesus and in which Jesus called him to be an apostle—an apostle to the Gentiles. At that point, he ceased his persecution of the Christians, but instead of going directly to Jerusalem to meet with the other apostles, he went first to "Arabia," and only after three years did he meet with Peter and James. He made only two additional trips to Jerusalem, one of them around 50 CE and the last around 56 CE. He is thought to have died in Rome around 64 CE, during the reign of Nero, along with other Christians who were blamed for setting fire to the city.

Except for the dates of Paul's birth and death, the foregoing details of his life can be gleaned from his letters. Additional details can be found in the Acts of the Apostles, written by Luke, the same person who wrote the Gospel sometime between 100 and 120 CE. But the stories in Acts are considered less reliable than those in the letters, and they are often discounted by scholars. The most famous such story is the one about Paul's conversion, where he was supposedly knocked off his horse while on the road to Damascus to persecute Christians under the authority of the Jewish high priest. If this event actually occurred, it would surely have counted as the high point in his life. But since Paul never mentions the story, not even once, in any of his letters, most scholars attribute it to an embellishment by

Luke. However, that Paul claimed to have visions throughout his life is not doubted. In one such vision, Paul says he was transported up to the third heaven, into paradise, where he heard inexpressible things, things that no one is permitted to tell. Whether Paul actually had such a vision and, if he did have it, what might have produced it is another matter.

Could Paul have received knowledge about the triune nature of the Christian god through these visions? Some believers do make this claim, and, of course, such a thing is possible in the sense that it involves no internal contradiction. But on the face of it, this would seem to be a perfect opportunity for applying Ockham's razor. If the details of Paul's account of the Christian god—where he got the basic idea of its triune nature—can be explained through natural occurrences, there is no need to appeal to miracles. What we have here is another instance where the essential core of a religion is said to be communicated through direct one-on-one contact with a divinity. In the case of Moses and the covenant, it was contact with Yahweh on the top of a mountain. For Paul, it was supposedly a one-on-one contact with the risen Christ through miraculous visionary experiences. In chapter 4, I attempted to show how Moses became acquainted with Yahweh through ordinary human experience. In this chapter, I hope to show the same sort of thing for Paul's ideas about the Christian god.

To pin down a naturalistic source of Paul's teaching about the Christian god, what we should look for first of all is a religious tradition or philosophical theory known to Paul where a deity is spoken of as a Father. The idea of God being a Father was obviously important for Paul because within the first few lines of every one of his letters, he makes reference to "God our Father" or "God the Father." Many more such references appear in the body of most of the letters. One possible source of this language is Jewish scripture. Paul was certainly well versed in scripture because he makes frequent reference to scriptural passages in his letters, and he boasts of having advanced beyond many of his contemporaries in the study of Judaism. Also, Jewish scripture does indeed make reference to the deity being a Father. For example, in Isaiah, we read, "But you are our Father, though Abraham does not know us or Israel acknowledge us; you, Lord, are our Father, our Redeemer from old is your name" (Isaiah 63:16). But scholars point out that this sense of "Father" is metaphorical, not metaphysical.[1] The word "Father" in "God the Father" has the same sense as "King" in "God our King." It means God as head of the Jewish people. It does not entail any special relationship to a Son. But this is precisely the sense that "God the Father" has in the letters of Paul. Thus, it is unlikely that Paul derived his knowledge of God the Father from his study of Jewish scripture.

Another possible source for Paul's teaching about God is his early contact with members of the Jesus movement. During the period that Paul spent persecuting the members of this movement, he very likely had the opportunity to talk to some of them, and this talk may have been the conduit to his learning about God the Father. The expressions "Heavenly Father" and "Father in Heaven" appear often in the Gospels, so they very likely occurred in the oral tradition that led to the writing of the Gospels. Indeed, the Lord's Prayer, put into the mouth of Jesus, begins with the words, "Our Father, who art in heaven" (Matthew 6:9–13). The prayer also contains an indirect reference to God the King through the words "thy kingdom come." If Paul spoke at all to the people he was persecuting, he most likely came in contact with this oral tradition. Could Paul have derived his knowledge of God as Father through his contact with this tradition? Again, the answer is probably not. As in Jewish scripture, the use of "Father" in the Gospels is metaphorical—which is to be expected given that the Jesus movement was a movement within Judaism. For Paul, God the Father is a father precisely through his having a son, and that son is none other than Jesus Christ. This is an existential, not a metaphorical relationship. As we have seen, the understanding that Jesus had of himself was not that he was the son of any god. If Jesus had claimed to be the son of Yahweh in anything other than a metaphorical sense, as a member of the Jewish people, he would have been branded a blasphemer and stoned to death. Yes, Jesus probably did think of himself as the future king of the Jews, but he did not think of himself as a god. The conclusion is that Paul did not get his idea of God the Father through contact with the Jesus movement.

## Paul and Egypt

Paul may have left a clue for solving the mystery when he said (Galatians 1:17) that after receiving his miraculous call to be an apostle, instead of leaving for Jerusalem to visit the other apostles, he left for Arabia. The purpose of this statement was probably to show how little he cared for the other apostles, but I think the mention of Arabia is significant for other reasons. In this particular passage, Paul leaves us guessing as to exactly what he means by "Arabia," but later in the same letter (Galatians 4:25), he tells us that Arabia is the location of Mount Sinai. Mount Sinai is situated at the southern tip of the Sinai Peninsula. This has led some scholars to conclude that for Paul, Arabia is the Sinai Peninsula. But for the past 5,000 years, since the first Egyptian dynasty, the Sinai Peninsula has been part of Egypt. So I would suggest that for Paul, "Arabia" means Egypt or at least the northern part of it. Even today, "Arabia" denotes a region that includes Egypt.

Assuming this conjecture is correct, that when Paul went to Arabia he went to Egypt, the next questions is, where in Egypt? Of course, it is possible that he went to Sinai, but it is hard to imagine why he or, for that matter, anyone else would want to go there. At that time, its most prominent feature was rocks and sand—and very hot sand at that. Paul's going to Sinai is especially hard to imagine in light of his apparent claim that he stayed in Arabia for three years. Three years in Sinai? It seems more likely that he went instead to Alexandria in the western Nile Delta. Why Alexandria? During Paul's lifetime, Alexandria was the second-largest city in the world (next to Rome). It was home to the largest urban Jewish community in the world, so Paul would have felt comfortable there. The Alexandrian Jews spoke Greek, which was Paul's native language. The Septuagint, the first Greek translation of the Old Testament, was produced there. Alexandria was a melting pot of Greek, Jewish, and Egyptian ideas, making it the most intellectually stimulating city in the world. It featured the world's largest library, which contained the work of every major thinker who had lived up to that time. It was also the home of Philo, one of the most prominent philosophers alive at the time. If a young man were interested in furthering his education, Alexandria would be an excellent place to do it. Paul would have had many reasons to go to Alexandria, and he could have easily reached it by boat from any major port city on the Mediterranean.

## Influence of Plato

Assuming Paul went to Alexandria for three years, let us spend a moment inquiring into what he would have encountered there. First off, he would have encountered a group of Jewish intellectuals who had become thoroughly imbued with the philosophy of Plato. More precisely, it was

Middle Platonism, the movement that flourished from 80 BCE to 220 CE and that was grounded in Plato's philosophy. So, to get an idea as to what this movement consisted of, it will be useful to review very briefly some of the central features of Plato's philosophy. The centerpiece of this philosophy is the theory of Forms (or Ideas), one of the most important theories ever created by the human mind. According to this theory, all natural objects—humans, dogs, cats, trees, fish, and so on—are what they are because they partake of a certain Form (or Idea) that defines their nature. For example, every human partakes of, or participates in, the Form called humanness; every dog participates in the Form of dogness; and so on, and this participation is responsible for the material thing's remaining essentially the same through the passage of time. The Forms are eternal, changeless, nonmaterial entities that exist outside the natural world and are knowable by the human mind. Given that the Forms are nonmaterial (not made of matter), they are invisible and not detectable by any of the senses. Obviously, the next question is, if the Forms are not detectable by the senses, how can they be known? Plato's answer is that knowledge of the Forms is innate in the human mind. Everyone has this knowledge from birth, and it is recovered through a process of recollection.

To grasp the plausibility of this theory, consider, for example, the Form of triangularity. This Form causes every triangle to be what it is—triangles drawn on paper, triangles made of wood, triangles carved in stone, and so on. Everyone knows what it means for something to be a triangle, so it is appropriate to ask, where did this knowledge come from? There are two possibilities: either it came through the senses, or it was always in the mind, even though we may not have been aware of it. Let us see what this knowledge consists of. A perfect triangle, the sort of thing studied in geometry, is a three-sided plane figure in which the sum of the three angles is equal to two right angles—not approximately equal but exactly equal. The three sides are perfectly straight and have no thickness at all. Obviously, such a thing cannot be seen by the eyes or detected by any of the other senses. Indeed, such a thing cannot exist in the natural world at all. Nothing in the natural world is exact, nothing is perfectly straight, and everything has thickness. Also, the properties of our ideal triangle are eternal: they have always existed and always will exist. But nothing eternal can be detected, as such, by the senses. Sensory experience is confined to the here and now. Thus, we are forced to conclude that our knowledge of triangularity was in our mind from the start. At birth, it lay in a kind of latent state. But gradually, our sensory experience with physical triangles and, later, our study of geometry led us to recall that knowledge, at which time it became fully conscious.

As already noted, the Forms are what make everything to be what it is. Every human is a human because he or she participates in the Form of humanness, every horse is a horse because it participates in the Form of horseness, and every white thing is white because it participates in the Form of whiteness. Taking this line of reasoning to the next level, we can ask, what makes every Form to be a Form? We can't say that every Form participates in the Form of formness because then Forms would be participating in themselves, which is impossible. In his published writings, Plato did not address this question, but he did in the so-called unwritten doctrine. Aristotle, who was Plato's most famous student and who knew Plato's theories as well as anyone, said that the One is what makes every Form to be a Form. The idea here is that every Form is an individual existing unit. Every Form is a "one," and it shares with every other Form this oneness. Thus, we can say that the One is Plato's ultimate metaphysical principle. The One is not a Form; it transcends the Forms. And it participates in nothing, not even itself. It cannot be related to anything because any kind of relatedness implies a reciprocal sharing. Also, it cannot be the cause of anything, at least not in the sense of being an agent, and it cannot suffer any influence from anything else. The One is not even knowable. Everything that is knowable shares something in common with the mind that knows it. The One is beyond mind, and its name cannot even be uttered. Since we are speaking of the One this very minute, our manner of speech can be only analogical at best.

Whether Plato actually held this unwritten doctrine has been a topic of debate, but what is undisputable is that the One was the central focus of attention for the principal philosophers in the Middle Platonic period, and they connected it with Plato. Also, when the Jews living in Alexandria at that time got hold of it, it produced a crisis of faith. The reason for the crisis is that the highest entity on the ontological scale (the One) should be identical with the highest religious entity, namely, God. For the Jews, this meant that the One should be identical with Yahweh. But it clearly was not identical with Yahweh. Yahweh was a creator god. As per

Genesis, Yahweh entered into countless causal and other relations with the created world. He set apart the light from the darkness; he separated the waters above from the waters below; he produced the sun, moon, and stars; he created all plant and animal life; and he created humans in his own image. He communicated with Moses, and he entered into a covenant with the Hebrews. He sent punishing plagues to Pharaoh, and he freed the Hebrews from their servitude. He created the Law, he rewarded the Hebrews when they obeyed it, and he punished them when they did not. The One, being absolutely transcendent, would have been infinitely above all of these engagements.

The status of Yahweh among the Alexandrian Jews was further eroded by the theory of creation presented in Plato's dialogue *Timaeus*. In the words of Gilles Quispel, "The *Timaeus* of Plato was the bedside book of every civilized and not so civilized man in the centuries before and after the beginning of our era."[2] The reason this book was so popular is that, unlike Genesis, which told a *story* of creation, the *Timaeus* gave a genuine *theory* of creation that addressed crucial issues, such as the source of order in the cosmos, the amenability of physical reality to the probing efforts of the human mind, and the applicability of mathematics in scientific explanation. In the process of presenting his theory, Plato introduces a figure called the Demiurge (*demiurgos* in Greek), which literally means "skilled craftsman." The function of the Demiurge was to get the process of creation started by bringing the Forms together with the material principle (the Receptacle) to produce physical objects and then fashioning both the soul of the world and human souls. The existential status of the Demiurge in Plato's account is probably little more than that of a literary device or perhaps a mythical figure. Plato never says that the Demiurge actually exists. But when the Alexandrian Jews read the *Timaeus*, they endowed the Demiurge with full-fledged existence, and they placed it side by side with Yahweh, the creator god of Genesis. In the wake of this comparison, Yahweh became demoted to a subsidiary role in the divine hierarchy. We are left with the One, which is seen as the principal god, and Yahweh, a lesser god, which, as a mere functionary, carries out the orders of the One. Obviously, in adapting Plato's theoretical machinery to this religious use, the One loses some of its original, utterly transcendent character.

## Influence of Gnosticism

Middle Platonism, as represented by thinkers such as Eudorus, who lived in Alexandria just before the time of Paul, was one of three streams of thought that led to the creation of a religious movement called Gnosticism. The word "Gnosticism" is derived from the Greek word *gnosis*, which means "knowledge." The movement can be very simply characterized by the expression that *the truth can be found within you.* In other words, by turning inward to one's innermost self, one can find all knowledge and even God. It is easy to see how this idea is related to Platonism. Plato held that knowledge of the Forms is discovered through a process of recollection (anamnesis). Recollection is a kind of turning inward by the mind, and the Forms are what underlie all knowledge. The One was the ultimate source of the Forms, so in reawakening our awareness of the Forms, we get at least a glimpse of the One (i.e., God). An added nuance stems from the fact that for many Middle Platonists, including Eudorus, the Forms were ideas in the mind of God.[3] Thus, in recalling our inner awareness of the Forms, we make intuitive contact with God. In its mature stage, Gnosticism was a spin-off from Christianity in the second century CE, and it was represented most prominently by the theologian Valentinus (ca. 100–160 CE). But the evidence is compelling that Gnosticism began as a movement within Judaism in the city of Alexandria. This early movement might best be called proto-Gnosticism because it evolved into full-fledged Gnosticism a century later.

One of the central tenets of proto-Gnosticism (Jewish Gnosticism) is that there are two gods in heaven. The chief god is the religious correlative of the One, and the lesser god is Yahweh, which is the religious correlative of the Demiurge. Since the One, for Plato, was identical to the Good, the chief god was considered to be the absolute expression of goodness, but since the One was also transcendent and unknowable, the chief god was referred to as the Unknown (and Unknowable) God. Further, since the Demiurge, in Plato's *Timaeus*, was said to create the most perfect cosmos possible, the lesser god in Jewish Gnosticism, Yahweh, was originally thought to be a highly perfect deity who worked in harmony with the Unknown God. As Jewish Gnosticism evolved into a movement within Christianity, Yahweh came to be thought of as an ignorant, bumbling fool who created a world riddled with flaws. One of the worst things that

Yahweh did, in the eyes of the Christian Gnostics, was to forbid Adam to eat of the tree of knowledge—which, for these Gnostics, was the ultimate good for humankind. Interpreting Yahweh as a force for evil in the world served to deepen the split between orthodox Judaism and early Christianity.

Oddly enough, it was only recently that scholars came to realize that a pre-Christian Gnosticism actually existed in Alexandria. In 1898, the Austrian theologian Moritz Friedländer wrote an important paper arguing in favor of this thesis, but his conclusions were discounted as being too speculative. The problem was that, at that time, there were no surviving documents authored by any proto-Gnostic writers. As happened with the Christian Gnostics a century later, any such documents, if they existed, may have been burned by orthodox opponents. But then, in 1945, a trove of writings, many of them Gnostic, were unearthed in Nag Hammadi, in Egypt, and this prompted a reevaluation of Friedländer's arguments. The most important spokesperson for Friedländer today is Birger Pearson, professor emeritus at the University of California, Santa Barbara. In a book published in 1990, Pearson reviews Friedländer's arguments, one of which relates to the Jewish philosopher Philo of Alexandria (ca. 25 BCE–50 CE). Philo, as the spokesman for Jewish orthodoxy, condemns certain heretics for apostasy. The problem is that we cannot be certain from Philo's writings alone that these apostates were specifically Gnostics living in Alexandria. But the Nag Hammadi texts tend to strengthen Friedländer's arguments. When these texts are taken into account, Pearson concludes, Friedländer "has been vindicated in his basic contention, that Gnosticism is a pre-Christian phenomenon that developed on Jewish soil."[4] Another scholar, the Dutch theologian Gilles Quispel, insists that Friedländer's thesis is correct, that a pre-Christian Jewish Gnosticism did exist in Alexandria. Quispel bases his argument in part on the Apocryphon of John, one of the writings in the Nag Hammadi collection. Despite its obviously Christian title, Quispel argues that this "crucial text of the so-called 'Gnostics'" was in fact authored by Jews in Alexandria. It describes a "constant struggle between Wisdom that bestows freedom of the spirit and allows consciousness to grow [a Gnostic ideal], and Jaldabaoth, a foolish demiurge, who forbids men to eat from the tree of knowledge."[5] Jaldabaoth is another name for Yahweh. Finally, Joseph Jacobs and Ludwig Blau, writing in the *Jewish Encyclopedia*, assert, "Jewish

Gnosticism unquestionably antedates Christianity . . . the principal elements of gnosticism were derived from Jewish speculation."[6]

## Influence of Hermeticism

Thus far, we have looked into two of the three streams of thought that commingled to produce Gnosticism. Hellenism contributed the theory of Forms, the One, Recollection, and the Demiurge, and Judaism gave a religious interpretation to these theories, converted the One and the Demiurge into gods, and made the One into an object of worship. The third stream of thought was Egyptian Hermeticism, which contributed the concept of God being a Father in a quasi-sexual sense. Hermeticism, an Egyptian religion, is said to be based on the writings of Hermes Trismagistus (thrice-great Hermes). Hermes Trismagistus was thought to be the incarnation of the syncretic union of the Greek god Hermes and the Egyptian god Thoth. Of course, these two gods are fictional, which leads us to suspect that Hermes Trismagistus is a fictional being as well. But there is a collection of writings called the *Corpus Hermeticum*, which is attributed to Hermes Trismagistus, and these writings are real. So some real person (more likely a group of people) must have written them.

Gilles Quispel argues that all the documents in the *Corpus Hermeticum* were written by the members of a mystery community, a sort of Masonic Lodge, in Alexandria at the beginning of the Christian era.[7] This Hermetic Lodge, which Quispel suspects is the birthplace of Gnosticism, consisted of Greeks, Jews, and Egyptians, none of whom was connected in any way with Christianity. One of the documents in the *Corpus* is a *Prayer of Thanksgiving*. It envisions an androgynous god having both male and female sexual organs, and the female half is invoked with the words "we know Thee, womb conceiving through the phallus of the Father."[8] So here, we have a Father in a more than metaphorical sense. The thirteenth treatise in the *Corpus* speaks of a male offspring, a Son, which is "born from the womb of spiritual Wisdom in silence, begotten by the sperm of God."[9] This Son is called *Anthropos* and is linked to the Platonic Form of Man. The first treatise in the *Corpus*, the *Poimandres*, tells how *Anthropos* is brought forth through a process of childbirth. Along these lines, some of the purely Jewish, non-Christian texts found at Nag Hammadi amplify the concept that the eternal Son of God is Man.[10] In another document written in Alexandria at about this same time, the Wisdom of Solomon, the Greek goddess Sophia (Wisdom) is represented as the spouse of the Lord and is called the Holy Spirit.[11] Thus, in Alexandria at the beginning of the common era, we have Hermetic/Gnostic traditions relating to all three components of the Christian god: Father, Son, and Holy Spirit. If Paul the apostle happened to visit Alexandria during these years, he likely would have made contact with the Jews in the Hermetic Lodge. He probably would not have seen them as heretics, as did Philo, but more as they saw themselves, as being on the cutting edge of an exciting Jewish intellectual movement.

## The Gnostic Paul

At this point, we can draw the provisional conclusion that it was Paul who created the basic building blocks of the Christian god. Paul did not get the idea of Father, Son, and Holy Spirit from any vision; he got it from his experience with proto-Gnostics, probably in Alexandria. However, this conclusion would be strengthened if we could identify additional pieces of information and features of Paul's message that show traces of Gnostic thinking. From the earliest days of Christianity, Paul had the reputation of being either a Gnostic or closely connected with Gnosticism. Tertullian, the second- and third-century Christian theologian and heresy hunter, labeled Paul the "Apostle of the Heretics," where "Heretics" means "Gnostics."[12] The accusation was based on the fact that the founder of *Christian* Gnosticism, Valentinus (100–160 CE), together with his followers, recognized Paul as a kindred spirit, one of their own. These followers claimed that Valentinus was a disciple of a man named Theudas, and Theudas was a disciple of Paul.[13] They read his epistles as susceptible to dual interpretations, one of which was intended for the pneumatics (the Gnostics, or the elect) and the other for the psychics (ordinary Christians). Taking her cue from this double way of reading Paul, Elaine Pagels, professor of religion at Princeton, wrote *The Gnostic Paul*, giving a Gnostic exegesis of all of Paul's letters that the Valentinians accepted as genuinely Pauline.[14] Numerous scholars consider Pagels's exegesis to make a great deal of sense of otherwise mysterious passages in Paul's letters.

If we look further at Paul's letters, keeping an eye out for every occasion in which he mentions the word "God," we find additional evidence of a Gnostic touch. For Paul, "God" always means God the Father. Not once, in all his letters, does he ever refer to a God the Creator of Heaven and Earth or, for that matter, God the creator of anything.[15] And this is exactly what we would expect if Paul's god rests on Gnostic ideas. As we have seen, the true god in proto-Gnosticism is not a creator. Rather, the true god is modeled after the Platonic concept of the One, and the task of creation is left to the Demiurge, which is an inferior deity generated, in some way, by the One. From this, it follows that Paul's god is not Yahweh, the Jewish god. For the Alexandrian Gnostics, Yahweh is the correlative of the Demiurge. Paul's god is the Platonic One made up into a Father who begets a Son. Of course, anyone familiar with the Apostles' Creed knows that the first line reads, "I believe in God, the Father Almighty, Creator of heaven and earth." Here, God the Father is linked up with God the Creator, but the Apostles' Creed was not written by Paul. It was written at least 300 years after Paul. The Nicene Creed starts out in much the same way, but that creed was not written by Paul, either. It stems from the Council of Nicea in 325 CE. Paul's God was not a creator god. It was God the Father.

## Paul's Trip to the Third Heaven

Another indication of a link between Paul's thought and thinkers in Alexandria is suggested by the famous passage from 2 Corinthians where Paul tells of a vision in which he was caught up to the third heaven:

> I know a man in Christ who fourteen years ago was caught up to the third heaven. Whether it was in the body or out of the body I do not know—God knows. And I know that this man—whether in the body or apart from the body I do not know, but God knows—was caught up to paradise and heard inexpressible things, things that no one is permitted to tell. (2 Corinthians 12:2–4)

Most scholars share the view that the "man in Christ" that Paul refers to here is none other than Paul himself and that the trip to the third heaven was identical to the trip to paradise. In other words, paradise is either in the third heaven or identical to it.[16] For a further explanation of the passage, we must know something of the context. It appears that from time

194

to time, Paul's legitimacy as an apostle was challenged for either of two reasons. The first arose from the fact that Paul had no contact with Jesus during the latter's life on earth. Jesus died at least two years before Paul's conversion, and there is no reason to think there was any contact before that event. To make up for this shortcoming, Paul claimed to have had visions of the risen Christ—eight in all—which were said to have more than qualified him as an apostle. The other challenge arose from what are thought to be a group of Christian Gnostics residing in Corinth. The Gnostics were known for having visions through which they claimed to receive all sorts of gnosis disclosing Christianity's hidden truths. The best visions were those that carried the subject up to heaven, to the Pleroma, the divine region from which the soul was supposed to have fallen in its descent to earth and to which it would hopefully return after death. If it turned out that Paul had never experienced any visions of this sort, he would be relegated to an inferior status in the eyes of the Corinthian Gnostics. The vision Paul reported in the passage quoted above appears to fit the bill perfectly. Not only did the vision take Paul up to heaven, but while there, he may have seen the face of the risen Christ.

## Why Three Heavens?

The only possible source of trouble is Paul's identification of his visionary destination as the *third* heaven. The problem is that the most common cosmological theory at the time, one accepted by practically everyone, featured seven heavens, not three. So if Paul's vision took him only to the third heaven, he arguably fell a long ways short of what the Gnostics in Corinth would have expected. In a 200-page study of this problem, Paula Gooder concludes that God permitted Paul to rise no higher than the third heaven to prevent him from becoming too conceited.[17] Along these lines, in 2 Corinthians 12:7, Paul speaks of having been given a "thorn in my flesh" to prevent such conceit. Yet this interpretation fails to accomplish what is arguably Paul's intended purpose, namely, persuading the Gnostics that he was as worthy as any of them. Morray-Jones takes a different approach by arguing that Paul was actually working with a three-heaven model so that in reaching the third heaven, he had indeed reached the uppermost level, the location of paradise and the Holy of Holies.[18] Yet Morray-Jones does not explain how it happened that Paul came to assume a three-heaven model in the face of what was surely the more commonly accepted one comprising seven heavens.

The explanation that I offer requires that we go back in time about 300 years and recall the theory underlying these various levels of heaven. Perhaps the shortest route begins with the theory of natural place developed by Aristotle (384–322 BCE). Aristotle accepted the theory invented by his predecessor Empedocles that everything in the cosmos is composed of combinations of four basic elements: earth, water, air, and fire. To this, Aristotle added the idea that each of these elements has its own natural place in the cosmos and that, if displaced from that place, the element will naturally return to it. In the center is earth, shaped in the form of a sphere. Surrounding earth is a spatially thick sphere of water, followed by a sphere of air and finally a sphere of fire. Thus, if a stone (composed mostly of earth) should be released in water, it will naturally descend to its natural place, beneath the sphere of water. If bubbles of air should be released in water, they will rise to their natural place above the sphere of water. And if a candle should be lit in air, the flame will strive to reach its natural place above the sphere of air. Amazingly, this theory was held until the seventeenth century, when it was replaced by Newton's theory of gravity.

The theory of natural place accounted for many terrestrial phenomena reasonably well. But there was one class of appearances that it did not explain at all. This class includes the heavenly bodies. Thus, if one should gaze upward at the moon on a clear night and see it as nothing but a large rock, according to Aristotle's theory, the moon should crash downward to the earth. Clearly, the theory needed modification. Aristotle did this by introducing a fifth element, called aether, into the theory. All the heavenly bodies, including the moon, sun, and the five known planets, were seen as composed of aether. The natural place of aether was above the sphere of fire, and unlike the other four elements, which tended to move either up or down, the natural motion of aether was circular. Also, unlike ordinary physical bodies that were subject to corruption, the heavenly bodies were eternal and incorruptible. Each of these bodies was conceived as being embedded in an invisible sphere, and the bodies move because the spheres rotate. So we have seven concentric spheres, each with its own motion, and all of them surrounding the spheres of fire, air, water, and earth. But what causes the motion of the invisible spheres? The principle of inertia, which depends on the concept of mass (invented by Newton), was unknown to Aristotle. For Aristotle, a moving body could remain in motion only as long as something moves it, just as an oxcart stays in motion only as long as the ox pulls it. Aristotle concluded that the spheres were moved by a nonmaterial, invisible, thinking substance (called a "mover" or "movent") that moves the spheres much as the soul of an animal moves the body of the animal.

Aristotle considered the entire realm of the heavens, including all the heavenly bodies and their associated spheres and movers, to be divine. Thus, when religious thinkers got hold of this theory, they converted the invisible spheres into levels of heaven. Since there were seven spheres, each attached to a heavenly body (the moon, Mercury, Venus, the sun, Mars, Jupiter, and Saturn), there were seven heavens. In addition, there was an eighth sphere for the fixed stars, and this was reserved by religious thinkers for the higher deities. A feature of Aristotle's theory that religious thinkers ignored altogether was the more than thirty-five additional spheres that were needed to account for the irregular motion of the planets. The idea of there being seven heavens was common throughout Paul's geographical milieu except, it seems, for one location: Alexandria. The switch from a seven-heaven model to one featuring three heavens can be seen as resulting from the work of Eudorus of Alexandria (first century BCE). Eudorus was steeped in the writings of Plato, and the most influential work of Plato at that time was undoubtedly the *Timaeus* (on which Eudorus wrote a commentary). In that work, Plato envisions the four fundamental elements as consisting of tiny particles shaped in the form of regular geometric solids.[19] Particles of earth have the shape of tiny cubes, and particles of water have the shape of tiny icosahedrons, with air and fire shaped as octahedrons and tetrahedrons, respectively. The fifth regular solid, the dodecahedron, which most closely resembles the perfect shape, the sphere, is assigned to the cosmos as a whole. This allocation of regular solids to the four elements had the effect on future thinkers of limiting the number of elements to four out of a priori necessity. Since, in addition to the dodecahedron, only these four solids existed, there could be only four elements. This means that there was no geometrical solid to assign to the aether, so Eudorus denied the existence of this element altogether.[20] As a result, for Eudorus, the highest sphere in the cosmos was that of fire, and all the divine heavenly bodies were thought to consist of it—fire in its purest form.

So, to summarize this line of thinking, Aristotle's cosmology envisioned four concentric spheres for the four elements (earth, water, air, and fire) and, surrounding all of this, seven concentric spheres for the seven known heavenly bodies. The seven concentric spheres were thought to be divine in some way. This led religious thinkers to conclude that there were seven heavens, and it became the most commonly accepted view at the time of Paul. But Eudorus, who was heavily influenced by Plato, modified Aristotle's theory by assigning all the known heavenly bodies to the sphere of fire. So now, we have only four concentric spheres, the highest one being the sphere of fire. Once these elements were connected with the four known geometrical solids, the number of spheres was limited to four by strict necessity. This means that above the earth, there are exactly *three* spheres, and it must forever be that way. This theory of Eudorus set the stage for the three-heaven model, which came a few years later.

Philo of Alexandria (ca. 25 BCE–50 CE), who was highly influential not only as a philosopher but also as a religious (Jewish) thinker, followed Eudorus in regard to the fundamental elements. But Philo conceives the spheres containing water, air, and fire as filled with more than mere material particles.[21] All three regions are filled with demons, souls, and angels, which sets the stage for later thinkers to see these spheres as levels of heaven. The third would then be the highest heaven. So the conclusion of this inquiry into the structure of the cosmos is that the source of the three-heaven model appears to be Alexandria. Accordingly, the fact that Paul was apparently operating with this model when he wrote of his mystical journey to paradise and the third heaven provides one more reason to think that he spent time in Alexandria during his younger years or at least was in contact with people who were influenced by Eudorus and Philo. Arguably, this would have put him in contact with proto-Gnostics and mystics. But Paul was not the only one to adopt a three-layer view of heaven. Gershom Scholem notes that the author of the *Slavonic Book of Enoch* describes Enoch as reporting how he was carried up to the third heaven and set down in the midst of paradise. The author of the apocryphal *Life of Adam and Eve* describes how God, following Adam's death, sends the archangel Michael up to paradise in the third heaven. And the author of the *Apocalypse of Moses* describes how Adam was carried into paradise up to the third heaven.[22] All three works are the product of Jewish mysticism that arguably has roots in Alexandria.

## Faith and Sin

Yet another way that Paul's writings are linked to Gnostic ways of thinking is apparent in his theory that salvation comes through faith alone, which is one of Paul's most important teachings. If we think for a moment about what this means, we see that it has profound implications for Paul's concept of God and God's relation to the believer. Suppose that someone should decide to accept Jesus as Redeemer but keep it a secret. If that person should die the next day, presumably that person would be saved. But how could such a thing happen if there is no outward manifestation of the believer's faith? There must be some nonmaterial (spiritual) channel of communication that links the mind of the believer directly to the mind of God through which God gets the message that the person in question is a believer. But this is very much a Gnostic idea. Plato's theory of recollection, adopted by Gnosticism, lays the groundwork for the idea that the human mind has access to the truth about everything through its contact with the mind of God (the locus of the Forms).[23] The human believer receives the gift of faith through its contact with the mind of God, and God knows who deserves salvation through his contact with the mind of the believer.

These ideas seem connected with what Paul says about the Holy Spirit in 1 Corinthians:

> For who knows a person's thoughts except their own spirit within them? In the same way, no one knows the thoughts of God except the Spirit of God. What we have received is not the spirit of the world, but the spirit who is from God, so that we may understand what God has freely given us. (1 Corinthians 2:11–12)

Here the Holy Spirit is linked up with the divine mind. Just as the thoughts of a person are known by that person's spirit, so the thoughts of God are known by God's Spirit—the Holy Spirit. And that Spirit is the channel through which we understand *what God has freely given us*. It is noteworthy that this same section of Corinthians connects the Holy Spirit with divine Wisdom (1 Corinthians 2:6–10). But that is exactly what the Alexandrian Hermeticists said about Sophia (Wisdom). Sophia, the spouse of the Lord, is the Holy Spirit.

The fingerprint of Gnosticism also seems to be evident in Paul's view of sin and salvation:

> I do not understand what I do. For what I want to do I do not do, but what I hate I do. And if I do what I do not want to do, I agree that the law is good. As it is, it is no longer I myself who do it, but it is sin living in me. For I know that good itself does not dwell in me, that is, in my sinful nature. For I have the desire to do what is good, but I cannot carry it out. For I do not do the good I want to do, but the evil I do not want to do—this I keep on doing. Now if I do what I do not want to do, it is no longer I who do it, but it is sin living in me that does it. (Romans 7:15–2)

Paul begins by saying there is a divorce between thought and action, between mind and matter, between what he knows is good and what he actually ends up doing. His thought is directed upward to the One (the Father), which is identical to the Good and the source of Truth (the Forms), but his actions are accomplished through the body, which is composed of matter, the creation of the Demiurge. The body (flesh) exerts a constant drag on the mind, confusing it and leading it into sin. All of this is pure Gnostic Platonism. (Recall that Plato spoke of the body as the prison of the soul.) Living the righteous life is a constant struggle between what the mind sees as right and what the body desires. Mind (spirit) and body are constantly out of sync because the Demiurge, as an inferior deity, is inevitably separated from and out of sync with the One. Given this conceptual backdrop, it becomes clear why Paul at times seems obsessed with human sexuality. Sexuality is the paradigmatic variety of bodily desire that operates independently of rational control. It is the perfect example of how the body operates in a state of disconnection from the mind. Whenever possible, Paul recommends that humans remain celibate (1 Corinthians 7:1, 8, 28, 32–34).

Salvation, for Paul, amounts to being released from this struggle between mind and matter, between the spirit and the flesh. Since sin consists in a separation from God (severing the channel of communication that exists between the human mind and the mind of God) and since it results from a kind of weakness (the inability of the spirit to withstand the constant pull of the flesh), salvation consists in a restoration of the connection to God and a release from the struggle with the flesh. At the resurrection, we will be given a transformed body, a "spiritual body" (1 Corinthians 15:44), a body not handicapped by the flaws it originally received through the clumsy craftsmanship of the Demiurge. This new body will be imperishable and in complete harmony with the Spirit.

Given this additional evidence, namely, the fact that Paul was known as the Apostle of the Heretics (Gnostics), that Paul's god is never the creator of the world (the Demiurge) but always the Father, that the Son of God appears linked up with the Platonic Form of Man and the Hermetic *Anthropos*, that the Holy Spirit is tied to a religious elaboration of Plato's theory of recollection by which a two-way channel of communication exists between the human mind and the mind of God, and that righteousness consists in overcoming the struggle between spirit and flesh, between the opposing forces of the One and the Demiurge, I feel confident in concluding that Paul is the one who created the basic building blocks of the Christian god: Father, Son, and Holy spirit. In so doing, Paul was inspired by a concrescence of three streams of thought: Middle Platonism, Judaism, and Egyptian Hermeticism.

## Jesus as Son of God

Paul also gets credit for an especially important innovation in regard to the Son of God. Paul interprets this deity as having a sole human instantiation in the person of Jesus Christ. Where did Paul get the idea that Jesus is the Son of God? Nowhere in any of his letters does he say that Jesus claimed to be the Son of God. This is significant because if Paul were aware of any such claim, he surely would have said so in his letters. Thus, the conclusion seems warranted that Paul did not get the idea from anything that Jesus said, either indirectly from his followers or directly from a vision. Going back to Paul's letters, Paul says that Jesus was appointed Son of God by his resurrection from the dead. In other words, he ties the Son of God attribution to the assumption that Jesus rose from the dead. And where did Paul get the idea that Jesus rose from the dead? Probably from conversations he would have had with Christians he had been persecuting. These conversations may have reported rumors grounded in collective memory that the man who died on the cross came back to life three days later. Thus, if such rumors were unsubstantiated, there would have been no reason in Paul's mind to conclude that Jesus was the Son of God.

A passage from 1 Corinthians supports the view that Paul received his information about the resurrection from other Christians. After reminding the Corinthians about the Gospel they had received from him, he says,

> For what I received, I passed on to you as of first importance: that Christ died for our sins according to the scriptures, that he was buried, that he was raised on the third day according to the Scriptures. (1 Corinthians 15:3–4)

Paul does not say from whom he received the information that he then passed on, but it would appear that there are two possible sources: a vision or a conversation with other Christians. What the passage does *not* say makes it likely that the source of Paul's information was *not* from a vision. The passage does not say anything about Jesus being the Son of God. But this is the single most important thing about the Christian message. If the information were from a vision, surely it would have contained this most important item (in addition to these three other items). Thus, the information that Paul speaks of most likely came from his contact with other Christians. According to New Testament scholar Bart Ehrman, there is good reason to think that this passage was originally part of a creed recited by the earliest Christians.[24] Assuming this to be the case, it provides evidence of what those early Christians believed and also of what they did not believe. What they believed is that Jesus died for our sins, that he was buried, and that he was raised on the third day. Missing from this belief is that Jesus is the Son of God. If these Christians had believed this, then surely it would have been stated in their creed. The upshot is that Paul received his information about Jesus' resurrection from his contact with the early Christians, but he did not receive the idea that Jesus is the Son of God from these people. And he did not receive it from a vision, either. Thus, the most likely source of the claim that Jesus is the Son of God is none other than Paul himself. Paul created it all by himself.

It is easy to see how Paul could have been led to draw this conclusion. Given that he made contact with some of the first Christians, Paul would have heard rumors or reports that Christ had appeared to some of his disciples. These appearances led some of them to conclude that Jesus had been raised from the dead. But these appearances were not like the sightings one might have of a friend or associate. The body of Jesus had not simply been resuscitated, as had Lazarus, who then lived a normal life and eventually died, but the appearances of Jesus were those of a mysterious entity who would show up for a few minutes and then miraculously go away. Jesus had no permanent location, no home, and he did not engage in the same activities as he had before death. He gave no sermons, forgave no sins, and never sat down with his friends to enjoy a common meal. The disciples probably thought that Jesus had been taken up to heaven, where he enjoyed a special relationship with God, and he came down from time to time to be with some of his disciples. When Paul put these stories together with what he had learned in Egypt, that God was in essence a Father, that the Father had a Son, and that the Son was linked to the Platonic Form of Man, he drew the conclusion that Jesus was the earthly instance of this Form of Man, that is, the corporeal instance of the divine Son. After Jesus was raised from the dead, God brought him up to heaven, where he adopted him as his Son. At the beginning of Romans, Paul speaks of

> [God's] Son, who as to his earthly life was a descendent of David, and who through the Spirit of holiness was appointed the Son of God in power by his resurrection from the dead: Jesus Christ our Lord. (Romans 1:3–4)[25]

Saying that Jesus was *appointed* Son of God is simply another way of saying that Jesus was the adopted son of God. Furthermore, Paul links this adoption to the resurrection. God the Father raised the earthly Jesus from the dead, brought him up to heaven, and then adopted him as his Son. This idea of Jesus being the adopted son of the Father was widespread in second-century Christianity, but the idea was later abandoned in favor of Jesus being the *begotten* son, which is the current view.

In coming up with the idea that Jesus is the Son of God, Paul, as a Roman citizen and as a speaker of Greek, may also have been influenced by several bits of Roman and Greek lore. In the ancient world, a number of prominent figures were thought to be the sons of some god or other. Alexander the Great was supposed to be the son of Zeus, Hercules was the son of either Jupiter or Zeus, and Romulus, the founder of Rome, was the son of Mars. Julius Caesar declared himself to be descended from gods, and Caesar Augustus, whose reign overlapped the early life of Paul, was called during his lifetime *the* Son of God.[26] Paul was certainly familiar with most or all of these traditions, so his identification of Jesus as the Son of

God had precedents that he was familiar with. We have already identified this belief that Jesus is the Son of God as part of the Jesus Illusion. It is purely a construction of Paul, and, of course, there is no certain reasoning or evidence to support it. Paul did not get the idea from his contact with the Jesus movement. Members of this community may have thought that Jesus had risen from the dead, but probably none of them thought that he was the Son of God. And certainly no member of the Jewish community thought any such thing. Jesus as the son of Yahweh? Such a thing would have been not only ridiculous but also blasphemous. Among these traditions, the most likely inspiration for the idea was probably Caesar Augustus. Just as Caesar Augustus was the Son of God in the corrupt world of the present, so Jesus was the Son of God in the perfect world to come.

Also included in the Jesus Illusion is the belief that Jesus died to reconcile humankind with God the Father (Romans 5:10–11). As we saw in the previous chapter, Jesus died because of a tragic miscalculation. He thought he was destined to become king of the Jews, but things turned out very differently. Jesus as reconciler is intrinsically connected with Jesus as Son of God. If Jesus is seen as an ordinary human, it makes no sense to say that he died to reconcile humans with a divinity. No ordinary human could accomplish any such thing. But when Jesus is recognized as the Son of God, all the pieces start to fall into place. Jesus' suffering and death now have a purpose, the effects of sin (chiefly death) may now be washed away, the divorce of humans from God is now mended, and humans can look forward to a life that is everlasting. The idea of Jesus as reconciler is also a fabrication of Paul, but admittedly, it does have a certain rational connection with Jesus as Son of God.

## Paul's Motives

Now that we have identified Paul the apostle as the creator of the basic components of the Christian god, there remains only one issue to determine: What motivated Paul in this grand endeavor? Could it possibly have been ambition? Something that would lead to great power in the future? I will argue that the answer is yes. However, I will also argue that something unique is going on in the case of Paul. The power that he expected to receive was not a power in this world. Rather, it was power in the next world, in the post-resurrection world. Proving this claim is complicated by the fact that there is no reason to think that Paul ever actually received this power. In other words, we have no evidence that Paul currently holds some high office in the heavenly realm. Also, most people who are motivated by power have some visible, tangible accomplishment that reveals this motivation. But Paul was never crowned king of any nation, he never won a single important battle over an opposing military force, and he never was the recipient of great wealth. Thus, to prove our thesis about Paul and the quest for power, we are limited to a search of his letters for hints that the power motive operated behind the scenes. This means that we must search for passages that say something about Paul's state of mind. An additional factor that complicates this search is my conviction that ambition and power were not the only motivators at work in the mind of Paul. It often is the case that important life decisions are motivated by more than a single concern, and I think this is certainly the case with Paul's decision to become the apostle to the Gentiles.

It is the considered judgment of E. P. Sanders that one of Paul's activities we can be absolutely certain of is his early persecution of the Christian movement.[27] Paul is completely clear about this in three of his letters.[28] In Galatians, he writes,

> For you have heard of my previous way of life in Judaism, how intensely I persecuted the church of God and tried to destroy it. (Galatians 1:13)

Paul tried to *destroy* the Christian movement. His persecution was *intense*. Sanders thinks that this persecution included persuading synagogues to administer thirty-nine lashes, the maximum amount allowed, to those Jews who had accepted Jesus as the Messiah.[29]

On the other hand, even a cursory reading of Paul's letters will reveal that a central part of his message, perhaps the most central part, has to do with love:

> Let no debt remain outstanding, except the continuing debt to love one another, for whoever loves others has fulfilled the law. The commandments . . . are summed up in this one command: "Love your neighbor as yourself." (Romans 13:8–9)

> If I speak in the tongues of men or of angels, but do not have love, I am only a resounding gong or a clanging cymbal. (1 Corinthians 13:1)

Love is patient, love is kind. It does not envy, it does not boast, it is not proud. It does not dishonor others, it is not self-seeking, it is not easily angered, it keeps no record of wrongs. Love does not delight in evil but rejoices with the truth. It always protects, always trusts, always hopes, always perseveres. (1 Corinthians 13:4–7)

So how do we reconcile Paul's original persecution of Christians against the backdrop of passages such as these about love? Tough love? Not a chance. Paul worked to destroy the church, not reform it. If Paul had the opportunity (and he might have), he could even have gone so far as to have these wayward Jews executed. Paul attributes his persecution of these people to zeal. If so, what made him shift from zeal to love? Could this have been brought about by some vision? After all, the author of Acts attributes Paul's conversion to a miracle: while on the road to Damascus, he was knocked off his horse, at which point he experienced a vision of the risen Christ. We have already observed that this miracle is not mentioned once in all of Paul's letters, and if it had occurred, it was exactly the sort of thing that Paul would have mentioned over and over. It would have been the single most important event in his entire life. Besides, Paul's teaching about love seems so heartfelt that it was not the sort of thing that could have been received through a vision. It seems that this teaching reflects the very essence of Paul's soul. So, instead of a vision, I would suggest that Paul experienced a crisis of conscience when he saw the results of his high-blown zeal. Here he was, rounding up these poor people only to have them tortured and possibly even killed. Amid all the action, Paul would have seen how these Christians loved one another. They were hardly the monsters that apostasy might connote. The awful sight of these events, wives being torn away from their husbands, children from their parents, must have triggered the realization that what he was doing was deeply wrong. It may have taken weeks or months for it to settle in, but when it happened, the realization would have been life jarring, like being knocked off a horse.

When Paul decided to change course and join up with the people he had been persecuting, the first thing we would expect him to do is connect up with the other apostles. After all, by his own acknowledgment, he was called directly by Jesus to be the apostle to the Gentiles. Presumably, he knew nothing about what it meant to be an apostle. Would it not have been wise to check in with those who had a few years of experience in the job? But no. Paul had other plans. "I did not go up to Jerusalem to see those who were apostles before I was, but I went into Arabia" (Galatians 1:17). Immediately, we sense an attitude of dismissal toward the other apostles. What could be the source of it? Obviously, from this passage, Paul knew that these other apostles existed. He may have learned about them from his contact with the Christians he had been persecuting. Or perhaps he learned something from his contact with the Jewish priesthood.[30] What might he have learned? The answer is clearly rooted in speculation, but he might have heard that the twelve apostles were each promised, in the next life, a governing role over one of the twelve tribes of Israel in exchange for their success in winning converts.[31] If so, the implication was that there would be no room at the table for a thirteenth apostle. Either Paul could work with one of the others to win converts, or he could forget about being an apostle altogether. But such a result was unacceptable. Paul insisted that he was at least as much an apostle as any of the others. He was the apostle to the Gentiles. That designation set him apart from the others.

Why the Gentiles? Paul's response was that through a vision, Jesus himself had appointed him apostle to the Gentiles (Galatians 1:15–16). I would argue that there is another, quite different explanation. If some kind of reward could be expected for winning converts, the opportunity was much greater among the Gentiles than among the Jews. Simply put, there were far more Gentiles in that part of the world than there were Jews. And Paul, as an educated man, had the skills to reach them. Paul could write letters. While the other apostles depended on baptism, a highly labor-intensive operation, Paul could convert thousands through a single letter. Quickly, Paul became the Henry Ford of early Christianity— mass conversions from an unlimited supply of candidates.

## Paul's Expected Reward

So we see, following his conversion, that another side of Paul becomes apparent: Paul the entrepreneur of religion. It was probably always there, even during the days when he was persecuting the Christians. He probably expected some reward for this work, but there are no letters from him to document it. Following his conversion, Paul saw a marvelous opportunity. The Jesus message was obviously popular. It captured the imagination of thousands. It promised hope to the poor and the powerless. For the first time in history, a religious leader (Jesus) comes along and tells ordinary folks that they are important. Up to then, the only important ones were the Jewish priests and the Roman aristocrats. Now the average guy has a chance. All that is needed is that they be given the message. And Paul had the intelligence and skill to hone the message for maximum effect. He had apparently heard a rumor that Jesus, the leader of the group he had been persecuting, had risen from the dead. Paul converted the rumor into an article of faith. Jesus had, without question, risen from the dead. This in itself was a compelling story, a good reason for prospective converts to sign up with the new movement. But how much more compelling would the story be if Jesus were elevated in status to the Son of God? Not the son of Yahweh but the son of a new god, God the Father of all, a god that Paul had managed to create. Paul then converted the image of the risen Christ into a model that every new convert could look forward to in the next life (Romans 5:5). Just as the risen Christ was no mere ghost but had a body extended in space and time, a body that could enjoy all the joys and pleasures of the present life, so every Christian could look forward to such a life but without the attendant aches, pains, and disappointments. And these joys and pleasures were just around the corner. "The hour has already come for you to wake up from your slumber, because our salvation is nearer now than when we first believed" (Romans 13:11).

The foregoing might be taken to imply that Paul was disingenuous in his teaching. Did he actually believe everything that he taught? There is good reason to think that he did believe it. After all, he endured numerous instances of persecution, including multiple imprisonments, beatings, being stoned and left for dead, and being shipwrecked. No one would have endured such insults on behalf of a teaching if there were any doubt in the believer's mind that the teaching was true. What was the source of this teaching? Paul claimed to have received it directly through visions of the risen Christ. Did he actually have those visions? Of course, it is possible that he may have had some of them. He may have been a mystic, and many mystics have visions. He may have acquired mystical abilities through his experience with the Egyptian Hermeticists, who were mystics. The claim that he was conveyed up to the third heaven is right out of the Gnostic playbook. He may have interpreted ordinary flashes of insight as visions. Or his visions may have been moments of ecstasy brought on by any number of possible causes. Whatever be the case, everything that he claimed to have received through visions can be explained through natural causes. We have already identified the probable source of the basic components of the triune God: Father, Son, and Holy Spirit. That the Son had an instance in the natural world could be inferred from the Middle Platonic theory of participation. The Son is the Platonic Form of Man, and Forms have instances in the natural world. That this instance was none other than Jesus Christ could be inferred from the idea that Jesus was raised from the dead. Paul suggests this when he writes that Jesus "was appointed the Son of God in power by his resurrection from the dead" (Romans 1:4). All of these inferences have loose ends, but when a message is repeated over and over, the loose ends tend to be ignored, and the thrust of the message is believed with nary a doubt.

Additional evidence supporting the idea that Paul expected a very significant reward for his work in winning converts can be found in several places in his letters. In the course of his ministry in Corinth, Paul was apparently challenged in regard to his legitimacy as an apostle. This, of course, was of the greatest importance because if Paul's apostleship was not legitimate, then he would get no credit for all the converts he had won. Paul replies to those attacking him:

> Are they Hebrews? So am I. Are they Israelites? So am I. Are they Abraham's descendants? So am I. Are they servants of Christ? (I am out of my mind to talk like this) I am more. I have worked much harder, been in prison more frequently, been flogged more severely, and been exposed to death again and again. Five times I received from the Jews the forty lashes minus one. Three times I was beaten with rods, once I was pelted with stones, three times I was shipwrecked, I spent a night and a day in the open sea, I have been constantly on the move. I have been in danger from rivers, in danger from bandits, in danger from my fellow Jews, in danger from Gentiles; in danger in the city, in danger in the country, in danger at sea; and in danger from false believers. I have labored and toiled and have often gone without sleep; I have known hunger and thirst and have often gone without food; I have been cold and naked. Besides everything else, I face daily the pressure of my concern for all the churches. (2 Corinthians 11:21–28)

Paul's reply, in effect, is, How dare you challenge my legitimacy? I have all the qualifications that you have, and more. Besides, I have worked much harder, tolerated more abuse, and suffered more hardships than any of you. For you to deprive me of my legitimacy would be the greatest injustice.

## A Threatened Man

Paul never says exactly who these people are who are attacking his legitimacy. Some have argued that it was the original twelve apostles or their representatives, others that it was a group of Gnostics in Corinth. For our purposes, the identity of these individuals is not particularly important. Rather, it is Paul's state of mind in confronting them. As will become even clearer in the selections that follow, Paul is clearly threatened by these forces of opposition. And why is he threatened? He is worried that his converts will be taken away from him. He is worried that someone else will take credit for them, in which case he will be deprived of his just reward. Paul expresses the same concern in this passage from Galatians:

> I am astonished that you are so quickly deserting the one who called you to live in the grace of Christ and are turning to a different gospel—which is really no gospel at all. Evidently some people are throwing you into confusion and are trying to pervert the gospel of Christ. But even if we or an angel from heaven should preach a gospel other than the one we preached to you, let them be under God's curse! As we have already said, so now I say again: If anybody is preaching to you a gospel other than what you accepted, let them be under God's curse! (Galatians 1:6–9)

One interpretation of this passage might be that Paul is concerned that the Galatians are accepting a Gospel other than the true Gospel. If the issue were merely what the true Gospel was, the proper response from Paul would be to schedule a meeting with these folks on the other side and come to some resolution on what the true message should be. But that is not the issue. Rather, Paul expresses his astonishment that the Galatians were deserting *him*—not the Gospel but the person who preached it. And why is this so important? Because Paul has a tremendous personal investment in the Galatian converts. The Galatians are money in Paul's heavenly bank account. The extreme emotional involvement Paul has with the matter is indicated by the language at the end of the passage. If anyone is trying to win you away from me, let them be cursed (damned)! And he repeats the curse.

This same level of involvement appears evident in the next selection. Referring to certain unnamed individuals who Paul sees as working against him, he writes,

> For such people are false apostles, deceitful workers, masquerading as apostles of Christ. And no wonder, for Satan himself masquerades as an angel of light. It is not surprising, then, if his servants masquerade as servants of righteousness. Their end will be what their actions deserve. (2 Corinthians 11:13–15)

Here, Paul accuses these opponents of being agents of Satan. They are false and deceitful. The language clearly suggests that Paul feels threatened by these pretenders.

The same defensive language is apparent in the next selection. Again, Paul responds to the charge that he is in some way illegitimate:

> I do not think I am in the least inferior to those "super-apostles." I may indeed be untrained as a speaker, but I do have knowledge. We have made this perfectly clear to you in every way. (2 Corinthians 11:5–6)

Here, it appears that Paul's opponents are the original twelve apostles. By sarcastically calling them the "super-apostles," Paul shows his apparent contempt. He insists that he is in no way inferior to them because, although he is not a great speaker, he has knowledge (gnosis). I read this assertion to mean that Paul claims for himself the special secret wisdom that he learned from the proto-Gnostics, probably in Alexandria. An alternate reading is that Paul had visions through which he experienced the risen Christ face-to-face. This might be in response to the claim that Paul was an illegitimate apostle because, unlike the others, Paul had never lived and worked with Jesus.[32] Paul could argue that the original apostles had an inferior acquaintance with Jesus because all they saw was the material, earthly image of him. Paul, on the other hand, saw the true, spiritual, heavenly reality of the man. The passage seems to show a clear Platonic influence.

A similar message appears to be conveyed in the next selection:

> I am not in the least inferior to the "super-apostles," even though I am nothing. I persevered in demonstrating among you the marks of a true apostle, including signs, wonders, and miracles. (2 Corinthians 12:11–12)

When Paul writes "even though I am nothing," he displays the ultimate in false modesty. He clearly thinks that he is superior to anyone else who might call himself an apostle. Yet he is desperate that his own status as an apostle not be undermined.

Again, in the same vein, Paul issues an appeal to the Corinthians:

> Am I not an apostle? Have I not seen Jesus our Lord? Are you not the result of my work in the Lord? Even though I may not be an apostle to others, surely I am to you! For you are the seal of my apostleship in the Lord. (1 Corinthians 9:1–2)

Another threat that Paul faced, in addition to the threat involving his legitimacy as an apostle, was the threat to his freedom in winning converts. As long as Paul could invite any and all Gentiles to join the incipient Christian movement without restrictions, he met with great success. But when certain elements in the movement tried to impose the requirement that potential converts first convert to Judaism, which required that males be circumcised, this created problems. Circumcising an infant is one thing. Circumcising a grown adult is quite another matter. There was the obvious physical pain, risk of infection, and recovery period. Furthermore, for the Greeks and those impacted by Greek culture, which comprised a sizable portion of the Gentile population, a circumcised phallus was aesthetically repulsive.[33] These two concerns, pain and aesthetics, were guaranteed to slow down the influx of converts. Paul observes how the requirement for prior conversion to Judaism arose in Galatia:

> This matter arose because some false believers had infiltrated our ranks to spy on the freedom we have in Christ Jesus and to make us slaves [to the Torah]. We did not give in to them for a moment, so that the truth of the gospel might be preserved for you. (Galatians 2:4–5)

Paul is referring here to the freedom that the new Christians have in not being subject to the Law incorporated in the Torah. This is largely a theological issue. But behind this theological freedom there lurks the freedom to invite new candidates into the movement without restriction. Paul reacted intensely to the requirement that his initiates be circumcised:

> Those who want to impress people by means of the flesh are trying to compel you to be circumcised. . . . Neither circumcision nor uncircumcision means anything; what counts is the new creation. (Galatians 6:12–15)

Furthermore, that Paul is using the word "circumcision" literally and not metaphorically is clear from the following blunt comment:

> As for those agitators, I wish they would go the whole way and emasculate themselves. (Galatians 5:12)

In other words, as long as these mutilators of the flesh are cutting off their foreskins, they should go the whole distance and cut off their testicles. Paul's emotional involvement in the issue is evident.

That Paul was concerned until the end of his life with requiring circumcision as a precondition for conversion is clear from his last letter written from prison:

> Watch out for those dogs, those evildoers, those mutilators of the flesh. For it is we who are the [true] circumcision, we who serve God by his Spirit, who boast in Christ Jesus, and who put no confidence in the flesh. (Philippians 3:2–3)

The terms "dogs" and "evildoers" indicate the intensity of Paul's loathing for those advocating conversion to Judaism as a condition for conversion to Christianity.

## Paul in the Afterlife

The final question is, what did Paul expect in return for winning all these new converts? I think the answer is linked up with his view of the afterlife. As already noted, Paul thought that in the next life, we would be given a spiritual body (2 Corinthians 15:44). We will have the same kind of body that Jesus had after the resurrection. Just as Jesus was visible and extended in space and time and could travel from place to place and communicate with other humans, so we will have the same attributes and capabilities. We will consist of neither a reanimated corpse nor a pure spirit but a glorified body that suffers none of the disadvantages of a natural body and that will never again die. Such a view of the afterlife is quite different from that held by many Christians today, for whom the next life will be that of a pure spirit without a body. The latter view is closely related to Plato's theory, and why Paul did not adopt it is an interesting question in itself given that he was heavily influenced by Middle Platonism.[34] But it is quite clear that Paul did not hold the pure spirit view. Those blessed with an afterlife will live in a society, probably here on earth, in a cosmos that has been thoroughly transformed.[35]

Such a society would require organization just as every human society does today. In a society of pure spirits, organization might be accomplished through some kind of ESP, where the Absolute Spirit (God) sends signals instantaneously to every finite spirit and thereby achieves perfect harmony among them. But in a society consisting of spiritual bodies, organization would depend on human communication, and this would entail a hierarchy of communicators. There would be governors, consuls, praetors, and so on in descending levels of power. I am reasonably certain that Paul envisioned himself in the role of some very high official in the heavenly society of Gentiles. Since there would likely be more members of this society than any of the twelve tribes of Israel (each governed by one of the other apostles), Paul would end up with more power than any of the other apostles. So in Paul, once again, we have a priest creating gods for the purpose of augmenting his own power, in this case a power in the life to come.

Albert Schweitzer, who wrote a book on Paul's mysticism, also thought that Paul expected some special reward in the next life. The Pauline scholar James Tabor agrees with Schweitzer:

> I am convinced, as Albert Schweitzer suggested, that Paul had come to believe in the latter years of his life that he would likely not live to see the return of Christ but that he was to receive a special reward immediately upon his death. Unlike others who "sleep in Christ," awaiting the resurrection at Christ's coming, Paul seems to believe that he will be raised up immediately out of Hades and taken to join Christ in heaven—being glorified together with him, as he has suffered and died with him.[36]

Assuming that Paul went to Alexandria after his decision to join the Jesus movement, he arguably would have come in contact with a melting pot of ideas. From Middle Platonism he would have learned about the

Platonic One, from Jewish Gnosticism he would have linked the One with a god of religion, and from Egyptian Hermeticism he would have heard that God is a Father who generated a Son and that the divine spouse was called the Holy Spirit. Further, this Father god was not identical to the Jewish god Yahweh, who was specifically a lower-level deity who created the world. After leaving Alexandria, Paul converted the rumor that Jesus had risen from the dead into an article of faith, and he identified the risen Christ with this Son, the offspring of the Father through the mediation of the Holy Spirit. If these observations hold true, Paul gets credit for the three building blocks of the Christian god.

Paul proceeded to preach this message to the Gentile community. As apostle to the Gentiles, Paul was in competition with the other apostles to win the most converts. He was the only apostle who had never laid eyes on the pre-resurrection Jesus, so he felt that this fact threatened his legitimacy in the eyes of the other apostles. He feared that the other apostles might take away his converts, and this fear led to a power struggle that lasted until the end of his life. Because this struggle undoubtedly intensified the fervor of Paul's preaching, the triune God can be said to be the product of power. But it is also the product of power in a different but related sense. Paul hoped to receive great power in the government of the hereafter, and he constructed the triune God in part to receive it. Since power is what motivated its construction, the triune God can be seen as the product of power. It was the product of power in regard to both its construction and its dissemination.

# CHAPTER SEVEN
# THE CHRISTIANS
## Trinity Completed

A t the very end of the Gospel of Matthew, there is a famous passage that reads,

> Then Jesus came to them and said, "All authority in heaven and earth has been given to me. Therefore go and make disciples of all nations, baptizing them in the name of the Father and of the Son and of the Holy Spirit, and teaching them to obey everything I have commanded you. And surely I am with you always, to the very end of the age." (Matthew 28:18–20)

This passage (along with the rest of the Gospel) was written at least fifty years after the death of Jesus. Its authenticity almost certainly depends in large measure on collective memory—the collective memory of the apostles and their successors—and, as we have seen, collective memory is a survival-enhancing mechanism (or process). Jesus is reported to be saying something that would help ensure the survival of his movement. With that in mind, we can ask, did Jesus really say this, especially the part about his having received all authority in heaven and earth? Of course, it is possible that he said something remotely similar to this, but his actual statement was massaged by multiple generations of speakers and listeners who had a vested interest in the survival of the church. Also, the fact that the statement is credited to the risen Jesus and not to the Jesus who lived and worked with the apostles has a bearing on its alleged authenticity. But the main question, for our purposes, is not whether Jesus ever said any such thing but whether the apostles believed the gist of the message as it existed in collective memory and as it came to be reported in the Gospel.

## The Power of the Bishops

In this passage, the resurrected Jesus says to his apostles that he has been given ultimate power (authority) over heaven and earth, and the implication is that he is transferring at least some of that power to them. So did the apostles believe that they had received certain powers from the resurrected Christ? I think the answer is clearly yes. Assuming this to be the case, the next question is, what powers did the apostles believe that they had received? I think the prima facie answer, in light of the quoted passage, is a set of three powers: the power to baptize, the power to teach, and the power to ordain/consecrate successors. The power to baptize is mentioned explicitly in the passage, the power to teach is implied by the command that the apostles go out and teach all nations, and the power to ordain successors is implied by Christ's promise that he would be with them until the end of the age. A single generation of apostles could never accomplish the assigned task. And then there is the additional power to do the things that Christ "commanded" them to do before his death, which included the power to celebrate the Eucharist.

Let us first consider the power to baptize. Our understanding of baptism goes back to the work of John the Baptist on the Jordan River:

> And so John the Baptist appeared in the wilderness, preaching a baptism of repentance for the forgiveness of sins. The whole Judean countryside and all the people of Jerusalem went out to him. Confessing their sins, they were baptized by him in the Jordan River. (Mark 1:4–5)

The idea is that baptism, which involves immersion in water, washes away sin (including original sin), but it must be combined with repentance. As per the Gospel message, the people first confessed their sins, and then they were baptized. But this leads us to ask, what about sins that would be committed after baptism? For these, at least initially, it appears that mere repentance was thought to be sufficient. After all, the kingdom of heaven was just around the corner. The first command that Jesus is reported to have issued is "Repent, for the kingdom of heaven has come near" (Matthew 4:17). However, as the years went by and the kingdom never arrived, the apostles and/or their successors concluded that something additional was needed.[1] Rebaptism was not possible because baptism was supposed to be a one-time-only occurrence. However, the fact that baptism resulted in the forgiveness of sins and the fact that the apostles had the power to baptize implied that the apostles had the power to forgive sins. It was probably reasoning such as this that led to the gradual introduction of what eventually became the sacrament of penance. This gradual introduction began late in the first century CE.

The Didache, the first Christian catechism, written around 100 CE, commands an individual confession during the worship service. "In the congregation thou shalt confess thy transgressions." Also, "On the Lord's Day come together and break bread . . . having confessed your transgressions that your sacrifice may be pure." Clement I, bishop of Rome, in his *Epistle to the Corinthians* (ca. 96 CE), urges sinners to "submit themselves to the presbyters and receive correction so as to repent" (Chapter 57). Another early bishop, Ignatius of Antioch, in his *Letter to the Philadelphians* (ca. 108 CE), says "that the bishop presides over penance." This shift from mere repentance to confessing one's sins to the bishop or presbyters amounted to a significant power grab by the bishops. Now, in addition to repenting, sinners had to "submit themselves" to the presbyters. The bishops and presbyters now had the say in deciding whether sins would be forgiven. To justify the change, the bishops noted that those who had committed grievous sins were getting off too easy by merely repenting.

The appropriation of power was rendered official a few years later (around 110 CE) when the author of the Gospel of John had the risen Christ say to his apostles,

> Peace be with you! As the Father has sent me, I am sending you. . . .
> Receive the Holy Spirit. If you forgive anyone's sins, their sins are forgiven; if you do not forgive them, they are not forgiven. (John 20:21–23)

It seems highly unlikely that Jesus ever said this because if he had, the apostles would have implemented the ritual of penance very shortly after they had supposedly received the power, that is, shortly after Jesus' reputed resurrection. But this did not happen. It took many years for the ritual to develop. What in fact the evangelist is doing here is making official a ritual that had already developed or was in the process of developing. The full significance of this passage may be grasped when it is read in conjunction with a passage from the Gospel of Matthew, which had been written several years earlier (around 80 CE):

> I will give you the keys to the kingdom of heaven; whatever you bind on earth will be bound in heaven, and whatever you loose on earth will be loosed in heaven. (Matthew 16:19)

The meaning of the key symbol is unmistakable. Keys open doors, and they lock them shut. In this case, the door is the gateway to heaven. Jesus tells Peter that he has the power to decide who gets into heaven and who does not. And Peter has this power precisely because he (along with the other apostles) has the power to forgive sins or not to forgive them. Those whose sins are forgiven will make it into heaven, and those whose sins are not forgiven will not make it. Sculptors and painters helped solidify this message by depicting Peter as holding one or two keys—the keys that grant access to everlasting life. The image and the message it conveys were so compelling that, as years passed, even princes and kings submitted themselves to the power of the Church.

That the apostles believed they had the power to name and ordain successors is implied by their actions, for they did indeed name them. Following the Gospel of Luke (Luke 10:1), Hippolytus of Rome (or Pseudo-Hippolytus) names seventy disciples of Jesus, fifty-three of whom are identified as bishops. In most cases, the apostle who had ordained them is not known, but there are exceptions. Prochorus, bishop of Nichomedia, was ordained by the John the Apostle; Urban, bishop of Macedonia, was ordained by the apostle Andrew; Narcissus, bishop of Athens, was ordained by Phillip; Jason, bishop of Tarsus, was ordained by Paul; and Anacletus, bishop of Rome, was ordained by Peter. Also, outside this list, Clement I, bishop of Rome, was ordained by Peter, and Timothy and Titus are thought to have been ordained by Paul. However, even those for whom details are lacking were almost certainly appointed or ordained by some apostle or his successor. The new bishop did not simply appoint himself to the post. The reason for this is that, from a very early date, the ordination ritual involved a laying on of hands. Through this subritual, the power of the Holy Spirit was thought to flow out of the celebrant doing the ordaining and into the person being ordained. This was not merely a symbolic gesture but also an existential process that accomplished an actual transfer of spiritual power. It was through the resultant indwelling of the Spirit that the new bishop would have the power to baptize and to celebrate the Eucharist. And the only way that the new bishop could acquire the Spirit was through another bishop who already had it.

The laying on of hands had a rich history in Judaism. Moses ordained Joshua by laying his hands on him (Numbers 27:15–23), and in the same way, he ordained the seventy elders (Numbers 11:16–25), who in turn ordained their successors. In Christianity, Peter and John laid their hands on the Samarians to invoke the Holy Spirit (Acts 8:15–19), and the apostles laid their hands on the group of seven disciples (Acts 6:5–6). Clement I, bishop of Rome, in his Epistle to the Corinthians, argues that everything should be done according to a certain order, namely, the order envisioned by God (Chapter 40). As concerns the Church, this order was fulfilled by Christ being sent by God, the apostles being sent by Christ, and the bishops being sent by the apostles (Chapter 42). When the bishops are no longer able to fulfill their duties, it is therefore appropriate that "other approved men should succeed them in their ministry" (Chapter 44). The most important consequence of apostolic succession is that all power is kept inside the club so to speak. All power in the early church is in the hands of selected individuals who appoint their own successors. However, in saying this, I do not mean to imply that spiritual power in the form of the Holy Spirit actually flows from God the Father, through Christ, through the apostles, and into the bishops but merely that the bishops believed this to be the case, and they succeeded in convincing the laity to believe it as well.

The power to appoint and ordain successors stands at the basis of what has come to be called apostolic succession. According to this belief, power that originated with God the Father was transferred to the Son through his incarnation. Jesus transferred it to his apostles through his words "Receive the Holy Spirit," especially at Pentecost, when the apostles were filled with the Holy Spirit, as evidenced by tongues of fire that appeared over them (Acts 2:1–4). The apostles transferred this power to their successors through the laying on of hands, and so the process continued through subsequent generations of successor bishops. Throughout the years, the question as to whether there really is an apostolic succession has been the subject of vigorous debate. But again, for our purposes, the question is not whether apostolic succession is actually grounded in fact but whether the successors to the apostles believed that it was.

The power to teach, which is implied by Jesus' command to go out and teach all nations, itself implies that the apostles were in possession of the truth. There would be no point in teaching something if that something were not true. And the power of truth (knowledge) rests on the same foundation as the other powers, namely, on the indwelling of the Holy Spirit. The apostle Paul spoke of the Holy Spirit as the great teacher of spiritual truths (1 Corinthians 2:13). Also, if we are correct in tracing the original concept of the Holy Spirit to Platonic proto-Gnosticism, the Holy Spirit was originally thought to be identical with Sophia, the Greek goddess of wisdom, the source of truth and knowledge. So when a bishop is ordained, he receives a special infusion of the Holy Spirit that provides a kind of access to the mind of God. Such is the sense of the passage from Luke that reports Jesus as saying to his disciples, "Whoever listens to you listens to me; whoever rejects you rejects me; but whoever rejects me rejects him who sent me" (Luke 10:16).

So the early bishops thought that they had been endowed with exceptional power. In his Letter to the Magnesians, Ignatius, bishop of Antioch, wrote, "the bishop, presiding after the likeness of God and the presbyters after the likeness of the council of the Apostles, with the deacons also who are most dear to me, having been entrusted with the deaconate of Jesus Christ" (6:1). Here Ignatius compares the bishop with God himself, and he also alludes to the beginning of a clerical hierarchy where the power granted to the bishop flows downward to the presbyters (an office that later became the priesthood) and then to the deacons. In his Letter to the Smyrnaeans, this analogy between the bishop and God the Father is reiterated: "See that you all follow the bishop, even as Jesus Christ does the Father, and the presbytery as you would the apostles; and reverence the deacons, as being the institution of God. Let no man do anything connected with the Church without the bishop" (8:1). In his Letter to the Corinthians, written around 96 CE, Clement, bishop of Rome, speaks of a quasi-military chain of command that links the bishops to the apostles and the apostles to God (Chapter 37). The laity must obey their bishop just as Christ obeyed the Father and the apostles obeyed Christ (Chapter 42). Ignatius, too, spoke of a duty to obey the bishop. In his Letter to the Magnesians, he wrote,

"Be obedient to the bishop . . . as Jesus Christ was to the Father, and as the Apostles were to Christ and to the Father" (13:2).

## Valentinus

Such was the prevailing backdrop when, around 136 CE, a Christian theologian named Valentinus (100–160 CE) arrived in Rome from Alexandria. Few details are known of Valentinus's life. He may have been born in Alexandria or perhaps Carthage, but he was certainly educated in Alexandria, a city that we earlier characterized as the cradle of Gnosticism. He was a disciple of a man named Theudas, who in turn was a disciple of the apostle Paul, so he arrived in Rome with a certain pedigree. He was highly intelligent and an excellent speaker and writer—facts acknowledged even by his opponents—and he very quickly attracted a wide following, so wide, in fact, that he came very close to being selected bishop of Rome. After being passed over for that office, he founded a school that was instrumental in spreading his views about the nature of Christianity, views that were not only widely accepted but also thoroughly Gnostic. It seems that at first the Valentinian interpretation of Christianity was accepted even among the bishops, who probably saw it as a highly spiritual and at worst harmless movement. But shortly after Valentinus's death, the bishops came to see that Valentinianism posed a lethal threat to Christianity, and they condemned it as a heresy.

What exactly was behind this shift in viewpoint by the bishops? A few years earlier, many of these bishops had supported Valentinus's being named bishop of Rome. Of course, as we will see, there were the usual theological reasons. But I will argue that the real reason behind the shift was that Valentinianism (Christian Gnosticism) threatened the power of the bishops. Worse than that, Valentinianism rendered the office of bishop all but irrelevant. A logical consequence of the Valentinian standpoint was that the bishops were a useless appendage on the Church that could easily be eliminated. This consequence was not apparent at first because Valentinus was a poet who wrote in mystical, metaphorical language. Also, from its beginnings in the Hermetic Lodge in Alexandria, Gnosticism was a movement shrouded in secrecy, and its doctrines were supposed to be kept hidden. But gradually, the realization set in among the bishops that Valentinian Gnosticism was a variety of Christianity that must be stamped out at all costs.

Let us consider the first of the powers outlined above, namely, the power to forgive sins through baptism and penance. This power depended on the interpretation of sin that had come from Judaism. Sin was a product of human willfulness that caused a separation from God. The first sin was committed by Adam, was passed down to his descendants, and must be washed away through baptism before the convert can gain entry to the Christian community. Subsequent sins were the result of evil decisions by the convert himself, and they must be washed away through penance before the sinner could gain entry to the kingdom of heaven. But the Christian Gnostics would have none of this. Sin was not the product of the sinner; rather; it was more the other way around: the sinner was the product of sin. Sin was a factor ingredient in created reality right from the start, and innocent human beings are its victims. Sin is the imperfect residue that was left over from the bungling efforts of the Demiurge in creating the physical world. It is like a fog that confuses the human mind from birth, leading it to stray off course into misery and unhappiness. What is needed to eliminate sin from one's life is not some sacrament called baptism or penance administered by bishops but a healing process that dispels the confusion and restores clarity of vision.

The Gnostic view of sin is a direct consequence of its theory of God. God the Father is conceived as being identical with the Platonic One. Let us consider, for a moment, what this involves. First off, the One, as pure unity, cannot change in any way. If the One were to undergo some kind of change (such as to grow or shrink), then, after the change, the One would have acquired a new attribute (increased or decreased size), and it would no longer be a "one"—it would be a "two." For the same reason, a One cannot be in time—that is, it cannot have a temporal dimension because whatever is in time is constantly changing. Also, of course, it cannot have a spatial dimension because whatever has a spatial dimension has parts, and whatever has parts is not a "one."[2] For these reasons, if God the Father is identical to the One, it cannot be a creator. If it were a creator, it would change during the creative activity. For one thing, it would go from being a noncreator to being a creator. Also, it is hard to see how something without a spatial dimension could create things (e.g., mountains and trees) that are spatial. Through reasoning such as this, the Gnostics concluded that God the Father did not create the universe; in fact, it did not create anything at all. It totally transcends the physical universe.

So if God the Father did not create the universe, then who did? Valentinus selected the Demiurge (the creator deity from Plato's *Timaeus*) to fill this role. Further, Valentinus envisioned the Demiurge as "flowing" from God the Father through a process called emanation, where emanation is not conceived as a creative activity (so it does not result in the Father being a subject of change). One emanation leads to another and that one to another, where each succeeding emanation is less perfect than the one before. Think of a series of cascading waterfalls in a large fountain, where the water gets dirtier with each succeeding cascade. The Demiurge comes at the tail end of a long series of emanations and is so far removed from the Father that it comes on the scene as an ignorant bungler. And the universe that the Demiurge produces reflects all the flaws of its maker. Where God the Father, who is absolutely perfect, is pure oneness, the universe is just the opposite: it is imperfect and suffused with multiplicity. Where the Father is immune from change, the universe is constantly changing; where the Father is outside space and time, the universe is extended in space and time; and where the Father is pure spirit, everything in the universe is made of matter. All this multiplicity and flux causes confusion in the minds of human occupants. These humans are engaged in a constant struggle to return to their home with the Father, but instead they get distracted by such things as the pursuit of wealth, fame, and physical beauty. What is needed is a reliable guide through the obstacle course of material distractions, and such a guide is to be found in the person and message of Jesus Christ, who was sent into the world precisely for that purpose. Individual Christians can find Jesus perfectly well by themselves without any help from the bishops.

Another way that Gnostic Christianity differed from the Christianity of the bishops was in regard to apostolic succession and the hierarchical arrangement consisting of bishops, presbyters, and deacons. The Gnostic community was thoroughly egalitarian, with no clear-cut distinction between laity and clergy and, within the clergy, no permanent distinction between priestly offices. The community did recognize the offices of bishop, presbyter (or priest), and deacon, but the class of individuals who occupied these offices was in constant flux. One day, a certain member of the laity might be called a bishop, another day a deacon, and another day a presbyter, without any special qualification for the office. And these offices were open to everyone without distinction—old men, young women, boys, girls, believers, and pagans. The Gnostic community apparently did recognize the ritual of ordination, but everyone was a candidate for every office. As can be imagined, this arrangement horrified the bishops of the regular church, who reveled in their elite status. Tertullian (ca. 155–240 CE), the early Christian apologist and spokesperson for the bishops, condemned the practice:

> Their ordinations are carelessly administered, capricious, and changeable. At one time they put novices in office; at another, persons bound by secular employment. . . . Nowhere is promotion easier in the camp of the rebels [Gnostics], where even the mere fact of being there is a foremost service. So today one man is bishop and tomorrow another; the person who is a deacon today, tomorrow is a reader; the one who is a priest today is a layman tomorrow; for even on the laity they impose the functions of priesthood.[3]

The Gnostics defended this egalitarian attitude toward religious office by the observation that it reduced envy by lower-status persons for those on a higher level.

A third way Gnostic Christianity differed from the religion of the bishops was in regard to religious truth. Earlier, I characterized Gnosticism by the simple maxim that the truth is to be found within you. The Gnostics claimed to obtain ultimate truth by turning inward to the core of the self. Exactly what this involved is uncertain, but presumably, it included meditation, reflection, and cultivating a receptivity for visions, revelations, and trances. The result was supposed to put the believer into direct contact with the mind of God, and it revealed profound truths that transcended anything that the bishops could claim to have received via apostolic succession. These profound truths are what is otherwise called *gnosis*. The Gnostics did not deny that the bishops had something valuable to teach; they simply held that it was an immature form of truth that could be surpassed through Gnostic practices. Heracleon (ca. 170 CE), a student of Valentinus, wrote "at first people believe because of the testimony of others," but then "they come to believe from the truth itself."[4] Marcus, another student of Valentinus, wrote that he had a vision in which a mystical presence said to him,

> I wish to show you Truth herself; for I have brought her down from above, so that you may see her without a veil, and understand her beauty.[5]

This Truth is none other than God himself. Pagels sums up the idea thus: "self-knowledge is knowledge of God; the self and the divine are identical."[6] Obviously, if Christians can obtain access to God himself simply by acquiring self-knowledge, they have little need for the bishops and their claims to truths derived from contact with the apostles.

Irenaeus (ca. 130–202 CE), bishop of Lyon and archcritic of the Gnostics, tried to shame his opponents by pointing out that their claims to gnosis put them on a higher level than the apostles themselves:

> They consider themselves "mature," so that no one can be compared with them in the greatness of their *gnosis*, not even if you mention Peter or Paul or any of the other apostles. . . . They imagine that they themselves have discovered more than the apostles, and that the apostles preached the gospel still under the influence of Jewish opinions, but that they themselves are wiser and more intelligent than the apostles.[7]

Far from being shamed, the Gnostics would reply that they had indeed gone beyond the apostles in that religious truth was something that continued to develop and blossom, and the Gnostics had access to the fuller truth through gnosis (inner vision). They point out that Christians are divided into two groups: the psychics and the pneumatics. The psychics are souls imprisoned in matter, and they operate on the level of sensory perception, but the pneumatics have escaped their imprisonment and as a result are able to reach deeper, more profound truths that transcend sensory perception. Ordinary Christians, including the bishops, function on the level of psychics, but the Gnostics, who have reached spiritual maturity, function as pneumatics. Because of their immaturity, the bishops are handicapped in two ways. First, they are incapable of grasping the higher truths through gnosis, and, second, they fail to comprehend the secret truths that Jesus communicated to his apostles. The Gnostics could point to the testimony of Mark the evangelist, who reports Jesus as saying to his apostles,

> To you has been given the secret of the kingdom of God, but for those outside everything is in parables; so that they may indeed see but not perceive, and may indeed hear but not understand. (Mark 4:11–12)

For the Gnostics, "those outside" are the psychics, the immature ones, the bishops. They do understand the parables on a superficial level, but the secret, hidden meaning behind the parables lies outside their grasp.

## Emergence of Heresy

The bishops' final response was to condemn the Valentinians as heretics and to burn all their writings—at least all that they could get their hands on. A few writings survived in a clay jar that was found in 1945 by a young man in Nag Hamadi, in Egypt, and these comprise most of the original source materials available to scholars today. This action by the bishops effectively shut down the Valentinian movement, at least for several years, it being hard to run a school when the course materials have gone up in smoke. But we should examine this final response of the bishops more closely, and we can do so by posing two questions: what motivated the bishops to take this final step, and what, exactly, does it mean for a doctrine to be declared heretical?

For the first question, the fact that the bishops burned the writings of the Valentinians strongly suggests that they were threatened by these people. Burning one's opponents' work is a drastic action. It goes far beyond the more moderate response of simply telling one's followers to avoid the Gnostics. Further, it should be clear at this point why the bishops would have been threatened. The Gnostics, who were highly popular, were on the verge of rendering the bishops completely irrelevant, a useless appendage on the Church. They were not needed to forgive sin because sin was not the sort of thing that could be forgiven. The most inconvenient byproduct of sin, guilt, could be relieved simply through acquiring gnosis. When the sinner sees the true cause of sin (the Demiurge) and realizes that he himself is not responsible for it, he no longer feels guilty. The radical egalitarianism of the Gnostics completely undermined the office of bishop and the need for apostolic succession. Anyone who wanted to be a bishop could be one. All that need be done is to spread the word, and that person could be named bishop for a day, for or a week, or whatever. And the bishops' claim to special knowledge through apostolic succession was vitiated by the Gnostics' assertion that gnosis offered a much higher form of knowledge than the bishops could ever hope for. The Gnostics had access to the very highest truth through their direct contact with the mind of God, while the best that the bishops could expect was a kind of indirect access mediated by predecessor bishops and the apostles. What bishop would not be threatened by such a movement? Thus, the response of the bishops to the ever-increasing threat posed by the Gnostics was an action to preserve their own power.

Granted that fear of losing power motivated the bishops to condemn the Gnostics, can we say that this was the *only* motivation? Was it not possible that theological reasons played a complementary role? Even a cursory reading of Irenaeus's massive five-volume work *Against Heresies* suggests that this might be the case. Throughout the work, Irenaeus is engaged in "proving" various theological points: There is but one God (2.1), The world was created by God the Father (II.2), The opinions of the heretics about the Demiurge are untenable and ridiculous (II.19), Perfect knowledge (gnosis) cannot be attained in this life (2.28), Jesus Christ is perfect God and perfect Man (3.19). This focus on proving things and the literary style that accompanies it show that Irenaeus was familiar with Greek logic. He was also at least vaguely familiar with the work of a few Greek philosophers (2.14). Further, his proofs aimed at destroying the doctrines of the heretics are generously sprinkled with emotionally charged language: "blasphemous," "wicked," "ignorant," "monstrous," "audacious," "evil," "deceitful," "nefarious," "impious," "absurd," and "foolish." The Gnostics are "wolves in sheep's clothing," "miserable little foxes," and "agents of Satan," and their doctrines are "filth." Such language gives a kind of steamroller quality to his argument, reinforcing the observation that *Against Heresies* is a thoroughly polemical work. So, this leads us to ask, what, exactly, does "theology" mean to Irenaeus? I think the answer is that for Irenaeus (and for other bishops of the time), theology was a polemical engine fabricated from Greek logic and Greek patterns of expression for the purpose of smashing the doctrines of opponents and thereby increasing their own power. It was not an unbiased theoretical instrument for deepening an understanding of religious beliefs and discovering new ones, although in some cases, this might have been a side effect. So, when we say that in condemning the Gnostics as heretics the bishops were motivated by theological reasons, what this means is that theology disclosed ways of attacking Gnostic doctrines that might not have been seen without it and provided the linguistic machinery to do it. Thus, by using theology to attack the Gnostics, the bishops simply availed themselves of an instrument tailored to increase their own power.

A third motivation that almost certainly operated in the minds of the bishops was that in burning the writings of the Valentinians and declaring them heretics, the bishops were acting to ensure the survival of the Christian church as they knew it. The bishops saw the Valentinians and other Gnostics as a threat to the very existence of the Church, and the main source of that threat was gnosis. For the bishops, gnosis was an inexhaustible source of new "truths," many of which were inconsistent with one another and with truths that had been handed down by the apostles. The Gnostics would enter into trances or experience visions, and immediately they would announce the discovery of something new and profound. The situation was totally out of control, with novel points of doctrine popping up everywhere. For Irenaeus, these so-called verities were little better than hallucinations: "every one of them generates something new, day by day, according to his ability; for no one is deemed 'perfect' who does not develop among them some mighty fictions" (*Against Heresies*, 1.18.1). But in acting to preserve the existence of the Church as they knew it, the operative words were "as they knew it." The Church as the bishops knew it was a quasi-military social structure headed up by bishops. Their pronouncements were to be believed and their orders obeyed as if they had come directly from God. So acting to preserve the Church meant acting to preserve the power of the bishops.

Turning to the second question about what is involved in the act of identifying someone as a heretic, we can begin by noting that religious doctrines in the second century CE did not come supplied with tags marked "heresy" and "orthodoxy." No amount of analysis by a religious scholar would have indicated in which category to place any particular doctrine, whether orthodox or heretical. Christianity was not sufficiently developed to have provided an established standard of orthodoxy. In regard to the bishops and the Valentinians, each side was convinced that his own doctrine represented the "true" Christianity. The bishops held that all authority flows through links in a chain that leads back to the apostles, and the Gnostics held that all authority flows directly from God through spiritual channels that connect the mind of every believer immediately to the mind of God. There is nothing intrinsic to either position that made one superior to the other. There was no Valentinian heresy or Gnostic heresy until some bishop (in this case mainly Irenaeus) stepped forward and declared these doctrines to be heretical. The Valentinians could have retaliated by declaring the bishops to be heretics, but, as we will see shortly, they did not have the clout to do this. So the Valentinian heresy was the creation of the bishops. It did not exist at all until the bishops came forth with their declaration, and when they did so, they raised a wall of separation between themselves and the Valentinians. At that instant, both heresy and orthodoxy came into existence as polar opposites. This action was exactly parallel to what happened in ancient Judaism when Moses erected a wall of separation between monotheism and polytheism, an act that we have dubbed the monotheistic demarcation.

Philosophers of language call declarations, such as the one that created the Valentinian heresy, performative utterances. These are expressions that effect some change or bring something into existence. They are manifestations of power. They are not statements, and unlike statements, they are neither true nor false. Thus, the original utterance by the bishops that the Valentinians are heretics is neither true nor false, but it is a speech act that creates the heresy. Christianity features quite a number of such performative utterances. In the Eucharist, the expressions "This is my body" and "This is my blood" are performative utterances because they are supposed to effect a change in what is originally bread and wine. The expression "I baptize you" is a performative utterance because it is supposed to effect a change in the religious status of the person being baptized. It converts that person into a Christian. The expression "I absolve you," when spoken by a bishop, is supposed to wash away sin from the penitent. The expression "I pronounce you husband and wife" is supposed to create a special relationship between the parties to the marriage, and the expression "I excommunicate you" is supposed to create a separation between the person being excommunicated and the body of the Church. All of these cases represent genuine instances of performative utterances, and the idea that they effect some kind of *symbolic* or *fictional* change appears unproblematic. However, those who believe that these utterances effect a change on the *existential* level open themselves to the charge that their belief amounts to an illusion. It would be an illusion that results from assuming that bishops have some *genuine* power to effect such changes. Arguably, the Valentinians were no more heretics after they were declared to be such than they were before the declaration, but in the eyes of believers accustomed to hearing other performative utterances from their bishops, the Gnostics really became heretics when they were declared to be so.

Why did the bishops win their battle with the Gnostics? Because they were more powerful than the Gnostics. And why were the bishops more powerful? Because they were organized and unified. This organization and unity rested on two factors: uniformity of teaching and a rigid social structure. Irenaeus is proud to point out that it made no difference where a person might be, whether in Germany, Spain, Gaul, Egypt, or Libya: that person would hear the same teaching from any Christian bishop. Just as the sun shining on many places on the earth is one and the same sun, so the teaching of the Church in any of these places is one and the same teaching (*Against Heresies*, 1.10.2). At the time these words were written, this uniformity of doctrine was just in its infancy, and Irenaeus's words were more an aspiration than they were a description, but with the passage of centuries, the aspiration became a reality. The social structure of the Church consisted in the established offices of bishop, presbyter, and deacon and in the requirement of apostolic succession. The relationship between bishop and presbyter and between presbyter and deacon was the same no matter where on the earth one might happen to be, and not just anyone at any time filled these roles. The persons who filled them were *permanently* ordained, and in being so, they were linked through a laying on of hands to earlier apostolic successors and ultimately to the apostles themselves.

These teachings and this social structure count as belief constructs and social constructs, respectively, and, as we have seen earlier, such constructs serve to enhance power. The Gnostics, on the other hand, had no such power enhancers. Their teachings, if not inconsistent, were certainly incoherent and exceedingly complicated, and their social structure was practically nonexistent. The deficient social structure stemmed from the fact that their connection with the deity was highly individualistic and based on individual dreams, visions, and trances. In addition, the bishops succeeded, via performative utterances, in *defining* their doctrine as the orthodox one and the doctrine of the Gnostics as the heretical one, and these definitions quickly took hold in the public mind. If, by chance, the Gnostics had won the battle with the bishops, it seems a virtual certainty that the Christian church would not have survived for long. But that fact has no bearing on our conclusion that the success of the bishops was re-

THE CHRISTIANS: TRINITY COMPLETED

ducible to power and to power alone. The power had different manifestations: sometimes it was raw physical power that burned books, sometimes it was power in the guise of theology, and sometimes it was political power aimed at organization building. But it was still nothing but power.

## Defining Orthodoxy

We are now prepared to introduce new and what I consider more useful definitions of the terms "heresy" and "orthodoxy." The problem with today's lexical definitions of these terms is that when they are projected backward to the second century CE, they become vacuous and question begging. "Orthodoxy: conforming to approved Christian doctrine." "Heresy: deviating from approved Christian doctrine." The problem is that there was no approved Christian doctrine in the second century to serve as a standard. Christian doctrine, including the meaning of the triune God, was in a state of flux. Determining whether a given doctrine was orthodox or heretical required waiting to see whether it emerged victorious in the battle to come. Unfortunately, sometimes the wait was very long, and one could never be completely sure when the battle was over. In place of the standard lexical definitions, I offer two substitutes based on priestly power. They may not provide the level of precision that one might hope for in a definition, but at least they are not completely vacuous:

> Heresy: A doctrine is heretical if, in the opinion of the bishops and their surrogates, it undermines or weakens priestly power.
> Orthodoxy: A doctrine is orthodox if, in the opinion of the bishops and their surrogates, it promotes and strengthens priestly power.

Definitions such as these are usually called theoretical definitions because they depend on a theory—in this case the theory that all religious doctrine (not just Christian) is the product of power. As we proceed through this short survey of Christian heresies, we will keep an eye out for whether these definitions help to make sense of the orthodoxy/heresy distinction. If they do help, and I think they do, that will serve to confirm the underlying theory on which they are based.

Turning to the language of the definitions, the bishops in question included Clement I of Rome, Ignatius of Antioch, Irenaeus of Lyons, and Polycarp of Smyrna. People who arguably stand as surrogates, or stand-ins, include Tertullian of Carthage, Hippolytus of Rome, Origen of Alexandria, and Justin Martyr. Irenaeus wrote the five volume *Against Heresies*, Tertullian authored *Against the Valentinians* and five books refuting the doctrine of Marcion, Hippolytus wrote the seven-volume *Refutation of All Heresies* (only fragments survive), and Justin wrote *Against Marcion*, among numerous other works. Because the declaration of heresy involved a power struggle that went on for many years, it sometimes happened that someone who was originally heralded as an opponent of heresy was later named as a heretic. Such was the fate of Tertullian, who was later in life declared to be a heretic because of his adoption of Montanism. Around the middle of the second century, the writings of individual bishops came to be supplanted by councils, which were gatherings where bishops would meet to discuss articles of faith and act in unison against what were perceived to be threats to the Church. Such councils included the Council of Rome (155 CE and 193 CE), the Council of Ephesus (193 CE), the Council of Carthage (251 CE), and the Council of Iconium (258 CE). The famous First Council of Nicaea (325 CE) declared Arianism to be a heresy.

## A Quartet of Heretics

One way of undermining priestly power is by impeding conversions. A priest with few followers has little power. Such was the effect of the doctrine created by Marcion of Sinope (ca. 88–169 CE). Marcion was a contemporary of Valentinus, and in some ways, his message overlapped the doctrine of the Valentinians and other Gnostics. He held for the view that there is a strict separation between Yahweh, the god of the Jews, and God the Father, the god of the Christians. Simply put, Yahweh is not the Father; they are two distinct gods. Yahweh is the jealous, vengeful god of the Old Testament who constantly punishes humans for their violations of the Law of Moses, whereas the Father is a god of love who treats humans with compassion and mercy and offers them salvation. Yahweh is identical to the Demiurge, the foolish, bungling creator of the universe, whereas God the Father, who resembles the Platonic One, is a completely transcendent entity who stands above the physical universe and all the evil it contains. Further, since Jesus shares the same nature with the Father, Jesus, too, is a transcendent being who stands aloof from the travails of the world. But this puts Jesus above the level of human concern. He is not the sort of person who would attract converts. His position was condemned as heretical by Tertullian in the five-volume work *Against Marcion.*

Marcion's doctrine is otherwise called Docetism, from the Greek *dokeo,* which means "to appear." According to this position, Jesus was a mere appearance. He had no real body. He was never really born; never grew up in a family with a mother and a father; never had childhood friends; never struggled through puberty; never experienced love and rejection, loyalty and betrayal, and pain and sickness; and never died on a cross. He was a kind of phantom, a mental image, that only *appeared* to the apostles. All of this makes sense on the supposition that Jesus was transcendent—not made of matter. However, no prospective convert could ever love anyone so removed from ordinary human experience. Thus, it was necessary that Marcion be condemned as a heretic. The bishops concluded that Jesus did have a real body, but at the same time, they held that he was transcendent. Since transcendent means being independent of matter, by all appearances, the bishops contradicted themselves. They were concerned more with winning converts than with maintaining logical niceties. Ordinary people are rarely troubled by contradictions, especially after they get used to the idea. But it was absolutely essential to maintain the flow of converts. Without it, the power of the bishops would quickly dissipate.

In condemning Marcion, the bishops also declared that God the Father was one and the same being as God the Creator. They synthesized the two gods, and this synthesis eventually made its way into the creed: I believe in one God, the Father almighty, creator of heaven and earth. Furthermore, by joining the two gods, the bishops made it easier to convert Jews, whose religion included the worship of Yahweh the creator. It would be easy for them to transition to God the Father. It would be like walking from one room into another.

Next in our quartet of heretics is a Christian convert named Montanus, and his doctrine is called either Montanism or the New Prophecy. Soon after becoming a Christian, Montanus claimed that he was a channel of the Holy Spirit, that the Holy Spirit spoke through him, and that, as such, he had the power to prophesy. His prophecies were supposed to clear up ambiguities in the message left by the apostles and to update that message. The practice ran parallel, in many ways, with what occurred in Valentinianism. The Holy Spirit in Montanism replaced gnosis, and it provided the basis for new knowledge in the form of prophesies. Just as the new knowledge for the Valentinians was alleged by the bishops to exceed what was taught by the apostles, so the prophesies of the Montanists were eventually found to go beyond the message of the apostles and even the message of Christ.

The prophesies of the Montanists tended to render the bishops irrelevant as teachers because the bishops had no control over what was being prophesized. Even the prophets themselves had no control over it because it was not the flesh-and-blood human who was testifying but rather the Holy Spirit who was testifying through them. As with the Valentinians, the Montanists were thoroughly egalitarian: anyone could be a prophet or a bishop, even women, and this undermined the sacrament of ordination. Even some of the language of the Valentinians turned up in Montanism. The Montanists called themselves *spiritales* ("spiritual ones"), analogous to the pneumatics for the Valentinians, and the ordinary Christians (presumably including the bishops) were *psychici*, analogous to the psychics for the Valentinians. To preserve their own power in the Church, the bishops had little choice but to declare Montanism a heresy. This declaration served to limit the power of the Holy Spirit to providing insights consistent with what the bishops knew to be true.

Another heresy that arose in the early years of the Christian era concerned the relationship between God the Father and God the Son. Theodotus of Byzantium promoted a doctrine called adoptionism whereby Jesus was said to be the adopted son of the Father as opposed to the begotten son. This view appeared to be supported by certain passages in scripture. Paul, in Romans, refers to Jesus, "who through the Spirit of holiness was appointed the Son of God in power by his resurrection from the dead" (Romans 1:4). Jesus was *appointed* the Son of God, and this happened at his *resurrection*. This language seems to suggest that Jesus was adopted by the Father. Further, Acts, quoting the second Psalm, has God saying to Jesus, "You are my son; today I have become your father" (Acts 13:33). The word "today" refers to the day of the resurrection. This passage, too, suggests that Jesus is the adopted son. Yet, in spite of this language, the bishops insisted that Jesus was the begotten son, and they condemned the teaching of Theodotus as heretical. Furthermore, they insisted that Jesus was the begotten son in spite of the fact that the Father lacked the sexual organs to beget anything.

Why was it so important to the bishops that Jesus be the begotten son? The answer seems to be that they considered the status of an adopted son to be something less than that of a begotten son. And why was this important? The answer can only be that as a begotten son, Jesus would be more attractive to potential converts. Jesus would be closer to God the Father and therefore a more appropriate object of worship. Given these considerations, a begotten son would win more converts, and, throughout time, this would augment the power of the bishops. A priest in charge of a large church is typically more powerful than a priest in charge of a small church. Thus, it seems likely that augmenting priestly power was a significant factor in the decision to condemn the doctrine of adoptionism.

One of the more interesting doctrines that arose in these early days of Christianity was the one popularized in Rome by a priest named Sabellius. The doctrine is alternately called Sabellianism, modalism, or dynamic monarchianism, and it holds that Father, Son, and Holy Spirit are not individual beings or substances but aspects, roles, or modes of a single person or substance. The great advantage the theory has is that it largely avoids the problem of tritheism that immediately arises in connection with Father, Son, and Holy Spirit. Each of these entities is said to be God, but since there are three of them, it would appear that there are three gods. However, if we say that these entities are not gods but rather aspects or modes of a single god, then threeness can be persevered while maintaining a monotheistic stance. The danger that confronts this position is the possibility that the three divine entities should coalesce or meld together so that threeness dissolves into oneness. Sabellius seems to have avoided this problem by having the one divine entity, God, fill the three roles at different times. First, God acted as Father (creator), then at a later time as Son (redeemer), and finally in the last stage as Holy Spirit.

To see what is wrong with this theory from the standpoint of a potential convert, imagine such a person asking about Jesus. "Who is Jesus?" she asks. "Is Jesus still alive? Will he answer my prayers?" The Sabellian bishop would reply, "You should not think of Jesus as a person. Jesus is only a role, an aspect, a kind of mask on the face of God. Also, this role may no longer be active. It may have passed over to the Holy Spirit. So, instead of praying to Jesus, perhaps you should address your prayers to the Holy Spirit." But every Christian is set on praying to Jesus, the one who suffered and died for them. If Christians should be told that there is no point in praying to Jesus, the flow of new converts would dry up in no time. With no new converts, the power of the bishops would evaporate. In 220 CE, Sabellianism was declared a heresy by the bishop of Rome, and Sabellius was excommunicated.

## Arius

Among all the doctrines that were declared to be heretical, the one that caused the most upheaval in the early church was undoubtedly the doctrine invented by an Alexandrian priest named Arius. He was opposed most immediately by his own bishop, a man named Alexander. The dispute centered on the relationship between the Father and the Son. Both Arius and Alexander held that both Father and Son were God and that the Son was begotten of the Father. But they differed in the way that Father and Son were said to be God. For Alexander, the Son was God in the fullest sense of being equal to the Father, but for Arius, the Son was God in a lesser sense for the simple reason that he was begotten. This difference follows from the different meanings that Arius and Alexander give to the word "begotten." Arius used the word in the ordinary sense of an activity that occurs in time, so if something was begotten, then there was a time before which that thing was begotten. Thus, since whatever is begotten does not exist before it was begotten, there was a point in time when the Son did not exist. Accordingly, the Son is somehow less than the Father: the Father is eternal, but the Son is not eternal. Alexander, on the other hand, used "begotten" in the sense of an attribute that, in the case of the Father–Son relationship, does not occur in time.[8] He held that the Son was begotten from all eternity. The Father is who he is, specifically a father, from all eternity, and therefore, since fatherhood entails having an offspring, the Father had an offspring (a Son) from all eternity.

Both positions can be seen as inherently inconsistent, that is, as being self-contradictory. Arius holds (along with Alexander) that the Father is "unalterable and unchangeable."[9] But if the Father begets a Son in time, he is subject to alteration and change. He goes from being a God who has not begotten anything to a God who has begotten a Son. This involves a change in status.[10] Also, the Father is said to be a One, a simple being.

He is not a composite of two beings. But if he begets a Son in time, he is a temporal composite. He consists of a God who has begotten nothing sandwiched together with a God who has begotten a Son. As for Alexander, I would argue that the act of begetting is intrinsically an activity that takes time. It is not possible to suck out the time element and then pretend that everything is okay. It is not legitimate to redefine something essentially temporal as something that is nontemporal and then use the new definition to deduce consequences about the original article. If the term "square" is redefined as having circular attributes, then it is easy to prove that square circles are possible. Alexander was apparently aware of this difficulty, for he says that attempts to understand the Son's relationship to the Father, along with many less important topics, are "beyond the capacity of the human mind."[11] It also lies beyond the power of language to express: "It has been shown that the nature of his [the Son's] existence cannot be expressed by language, and infinitely surpasses in excellence all things to which he has given being."[12] Generalizing Alexander's procedure, whenever we are confronted with a contradiction in our theology, all we need do is say that the issue lies beyond the capacity of the human mind to grasp and then proceed as though the problem has been solved.

If we set aside these logical infelicities (after all, there is no indication that the bishops paid any attention to them), we see that each position has its own distinct advantages. Arius's theory (we might call it the *strong Father* position) undoubtedly made the most sense to the average person. It involved no distortions of language, and it interpreted the Father–Son relation in much the same way that human fathers are related to their sons. The human father is the cause of the human son, so, since causes always precede their effects, it is easy to see that the divine Father precedes the divine Son. The divine Father is eternal, whereas the divine Son is not. The divine Father is God in an absolute sense, whereas the divine Son is God in a less-than-absolute sense. Alexander's theory (we might call it the *strong Son* position) does just the opposite. The Son is made equal to the Father in every way. The Son is God to the fullest extent. This makes Jesus, who is identical to the Son, completely and totally God. Therefore, when Christians are worshipping and praying to Jesus, they can rest assured that they are worshipping and praying to God and nothing less than God.

Recalling the definition that orthodoxy is the position that strengthens the power of the bishops, it is clear that both sides could claim to be the orthodox one. Arius could say that his theory would bring more people to church since potential churchgoers must first understand the nature of their god before they pray to him, and his was the theory grounded in common sense. Alexander could say that churchgoers want to pray to a full-fledged god, not a second-rate one, and only his theory offered such an option. Thus, it should come as no surprise that the Arian controversy split the community of bishops right down the middle. But this is a bit of an exaggeration since, as will become clear presently, it appears that the vast majority of bishops did not care a great deal about these theories. But among the bishops who did care, each theory could boast a substantial number of supporters. Assuming that these bishops were the movers and shakers in the Church, there was a genuine sense in which the Arian controversy did split the Church in two. But the one person who was most distressed by this situation was not a bishop at all. It was the emperor Constantine. In 324 CE, Constantine defeated his rival Licinius in the battle of Crysopolis, thus uniting the empire of the east with the empire of the west. But although the Roman Empire was now united geographically, it was not united spiritually, and the lack of such unity could pave the way for political divisions in the future. So Constantine took it on himself to heal the fissure caused by Arianism. Furthermore, since by that time Constantine had become a supporter of Christianity and friendly with many of its bishops, he was in a perfect position to take on this task.

## Council of Nicaea

In the year 325, Constantine issued an invitation to all the bishops in the empire to gather together in the city of Nicaea, in Turkey, about fifty-five miles southeast of today's Istanbul. The invitation went out to 1,800 bishops, and Constantine offered to pay the cost of travel and lodging, but even with that offer, only an estimated 318 bishops showed up—about one-sixth the total number of those invited. For whatever reason, very few bishops from the western empire showed up. Even the bishop of Rome stayed at home. Most of those who came were from the east—Egypt, Palestine, Syria, Asia Minor, and Mesopotamia. One reason for the low turnout could have been lack of interest. Theological technicalities have little relevance to the day-to-day task of running a diocese. The chief purpose of the council was to settle the dispute between Arius and Alexander, and, after a month of contentious debate, the bishops excommunicated Arius and declared his doctrine a heresy. The bishops preferred a strong Jesus to a strong Father. But this decision hardly settled the matter. Constantine gladly accepted the outcome, as he would have if the vote had gone the other way. His chief interest was unity in the sphere of religion, which strengthened the unity of the empire. But Constantine's successor, Constantius II, came out solidly in favor of Arianism or at least a weakened form of it. He drove into exile bishops who favored the outcome at Nicaea, one of whom was Athanasius of Alexandria, who had succeeded Alexander. In the year 357, the third Council of Sirmium reversed the relevant parts of the Nicaea decision, declaring that God the Father is greater than God the Son. The battle between the pro- and anti-Arians continued to rage until the year 381, when the Second Ecumenical Council in Constantinople reaffirmed the doctrine accepted in Nicaea that the Son is equal to the Father.

Arguably, the most important outcome of the Council of Nicaea is that it marked the emergence of political power in Church decision making. Earlier disputes involving charges of heresy had involved one or more bishops against non-bishops, but at Nicaea, it was bishop against bishop. What is political power? Usually, the term refers to the power exerted by nation-states. But political power also exists on the level of individual humans. On this level, political power means having diplomatic skills, knowing how to maneuver; it includes craftiness, elocutionary skills, and knowing how to use coercion effectively and how to strike a bargain. It involves the ability to win trust and make friends and knowing how to cash in on personal debts and how to use friendships to one's advantage. It includes communication skills and knowing how to galvanize a crowd. It includes debating skills, the ability to think on one's feet, and knowing how to put together a good argument. All of these sources of power coalesced at Nicaea to lay the groundwork for the theory of the Trinity. But political power, more than any other kind of power, involves an element of chaos, of unpredictability. What would have happened if more bishops from the west or just more bishops overall had showed up? An analogous question is asked today after every election. Those absent bishops had ideas that were left out of the final equation. What would have happened if such and such bishop had not been so appealing on the podium or had been more effective at framing an argument?

A year prior to the reign of Constantine, the eastern empire was ruled by Diocletian, who subjected Christianity to the bloodiest persecution in its history. When Constantine became emperor, relations with the empire reversed course. In 313, Constantine, together with his coruler Licinius, issued the Edict of Milan, which decriminalized the Christian religion and brought an end to the persecution. Christians, of course, were delighted with this turn of events, and they felt they owed Constantine a huge debt of gratitude. When the Council of Nicaea convened twelve years later, the bishops knew that Constantine wanted a unified church, and they wanted to cooperate with him in bringing this about. But they disagreed among themselves on how this should happen. About twenty-two bishops favored the Arian doctrine, an unknown number (probably sizable), were on the side of Alexander, and what was most likely the majority were undecided. The council was in session for one month, and those days witnessed an intense struggle to gain a majority. Actually, the struggle began even before the council met since it was originally set to open in the city of Ancyra (today's Ankara), but since the bishop of that region was a staunch opponent of Arianism, the Arians persuaded Constantine to switch the location to Nicaea. When the big day arrived, Constantine entered the chamber like a god bedecked in purple, gold, and precious stones and seated himself amid the bishops.[13] One can only imagine the fawning and the posturing to appear in good stead with the emperor. Perhaps if one plays his cards right, he will win a special office in the royal palace or some other plush job. And how best to accomplish that? Come up with a winning formula to solve the Arian problem. The competition was intense, and the more capable bishops used every device they could think of to secure a win. In the end, only two bishops dissented from the majority opinion, and these were banished, and every copy of the *Thalia*, the book expressing Arius's teaching, was burned. The final outcome of the Council of Nicaea was the product of multiple forms of power, all pulling in different directions.

## Nicene Creed

The documentary product of the Council of Nicaea was the first version of the Nicene Creed, a statement of belief incumbent on all Christians to profess. During a span of several years, this first version underwent multiple revisions until it reached today's familiar form. The original version read as follows:

> We believe in one God, the Father, almighty, maker of all things visible and invisible;

This first clause relates to Marcion, who held for two gods, one a transcendent being, the other the Demiurge, an inferior creator god. The bishops are here saying that there is only one god who is also the creator. The problem as to how the Father can remain transcendent while becoming involved in the activity of creating is ignored. The creed continues:

> And in one Lord Jesus Christ, the Son of God, begotten from the Father, only begotten, that is, from the substance of the Father, God from God, light from light, true God from true God, begotten not made, of one substance with the Father, through whom all things came into being, things in heaven and things on earth, who because of us humans and because of our salvation came down and became incarnate, becoming human, suffered and rose on the third day, ascended to the heavens, will come to judge the living and the dead;

In this lengthy clause, the word "begotten" appears three times. How the Father, who lacks sex organs, can beget anything at all is left unanswered. The only kind of begetting that we are familiar with is what is done by humans (and animals), and if the bishops did not intend this, then they should have used a different word to identify the relation between Father and Son. Moving on, the phrase "begotten not made" distinguishes the act of begetting from the act of making. Arius held that begetting was a kind of making, which occurred in time. The bishops are saying that the begetting they have in mind is one that occurs from eternity. They say nothing about how an activity that is *essentially* temporal can occur outside of time. The word "substance" occurs twice, and it derives from Constantine's apparent suggestion (discussed presently) that the bishops interpret the Son as having the "same substance" as the Father. The phrase "true God from true God" responds to Arius's claim that the Son is not a "true God" in the sense that the Father is but only a god in a less-than-true sense. The phrase "light from light" appears to be a reference to the book of Wisdom 7:26, where God is compared with an eternal light. Continuing,

And in the Holy Spirit.

At this point in time, the bishops have no idea what to make of the Holy Spirit. Is it part of the one God, a god unto itself, or something else? Obviously, the bishops have not yet come up with a theory of the Trinity, so they are unable to do anything more than append this brief phrase referring to the Spirit. The creed concludes with a list of anathemas (doctrines declared to be heretical):

> But as for those who say, "There was when he was not" and "Before being born he was not" and that "He came into existence out of nothing" or who assert that the Son of God is of a different hypostasis or substance or is subject to alteration and change—these the Catholic and Apostolic church anathematizes.

All of these positions declared to be heretical were advanced by Arius. Arius held that there was a point in time when the Son of God did not exist, that he was created out of nothing just as things in the world were created, that his substance is not identical with the Father's, and that he was subject to alteration in time. According to this last anathema, the Son is not subject to alteration, but this appears to be inconsistent with the earlier statement that through the Son, "all things came into being, things in heaven and things on earth." Things on earth did not always exist. Therefore, before they existed, the Son was not a mediator in creating the earth, but then he became such a mediator (or cause). This implies alteration. Finally, in this passage, the word "hypostasis" is literally synonymous with "substance." It derives from the two Greek words *hupo* ("under") and *stasis* ("standing"), while "substance" derives from the two Latin words *sub* ("under") and *stare* ("to stand"). I will argue presently that the appearance of "hypostasis" in the creed results from the influence of the Neoplatonic philosopher Plotinus.

Constantine's role at Nicaea was that of supreme civil authority in the empire, and as such, he did not enter into the deliberations, which were about religious matters. But there may have been an exception to this rule. When the discussion turned to the relation between the Father and the Son, to facilitate a resolution to this problem, Constantine appears to have tossed the term *homoousios* into the conversation.[14] The term derives from two Greek words, *homos* (meaning "same") and *ousia* (meaning "substance"). The suggested idea is that the Father is the same substance as the Son. Where did Constantine get this word? I can offer only a likely conjecture. Constantine was an educated man, and he was fluent in both Latin and Greek. He may have studied the philosophy of Aristotle, where the theory of substance is a central (if not *the* central) idea. In any event, the bishops wanted to do whatever they could to please the emperor (besides being their protector, he had foot the bill for the entire council), and that may have motivated them to take the idea seriously. As it turned out, Constantine got what he wanted. *Homoousios* broke the logjam, and in no time the bishops were saying that Father and Son were related as being of the *same substance*. They clinched their "solution" by putting it into the creed. The bishops probably gave little thought at the time to what they were doing since the proposed solution amounted to selecting the central idea in a heathen philosophy and injecting it into the heart of the Christian God. This concern would come back to haunt them a few years later when the complaint was raised that *homoousios* had no grounding in scripture. But after all the storms had passed, *homoousios* emerged as a permanent fixture in the creed.

A more serious concern is that the appeal to *homoousios* really solves nothing at all, and it even exacerbates the problem. To say that two things have identically the same *ousia* is to say that they are literally identical. To say that the Father has the same *ousia* as the Son is to say that the Father *is* the Son. An alternate translation for *ousia* is *being*. If *A* and *B* have the same being, then they are absolutely identical. They differ only in name. No amount of linguistic trickery or obfuscation will rescue the bishops from this result. Adopting the *ousia* terminology effectively forces the bishops back into Sabellianism. If Father and Son should be interpreted as different *modes* of one and the same substance, then some small distinction could be maintained between them. But apart from that, it appears there is no way of preventing Father and Son from commingling. Another possible solution of sorts is to say that Father and Son are *similar* in substance instead of the *same* in substance. This alternative was indeed discussed, but it was rejected because it failed to accomplish the intended result: ensuring that the Son be absolutely equal to the Father.

## Return to Arianism

In 337 CE, Constantius II succeeded his father Constantine I, and because the Arian dispute had erupted once again, in 358 he requested two church councils to again resolve it, one in the east, the other in the west. The council in the west met at Ariminum, and the majority rejected the decision reached at Nicaea and held that the Son was merely similar to the Father. The council in the east met at Seleucia, where the two sides were so bitterly divided that no real decision was reached. The deliberations were fraught with intense political wrangling, many bishops condemned their opponents as being heretics, and at least one bishop was sent into exile. To resolve the split at Seleucia, Constantius ordered yet another council, which met in Constantinople in 360. The council decided to reaffirm the earlier decision reached at Ariminum that the Son is merely similar to the Father, and it also rejected altogether the "substance" language adopted at Nicaea (that the Son is of the same substance as the Father). Interestingly, the council criticized this language as "not being understood by the people"—which, of course, makes sense because putting this language into a creed requests that believers accept a contradiction. The council also rejected the "substance" language as not being grounded in scripture.[15] As a result of the work of this council, Arianism became the new orthodoxy, at least in the eastern empire. This result certainly pleased the emperor because he was himself an Arian (or very close to it).

Still, the Council of Constantinople (360) failed to address the divine status of the Holy Spirit. All it said is that we believe "also in the Holy Spirit, whom . . . Christ our Lord and God, promised to send to mankind as the Comforter." Nineteen years later, the eastern empire had a new ruler, Theodosius I, who was committed to Nicene Christianity. Almost immediately, he took action to eliminate Arianism from the eastern empire by calling for an ecumenical council (which was the second such council, Nicaea being the first) in the city of Constantinople. This was given the name of the First Council of Constantinople, and it met in 381. To ensure that it achieved the "right" result, Theodosius paved the way by making certain political adjustments. Constantinople was solidly Arian, as was its incumbent bishop, Demophilus. Theodosius offered to confirm Demophilus only on condition that he abandon Arianism and accept the Nicene Creed. When Demophilus refused, Theodosius expelled him and appointed Gregory Nazianzus, also committed to Nicene Christianity, in his place. Next, when a group of thirty-six Macedonians (Semi-Arians) showed up, they were refused admission when they declined to accept the Nicene Creed. They surely would have voted the "wrong" way. The third maneuver was to eliminate the threat posed by a certain Maximus, who claimed to be bishop of Constantinople in opposition to Theodosius's appointment of Gregory. Maximus would likely have supported the Arian cause. Once the council was in session, the first order of business was to invalidate Maximus's consecration as bishop. The intensity of the political wrangling is evident in the irregular way that Maximus had been consecrated. One night, prior to the opening of the council when Gregory was ill, a group of conspirators broke into the cathedral and, in complete secrecy, completed the consecration ceremony. They seated Maximus on the Episcopal throne just as dawn was breaking.

The body of delegates having been properly sanitized, the council proceeded to fulfill the emperor's wishes. The Nicene Creed was re-instated as expressing the orthodox position of the entire empire. The words describing the Son as "being of one substance with the Father" were retained, just as in the original Nicene Creed. But new language was inserted describing the Holy Spirit as "the Lord and Giver of life, who proceeds from the Father, who with the Father and the Son together is worshipped and glorified, who spake by the prophets." The Spirit is thus now recognized as the third component in a Trinity, and there is at least a suggestion that the Spirit is equal to the Father and the Son.

## Influence of Plotinus

The word "hypostasis" does not appear in this version of the creed as it does in the original Nicene version because the statement of anathemas (where the word was included) has been deleted. But it was soon adopted to explain the identities of Father, Son, and Spirit. As a result of using *homoousios* to explain the underlying reality of Father, Son, and Spirit, the three tend to merge together into a single undifferentiated unit. To give each of them a distinct identity, they were each said to be a hypostasis, where "hypostasis" was equated with "person." Thus, we end up with a Trinity consisting of three *persons* in one God. Credit for the work of using "hypostasis" to explain this feature of the Trinity goes to three bishops known as the Cappadocian fathers.

The Cappadocian fathers, who were all about the same age, were Basil of Caesarea, his brother Gregory of Nyssa, and their close friend Gregory of Nazianzus (who had been appointed patriarch of Constantinople by Theodosius). The three bishops were well versed in Greek philosophy, and as such, they were almost certainly familiar with the work of the Neoplatonist philosopher Plotinus (203–270 CE). Plotinus's work is very closely tied to the work of Plato, and overlaps it in many ways. According to Plotinus, the ultimate principle of reality is what he calls the One. From the One, a second principle emanates, called Intellect, and from Intellect emanates a third principle called Soul. Each of these principles is called a hypostasis, where "hypostasis" has the same etymology in Greek as "substance" has in Latin.[16] Now a loose reading of the central work of Plotinus, the *Eneads*, might lead one to see a resemblance between these three principles (which are a little like divinities) and the Father, Son, and Holy Spirit of the Christian Trinity. I think it highly likely that is exactly what the Cappadocians did, and that is what led them to apply the term "hypostasis" to the three members of the Trinity for the purpose of keeping them distinct. In a letter to a certain Count Terentius, Basil wrote,

> I shall say that essence (ousia) is related to person (hypostasis) as the general to the particular. Each one of us partakes of existence because he shares in ousia while because of his individual properties he is A or B. So, in the case in question, ousia refers to the general conception, like goodness, godhead, or such notions, while hypostasis is observed in the special properties of fatherhood, sonship, and sanctifying power. If then they speak of persons without hypostasis they are talking nonsense.[17]

In reference to the Trinity, what Basil is saying is that Father, Son, and Holy Spirit exist insofar as they partake in *ousia*. In this respect, they are the same. But they are individuals insofar as they are hypostases. In this context, a hypostasis is a kind of second-level substance that sits on top of *ousia*, the primary substance. Every kind of substance confers individuality. Thus, the Trinity, as grounded in *ousia*, is an individual unto itself. But the components, Father, Son, and Spirit, insofar as they are hypostases, are individuals within the larger unit. Basil links the idea of hypostasis with the idea of person almost by definition. Within the Trinity, "hypostasis" is synonymous with "person."

So does this maneuver involving *ousia* and hypostasis save the Trinity from being rationally inconsistent? I think not. From the quoted passage, it is clear that Basil is interpreting the problem of the Trinity as a case of the ancient problem of the one and the many—which it may well be. Cast in terms of language, the problem is, how can we use a single term, such as "man," to refer to many individuals, such as Tom, Dick, and Harry? "Man" is the *one* general term, "Tom," "Dick," and "Harry" are the *many* particular terms. Both Plato and Aristotle worked on this problem. Aristotle answered it in terms of his theory of substance and accidents. One substance, call it "manness," can receive many accidental forms (accidents), such as location, size, color, shape, weight, having a skill, being educated, and so on. Depending on the accidents that the substance receives, the substance becomes Tom, Dick, or Harry. The substance serves as the *substratum* for the accidents; in other words, it stands under the accidents—which, as we have seen, is the meaning of "substance" (*sub + stare*). Plato addressed the problem of the one and the many in terms of his theory, presented in the *Timaeus*, of the receptacle and the forms. One receptacle can receive many different combinations of forms. This theory was undoubtedly the inspiration for Aristotle's theory.

Basil is attempting to solve the problem of the Trinity in basically the same way. He is using *ousia* as the one substratum for the many (in this case three) hypostases. But there is a significant difference between what Basil is doing and what Plato and Aristotle did hundreds of years before him. For Basil, one substance (*ousia*) serves as the substratum for other *substances* (the three hypostases). This would be like saying that one actual man could underlie three actual men (Tom, Dick, and Harry). It is like saying that there is one actual being called manness or humanity and that every individual man rides piggyback on top of it twenty-four hours per day. It is nearly impossible to imagine such a thing. And this may be the reason why neither Basil nor the other two Cappadocians developed any theory to explain how it could happen. It would have to be a theory to explain the impossible. Another important point that Basil sloughs over is the identification of hypostasis with person. In what way can "hypostasis" be synonymous with "person"? From its etymology, "hypostasis" is synonymous with "substance." But surely, "substance" and "person" are not synonymous. Granted, Plotinus, who was probably the inspiration for Basil, used "hypostasis" in a special way to denote One, Intellect, and Soul, but he gave an extensive explanation for this use. Basil gives no explanation for identifying "hypostasis" with "person." The upshot of this analysis is that the work of the Cappadocian fathers fails to assure the individuality of the three components of the Trinity or to explain their identity as persons.

We are left with the inevitable conclusion that the Christian notion of the Trinity is mired in inconsistency. We are left with three entities, Father, Son, and Holy Spirit, who are said to be one God. They are of the same substance, *homoousios*. They have the same *being*. This can only mean that they are identical, and they differ only in name. We must accept the conclusion that three is one—which in any language is self-contradictory. But this conclusion is basically acknowledged by Church thinkers when they say that the Trinity is a mystery. The two greatest theologians that Christianity has produced, Augustine and Thomas Aquinas, agree on this point. Augustine holds that sin has corrupted the human mind so that we cannot understand the doctrine of the Trinity, but we can hope to understand it in the next life.[18] He admits that "among all these things that I have said about that supreme trinity . . . I dare not claim that any of them is worthy of this unimaginable mystery."[19] According to Aquinas, "It is impossible to attain to the knowledge of the Trinity by natural reason."[20] Such knowledge is an article of faith. In response, I would argue that it is extremely dangerous to hold that important truths are beyond the capacity of the human mind. Could it possibly be true that square circles exist but that our minds are too week to grasp this truth? If we admit such a thing, then we undermine all mathematics, all logic, and human communication becomes impossible.

However, to cut some slack for those bishops, who, during a span of three centuries, worked to produce the formulation of the Trinity, an argument can be made that they were simply not concerned with rational consistency. What they were concerned with is human feeling. Such a conclusion is supported by every declaration of heresy that we have considered. These include Valentinianism, Marcionism, Adoptionism, Sebellianism, and Arianism. According to Valentianism, God is modeled after the Platonic One and is so far removed from ordinary life that it is not even conceivable by the human mind. No such God could ever be the object of human feelings. For Marcionism, Jesus had no real body, he never suffered a horrible death, and he never experienced things the way ordinary people experience them. Potential converts could never relate to such a person. Adoptionism held that Jesus was the adopted son, as opposed to the begotten son, of the Father. As an adopted son, Jesus was thought to have no "real" connection with the Father, so in praying to such a Jesus, one is not "really" praying to God. Much better to have a Jesus who is a begotten son. Such a Jesus is the real thing. Sabellianism taught that Jesus is not God, in any complete sense of the term, but just a mode, or mask, that appears on the face of the Father. It is impossible to have feelings of love or tenderness for a mask or role, so this theory had to go. Finally, Arianism held that Jesus was not absolutely equal to the Father because he was not coeternal with the Father. He was created by the Father, just like other creatures, and as such, he would not elicit the strongest feelings. Praying to Jesus would not be quite as good as praying to the Father, but it is Jesus, not the Father, who is supposed to be the central figure in Christianity.

In opting for feelings over logic, the bishops made the right decision as concerns self-preservation. Today, more than a billion Christians revere the deity called the Blessed Trinity, and they give nary a thought to whether they are worshipping a contradiction. The Father is the divine protector, creator of heaven and earth, who loves every one of his human creatures. Jesus is the savior who died for sinners and who brings salvation to those who believe in him. And the Holy Spirit is the comforter who brings solace to those in despair and wisdom to guide them on their pathway through life. The Christian god, the Trinity, was assembled specifically for the purpose of calling forth good feelings, and it is immensely successful in doing this, even though it makes no sense. The good feelings elicited by the Christian god are one of the chief reasons for Christianity's survival through 2,000 years, and the bishops have been among the principal beneficiaries.

## Summary and Conclusions

According to the account given here, the Trinity is a construct, a fabrication of human creativity stretching over 300 years. The story begins with the work of Paul the apostle, who assembled the three basic components from materials taken from renegade Judaism, Middle Platonism, and Egyptian Hermeticism. Paul introduces these components in his epistles, which are the earliest writings in Christianity. Most of the epistles mention every one of them, where they are presented as objects of prayer, worship, and sacrifice. But by the end of his life, Paul left no explanation as to what, exactly, these three components were. Were they gods? Were they features of a single god? Were the Son and the Spirit creations of the ineffable Father? It took 300 years for the bishops to work out answers to these questions, and much of this work involved declarations of heresy. Each such declaration was an incremental step in the fabrication of the Christian god. The Valentinian heresy settled the question of whether God is absolutely aloof from the world, the response to Marcion held that the Father created the world and that the Son is actually involved with the world and not a mere appearance, and the heresy of Theodotus settled the question of whether Jesus is the begotten son or the adopted son of the Father. Declaring the position of Sabellius a heresy implied that the Father, Son, and Holy Spirit are not mere modes of existence, and the Arian heresy resolved the issue of whether the Son is in some way less than the Father or is absolutely equal to the Father. With each of these steps, one more piece was added to the puzzle that became the Christian god, and all of this implies that the Christian god is a construct fashioned by human hands.

In opposition to this conclusion that the Christian god is a construct, one might argue that there is an independent deity who quietly worked behind the scenes guiding the bishops in their thinking and ensuring that they reached the right decision about all these heresies. It is this entity, it will be argued, that is the true Christian god. But such an argument is clearly circular. It implies that we know something about the Christian god apart from the 300-year-old process that led to its formulation. It implies that we somehow have access to this deity without referring to all the arguments that tell us what it is. Any circular argument is fatally flawed. However, if we ignore the circularity problem for a moment, the argument also violates the principle underlying Ockham's razor: if an event or series of events can be explained in terms of natural causes, then that is the explanation we should accept. In accord with this principle, it makes perfectly good sense to say that the triune God of Christianity was literally brought into existence through the wrangling of the bishops during a 300-year period. There is no need to assume that another God exists alongside the bishops that guided their thinking. The bishops by themselves were quite capable of reaching the decisions that they reached without any help from the outside. The overall conclusion is that the Christian god is a construct, a construct created by the bishops, and not some hidden entity lurking behind their work.

Further, the Christian god is the product of power, specifically the power of the bishops. The bishops exercised their power in many ways. Anyone who disagreed with them or who worked to undermine their power was declared to be a heretic, and the heretic was excommunicated. If a heretic had written anything, the bishops burned it. After Nicaea, the power of civil authority reinforced the power of the bishops. Constantine assisted the bishops in burning the writings of the Arians and in banishing those bishops who supported this doctrine. Another way the bishops exercised power was to convince the faithful that they actually had the powers that they claimed to have. The bishops claimed to have the power to forgive sins and to excommunicate heretics, and that implied the power to shut the gates of heaven to anyone who disagreed with them. The bishops claimed to be the voice of God, so they appeared to the faithful as the definers of absolute truth. Further, the bishops claimed to have the exclusive power to consecrate new bishops, so they had the power to ensure that their views of orthodoxy were maintained into the future. The creation of the triune God of Christianity exemplifies the theory developed by Michel Foucault that power produces knowledge. (This theory is discussed in the next chapter.) The doctrine of the triune God is purported to be knowledge, and this doctrine is the product of power—the power of the bishops who created it.

According to the theory advanced in this book, the belief that the Christian god is an actually existing entity not dependent on the power of the bishops is an illusion. How did this illusion become so ingrained in Christian culture? The doctrine of the Trinity entailed an outright contradiction, but countless bishops during a period of 300 years assured the faithful that it was true, and everyone believed the bishops. Also, it was included in prayers such as the Nicene Creed and the Apostles' Creed (prayers that were repeated over and over), it was mentioned in liturgical practices that were attended regularly, and the threat of excommunication and the loss of a heavenly reward terrified anyone who might dare to doubt it. All of these influences led to the general acceptance of the Trinity. Parents would teach it to their children, friends and relatives would assure one another of its truth, and every catechism referred to it as a core belief. Since all heretical writings had been destroyed, there was nothing that anyone could point to that might challenge the belief. In due course, belief in the existence of the triune God became a truth that was considered obvious. Is the sky blue? Of course it is. But if belief in the triune God is an illusion, then every belief that depends on it is equally an illusion. These include believing that the bishops have the power to teach, the power to forgive sins, the power to ordain, the power to excommunicate, the power to declare a doctrine heretical, and the power to celebrate the Eucharist. All of these beliefs feed into the hope for a heavenly reward after death, and they assuage the fear of burning in hell. In the terminology introduced earlier, belief in the independent existence of the triune God is called a factitious illusion because it is created by humans (bishops). Further, because its principal object (God) involves no empirical content, this kind of illusion is especially difficult to undermine. There is no sensory evidence that might falsify it, which is what most of us depend on in our daily lives to validate or invalidate something.

Claiming that the Trinity is the product of priestly power and that it was created for the purpose of promoting priestly power might suggest that all bishops are power-driven fanatics. There are at least two ways of looking at this issue. First off, from the earliest days of Christianity, the bishops were as much victims of their illusion as they were causes of it. The vast majority of bishops were fervent believers in the message of Christianity. From the time they were little boys, they were taught that Jesus came down from heaven, became flesh, and died to save humankind from sin. They were taught that the Christian church exists for the purpose of continuing the process of salvation and that bishops play a key role in this process. Thus, when they agreed to become bishops themselves, they saw themselves as stepping into one of these roles. They envisioned a life of self-sacrifice devoted to the goal of getting souls into heaven. Yet, perhaps unbeknownst to them, when these men signed on to becoming bishops, they were tying themselves to an institution that was aimed at promoting priestly power, and even if they were vaguely aware of that fact, there was nothing they could do to change it. Thus, in spite of their saintly motives, the bishops would be working unwittingly to promote their own power. Every official task they would perform, every celebration of the Eucharist, every sermon they would give, every ordination they would participate in, every sin they would forgive would strengthen the institution they had joined, and it would thereby promote the power of the bishops who were pivotal to its operation. Also, as the institution got stronger, so did belief in the triune God that stood at the very center of it. Thus, we have here another confirming instance of our overriding theme that the chief function of every priest is to create gods and to sustain them in existence.

The other way of looking at the power issue recognizes that some bishops were indeed power-hungry fanatics. In 1492, Rodrigo Borgia paid enormous bribes to become bishop of Rome (Pope Alexander VI), and he used the office to enrich himself and his family, becoming one of the most powerful men on earth. Pope Urban VI (1378–1389) was so intoxicated with power that when he got word of a conspiracy to depose him, he had six cardinals arrested, tortured, and executed. These are just two examples out of many that could be cited, but they point up the fact that for many bishops, power was the whole point of holding office. In light of the adage that power corrupts, we should hardly be surprised at this outcome. But from the earliest times, even lower-echelon bishops enjoyed the benefits of their office, so it is likely that they, too, had a thirst for power. One kind of power that every bishop could look forward to having is what might be called the power of importance. By wearing distinctive garments and an impressive-looking hat, bishops advertised the message, We aren't just ordinary folks; we are important; we speak to God. Bishops had social status. Everyone respected them, even officials in civil government. They were invited to important events, state dinners, public affairs of all sorts, coronations (where they officiated), funerals, holiday festivities, weddings, and, of course, religious councils and festivals. They could expect gifts and honoraria for prayers, masses, and favors bestowed. Everyone wanted to be their friend and to be seen in their company.

In 313 CE, Constantine issued the Edict of Milan, which decriminalized the Christian religion. This action broke down the wall of separation that had existed between Christianity and civil government. Following the First Council of Nicaea (325 CE), which declared Arianism to be a heresy, Constantine acted in the spirit of this edict when he drove Arius into exile along with the two bishops who followed his teaching. This marked the first time in history that secular power was used to enforce Christian doctrine. Several decades later, in 380, Theodosius, who was committed to the Nicene version of Christianity, together with his two corulers, issued the Edict of Thessalonica, which declared Nicene Christianity to be the official religion of the Roman Empire. From that date forward, given the cooperation of the emperor, the bishops had at their disposal the most powerful military force on the planet. Theodosius himself acted to suppress all deviant forms of Christianity that opposed Nicene orthodoxy. These sects were not allowed to assemble, to spread their teachings, or to ordain bishops. He also suppressed all forms of polytheism, including worship of the Roman gods, by abolishing their holidays and closing their temples. These actions obviously promoted the growth of orthodox Christianity and increased the power of its bishops. The Edict of Milan also worked to augment the power of the bishops by allowing the Church to own land openly and legally. This paved the way for gifts of land by kings, emperors, and wealthy individuals as a kind of payback for favors rendered and perceived benefits received. The Lateran Palace in Rome is thought to have been a gift from Constantine.

Prior to the Council of Nicaea, Constantine probably had an understanding with the bishops, at least an implicit one, whereby if they assisted him in settling the Arian controversy and unifying the empire spiritually, he would assist them in promoting orthodox Christianity throughout the empire. This was the first step in what would become a grand symbiotic relationship between civil authority and religious authority that lasted for centuries. The way it would often work is that the bishops would confer God's stamp of approval on a certain ruler in exchange for gifts of land and property. The stamp of approval was given by having a bishop anoint the designated ruler at the beginning of his reign and then receive the gift later on. The anointing ritual would often involve the bishop placing a crown on the head of the ruler, as depicted in countless paintings and works of art. This arrangement paid off in a big way hundreds of years later when Pope Stephen II traveled all the way to Paris to anoint Pepin the Short (the son of Charles Martel and the father of Charlemagne) as king of the Franks. Pepin reciprocated two years later (in 756) by donating to the Church a very large section of land stretching from Ravenna (close to the eastern coast of today's Italy) to Rome (close to the western coast). This land grant, which has come to be called the Donation of Pepin, marked the first time that the pope became an official temporal ruler, and it set the stage for the creation of the Papal States. By this time, the Church of Rome was well on its way to becoming one of the most powerful and richest organizations on earth.

# CHAPTER EIGHT
# POWER

The word "power" is one of the most commonly used words in the English language, but users of the word rarely have any understanding of its exact meaning, nor have they even thought about it. Plato, in one of his later dialogues, ties the meaning of the word to the concept of being. He equated being to the power of acting and being acted on:

> Anything which possesses any sort of power to affect another, or to be affected by another, if only for a single moment, however trifling the cause and however slight the affect, has real existence: and I hold that the definition of being is simply power.[1]

In other words, if something exists, then it has the power to act on something. And if something has the power to act on something, then it exists. Plato does not develop this idea any further, and he raises the question in only one dialogue, but the insight has profound implications. Being is intrinsically active. This thought underlies the interactive theory of perception introduced in the next chapter.

In this chapter, I present a brief sketch of the theories of four philosophers who are known for their theory of power. These are Thomas Hobbes (1588–1679), Friedrich Nietzsche (1844–1900), Michel Foucault (1926–1984), and Alfred North Whitehead (1861–1947). The first three disclose the connection between power and human life, including human subjectivity. Whitehead's theory resembles Plato's later insight in that it extends to all of reality, but only the part of the theory that relates to miracles and divine power is considered in this chapter. The purpose of this inquiry is not just to place in historical context the treatment accorded in this book to the concept of power but also to provide additional insights that may serve to enrich it.

## Hobbes

Thomas Hobbes is known for having authored *Leviathan*, universally recognized as one of the most influential books on political philosophy. Arguably, the central concept in *Leviathan* is that of power:

> I put for a general inclination of all mankind a perpetual and restless desire of power after power, that ceaseth only in death. (*Leviathan*, 11)

The reason why Hobbes sees power as something everyone wants is because power is needed to satisfy the passions. The two chief passions are desire, which draws a person toward something, and aversion, which repels a person away from something. Just as good is the object of desire, so evil is the object of aversion. Good and evil are equivalent, respectively, to pleasure and pain. So the way it works for Hobbes is that the passions provide the *object* to be obtained or avoided, and power provides the *means* for actually obtaining or avoiding that object. For example, our passion called desire might identify an article of clothing as something to be obtained, but we need power (in this case money) to actually obtain it. Every person alive is the subject of desires and aversions, and the operation of these passions is just as necessary as the operation of a machine. We cannot choose that our passions suddenly stop working, and as long as we are alive, they determine how we behave in every situation.

Hobbes spends a good deal of time in *Leviathan* showing how a person should grow and expand his or her power. Most people start out with a certain amount of natural power, which consists of "the eminence of the faculties of body or mind; as extraordinary strength, form [beauty], prudence, arts, eloquence, liberality [generosity], nobility" (*Leviathan*, 10). These can be used as the basis for acquiring additional powers, which are called instrumental powers. The greatest of the instrumental powers is acquired by attaching to oneself supporters of various kinds. "Therefore, to have servants is power, to have friends is power: for they are strengths united" (*Leviathan*, 10). Additional instrumental power is to be had through riches, reputation, success, affability, knowledge of the sciences, and the acquisition of instruments of war, such as fortifications and weaponry (*Leviathan*, 10). All of these generate either love or fear in the minds of others, and both are varieties of power. In terms of the theory I am advancing in this book, groups of friends, money, reputation, weapons, and so on are all constructs of one kind or other. So what Hobbes is doing here is showing how constructs can be used to augment one's power.

One of the best ways of expanding one's power is by appropriating it from others. Hobbes lists a great number of measures we may take to accomplish this (*Leviathan*, 10). We can ask them for help, obey them, give them gifts, flatter them, show them signs of love or fear, praise them, appear humble before them, believe (or appear to believe) what they say, rely on them, ask them for advice, agree with them, and imitate them. What this comes down to is that we appropriate the power of others by manipulating them. Manipulation involves creating illusions, being disingenuous, pretending to be other than what we are. So creating illusions is a natural outcome of power maximization. All of us are compelled, as if by a law of nature, to maximize the meager power that we are born with, and this leads us to create illusions.

In a remarkable passage from one of his books, *De Homine* (IX, 21), Hobbes compares human life to a long-distance footrace, a footrace that ends only in death. He renders this comparison plausible by showing that we experience the same emotions in everyday living as a runner experiences on the track. We feel glory when we notice that we are ahead of others, we feel humility when we notice that others are ahead of us, we feel hatred when we are beholden to another runner, we feel repentance if we should have to turn back, we feel hope when we get a spurt of new energy, we feel despair when we are weary, we feel envy when we think of ourselves in the place of a runner ahead, we feel anger when we are confronted with a sudden obstacle, we want to weep when we fall down on the track, we want to laugh when we see another runner fall, we feel pity when we see another runner lose ground unfairly, we feel misery when we continually see others pass us up, we feel felicity when we see ourselves continually pass up others, and if we should leave the course altogether, we die. Hobbes's point is that life is constant competition. We are all stuck in this race to the death, and there is nothing we can do about it. Winning is everything, and we will do absolutely anything within the realm of the possible to accomplish that goal.

Competition is a sure sign of the operation of power, and we can see it in religion as much as in other avenues of life. Going back in time as far as possible, there was almost certainly competition among rainmakers and among those who would cure disease. When rain or the restoration of health did not come after an impressive performance, the loser would be replaced by someone with more powerful gods. In ancient Egypt, there was intense competition between Akhenaten and the pharaohs who promoted Amun, Re, and the standard pantheon. This is evident by the way Akhenaten sent workers out in the field to deface the images of these other pharaohs. The same thing happened in reverse when Tutankhamun assumed power and his sculptors defaced the images of Akhenaten. Among the ancient Hebrews, there was competition between Moses and the proponents of Baal, and many lives were lost over the struggle for monotheism. In Christian times, there was competition between the members of the early Jesus movement and the Jews whom the former were instructed to convert, and even within the Jesus movement, there was competition between Paul and the other apostles. After the Reformation, the competition between Protestants and Catholics is familiar to everyone. Thus, the idea that religion operates in an atmosphere of peace and harmony without the element of power belies the facts.

In any kind of competition, the one with the greatest power is the one who wins. It is therefore essential to have power. Thus, it is no wonder that Hobbes describes the general inclination of mankind as "a perpetual and restless desire of power after power, that ceaseth only in death" (*Leviathan*, 11). Yet for many people, having power seems not to be a major concern. They care practically nothing about how much power they have. How is this to be explained? The simplest answer may be to appeal to the footrace metaphor. When those in the lead see someone approaching from the rear, they give an extra spurt of energy to stay ahead. This teaches those behind that it is pointless to strive to get ahead because whatever they do will be matched by an extra effort from the leaders. Those bringing up the rear eventually come to see themselves as losers, and they never do very much to improve their position in the race. But for those in the front, power is all-important. If someone ahead should falter, that leaves an opening for a runner behind to move up. It creates a power vacuum just waiting to be filled, and the leaders are always alert to the occurrence of a power vacuum because it presents an opportunity that may not come along again.

The same thing is to be found in religion. Rank-and-file religious leaders are often unconcerned about power, and they go about their duties like those filling any ordinary job. For this reason, the laity see the role of the priest as the epitome of relaxation and tranquillity. But for those holding the higher offices, the competition can be intense. Bishops, both Catholic and Protestant, have been competing among themselves for centuries regarding such issues as what constitutes orthodox teaching, who should be promoted to some higher office, and who would be elected pope. In ancient times, the Jewish high priest was in competition with Roman officials and later with members of the emergent Jesus movement. With Protestant evangelicals, competition is most evident among the televangelists, where the primary goal is bringing in the most money. There we see marketing strategies, brand names, punch lines ("ask big, receive big"), project managers, full-time accountants, lawyers, and software designers whose goal is to make raising money online as simple and as easy as possible.

Hobbes's view of life as competition is illustrated in the likely way that religion first emerged. The people in the Neolithic period were driven to augment their power in the tribe in any way possible. Those with ordinary skills constructed farm implements and spears, while the more creative ones invented imaginary beings called gods. These inventors then created the illusion that the gods really existed, that they controlled the weather and the fertility of seeds, and that they (the inventors) had the unique ability to bargain with the gods for the benefit of the tribe as a whole. This illusion greatly augmented their power in the tribe, and they expanded it further by creating fetishes, ritual dances, rattles and drums that would attract the attention of the gods, and special garments made of animal skins and bones that alerted everyone that the wearer was endowed with special abilities. These latter artifacts Hobbes called instrumental powers. The religions that came later featured more gods and a countless number of instruments, including temples, rituals, prayers, sacred books, and holy artifacts.

From a Hobbesian standpoint, religion is a product of the combined operation of power and the passions. The passions, for Hobbes, are the result of the motion of tiny particles in the human body, and the motion of these particles, Hobbes argued, is governed by the laws of nature. It would appear, then, that religion, too, is somehow governed by the laws of nature. This idea leads us to ask whether religion arises in history with the same kind of regularity as avalanches in snowy mountains and flowers in spring meadows. The invention of gods presents such an obvious opportunity for a clever person to increase his or her power that it seems almost necessary that someone would eventually come up with the idea. Once this person has convinced his fellows that he has the power to bargain with those gods for their benefit, unlimited riches can be expected. Con artistry has been around practically from the beginning of time, and religion is just a subtle form of that ancient craft. The practice of con artistry will likely be around for many years to come, and so will religion.

## Nietzsche

Power plays as big a role in Nietzsche's later philosophy as it does in Hobbes's thought. One of the main differences between the two theories is that for Hobbes, power is a means to an end, while for Nietzsche, power is an end in itself. Toward the beginning of one of his later works, there is an often-quoted passage that reads,[2]

> What is good? Everything that heightens the feeling of power in man, the will to power, power itself.
>   What is bad? Everything that is born of weakness.
>   What is happiness? The feeling that power is *growing*, that resistance is overcome.
>   Not contentedness but more power; not peace but war; not virtue but fitness (Renaissance virtue, *virtù*, virtue that is moraline-free).

Here, Nietzsche identifies the good with power. Power is good because it feels good, it enriches life, it intensifies life, it makes life worth living. Power itself and the feeling of power are closely related, but they are not identical. A person can have power but not feel anything, as, for example, if the person is asleep or daydreaming. But normally, people who have power also experience the feeling of power on many occasions. Having power is what causes the feeling of power. This passage also ties power to the activity of willing. The phrase "will to power" was undoubtedly suggested to Nietzsche by Arthur Schopenhauer, whose book *The World as Will and Representation* was highly influential on the young Nietzsche. Schopenhauer held that will is the only truly real thing we can know. For Nietzsche, will became the source of power and the foundation of life. "Life simply *is* will to power."[3] Also, it is through willing that we become aware of our power. For example, digging a large rock out of a flower bed requires a concentration of the will. We may pry at the rock from many different angles, and only after a lengthy struggle does the rock come loose.

Nietzsche says that happiness is the feeling that power is growing and that resistance is being overcome. For an example, consider the activity of climbing a mountain. At the beginning of a climb, things are usually easy, but soon the grade becomes steeper, and impediments abound. Exhaustion sets in. Putting one foot ahead of the other demands the greatest strength of will. Eventually, the mountain is conquered. Actual climbers have reported, "When you reach the top, you feel incredible." "You feel empowered and as though you could do anything." There is "an awesome sense of accomplishment and freedom." The experience is "life affirming, one of my proudest achievements." "Nowhere else in life do I feel more alive." This is the happiness that Nietzsche speaks of that results from striving to overcome resistance. Of course, it represents an extreme form of it. Other forms of the very same experience come from raising a child and attending her wedding, carving a statue from a block of stone and then standing back to appreciate it, writing a poem and reading it afterward, building a room addition on one's home and then living in it, developing a business and enjoying its success, or running for political office and winning. All involve will to power overcoming resistance.

The last sentence in the passage quoted above suggests that will to power is closely associated with values. The title of Nietzsche's unfinished book on the subject was *The Will to Power: Attempt at a Revaluation of All Values*. When Nietzsche equates happiness not with peace but with war, he does not mean a war involving guns and bombs but a war of thinking people against what he considers the false values of the age. These false values include anything that undermines the wholesomeness of life, including holiness, pity, whatever devalues the human body, meekness, humility, pettiness, envy, resentment, revenge, otherworldliness, self-sacrifice, faith, unquestioning obedience, piety, and herd values. All of these amount to cases of resistance that will to power must fight to overcome.

Nietzsche recommends replacing false values with what he calls Renaissance virtues, meaning the virtues and values of ancient Greece and Rome that were reintroduced into European culture during the Renaissance. In Italian, *virtù* (Latin *virtus*) means "power." By virtues that are moraline-free, Nietzsche means virtues free of corrupt morals. These Renaissance virtues include respect for reason and science, freedom, cheerfulness, graciousness, honesty, pride, nobility, courage, magnanimity, health, beauty, and strength.

Not every person manifests the same level of power, and those who direct their power to self-mastery and the striving for excellence have the greatest will to power. Those who are seriously deficient in will to power are deemed to be corrupt:

> I call an animal, a species, or an individual corrupt when it loses its instincts, when it chooses, when it prefers, what is disadvantageous for it. . . . Life itself is to my mind the instinct for growth, for durability, for its accumulation of forces, for *power*: where the will to power is lacking there is decline.[4]

Corruption is the result of will to power working against itself, against its own interests. When this occurs, the result is an overall diminishment of power. Corruption of this sort is most manifest in what Nietzsche calls *slave morality*. Within a social context, slave morality can be seen as a reaction of a weaker culture to a stronger and dominant culture whose morality then becomes the master morality. It is exemplified by the reaction of early Christianity to the dominant influence of the Roman Empire. The weak, powerless Christians reacted to the strong, powerful Romans with what Nietzsche calls *ressentiment*. This is a French term that is sometimes said to have no adequate translation in English, but it means roughly a combination of resentment, envy, hatred, hostility, cynicism, revenge, vilification of one's oppressors, and devaluing what the oppressor values:

> The slave revolt in morality begins when *ressentiment* itself becomes creative and gives birth to values: the *ressentiment* of natures that are denied the true reaction, that of deeds, and compensate themselves with an imaginary revenge. While every noble morality [i.e., master morality] develops from a triumphant affirmation of itself, slave morality from the outset says No to what is "outside," what is "different,"

what is "not itself"; and this No is its creative deed. This inversion of the value-positing eye—this *need* to direct one's view outward instead of back to oneself—is of the essence of *ressentiment*: in order to exist, slave morality always first needs a hostile external world; it needs, physiologically speaking, external stimuli in order to act at all—its action is fundamentally reaction.[5]

Nietzsche's argument here is that a healthy person responds to an oppressor by directing his attention inward toward himself. He builds up his strength until he has the power to muster a counterattack with deeds. A sick person, on the other hand, a person of *ressentiment*, responds right from the start with an imaginary attack on the oppressor. He imagines that the oppressor is evil and that all his values are evil. He says no to these values, and he proceeds to create for himself a new set of values that are the opposite of the oppressor's values. Since the oppressor's values include courage, strength, truthfulness, and other life-affirming values, the person of *ressentiment* takes for himself values that include timidity, weakness, lies, and other life-denying values. The person of *ressentiment* thus becomes even sicker than he was before. His life becomes a self-contradiction. On the one hand, this person is alive, but he adopts for himself values that deny life. In such a person, will to power cancels itself out, and the result is a person highly deficient in will to power.

## Nietzsche (cont.): Ressentiment and Religion

When a whole society does this sort of thing, the result is a very sick society. Such was the society that Nietzsche found himself surrounded by in nineteenth-century Europe. He asks himself,

Where does it come from, this sickliness? For man is more sick, uncertain, changeable, indeterminate than any other animal, there is no doubt of that—he is *the* sick animal: how has that come about?[6]

The answer is that all this sickness comes from *ressentiment*. In particular, it comes, he argues, from Christianity, which he sees as a religion of *ressentiment*. And the sickness is maintained by sick priests. The priest is a sick shepherd nursing a flock of sick sheep:

We must count the ascetic priest as the predestined savior, shepherd, and advocate of the sick herd: only thus can we understand his tremendous historical mission. *Dominion over the suffering* is his kingdom, that is where his instinct directs him, here he possesses his distinctive art, his mastery, his kind of happiness. He must be sick himself, he must be profoundly related to the sick—how else would they understand each other?—but he must also be strong, master of himself even more than of others, with his will to power intact, so as to be both trusted and feared by the sick, so as to be their support, resistance, prop, compulsion, taskmaster, tyrant and god. He has to defend his herd—against whom? Against the healthy, of course, and also against envy of the healthy [i.e., against envy that the sick have for the healthy].[7]

The ascetic priest is the priest who takes himself seriously. This would exclude "priests" who know they are fakes, such as many televangelists today. It would also exclude priests who have taken the job simply because it provides perks, such as little or no manual labor and some degree of prestige. The ascetic priest operates with a moderate level of will to power—enough to command respect from members of the flock and to support them in times of weakness, as when their envy of the healthy tempt them to leave the herd for a better life. But no priest has as much will to power as anyone who is truly healthy. The truly healthy are marked by life-affirming values, whereas every priest has life-denying values, values such as meekness, holiness, and otherworldliness.

Judging by the number of references in his published writings, Nietzsche's favorite Christian priest was Paul the apostle. Paul, he thought, was a man singularly driven by hatred:

On the heels of the "glad tidings" came the *very worst*: those of Paul. In Paul was embodied the opposite type to that of the "bringer of glad tidings": the genius in hatred, in the vision of hatred, in the inexorable logic of hatred. *How much* this dysangelist [bringer of ill tidings] sacrificed to hatred! Above all, the Redeemer: he nailed him to *his own* cross. The life, the example, the doctrine, the death, the meaning and the right of the entire evangel—nothing remained once this hate-inspired counterfeiter realized what alone he could use. *Not* the reality, *not* the historical truth! And once more the priestly instinct of the Jew committed the same great crime against history—he simply crossed out the yesterday of Christianity and its day before yesterday; he *invented his own history of earliest Christianity.* Still *further*: he falsified the history of Israel once more so that it might appear as the prehistory of *his* deed: all the prophets spoke of *his* "Redeemer."[8]

What was it, exactly, that Paul hated? Nietzsche answers, Everything wholesome in life—everything that was natural, everything that brought pleasure to people, and especially everything that involved sexuality. Reading Paul's epistles would bring on, in any healthy person, what Nietzsche called an episode of nausea. Nietzsche accuses Paul of falsifying the message of Jesus, a message that he, incidentally, agreed with. He says that Paul also falsified the history of early Christianity for the purpose of benefiting himself, and he did the same with the history of Israel by making it appear that he himself was the beneficiary of the early prophesies. All of this, Nietzsche argues, Paul did to increase his own power:

> At bottom, he had no use at all for the life of the Redeemer—he needed the death on the cross *and* a little more. . . . What he himself did not believe, the idiots among whom he threw his doctrine believed. His need was for power; in Paul the priest wanted power once again—he could use only concepts, doctrines, symbols with which one tyrannizes masses and forms herds.[9]

Power, of course, is the ultimate good for Nietzsche, so if Paul had used his power to achieve self-mastery and personal excellence, he would have been the most noble of humans. But no. Paul used it to tyrannize other people. He was little better than a slave owner. His power was a power corrupted by *ressentiment*, a power turned against itself. He cared nothing for the real Jesus, the Jesus who preached and labored before dying on the cross. Rather, he cared only for the fictional Jesus, the one he had fabricated post-resurrection, and he used it only to augment his own power.

In general, priests derive their power by controlling others. In Nietzsche's words, they exercise "dominion" over others; they "tyrannize" the masses. Such people have only limited will to power, an inferior will to power. The people who have the greatest will to power are those who are masters of themselves. They strive to perfect themselves by creating values for themselves. They strive to create a life that is this-worldly and life affirming, so life affirming that the individual could choose that his or her life be lived over and over again without any changes. This choice reflects the famous idea of the eternal recurrence of the same situation. Such a life is depicted by those statues (and there are several versions of them) that show the sculptor, hammer and chisel in hand, carving himself out of a block of stone. Nietzsche calls such a person an overman (German: *Übermensch*, "overperson"). The overman operates in a state of radical freedom, and it is not possible even to imagine what such a person would be like because he or she is not a product of any set of preexisting ideals. The values that constitute this person are new and did not exist in any sense before they were created by the overman himself (or herself).

As a counterargument, religious believers would probably hasten to point out that they themselves do not experience power as a significant motivator in their own lives, so why should it have been a motivator for these ancient figures? "Power? It counts for nothing in my life," they might say, nor did it in the lives of Moses, Jesus, Paul, and others. Nietzsche could reply that this reaction is normal given the influence of *ressentiment*. The immediate effect of *ressentiment* is a shift in values. Today's believers do not notice the role of power in their lives because their values have changed. They no longer see power and the feeling of power as the ultimate good. This shift in values probably did not happen to them immediately. It happened to their ancestors, and these ancestors passed on their values to them through dozens of generations. However, what today's believers will acknowledge is will to power working in another way, namely, as a reaction to values they oppose. This reaction manifests as a hostility to whatever stands in opposition to their own values. They may hate any religion that is different from their own, or at least they are suspicious of those other religions. They hate any political party or government policy that conflicts with their views. They avoid associating with anyone on the outside, anyone who sees things differently from the way they do. They refuse to dress like those other people or act like them or think like them. All is done as a reaction to what is on the outside, which, according to Nietzsche, is will to power operating in a corrupted way, as *ressentiment*.

Nietzsche's theory of *ressentiment* helps explain why the god idea is so resilient, why many believers cling to it so desperately once it has taken root in their worldview. The god idea defines the ideal of value for these believers. Anything is good and valuable to the extent that it agrees with this ideal, and anything is evil to the extent that it disagrees with it. When the god idea is very different from ordinary things, when, for example, it is all-powerful, all-knowing, and transcendent, then the believer adopts values and behaviors in response to these attributes. These are slave values and slave behaviors. The believer becomes submissive, reverential, and meek in relation to the god and comes to value such things as holiness, the sacred, and the blessed. At the same time, the believer defines himself in opposition to the world. He comes to hate and vilify whatever is of the world, and this in turn strengthens his belief in the god. If anything should happen to undermine belief in the god, the believer's entire system of values would collapse. Nothing would have any meaning, a condition that Nietzsche calls nihilism. To avoid the threat of nihilism, the believer clings ever more tightly to the god idea. As an antidote to nihilism, Nietzsche proposes his revaluation of values, a restructuring of values in accord with what he considers to be truly wholesome in life.

## Foucault

Among the philosophers who influenced Foucault, the most important may have been Nietzsche. Foucault said that reading Nietzsche was "a philosophical shock . . . a revelation."[10] Thus, it is not surprising that the idea of power is as central in the work of Foucault as it is in Nietzsche's. But Foucault's treatment of power is quite different from Nietzsche's. One difference is that for Nietzsche, power is an end in itself. Power is good. The feeling of power is good. The feeling that power is increasing is good. Foucault never talks this way. There is nothing intrinsically good about power. Power is good only as a means to an end. Also, for Nietzsche, every human being is a point source of power. Power flows forth from these point sources and disperses out into the world. Also, power is not a social phenomenon for Nietzsche. A person all alone on an island could experience the feeling of power just as much as a person in a big city. However, for Foucault, power is a thoroughly social phenomenon, and it flows in two directions in humans: inward and outward. Power is essentially relational. Every person in a society of humans is linked with other humans through power relations.

For Foucault, the human subject is *constituted* by power relations. Power relations are literally what make up every human subject. Accordingly, we can derive an understanding of what a power relation is by analyzing any human subject. Suppose I ask the question, "Who am I," and suppose my response is, "I am a parent." The answer discloses the power relation between me and my child or children. The relation is one of authority and responsibility, and the power flows from me to my children. Suppose a further answer is, "I am an employee." Then power flows to me from my employer. If a further answer is, "I am a supervisor," then power flows from me to all those I supervise. Additional possible answers are, "I am a teacher," "I am a student," "I am a doctor," "I am a patient," "I am a wife," "I am a husband." Each answer reveals something about the personal identity of the respondent, who the person is as a subject, and what the power relation is. Foucault says that all of us become subjects by subjecting ourselves to power relationships. We do this by choosing to enter into them. The relationships constitute the subject and define our daily concerns. As a parent, we spend much of our time during the day thinking about our children; as an employee, we spend much of our time thinking about our jobs; and so on. Each of us is locked into a network of power relations, a kind of grid work, linking us to a great many other subjects. I am who I am because of my power relations to X, Y, and Z. X is who she is because of her power relations to P, Q, and R and so on. All of this reveals that any society of subjects is composed of a huge number of such relations linking all the members to other members. A society is a kind of substratum of power relations.

What Foucault means by a power relation is exemplified by the relations between spouses. Probably the healthiest of spousal relations are those that have a balance of power. In these, there is a constant flow of power back and forth. Now one spouse seems to have the upper hand, now the other. Now power flows in one direction, now in the other. Almost all squabbles, disagreements, and fights between spouses are about power. You do the dishes tonight. No, you do them; I did them last night. Why is it that I always do the work around here? Please give me the TV remote. There's a movie I want to watch. No, you always get to pick. At least for once, the choice should be mine. Would you please get up and feed the baby? She's screaming, and I think she's hungry. Why me? I have to get up early in the morning. At least you have the luxury of sleeping in. If all the power should end up in the hands of one spouse, the other may simply shut down or abandon the relationship.

Power, for Foucault, is the action of controlling other people. Power is getting other people to do what you want them to do. But power is not the same thing as physical coercion. Physical coercion overrides the freedom of the person being controlled and is therefore not a genuine power relation. A true power relation controls the actions of others while at the same time recognizing their freedom. So a genuine power relation is a kind of persuasion. "It incites, it induces, it seduces, it makes easier or more difficult; it releases or contrives, makes more probable or less."[11] Another way of putting it is that power is management, and all good management recognizes that those being managed are free agents who can either rebel or completely shut down. To prevent this from happening, the good manager develops strategies to ensure that the job gets done while at the same time ensuring that those doing the job participate of their own free will.

A good example of power in action is raising children. Practically any parent would agree that this is a problem of management, and strategies constantly come into play. One strategy is negotiation: If you clean up your room, then you can go out with your friends. If you wash the car, then I'll give you five dollars. No? Okay, seven dollars. Engaging children with chores around the house situates them in a network of power relations not only with parents but also with siblings. It creates bonding, and bonding relations rest on power relations. Another strategy is teaching skills: how to bake brownies, how to use tools, how to ride a bicycle. Skills shape and mold the subjectivity of the child. They develop the child's self-identity. The child comes to see himself or herself as a baker of brownies, a user of tools, a rider of bicycles. By developing skills, children fit themselves into the power structure that constitutes family life.

As this example shows, power, for Foucault, means shaping the subjectivity of those being managed. And this is accomplished by placing the subject in a network of power relations. These power relations are literally what make up the subject. Cases of this are widespread throughout society. Practically any kind of training accomplishes this goal. Corporations train their employees to do their jobs in the way they see fit. They assign them a workplace, tell them what is expected of them, and subject them to regular evaluations. The employee comes to see herself as someone who fulfills the description of the job. Every military organization trains its recruits and teaches them about the chain of command, how to follow orders, and the meaning of honor and duty. Every recruit is given a uniform and assigned a rank in a power structure. All of this molds the recruit's self-image.

Schools mold the subjectivity of students through the instructors they hire, through the design of the curriculum, through mandatory examinations and final grades. Students who succeed experience an enhancement of self-worth, while those who fall short of the mark come to see themselves as failures. Prisons shape the subjectivity of inmates (they reform them) by restricting their movement, by requiring that they participate in regimented activities, and by teaching them skills. This was one of Foucault's selected areas of research. Another area that interested him was how psychiatric hospitals and the psychiatric profession in general shaped the self-identity of thousands of people in regard to their own sexuality. Many years ago, certain sexual practices, including child sexuality and homosexuality, came to be evaluated as irregular, the result being that many homosexuals started seeing themselves as perverts.

Ensuring efficiency in management is always a goal of power. The greater the efficiency, the greater the power. This fact explains Foucault's fascination with an architectural design for a prison, invented by the English philosopher Jeremy Bentham (1748–1832). The design is called a panopticon, and it consists of a ring-shaped building having one or more stories divided into cells for housing prisoners. Each cell has a large window facing inward toward the center of the circle and another window facing outward to allow light to enter the cell. In the center of the circle is a guardroom (a tower if the circular building has multiple stories) with windows facing in all directions. The windows are fitted with blinds or some other apparatus to allow the single guard to see out but no one on the outside to see in. With such a prison, a single guard could keep watch on all the prisoners without their knowing for sure if the guard was watching them. The guard could not watch all of the prisoners simultaneously, but since no prisoner would know at any one time whether he or she was being watched, the prisoners would act as though they were being watched at all times. The person in the tower could be asleep, and still the inmates would think they were being observed. The panopticon represents an ideal of managerial efficiency since, at least in theory, it could be run by a single individual.

A signature feature of Foucault's theory of power is that power produces knowledge. For Foucault, important knowledge always arises in a context of struggle, and struggle is the earmark of the operation of power relations. The controversy leading to the acceptance of Darwin's theory of evolution is an example. In the middle of the nineteenth century, Charles Darwin wrote a book arguing that animal species, including humans, were not fixed and immutable, as had been previously thought, but were the product of an evolutionary process called natural selection. This theory not only violated what biologists had held sacrosanct for centuries—it went back to Aristotle, considered to be the founder of biology—but also violated Holy Scripture. It directly contradicted the account in Genesis, and it appeared to undermine the role of God as creator. Religious leaders and conservative-leaning biologists wanted the theory tossed to the flames, but more thoughtful members of the scientific community wanted it retained. All of these individuals were terminal points in a complex network of power relations. Gradually, through numerous books, countless articles published in professional journals, papers read at conventions and meetings, and debates held in both public and private settings, the vast majority of professionals accepted the theory as knowledge.

It never happens that a scientist announces some theory and instantly, almost by magic, the entire scientific community accepts the theory as true. Almost always, the announcement triggers a struggle. Some scientists are inclined to accept the theory, and some are not. Any kind of unanimity may require years of experimentation, thoughtful reflection, and debate, and only after the dust has settled does the theory count as knowledge. Other, well-known examples where a lengthy struggle preceded the general acceptance of a theory include the heliocentric theory in astronomy, the special and general theories of relativity, quantum mechanics, and non-Euclidean geometries.

## Foucault (cont.): Religion

All religions arise through the creation of what is thought to be a three-way power relation between priests, gods, and ordinary people. Power is thought to flow from the priests to the gods—the priests bargain with the gods—and from the gods to the people—the gods judge the people. However, if what is said in this book is correct, the gods are merely a fiction created by the priests. Thus, there is in fact only a two-way power relation, that between the priests and the people. Power flows from the priests to the people: the priests control the people.

Just as the power relation joining a woman with her child shapes the subjectivity of both mother and child and the power relation joining the employer with the employee shapes the subjectivity of both, so the power relation joining the priest with a believer shapes the subjectivity of both people. The child willingly obeys the mother because the child sees herself as nestled in a power relation that defines who she is. The child *is* an obeyer of her mother. Similarly, the lieutenant obeys orders from the captain because the chain of command defines the lieutenant to be someone who obeys an officer of higher rank. For this reason, obedience is automatic and freely given. The person obeying is simply acting according to that person's internal nature. In the same way, the religious believer is an obeyer of divine commands as expressed by the priest. This is the way that priests control believers. They control them by calling into play the power relation that joins the parties together.

Shaping the subjectivity of the religious believer is accomplished in basically the same way as it is in other professions. For the surgical nurse, this involves preparing patients, sterilizing tools, and administering medication; for the paralegal, it involves preparing pleading papers and typing letters to clients; for the store clerk, it involves providing assistance to customers and checking out items that are purchased; and for the military recruit, it involves following orders on the marching field. By engaging in these activities, the nurse, the paralegal, the store clerk, and the military recruit come to see themselves as someone whose existence is defined by the job at hand. The subjectivity of the religious believer is shaped by participating in rituals, engaging in public and private prayer, reading holy books, attending church services, and meditating on religious themes. Through these activities, the religious believer comes to see himself or herself as intrinsically religious and as being subservient both to the god and to the priest.

For every priest, the goal is to achieve control over the maximum number of believers with the least possible expenditure of effort. The idea captured in the panopticon shows how such a goal may be reached. The priest creates and sustains a god that sees the innermost thoughts and desires of believers, just as the guard in the tower sees the prisoners in the cells. This god is like a spiritual panoptic eye who sees inside human souls. The first priest to suggest the existence of any such god was probably Moses. Moses created the Ten Commandments, which proscribed many of the same infractions as the Egyptian Principles of Maat, but the commandments differed in an important way from the Egyptian rules. The commandments included proscriptions against *mental* acts. The commandment against bearing false witness forbids the intentional act of deceiving someone about another's behavior. It therefore also covers lying. The essence of telling a lie is the intent to deceive. To tell if a person is lying, one must examine that person's state of mind. The commandments also include two or three items related to coveting. "Thou shalt not covet." Coveting is a mental act; it is a kind of strong yearning. And the only way one can tell for sure if a person covets something is to peer inside that person's mind and examine what is going on. The fact that Moses included these prohibitions in the commandments implies that he conceived Yahweh as a being who has access to the minds of believers. Yahweh is the central eye of a spiritual panopticon. In writing these commandments, Moses had created the perfect control mechanism, the perfect expression of power. There was now no need (at least in theory) for the priests to keep a close eye on the people to see if they were behaving themselves. The people would now control themselves. Priestly power had become internalized.

Christianity follows in the footsteps of Judaism, but the Christian god is even more of a panoptic eye than the Jewish God. In commenting on the commandments, Jesus said that they are reducible to two: love of God and love of neighbor. But love, just as is coveting, is a mental act, and to know with certainty whether a person truly loves, one must have access to that person's mind. But the reasoning goes further than this. A central tenet of Christianity is that salvation is based on faith. To be saved, one must have faith in Jesus and believe his teachings. Faith, however, is very much a mental act, and to know whether a person believes something, one must know what is going on inside that person's mind. The Christian god must therefore constantly be spying on everyone, spying on their most private activities, their thoughts and desires. Thomas Aquinas, one of the two most important Christian theologians (the other being Augustine), addressed this question in connection with whether angels know "secret thoughts." The word "secret" emphasizes the point. Aquinas answers that angels cannot know secret thoughts, but only God knows these things. More specifically, God knows both thoughts "as they are in the mind and affections as they are in the will."[12]

Whether God knows our secret thoughts is immediately pertinent to sins other than lying and coveting. In Christianity, lust is a sin committed merely by assenting to certain thoughts. But if God can detect the sin of lust, he can obviously detect sins committed in secret that involve outward actions. Such sins include masturbation, murder by poisoning, various forms of theft including embezzlement and shoplifting, and sins where only a preliminary plan is carried out, such as plans for arson and robbery. The priests assure the members of the flock that God sees all, like a great panoptic eye that never sleeps, and this goes a long way toward making sure the people abide by the moral laws and other regulations created by the priests. In this capacity, the god of Christianity is a perfect mechanism of power that operates without any actual expenditure of power.

In passing, I note that a similar mechanism exists in Islam. According to the Quran and Islamic tradition, every living human being is constantly accompanied by two angels.[13] One sits on a person's right shoulder, the other on the left. During every day of a person's life, the angel on the right records every good action that this person performs, and the angel on the left records every bad action. At the end of the person's life, the record is submitted to Allah, who consults it in deciding whether to send the person to paradise or purgatory/hell. The graphic imagery testifies to the likely effectiveness of this mechanism of power. One can only wonder how many children it has deterred from stealing candy from the corner store.

Turning to Foucault's idea that power produces knowledge, we can see many instances of this idea at work in religion. As always, knowledge results from a struggle. In regard to Judaism, what probably counts as the single most important piece of knowledge is that there is only one God. This knowledge resulted from a struggle lasting hundreds of years. The ancient Jews continually vacillated between monotheism and polytheism, and they settled on monotheism only after countless threats, condemnations, warnings, and punishments by Moses and other leaders. All of these threats were met with resistance from the ordinary people, and resistance is always an indicator of struggle. Thus, from this standpoint, the most basic truth in Judaism is a product of power.

In Christianity, a series of struggles lasting more than 300 years led to the production of the Christian god. These consisted of the many declarations of heresy that served to define Christian orthodoxy. They include docetism, adoptionism, Sabellianism, Montanism, Arianism, and others, and they are treated in chapter 7. The struggles usually resulted in the heretic (or a group of heretics) being excommunicated, and they often created a split in the body of believers, with some following the so-called heretic and others the bishop, who was always on the side of orthodoxy. In virtually every case, any books the heretic may have written were burned, and sometimes he was banished to a foreign land. The triune God of Christianity is as much the product of a power struggle as is the monotheistic God of Judaism.

The Protestant Reformation also illustrates Foucault's idea of power producing knowledge. The movement started in 1517 and included a cast of characters numbering in the hundreds, including Luther, Melanchthon, Pope Leo X, Zwingli, Calvin, Schnepf, Karlstadt, Benz, Bucer, Amsdorf, von Hutten, Vasa, Henry VIII of England, Cranmer, and Cromwell. All were linked to one another by power relations, and all were participants in a great struggle that involved the execution (murder) of hundreds of people in England. The truths that resulted from the struggle included the doctrines that Christians are justified by faith alone, that salvation is not merited by believers but comes from grace, and that scripture alone must be the source of all church teaching. When considered in this light, the basic foundation of Protestantism is the product of power.

Another example of power producing knowledge is offered by religious fundamentalists who struggle to keep their adherents from coming in contact with the outside world. These include the Hassidic Jewish community in New York, the Amish community, the Mormon Fundamentalist Church, and various forms of Protestant fundamentalism. The leaders of these movements restrict everything their followers read and whom they associate with and often prevent them from watching television or using computers. The Catholic Index of Forbidden Books, which technically remained in effect until 1966, represented a similar effort. The effect of these measures was to limit access to any point of view that differed from the official one so that the followers would have no basis to challenge it. In this way, the leaders controlled what their followers took to be true about everything and what ultimately counted as knowledge for them. To some extent, every religious leader does the same thing to keep believers in line.

## Whitehead

Alfred North Whitehead (1861–1947) stands out from the three other philosophers covered in this chapter in that he is the only theist. Nietzsche and Foucault were clearly atheists, and while Hobbes gives lip service to God and religion in *Leviathan*, for all practical purposes, he was an atheist, too. Whitehead is recognized at the founder of a movement known as process theology. Nevertheless, even though Whitehead is a theist, his theory does not lend much support to conventional religion. In what follows, I look briefly at how this theory bears on the possibility of miracles and divine power.

Miracles are an important part of conventional religion because they are cited as evidence that a god exists who cares deeply for those who believe in him. Judaism started out with a series of miracles (or apparent miracles). Yahweh sent plagues to the pharaoh to persuade him to release the enslaved Hebrews; he sent the Law to Moses atop Mount Sinai, he parted the waters of the Red Sea, he brought down the walls of Jericho, and he halted the motion of the sun in the heavens. Christianity, too, has its share of miracles. Jesus was born of a virgin, he made the blind to see and the deaf to hear, he walked on water, he rose from the dead, and he ascended to heaven forty days later. As I have argued earlier in this book, none of these alleged events ever occurred, but many people believed they did, so we should examine what is involved in the supposed occurrence of a miracle. This will involve taking a look at what some people believe about miracles.

A miracle is an alleged occurrence that interrupts the normal flow of things and that is said to be caused by God. For an example of such an occurrence, suppose that I stretch out my hand and pick up a small stone. I raise it a few feet above the ground and then drop it. It falls. Then I do this again. It falls. I do this fifty times. It falls every time. Then suppose I do this one more time, but the stone fails to fall. It simply stays suspended in midair. If I then claim that this unexpected occurrence happened because God interceded and prevented the stone from falling, I would be asserting the existence of a miracle. Most miracles, of course, happen to benefit someone. If we insist on some such benefit, it is easy to alter the example and imagine that the rock is very heavy and about to fall on someone's head.

How could the failure of the rock to fall be explained? One way is to assert that God suspended or violated the law of gravity. He simply abolished the law of gravity in the region surrounding the rock. Another way, which involves a weaker claim, is to say that God stretched out his invisible hand (assuming he has a hand) and prevented the rock from falling. And how could God do either of these things? God is all-powerful, so God can do anything. God made the law of gravity, so, of course, he can suspend it, and it's easy to imagine God's holding up a rock. Both explanations involve the assumption that God can interact with the world. In other words, God is causally efficacious as concerns physical events.

The claim that God is all-powerful is part of the conventional religious view that God is omniscient, omnipotent, and omnibenevolent (all-knowing, infinitely powerful, and all-good). Where this idea first arose may not be known, but the separate ideas of goodness, power, and knowledge have distinctly Platonic connotations. In chapter 1, there is the warning about blending religious belief with philosophical theories. Doing so often leads to bad results, and this case is no exception. One such result is the famous problem of evil, and it results from combining these three ideas into a single being that we then name "God." The problem goes like this. Given that there is evil in the world, a good God would want to eliminate it, a knowing God would know how to do it, and an all-powerful God would have the capacity to do it. Yet evil remains. The apparent conclusion is that there is no being that is all-knowing, infinitely powerful, and all-good. In my view, there is no solution to this problem.

Another problem with the conventional view of God is that there is no common ground between the finite and the infinite. This leaves no room for any interaction between the two. One aspect of this problem is that a finite mind (i.e., a human mind) is not capable of knowing an infinite being. Thomas Aquinas tried to address this problem by saying that we know God through analogical reasoning. We know limited forms of goodness, justice, wisdom, and power in this world, and from that, we make the leap to the infinite goodness, justice, wisdom, and power of God. But I would suggest that no analogy can bridge the gap between the finite and the infinite. The finite is not in any way similar to the infinite. Further, people think that if they behave in certain ways, they will please God. But how can a finite action affect an infinite being? It's as if throwing a grain of sand into the ocean will raise the level of the sea worldwide—but worse.

The ocean is not infinite. The problem is almost as bad going in the other direction. Intuitively, it seems that if an infinite being acts on something finite, the finite being would be overwhelmed or destroyed.

Yet another set of problems centers on whether God is subject to change. If God is subject to change, it would seem that he is not totally perfect because anything that changes is different after the change than it was before. If God was absolutely perfect before the change, he would be less so after the change. But if God created the world, it would seem that he changed in the process of creating it. Before the creative act, God was a non-creator; but after it, God was a creator. Besides creating the world, the Bible reports numerous cases where God has interacted with humans. God becoming human in the person of Jesus is an extreme case. All of these seem to entail change on the part of God, and they therefore imply a lack of perfection after the change. If one responds that God acts outside of time (and therefore does not change), we are confronted with the question of how any kind of acting can happen outside of time. If such acting can occur, it is not conceivable by the human mind, so we are left with a mystery. A mystery supports no conclusions of any sort.

Finally, there is the problem of how a thing that is not made of matter or connected in any way with materiality can act on physical things. God is usually conceived as something not made of matter. God is not visible, tangible, or detectable by any sense. But if God is not made of matter, then how can God act on material things? This is the correlative to the famous mind–body problem that relates to how a nonmaterial mind (soul) can act on a material human body and how a material human body can act on a nonmaterial mind. It is said that such interaction does take place because the body seems to send sensations to the mind, and the mind seems to exercise free choice by telling the body what to do. But how can this happen when there is no point of contact between the two? All physical agency appears to occur via the transmission of some kind of energy or force through a point of contact. If there is no point of contact, there is no transmission. In the same way, if there is no point of contact between God and the world, how can God act on the world by performing miracles, and how can people act on God through prayer and worship? It won't help to say that these interactions are miracles because that is precisely what we are trying to do here: explain how miracles are possible.

Whitehead attempted to avoid all of these problems by developing a philosophical theory that explains the world without any reference to a being that is omniscient, omnipotent, and omnibenevolent. This theory incorporates a first principle named "God," and I take this name to be unfortunate because it immediately invites confusing it with the religious entity by the same name, but with that understanding, we can give a brief sketch of what Whitehead's "God" consists of. As concerns the problem with a nonmaterial being interacting with a material being, Whitehead's God has both a material aspect and a nonmaterial (mental) aspect. So materiality and mentality are built into God right from the start, just as they are with every other particle of reality. God is not an exception to the rules but an instance of the categories or axioms that set up the system. Mentality and materiality are suffused throughout the universe. In this way, Whitehead proposes to solve the mind–body problem as well as the problem of how God interacts with the world.

As concerns the problem of God's changing, Whitehead's God is perpetually engaged in change (or process). God is constantly influencing the world, and the world is constantly influencing God. God never forces himself on the world, but by acting as a lure, God slowly guides the world to higher levels of order and new forms of interrelatedness. Also, to prevent radical loss from the advance of time, God takes up within himself the accomplishments of human beings who have perished. The world has always existed, and God exists alongside it, so to speak, as a fellow traveler. God continually learns from the world and adjusts his influence on the world based on what he learns. God does not select out small parts of the world, such as individual humans, for special treatment, but he acts on the world as a whole, and human beings are affected only insofar as they are part of the world. As a result, there are no miracles. But this is exactly what we find in real life. No avalanche is ever halted midway down the mountain before it buries the little village, and no tsunami is ever stopped at the shoreline before it drowns the people on the beach. Also, extremely wicked people rarely die in their sleep before they can wreak havoc on the human race.

The conclusion of this brief inquiry into the power of God is that there is nothing necessary about the God of Christianity (or the God of any other religion) being all-powerful. The Christian God is not omnipotent as a matter of definition. The reason why the conventional God of Christianity is omnipotent is because some priest at some point in time long ago selected certain ideas from ancient Greek philosophy, assembled them together, and then injected them into the Christian religion to produce the God that we have today. The outcome was generally bad in that it yielded many unsolvable problems, such as the problem of evil and the others just discussed. If this priest had selected ideas from some other philosophy, such as the one developed by Whitehead, these problems would not have occurred. But then there would be no miracles. A good deal of scripture would have to be excised or reinterpreted. Also, Whitehead's God does not lend itself to prayer, worship, and sacrifice, so the theory would have to be twisted in some way to make it more appealing in this regard. The selection by this priest (or priests) of the attributes of omniscience, omnipotence, and omnibenevolence for the Christian God is just another aspect of priests creating gods.

## Final Comment

I expect that the chief objection to what I have said in this chapter is that I have proved nothing. Hobbes, Nietzsche, Foucault, Whitehead—these people are just philosophers, and what they said are just theories. What if these theories are wrong? If they are, what they say proves nothing. This, of course, is true. But the purpose of philosophy is not to prove things. The purpose of philosophy is to disclose ways of looking at things. Its purpose is to focus attention on aspects of experience that are often overlooked or taken for granted. Philosophies can be seen as invitations to look at the world in new ways, ways that lead to unforeseen conclusions. Hobbes's statement that human life exhibits a restless desire of power after power and his comparison of life with a long-distance footrace can be seen as a proposal to look at life as a field of competition and all decisions as affected by a concern for winning. Nietzsche's claim that the feeling of power is an ultimate good and therefore that all people seek power can be seen as a proposal for interpreting the driving force behind all human action. Foucault's claim that human subjectivity is constituted by power relations, that all of us are locked into a power network, and that power often determines what we take to be knowledge is a proposal for understanding the human condition and the way that religion shapes how we see ourselves. And Whitehead's theory about the entity he calls "God" is an invitation to look at religious god constructs in new ways.

## CHAPTER NINE

# ILLUSION

The subject of illusion is not one that lends itself to an automatically structured inquiry, as is the case with a lesson in mathematics. There are no elementary topics that must be studied first in preparation for studying its complex formations. The subject is multifaceted and susceptible to multiple approaches. What follows is a discussion of some loosely connected topics related to religion and illusion.

## Two Theories of Illusion

Sigmund Freud was the first prominent writer to interpret religious belief as an illusion, an idea that he develops in his 1927 book *The Future of an Illusion*. According to Freud, religion is a neurotic reaction to the experience of helplessness encountered in childhood. To alleviate this feeling, we invent a God who is supposed to protect us against the threats posed by nature, together with the inevitable approach of death, in the same way that our father protected us against threats in our childhood years. God is modeled after the person of the father, which explains why God is often addressed as Our Father. But this God does not really exist. It is a mere fiction, the product of what Freud calls wishful thinking.

Freud cites the example of a young middle-class girl who dreams that one day a prince will come to marry her.[1] If she spends a great amount of time caught up in this dream, she is living an illusion. Of course, it is possible that this prince will turn up to marry her, but the chances are infinitesimally small. For Freud, the wish that there be a God to protect us is similar to the girl's wish that a prince will come to marry her. The motivating force behind the God illusion is the believer himself, just as it is with the girl who creates for herself the imaginary prince.

The theory developed in my book agrees with Freud's theory that religious beliefs are illusions, but it disagrees with him as to the cause of that illusion. In the place of a neurotic reaction, my account sees religion as caused by other people. These other people, whom I call priests, are the motivating force. Hence, the kind of illusion envisioned here is called factitious illusion, which expresses the idea that it is manufactured by others. Nevertheless, the effects of factitious illusion are similar to the effects of Freud's neurotic illusion.

In chapter 1, I created a scenario in which a person asks to borrow $10,000 and promises to pay back $20,000 in three months. You lend him the money, and every day, you dream of the possible things you might do with the extra $10,000. You might go on a cruise, or perhaps you might buy an expensive piece of jewelry. You dream about the wonderful times you will enjoy on the ship or the admiring glances from your friends when they see you wearing the jewelry. Your experience is like that of the young girl who dreams of marrying a prince. But your hopes are dashed when the borrower uses the money to buy drugs. Before lending the money, you should have taken some precaution to ensure that the borrower was not a drug addict.

Generalizing from this scenario, a factitious illusion is a mistaken belief resulting from an error in judgment. The error in judgment is induced by some other person who plays on the believer's hopes and fears. In the loan example, the borrower plays on the lender's hope to earn an easy $10,000. In the case of religious illusions, the inducers are called priests, and, in ancient times, the anticipated payback was in the form of fertile crops, an afterlife, land, and protection. Further, in the loan example, right from the start, the borrower never intended to repay the loan. Such borrowers are usually called con artists. In ancient times, some of the first con artists were priests. Religion deals with gods that are invisible and undetectable by any sense, and they thus provide the perfect medium for the con artist.

## Sources of Vulnerability

In every case of factitious illusion, there is something that renders the victim vulnerable to the trickery of the inducer. In the case of the loan, it was the victim's dream of gaining a relatively quick $10,000. If the victim had not been both greedy and gullible, he would not have lost his money. For the victims of priests in ancient times, it was, as Freud argues, fear of the powers of nature and the fear of death. Thanks to the accomplishments of modern civilization, people today are very well protected, and they hardly ever think about these threatening powers. Also, we do our best to insulate ourselves from the fear of death. When a friend or acquaintance dies, we may attend the funeral, but the corpse is always dressed in fine clothing and placed in a beautiful satin-lined casket. Everything is very pleasant and agreeable. As concerns our own death, we try our best to avoid thinking about it, and this is easy to do when its date is uncertain and some time off in the future. Only when death is right around the corner, as it is with condemned prisoners and those with a terminal illness, is the thought of one's own death unavoidable. These are the people who are most vulnerable to the inducements of the priest.

A generic form of vulnerability, one that is not generally avoidable, comes from what Freud called feelings of the uncanny.[2] The word "uncanny" translates the German word *Unheimliche*, which means literally "out of the home" (*Heim*). The word refers to the feeling we have of being displaced from our home, of being subject to hostile forces that beset us from every side, producing a feeling of anxiety that is normally suppressed. Suppose, for example, that a fire should come out of nowhere and burn our home to the ground. When the embers have cooled, we sit on the porch step and watch the family across the street enjoying a happy meal together. Only a couple of days earlier, we were doing the same thing ourselves, but now we are left with nothing to enjoy. Or imagine the feelings of a child whose father has died. As she rides in the hearse to the funeral, she looks outside the window and watches other children playing and having fun. She remembers the times she was doing the same thing herself. The feeling is strange and perplexing.

Feelings of the uncanny can also be evoked by books, films, and other works. Poulenc's opera *Dialogues of the Carmelites* reenacts events in the lives of sixteen Carmelite nuns who were sent to the guillotine during the French Revolution. At the end of the opera, the nuns are lined up to encounter their fate. They are singing hymns when the audience hears a "ka-thunk," which signals that the blade has dropped and the first head fallen into the basket. More singing and then another "ka-thunk." A few minutes later, only one nun is singing. The effect on the audience is eerie and unsettling. Another example, drawn from motion pictures, is the film *Never Let Me Go*. The film is based on the novel (same title) by the Nobel Prize–winning author Kazuo Ishiguro, and it tells the story of a group of young people who were produced through genetic engineering for the purpose of providing vital organs for people suffering from organ failure. Every day of their lives, these young people are haunted by the realization that as they enter their mid-twenties, their organs would be selectively removed until, after three or four "donations," their lives would reach "completion." The story of these young people is a model for human life in general. Everyone's life is limited to around ninety years, more or less, and the time of death is usually uncertain. But in the movie, the time of death is highly programmed, and it happens in the very prime of life, when young people tend to fall in love. The feelings generated in those watching both the opera and the movie are feelings of the uncanny.

Freud argues that religious belief makes us feel "at home in the uncanny."[3] My own theory agrees with Freud on this point. The priest offers us shelter from feelings of the uncanny that constantly lurk beneath the surface of conscious awareness. There is a God, the priest says, who will rescue us from the threats posed by nature, disease, and the inescapable approach of death. To receive these benefits, all we need do is offer prayer, worship, and sacrifice. What the priest does not say is that this God is a manufactured construct, the product of his own ingenuity or, more likely, the ingenuity of his predecessors. Therefore, the belief that religion offers us a genuine home in the midst of the uncanny is an illusion.

## The Meaning of the Real

Any discussion of the concept of illusion would be incomplete without an accompanying discussion about that which is not an illusion—that is, about what we can take to be real. To initiate it, consider an incident that occurred many years ago amid a conversation that the English writer Samuel Johnson had with his biographer James Boswell. The subject of the conversation was the theory of the Irish philosopher George Berkeley. Berkeley was an Anglican bishop concerned about the number of believers who had drifted away from the true faith because of the influence of materialism. He figured the best way to draw them back and prevent others from going astray was to develop a philosophical system that denied the existence of matter. The system that he developed was clever to the extreme in spite of its being a bit outlandish. In an attempt to disprove the part about matter, toward the end of the conversation, Johnson drew back his foot and struck a large stone with such force that he rebounded away from it. Then he said, "I refute it *thus*."[4] Whether Johnson succeeded in refuting Berkeley's theory is not our concern. Rather, our concern is with the basic insight captured in Johnson's demonstration. The best way to test whether something is real or not is to interact with it. And this is what I would offer as the best way of determining whether a belief is an illusion: attempt to interact with whatever the belief is about.

As concerns human experience, there are basically two kinds of interaction: physical interaction, as Johnson experienced in kicking the stone, and verbal interaction, as one would have in talking with one's friends or associates. Physical interaction is so compelling that practically no illusion can withstand it. Whatever we can interact with physically we can take to be real. The reason for this is that physical interaction engages our muscles, an integral part of our body. We can feel our muscles working and straining against something that resists them. Nobody would take his own body as being illusory (Descartes being a possible exception), so it follows that whatever our body engages with in this way we take to be real. A good example is furnished by tools, such as the hammer and saw used by a carpenter, the wrenches used by a mechanic, and the spoons and spatulas used by a cook. Such people use these tools nearly every day of their lives; they hold them in their hands, turn them over, and get a feeling for how they work. Unlike Johnson's encounter with the stone, which was a one-time event, carpenters and cooks use their tools over and over in numerous times, places, and situations. If Johnson's encounter with the stone served to convince him of the stone's reality, how much more so are carpenters and cooks convinced of the reality of their tools.

The same line of reasoning, of course, extends to countless things in our lives: the food we chew and swallow, the implements and utensils we use in preparing that food, the furniture in our homes that we move about from room to room, the chairs we sit on and the beds we lie on, the houses that we constantly clean and maintain, the clothing we wear and continually adjust for fit and appearance, the water we bathe in, the dirt in our garden that we dig up for planting flowers and vegetables, the cars and trucks that we drive and negotiate through traffic, the streets and highways we drive them on, and the sporting activities we engage in— baseball, tennis, football, soccer—and the opponents we struggle against. All of these things and activities engage our muscles, and no one would doubt their reality for a moment. At least as important as all of these are all the people we interact with: the infants we feed and care for, the toddlers we pick up when they have fallen down, the little leaguers we teach to throw a ball and swing a bat, the girlfriend or boyfriend we hold hands with while strolling through a park or watching a movie, the partner we swing on the dance floor, and the spouse we kiss and fondly touch. It was Descartes who said that the clear and distinct perceptions, which are chiefly visual, are the trustworthy ones. But when it comes to distinguishing illusion from reality, it is the tactile perceptions and the sensations of the activity of our muscles, all of which are the least clear and distinct, that are the most important.

While physical interaction involves the interplay of our bodies with things in the outside world, verbal interaction involves the interplay between our minds and the minds of others. It is impossible to climb inside the mind of another person to see what is going on in the interior, but we can do it indirectly by communicating verbally with that person. As with physical interaction, verbal interaction is not a passive phenomenon. Our minds are active in the process, just as our bodies, with their muscles, are active in physical interaction. Verbal interaction during a lengthy period of time leads to a kind of union between one mind and another. It is precisely this union that leads us to trust the other person and possibly even become intimate with that person. Prior to marriage, most couples engage in extensive verbal exchanges. They converse on topics such as values, interests, political persuasions, ambitions, hobbies, children, and plans for the future. They kid each other, they tell jokes to each other, they tease each other, they flirt with each other, they laugh with each other, they persuade each other to try something new, they recall fond memories to each other, and they tell stories to each other. These verbal interactions increase the likelihood of a successful marriage. But verbal interaction is not as foolproof as the physical type. After years of marriage, one spouse may admit never to have really gotten to know his or her mate. The disappointed party may acknowledge that the entire relationship was like an illusion. Often, such an outcome results from one of the parties having kept part of his or her inner life secret from the other party. But most of the time, verbal interaction is successful in revealing how others think and feel.

Many people, when asked what they are most certain about, will answer that they are absolutely convinced that there is a God whom they pray to and who is there always to protect them against danger and comfort them in adversity. This answer is positively remarkable in light of the suggestion that physical or verbal interaction is the ultimate key to distinguishing illusion from reality. Humans are not capable of interacting either physically or verbally with this God. We cannot shake hands with it, play football with it, snuggle in bed with it, or engage with it on the dance floor. We cannot tell jokes to it, cannot laugh with it, and cannot commiserate with it about our shared worries and concerns. Some people claim to be able to communicate with God, but any such communication is a sham compared with real communication and is indistinguishable from hallucination. In real communication, there is a shared energy, a give and take of mental activity, a mutual enrichment, and a tugging back and forth that often results in a shifting of viewpoints. The forces of religion operating in every corner of society have so contaminated the public mind that many people are persuaded that a fiction is more real than the furniture in their homes, than the clothing on their backs, than the tools and implements they use every day of their lives, and than the spouse or lover that they hold and caress. The fundamental intuition that all of us use instinctively to separate reality from illusion has been turned upside down and inside out.

Any society that has lost touch with this basic intuition is fertile ground for any con artist who happens to come around. Such was the mental state of the people living in upstate New York in the early years of the nineteenth century. In 1830, Joseph Smith announced to the people of Palmyra that he had unearthed a set of golden plates inscribed with Egyptian hieroglyphics, that the strange print could be deciphered only by a person wearing divinely empowered spectacles, that he himself had succeeded in translating the message on these plates, that the message laid out the blueprint for a new religion, and that the plates themselves were returned to the angel who had originally told him of their location deep beneath a rock on the side of a mountain. As it turned out, the plates were never seen by human eyes from that time forward (if, indeed, they were ever seen by anyone). What, it may be asked, was the reaction of those people who read this story? Some, of course, reacted as would be expected: that it amounted to nothing short of lunacy. But many sucked up the words with great enthusiasm, much in the way that goldfish in a bowl suck in particles of food as they drift down from the surface of the water. And how could this have happened? The answer can only be that those people were so conditioned by stories of miracles and divine revelations that they would believe anything phrased in biblical-sounding language.

## The Logic of Religion

Further evidence of the illusory character of religious beliefs is offered by the character of religious reasoning. Many people are religious because of their upbringing. Their parents have told them that there is a God who wants to be worshipped and that if they behave themselves and go to church, they will be rewarded in the end. They reason that their parents have always been correct about mundane concerns such as looking in both directions before stepping off the curb and never talking to strangers. If they have been right about these things, why shouldn't they be right about religion? However, one's parents are hardly experts on questions relating to the existence of a deity. Indeed, there are no experts at all in this area. There is no course of studies that will render a person an expert about the existence of God as there is for the existence of tectonic plates or DNA molecules. The reason why the parents are believers is most likely because their parents were believers and so on back for generations. But the fact that a religious belief has an established family history is not a good reason for thinking it to be true.

Parental influence is reinforced by society at large. Belief in God is common, and its manifestations are everywhere, in books, motion pictures, TV shows, billboard ads, artworks, crosses worn around the neck, and holiday festivities. The ubiquitous sight of churches, synagogues, religious schools, and charitable organizations testifies to the importance of religion in society. Whenever a tragedy of any sort occurs, whether it be a fire, a flood, an earthquake, or a plane crash, public figures urge viewers to pray for the victims. Surely, there must be a God who listens to all these prayers. The average individual is bombarded night and day and from every direction by the forces of religion. But the question is, do any of these influences provide adequate support for the conclusion that there is a God who wants to be worshipped and who answers prayers? The answer is that they do not. The sheer fact that millions of people happen to believe something is not a logical reason to conclude that this something is true. A single person can believe that two plus two is five, but that does not mean that two plus two really is five. And it makes no difference whether one person believes it or millions do.

Another reason people give for their religious belief is that they "feel" the influence of God in their lives. Others claim to have seen visions of religious figures, and sometimes those figures issue commands that the person receiving the vision do something, such as build a chapel or church or perhaps something less edifying. But it is a well-known fact that people feel and see what they expect to feel and see. In other words, beliefs influence perceptions. It never happens that a devout Muslim or devout Hindu would see the face of Jesus in a cloud formation or that a devout Christian would receive messages from Allah or from the Buddha. Furthermore, just because one person happens to feel or see something when others cannot is not a good reason for everyone else to go along. Someone sharing the religious beliefs of the person receiving the vision might be tempted to do this, but it is very unlikely that someone not sharing those beliefs would do so.

Yet another reason people give for their religious belief is "faith." They simply have faith that these beliefs are true, and they hasten to point out that faith serves a large purpose in life. When a schoolchild is told that aluminum conducts electricity, he or she takes it on faith that this is so. The same is true of the youngster who is told that sodium chloride (table salt) is soluble in water. Why shouldn't we take it on faith that there is a god who wants to be worshipped? Anyone who accepts this reasoning commits another error in reasoning. The fact is that there is a world of difference between these two kinds of faith. The facts that the schoolchild is told to believe are readily susceptible to empirical testing. For the salt example, all the child need do is drop a pinch of salt in a glass of water and see if it dissolves, and another simple test will determine if aluminum conducts electricity. But faith in the God of religion admits of no test at all. Why should anyone believe such a claim?

The religious believer is likely to reply that religious faith is a special case. There is a communications channel that runs from the mind of the believer to the mind of God, and through this channel, the believer receives the gift of faith. Such reasoning commits yet another logical error: circular reasoning. It is only through faith that the believer knows that God exists, so the believer cannot use the assumed existence of this God to prove the veracity of his faith. In fact, faith is not something delivered through a special channel or pipeline connected to a divinity, nor is it like a sixth sense. It merely means accepting some claim without evidence. When evidence is readily obtainable, as it is with the pieces of information taught to the schoolchild, faith is justified. But when no evidence is obtainable, not even in principle or theoretically, then faith is not justified. Such is the case with faith in a religious God.

The concept of faith causes as many problems for the religious believer as it solves, for it raises the question as to why the God of religion did not send the same beliefs to everyone. Some people are Muslims, some are Buddhists, some Christians, some Jews, some Shintoists, and so on. Couldn't this God ensure that everyone got the same message? This question is extremely important, but most believers simply slough it off as if it were not relevant to them—as if religious belief were like the color of one's hair or the shape of one's nose. Faith is not like hair color or nose shape. Faith is supposed to be an expression of the truth. Facial features have nothing to do with the truth. But the religious believer might respond in another way. Deep down, these faiths are really all the same: multiple expressions of one basic truth. And their concepts of God, while superficially different from one another, are really identical. This was a view popularized by Houston Smith in the 1950s, but it has now been largely discredited.[5] The better view is that these various religions are not the same at all, nor is their concept of a divinity, if they have such a concept at all. In fact, religious faith is unique to each believer. It is a private sort of thing that cannot be analyzed or explored from the outside. How could anyone possibly prove that all these faiths are ultimately the same?

Religious documents (the Talmud, the Bible, the Quran, and so on) provide another reason why many people become believers. They take these documents to be expressions of the final and absolute truth about things. The inducers of illusion claim that these documents are true, but should we simply take these people at their word? How do we know that what the documents say really is true? Most believers never ask this question. They simply take the truth of their favorite document for granted. Those who do ask the question may reason that these documents are so very old they must be true, but truth has nothing to do with age. Others are overwhelmed by the sheer number of these books in print—possibly as many as 5 billion for the Bible. But the number of Bibles in print has nothing to do with the truth of its content. Others may reason that the documents are so visually impressive with engraved covers and pages illuminated by beautiful artwork, but again, these features are unrelated to truth. Yet others reason that these documents express the truth because they are the revealed word of their personal God. But this answer depends on yet another case of circular reasoning: we know the Bible (or Talmud or Quran) is true because it is the revealed word of God. We know that God exists because it says so in the Bible (or Talmud or Quran).

One of the more emotionally persuasive lines of reasoning in support of the existence of a religious God depends on a kind of moral intuition. The reasoning goes like this. Some people, perhaps a majority, live their lives in accord with moral principles. They don't lie or cheat, they don't steal, they are faithful to their spouses, they pay their taxes, they contribute to charitable causes, but they just manage to scrape along. No summer home in the Hamptons, no European vacations, no around-the-world cruises, and no Mercedes-Benz in the garage. Others live lives of moral dereliction: they lie, cheat, and steal and are unfaithful to their spouses, never contribute a dime to charity (unless it improves their image), live in fancy homes, drive Porsches, and take great vacations. Isn't this arrangement basically unfair? Surely, there is a moral god who will set it all straight in the end. Those who got cheated in this life will get their just reward in the next. But how do we know that life is necessarily fair? We can be assured of its fairness only by the existence of a moral God who regulates it. We know that this God exists because without such a God life would be fundamentally unfair. The argument begs the question.

The occurrence of miracles triggered by prayers is sometimes cited as evidence for the existence of the God of religion. Society at large has been prepared in advance to expect miracles by the reports in religious documents. Therefore, when people pray for a miracle—perhaps for the restoration of one's eyesight or the recovery of a lost article—and the hoped-for outcome occurs, the result is dubbed a miracle and therefore as evidence for the existence of God. This line of reasoning is defective for two reasons. First off, without the widespread belief in miracles, no one would ever attribute the restoration of one's eyesight or the recovery of a lost article to a miracle. The thought that a miracle had occurred would never come to mind. Second, just because one thing happens after something else does not imply that the first thing caused the second thing. If someone sneezes and then a robbery occurs at a nearby bank, no one with any sense would say that the sneeze caused the robbery. Analogously, if someone prays for something and later an event occurs (such as the recovery of the lost article), no one should conclude that the prayer caused or triggered the event. The event might have been caused by any number of natural occurrences.

The fact that none of these lines of reasoning qualifies as logically acceptable is remarkable in itself. What is even more remarkable, though, is that when this fact is pointed out to believers who use these forms of reasoning, they do not care in the slightest. They simply slough off the critique and continue to maintain their beliefs as if nothing was wrong. One can only wonder why this is the case. It probably has something to do with the emotional element in these beliefs. They love their beliefs so much that they cannot part with them no matter what. This leads us to question whether religious beliefs are supported by anything more than emotion.

## The Appeal to Philosophy

A type of reasoning that some people use to justify belief in a religious God is exemplified by the arguments of Thomas Aquinas. I contend that this reasoning is defective first and foremost because the God whose existence it is supposed to support is not even remotely similar to the God that believers worship. One of Aquinas's more interesting arguments is the one based on necessity and contingency. It goes like this. Ordinary things we experience in our day-to-day lives are contingent in the sense that it is possible for them not to exist. Consider, for example, the apple sitting on my desk. If I simply leave it there, without eating it, after a certain length of time, it will simply disintegrate; in other words, it will no longer exist. But if the entire universe is contingent like the apple is, at some point in time, it, too, will no longer exist. And if the universe has been around for an infinite period of time, that point in time has already been reached, which means the universe no longer exists. However, it is obvious that the universe does exist, so it follows that its existence is sustained by a necessary being, which cannot pass out of existence.

Aquinas equated this necessary being with the God of Christianity, but in fact, no two things could be more different. A necessary being is one whose very nature is to exist; it expresses the fullness of reality. This means that it cannot acquire anything it does not already have, and this means that it cannot change. Any change involves the acquiring of a new perfection or attribute. If it cannot change, it cannot think since thinking involves a flow of ideas, which is a kind of change. If it cannot think, it cannot love, nor can it desire anything. Desiring implies wanting something that one lacks, and a necessary being lacks nothing. Since a necessary being already has every perfection, it is infinitely perfect. A necessary being cannot enter into any relationships with anything else because it would then be dependent in some way on whatever it is related to, and this means that it cannot cause anything or create anything. A necessary being exists outside of space and time because anything in time is constantly changing, and anything in space can move, which is a kind of change. A necessary being simply is, or exists, if we can even say that of it. We might call this necessary being a God of reason. Most philosophical arguments in support of the existence of some kind of God end up with a God of reason similar to Aquinas's.

The God of every religion, on the other hand, is terribly different from this God of reason. Every religious God is imperfect in multiple ways. It can change, and it is affected by things around it. It can think, and it desires things (which means that it lacks these things). It thinks about people, and it desires praise, worship, and sacrifice. It loves people, it wants to be loved and pleased, and it favors people who love and please it. It can also be angry with people, and it can punish them for doing wrong. It exists in time (and possibly in space), and it enters into relationships with multiple things. It causes change in the world, it cures disease, it produces miracles of many kinds, it guides people through life, and it rewards them with an afterlife. It comes to the aid of people in need, it comforts people in distress, and it rewards them with material blessings. In short, the God of religion can do—and allegedly does—practically everything that the God of reason cannot do. Any attempt to equate the two kinds of Gods, as many philosophers and theologians have done, is to violate the most fundamental principle in logic, the principle of contradiction.

295

## Ritual

The chief purpose of all religious ritual is to sustain belief in God or belief in the multiple gods, on which every religion rests. Ritual is real, but the God of religion is not, at least not in the same sense. This God derives its reality through being associated with ritual. The problem is that the God of religion is so fragile. It cannot be seen, heard, or detected by any other sense. It is not a physical thing at all, does not take up space or time the way physical bodies do, and does not interact in any verifiable way with human beings. Humans, on the contrary, are very much in space and time. They have their projects, they travel to work, they enjoy themselves at barbecues and picnics, they worry about paying bills, they get married and have children, they take their kids to soccer practice, and they engage in countless other activities. All of these activities take time. Without religious ritual, these activities would quickly snuff out the life of God and any religion it supports. There would be no time for it. Without ritual, all religious belief would soon melt away. To save God, what is needed is something very much in space and time that will carve out a place for God. It will make a place by elbowing out some of these other activities. This something is ritual. According to the position taken in this book, the God (or gods) of religion has no existence at all apart from human belief. So the chief purpose of religious ritual is literally to sustain the (fictional) existence of God (or the gods). Without ritual, God would soon pass out of existence entirely. It would not even have a fictional existence.

Ritual carves out a place for God by capturing the believer's interest and attention. One way it does this is by engaging the body of the believer. A ritual that occurs in many religions is going to a place of worship: a church, temple, mosque, chapel, synagogue, or other place. This activity imposes a structure on the body. It requires that people go to a certain place at a designated time. Once there, most people engage in prayers of various sorts. These prayers are actions that are usually repeated in regular intervals. The repetition creates habits in the body. Many people pray regularly throughout the day, prayer becoming very much a thing of habit. In this way, religion invades and becomes one with the body. Another activity that engages the body is worship. Worship usually involves assuming certain postures, such as bowing, kneeling, and outstretching one's arms. Some believers worship by rolling on the floor and others by bowing low and touching their head to the floor. Yet another activity is sacrifice. In ancient times, sacrifice involved acquiring an animal, killing it in a prescribed way, and offering it on an altar to a deity, all bodily activities. Today, the sacrifice is symbolic and often in the form of a monetary gift. The money is usually earned through bodily work. Other ritual activities that engage the body are genuflecting, making the sign of the cross, walking in processions, singing hymns, participating in pilgrimages, and visiting religious sites, such as Mecca, Rome, Jerusalem, Lourdes, and Fatima. Through all of these activities, religion becomes part of people's lives.

Another way that religious ritual becomes part of life is by creating bonds between people. Ritual ties people to other people. Many rituals involve group activities, and through participating in them, people get to know one another, and this leads to conversation and shared activities, such as eating together in a group and working together on common projects. Religion addresses hopes and fears, and when people get to know one another, individual hopes and fears become shared hopes and fears. Shared hopes and fears are basic to human bonding. People begin to pray for the realization of the hopes of others and for the easing of their fears. Shared beliefs about important subjects, such as the purpose of life, the meaning of death, the possibility of an afterlife, and what constitutes righteous behavior, are also fundamental to human bonding. These subjects become central to countless conversations and shared pursuits. Further, many rituals are gender specific; men do one sort of thing, and women do something else. Gender-specific roles lead men to bond with other men and women with other women based on their shared gender and their roles in ritual. Bonds work to define personal identity. We are who we are in large measure because of our ties with other people. Also, given the importance of gender to personal identity and the connection between religious beliefs and gender, we come to identify ourselves in terms of our religious beliefs. I am a Protestant, a Catholic, a Jew, or a Muslim. This is literally who I am. So ritual works to define who we are as human beings.

Religious ritual is also linked up with rites of passage. The most important times in our life are when we are born, when we survive puberty, when we marry, and when we die. Religion has successfully invaded these life transitions, and it has done so through ritual. In Judaism, boy babies are circumcised on the eighth day after birth, a ritual that symbolizes the boy's becoming part of the covenant with God. At the age of thirteen, the boy celebrates his bar mitzvah, which symbolizes that he is now a full-fledged member of the Jewish community. A similar ritual, bat mitzvah, is held for girls at the age of twelve. Jewish weddings celebrate unions thought to be made in heaven, and they are usually presided over by a rabbi. These rituals are especially important because they lay the foundation for new members of the Jewish community. At death, the funeral ritual celebrates a life thought to be holy, and it usually includes prayers and the reading of psalms. In Christianity, ritual rites of passage are sacraments. Baptism is the sacrament that washes away sin, is usually performed by a priest soon after birth, and introduces the newborn into the Christian community. Confirmation, performed by a bishop around the time of puberty, is supposed to strengthen a young person in faith at a time of new temptations. Matrimony is the sacrament that joins a couple in a holy union recognized by God, and extreme unction, offered at the end of life, opens the way for the soul to enter heaven. Not all Protestant denominations recognize all of these sacraments, but all of them recognize baptism. In Islam, circumcision (called khitan) is practiced widely as a sign of membership in the Muslim community, and it is even practiced on girls. There is nothing in Islam analogous to baptism, but ritual ablutions occur throughout life before prayer. At puberty, the ritual of Salah, praying five times per day at designated times, becomes obligatory. Muslim weddings are rituals filled with religious significance, and they are usually conducted by a Muslim cleric in a mosque. Funerals are also conducted by a cleric, and they include prayers to Allah to admit the soul of the deceased into paradise.

## Festivals

Festivals stand alongside rituals as crucial practices in sustaining religious beliefs. Festivals foster good feelings, and believers connect those feelings with the beliefs. The effect was especially pronounced among the ancient Egyptians. Direct participation in the temple rituals was forbidden to ordinary people, but this was not the case for the festivals. The Egyptians loved their festivals; they were central to the life of the community. Since the pharaoh was not only the head of state but also the highest of high priests, the secular and the religious were thoroughly blended. There was no distinction between secular festivals and religious festivals. The largest and grandest was the festival at Opet (Luxor), which honored the principal god Amun. It began with a huge procession in which the sacred image of the god, the cult statue, was placed in a little shrine situated in a small barque carried on the shoulders of several priests. As the procession wove its way through the massive crowds, onlookers strained to catch a glimpse of the god. This festival was held only once per year, so it marked a rare opportunity. A team of sensors purified the way, followed by priests carrying giant ostrich feathers that offered shade for the god. The god's consort, Mut, followed in a barque close behind, and this god was followed by a third barque carrying Amun's son, Khonsu. A band of musicians playing drums, pipes, and tambourines enhanced the overall experience. When the procession reached the bank of the Nile, priests loaded the three barques onto barges intended for the water. They were some seventy yards long, made of the finest Lebanon cedar, and bedecked with gold and jewels. As the procession continued upriver, mobs of spectators lined both banks. Eventually, the procession ended at a temple, where the gods were settled in for the night.[6]

Dozens of other festivals were held throughout the country at different times of the year, and what ordinary Egyptians may have loved most about them was the vast quantities of food, beer, and wine that were served. Herodotus, the Greek historian, wrote about the festival at Bubastis. He said that "more wine is consumed at this one festival than during the whole rest of the year." He speaks of 700,000 people (probably an exaggeration) enjoying one great celebration. Women play castanets, men play pipes, they clap their hands to the music, dancing girls entertain the crowds, everyone sings, and as the wine and beer go down, the festive spirit intensifies. Some of the women get so excited that they expose themselves to the revelers. One of the best things about the whole experience was that all the food and drink was free. It had been paid for by the god (i.e., by the pharaoh), so the people were certainly appreciative. It must have revitalized their religious fervor. But this, of course, was the whole idea. Not only did the gods sustain the life of the nation—they were thought to be responsible for the annual rise of the Nile, which was the source of all agriculture—but they also preserved all order in the cosmos. What better way to ensure belief in and appreciation for the gods than to hold sumptuous festivals, paid for by the gods, that the people would look forward to and come to love?

Judaism originated in Egypt, so it is virtually certain that the first Jewish priests were familiar with the Egyptian festivals. In some ways, the Egyptian festivals probably served as a model for the Jewish ones. Certainly, the purpose of these holidays was the same in both religions: to establish and solidify a connection between the people and their deity/deities. However, in contrast with the Egyptian festivals, where the consumption of alcohol was essential, the Jewish festivals tend much more toward contemplation and intellectual awareness. The most important Jewish holiday is Yom Kippur, the Day of Atonement, and it originated, according to tradition, when Moses descended from Mount Sinai and found his followers worshipping a golden calf. Moses prayed for forgiveness, and this prayer captures the sentiment of Yom Kippur. It is a day of reconciliation with God, of reconnecting with God. Other festivals include Sukkot, which involves mental reflection on God as protector; Rosh Hashanah, which celebrates God's creation of the world; Purim, which commemorates the day Esther saved the Jewish people from execution; and Passover, which recalls the time when the Jews are thought to have been enslaved in Egypt. Yahweh sent plagues to persuade the pharaoh to release them. All of these festivals include festive food, good wine, and happy feelings.

Christianity celebrates many minor festivals, such as Pentecost and the feast of the Ascension, but there are two major ones that dominate the others: Christmas and Easter. Christmas, which commemorates the birth of Jesus, mixes religious thoughts with colored lights, decorated trees, countless presents packaged in colorful wrapping, TV shows, musical performances, carols, parties, turkey or prime rib for dinner, and alcoholic drinks of all sorts. Commingled with all the festivities are the verses from the Gospel of Luke that describe the birth of an infant king in a stable surrounded by cows and sheep while, in the hills, hosts of angels announce the event to shepherds tending their flocks. The contrast of the lowly with the exalted and the rich with the poor is palpable, and it evokes the strongest of feelings. Easter, which is technically more important than Christmas, celebrates the resurrection of Jesus, and it combines thoughts of salvation with symbols of newness, including new clothes and the emergence of new life. As with Christmas, Easter includes elegant food and drink, and it induces believers to associate the religious significance of the occasion with happy times and joyful memories.

Islam is the setting for several festivals, but only two are official: Eid al-Adha and Eid al-Fitr. The first is considered to be the holier of the two, and it celebrates Abraham's willingness to sacrifice his son in obedience to God's command. The festival coincides with the end of the Hajj, the pilgrimage to Mecca. Muslims celebrate it by sacrificing an animal, usually a sheep, cow, goat, or camel, and sharing it with friends, family, and the less fortunate. They dress up in their finest clothing, exchange gifts, and enjoy other foods, such as specialty pastries and cookies. The other festival, Eid al-Fitr, occurs at the end of Ramadan. After the monthlong fast, which is intended to deepen faith in Allah, everyone is ready to celebrate. They decorate their homes, buy new clothing, gather with friends and family, give money and other gifts to children, and enjoy a sumptuous meal that includes lamb dishes, pastries, baklava, and chocolates. Neither of these festivals is mentioned in the Quran. They were almost certainly originated by early Islamic priests for the purpose of strengthening the ties between Muslims and Allah and thereby augmenting their own power. By all appearances, they succeed very well in accomplishing this purpose.

## Benefits and Harms of the Religious Illusion

Most people are of the opinion that religion is the source of many benefits, and they are probably correct about this. Religious organizations help the needy by directing attention to the problem of poverty, by reminding followers of the mandate to give to the less fortunate, and by transferring billions of dollars in contributions to alleviate poverty. Members of religious organizations dedicate their lives to teaching basic arithmetic, reading, and grammar to young children and to caring for their health and nursing them through illnesses. Religion promotes the well-being of believers by giving them a sense of purpose in life, by structuring their worldview, and by assuring them that they count for something in the eyes of God. Religion replenishes hope for people in despair, reassures them in times of uncertainty, and comforts them following the death of a friend or family member. It strengthens families by creating bonds among the members and instilling a sense of responsibility that they should feel for one another. It sets limits for children and gives order to their lives, which promotes good behavior. It even improves health by relieving anxiety and stress. Believers cite statistics to show that people with religious commitments live longer than those without. Religion provides moral guidance by teaching sets of maxims such as the Ten Commandments, and religion seems to make people happier by convincing them that they are living the way God intended them to live. All of these benefits serve as inducements for people to practice religion.

Yet religion is also responsible for producing a great deal of harm. Religion causes personal distress when believers discover that everything they believe amounts to an illusion. They become nihilists and believe nothing. Religion causes anxiety and worry in people who are afraid they might not make it into heaven. It disrupts communities by causing divisiveness: Protestants hate Catholics, Buddhists hate Muslims, and Muslims hate Hindus. The Ku Klux Klan, which is driven by religious beliefs, hates Jews and Black people. Religion enslaves women by restricting their movements and lifestyles, by forcing them into child marriages, and, in some countries, by requiring that they wear burqas and punishing them with flogging if they deviate from the rule. It destroys the possibility of female sexual fulfillment by subjecting women and girls to genital mutilation, and it paints them as sinful and as causing the downfall of the human race. The Christian theologian Tertullian described women as the gateway to the devil. It condemns homosexuals as being perverted, and in some countries, it executes them for engaging in same-sex practices. Religion corrupts the political system of democratic countries by demanding that laws conform to religious norms, and it interferes with the electoral process by illegally supporting favored candidates. Religion obstructs and undermines the progress of science, as evidenced by the religious response to the discoveries of Galileo and Darwin. If religion has all the answers, there is no need for science. Assuming that religious beliefs are illusions, most of the money and resources spent on supporting churches and their leaders is wasted money and wasted resources. Further, most of the time spent on religious rituals and the study of religious documents is wasted time that could be spent on more productive and rewarding pursuits.

One of the more harmful effects of religion is its impact on the human thinking process. It does this by contaminating the thinker's worldview, by persuading the thinking subject that certain things are real when in fact they probably are not. For example, the person who believes in miracles is likely to account for the occurrence of many things taken to be good as having happened because of a miracle. The inevitable result is an erosion of this person's understanding of causal connections. If the believer should desire some outcome, such as recovering from a life-threatening illness, the best way of getting it is to pray for a miracle instead of seeing a doctor or going to a hospital. The believer in demons will attribute the occurrence of something bad to the work of a demon and will not bother to find out why it really happened. The end result is an inevitable slide into magical ways of thinking. Further, because religion invites belief in contradictions, the believer will cast aside even the most basic principles of logic and draw conclusions that are totally absurd and contrary to the given evidence. A contaminated worldview will also persuade a religious believer to place undue trust in someone who is totally unqualified—for example, to trust the pronouncements of a TV personality about the cause of some disease against the considered judgment of qualified physicians or scientists. However, what may be the worst effect of religion on human thinking results from believing that there is a deity who holds the final truth about everything and that this truth is revealed in a select set of religious documents. The believer will become steeped in the pertinent documents and then attempt to enforce his or her understanding of these truths on everyone else. Such is the thinking behind every holy war and large-scale effort to impose personal religious beliefs on others by force.

## Murder and Mayhem

The Crusades were a series of religious wars between Christians and Muslims aimed at improving relations with the Eastern church and wresting the Holy Land from Muslim control.[7] The first Crusade, launched in 1095 by Pope Urban II and nearly 200 bishops, archbishops, and abbots at the Council of Clermont, had as its principal objective the capture of Jerusalem and its return to Christian control. As many as 100,000 souls, including princes, knights, foot soldiers, and common folk from throughout Western Europe, answered his call. The pope had assured them that God demanded they act by becoming soldiers of Christ, and it was said that he granted all who would participate a plenary indulgence, which means that any who would die along the way would go directly to heaven on condition that they had confessed their sins. The pope and his predecessor, Pope Gregory VII, had succeeded in sanctifying violence conducted on behalf of the Christian religion, and the violent action he had launched in that year was nothing short of a holy war. The first fruit of that violence was the slaughter of a great many Jews (perhaps thousands) living in the Rhineland, through which many crusaders marched en route to Jerusalem. These murdering crusaders were not a mere band of ruffians who had run amok but were under the strict command of Count Emicho of Leiningen. They beat down the doors of the houses and killed every Jew they could lay their hands on including men, women, children, and tiny infants. The justification given for their action was that the Jews were the enemies of God who had crucified Christ, so they deserved to die. Further, their money would help fund the Crusade. Yet some were allowed to live if they converted to Christianity.

After crossing the Bosporus at Constantinople, the first group of crusaders, known as the People's Crusade, under the command of a popular preacher named Peter the Hermit, roamed the countryside plundering every Muslim village in sight. They killed the inhabitants, tortured the elderly, and entertained themselves by roasting Muslim infants over open fires. A Muslim army retaliated by slaughtering nearly every one of them, but Peter managed to escape. The main army of crusaders, led by princes, followed close behind, and this army proceeded to conquer, with great loss of life, all the main cities of the area, including Nicaea and Tarsus. The largest city was Antioch, and overcoming its fortifications took eight months, with tens of thousands killed on both sides. Thousands of crusaders from society's lower classes died from starvation, disease, and hypothermia when they ran out of food and were forced to withstand a bitterly cold Turkish winter. On reaching Jerusalem, three years after having commenced their journey, the crusaders finally succeeded in scaling its walls by using two massive fifty-foot-high siege towers on wheels. There followed a slaughter the likes of which no one had ever seen. Thousands of Muslims and Jews took refuge in and around the structures on the Temple Mount, and the crusaders slaughtered every one of them, including women, children, and infants suckling at their mother's breast. Infant children who did not suffer being stabbed or decapitated were grabbed by the feet and swung against the stone walls, shattering their skulls and scattering brain tissue in every direction. The blood ran so high that it covered the ankles of the invading soldiers. After their job was finished, the crusaders, covered with blood and weighed down by as much silver and gold booty as they could carry, gathered inside the Church of the Holy Sepulcher. This was considered the holiest place in the entire Holy City, and it commemorated the death, burial, and resurrection of Jesus. There, the crusaders gave thanks to God for having blessed the siege with a successful climax.[8]

Another great crime committed in the name of religion was the Spanish Inquisition.[9] It began in 1478 by order of Ferdinand II of Aragon and Isabella I of Castile, the same rulers who funded the expedition to the New World led by Christopher Columbus. The purpose of the Inquisition to was to establish uniformity of religious belief throughout Spain. In 1481, six heretics were executed by burning them alive. Three years later, the two monarchs appointed the Dominican priest Tomás de Torquemada as grand inquisitor, at which point he enthusiastically commenced his mission to eliminate all heretics from the country. In 1478 and 1502, royal decrees were issued expelling from Spain all Jews and all Muslims, respectively, but they were allowed to stay if they converted to Christianity. A great many chose to do this. However, as would be expected given the circumstances, many of them secretly maintained their Jewish and Islamic beliefs and practices. Since the Inquisition had no authority over non-Christians, it was precisely these Jewish and Muslim converts who were the principal target of the Inquisition. Torquemada invited anonymous informants throughout the land to spy on their neighbors and to submit any kind of information that might lead to their conviction as heretics. Various kinds of torture—most commonly a modified form of waterboarding and the rack—were used to extract confessions and information about fellow heretics. Any torture involving the shedding of blood was not allowed. Also, it was widely recognized that confessions obtained under torture were not reliable, but if the accused confessed immediately after being tortured, the confession was accepted. Any information leading to the identification of other heretics was acted on. The Spanish Inquisition remained in operation for more than 300 years, and all successor grand inquisitors were priests of some sort, almost all of them bishops. It is estimated that 150,000 individuals were prosecuted and that 3,000 to 5,000 were executed.

The usual form of execution was being burned at the stake. In a few cases, the condemned individual was mercifully strangled to death before the pyre was set aflame. Perhaps this individual had been especially remorseful for having committed such grievous sins. But most were burned alive. In virtually all cases, the execution was preceded by an auto-da-fé, which was a religious ceremony featuring prayers and a Catholic Mass, during which the accused would be paraded about in colorful garments and tall pointy hats. The colors and designs on the costumes indicated the nature of the crime supposedly committed. At the end of the ceremony, the sentences of the accused would be read, the crowd would cheer, the fires would be lit, and the condemned would start to burn. As the flames leapt higher, their hair would catch fire, and they would cry out to God for mercy. These ceremonies were extremely popular, as they were rivaled only by bullfights. Today, hardly anyone alive would fail to be horrified by such displays. Everyone has a right to freedom of thought, we believe, and nobody should be subject to such ridicule and torture. But the idea that all human beings have rights simply by virtue of their being human was not recognized at that time and place. The Church was the representative of God on earth, and any action it took reflected the will of God. Inquisitions of this sort occurred on a lesser scale throughout Europe, and they even took place in Islamic countries where Muslims burned Christians and Jews.

Christian hostility toward Jews and Judaism continued into the Reformation. Martin Luther, the Great Reformer, had a visceral hatred for Jews. Yet in the early years of his ministry, he wanted desperately to convert them to his version of Christianity. For this purpose, in 1523, he wrote a short treatise titled "That Jesus Christ Was Born a Jew." The treatise went overboard to cast the Jews in a favorable light. His strategy was to be nice to the Jews so that they would convert. Luther said he would maintain this stance until it was clear what effect the treatise had.[10] Twenty years later, after the Jews failed to convert, he wrote "On the Jews and Their Lies." This treatise is a work of sheer hatred, and it reflected its author's true feelings about the Jews. The immediate impact was less than earthshaking due to the fact that Lutheran leaders did their best to suppress the work by ignoring it. The flames of divisiveness ignited by the treatise smoldered for more than 300 years until it was discovered by the Nazis in the early twentieth century. Then Luther was hailed as the greatest anti-Semite that Germany had ever produced, a true national hero, and the treatise helped to persuade thousands of Lutheran Christians to align themselves with the Nazi cause. The final effect was the slaughter of millions.

In the 100 years following Luther's split from Rome, Lutheranism spread widely through central Europe. Many towns and principalities converted to Lutheranism, while others held steadfast with Roman

Catholicism. In the meantime, French theologian John Calvin began preaching his own version of Protestantism in the 1530s, and it also spread widely. In 1618, Ferdinand II, king of Bohemia and future Holy Roman emperor, attempted to impose Roman Catholicism absolutely and exclusively throughout the empire, at which point the Protestant nobility rose up in revolt. Thus commenced the Thirty Years' War, which soon involved most of Europe. The war became a struggle to determine whether Roman Catholicism, Lutheranism, or Calvinism would have dominion in central Europe. Religion was not the only cause of the war (politics and commerce were also important), but it was a highly significant factor, and it induced the combatants to see their opponents as the agents of Satan. As a result, the fighting was exceedingly brutal, with horrendous crimes being committed against the peasant population. As was customary in most wars of the Middle Ages, the right to rape female captives was considered one of the perks of a soldier's job, and this right was exercised with gusto during the Thirty Years' War. All of the actual fighting occurred in what was then Germany, and it resulted in the death of some 8 million people. Possibly half of Germany's population perished.

## More Murder and Mayhem

Another great harm that took root in the West during the fifteenth and sixteenth centuries relates to slavery. Specifically, several religious leaders were instrumental in promoting the Black African slave trade in Portugal, Spain, and the Americas. In 1452 and 1455, Pope Nicholas V issued papal bulls (decrees) authorizing King Alfonso of Portugal to place in "perpetual slavery" pagans and Muslims living in Africa. Pagans included Black Africans. This authority was expressly confirmed by Pope Callixtus II and Pope Sixtus IV, it was implicitly confirmed by Pope Alexander VI, and it was expressly confirmed by Pope Leo X. Further, Pope Alexander VI (a Spaniard) paved the way for Spain to engage in the transatlantic trade in Black African slaves, and Pope Leo X implicitly permitted this trade.[11] These popes were not troubled by the obvious harm caused by their edicts because the belief was common at that time that Black Africans bore the biblical curse of Ham or that they were the children of Satan, so it did not make much difference how they were treated. After the Reformation, support for Black slavery became rampant in the Anglican Church, and the devout Elizabeth I, official head of the Church, together with Sir John Hawkins, created the British slave trade. This industry, which was supported by successor British monarchs (all heads of the Church), flourished until 1807, and it resulted in the capture and transportation of more than 10 million Black African slaves to the New World. Conditions aboard slave ships were worse than abominable, and when a slave died, the body would be cast overboard to the sharks. So many died that schools of sharks followed the ships all the way from embarkation to their final destination.

As exemplified by the Crusades and the Spanish Inquisition, the Jews have often been the victims of those committed to other beliefs. However, this does not imply that victimizing others was not above them. If Deuteronomy can be taken seriously, the Lord issued the following command to the Israelites:

> If you hear it said about one of the towns the Lord your God is giving you to live in that troublemakers have arisen among you and have led the people of their town astray, saying, "Let us go and worship other gods" (gods you have not known), then you must inquire, probe, and investigate it thoroughly. And if it is true and it has been proved that this detestable thing has been done among you, you must certainly put to the sword all who live in that town. You must destroy it completely, both its people and its livestock. You are to gather all the plunder of the town into the middle of the public square and completely burn the town and all its plunder as a whole burnt offering to the Lord your God. That town is to remain a ruin forever, never to be rebuilt. (Deuteronomy 13:12–16)

You must put to the sword all who live in that town. You must destroy it completely. Presumably, this includes women and children. And the command continues:

> When you march up to attack a city, make its people an offer of peace. If they accept and open their gates, all the people in it shall be subject to forced labor and shall work for you. If they refuse to make peace and they engage you in battle, lay siege to that city. When the Lord your God delivers it into your hand, put to the sword all the men in it. As for the women, the children, the livestock and everything else in the city, you may take these as plunder for yourselves, and you may use the plunder the Lord your God gives you from your enemies. This is how

you are to treat all the cities that are at a distance from you and do not belong to the nations nearby. However, in the cities of the nations the Lord your God is giving you as an inheritance, do not leave alive anything that breathes. Completely destroy them—the Hittites, Amorites, Canaanites, Perizzites, Hivites, and Jebusites—as the Lord your God has commanded you. (Deuteronomy 20:10–17)

If the people of the city accept your peace offer, you can reward them by making slaves of them. If they do not accept your offer, kill the men and do as you please with the women and children. But if the city happens to be one that the Lord is giving you, kill everything that breathes. Such is the command of Yahweh, the God of Israel. Obeying it could produce results as bad as what the Christians did in the Spanish Inquisition.

Islam is a religion that was born in violence, a condition that has remained with it for more than 1,300 years. Muhammad, the founder of Islam, was an illiterate merchant and warrior who, while praying in a cave, claimed to have received revelations from Allah via the angel Gabriel. This occurred in 610 CE, when he was forty years old. After preaching the message he had received in the cave, he acquired a number of followers, and when this number had increased to several hundred, he formed a unit of warriors to spread his message through military victory. One of the first engagements was the Battle of Badr, which began as a raid on a caravan of merchants and ended with victory over a much larger force of soldiers who had arrived from the city of Mecca. The outcome encouraged the belief that Muhammad had Allah on his side. During the next twenty years, Muhammad engaged in additional battles, including the Battle of Uhud, the Battle of the Trench, and the Battle of Khaybar. In 630, he led a group of 10,000 warrior converts against the city of Mecca and took control of the city. Later battles led to the control of most of the Arabian Peninsula, with most of its inhabitants converting to Islam.

After Muhammad died in 632, a dispute arose as to who should succeed him. His trusted friend and collaborator Abu Bakr thought that succession should be through qualified individuals, while his grandson Husayn ibn Ali thought it should be through bloodline. This dispute eventuated in a schism, with the group favoring personal qualifications becoming Sunnis and the group favoring bloodlines becoming the Shiites. Events that led up to the schism included the murder of a man named

Uthman, who was a successor of and son-in-law to Muhammad. When Ali ibn Abi Talib, another son-in-law, failed to avenge this murder, Muhammad's favorite wife Aisha and her army attacked him and his army in the Battle of Jamal. Aisha lost, from which arose the lesson that women should stay out of men's business. A second event was the Battle of Siffin, in which Ali, the victor at Jamal, fought a successor to Muhammad named Muawiya. The dispute concerned when to bring Uthman's murderers to justice, and after 70,000 lives were lost, the battle ended in arbitration. Four years later, Ali was murdered by being stabbed with a poisoned sword, and he was succeeded by his son Husayn. Several years later, Muawiya died and was succeeded by his son Yazid. These two then met in the Battle of Karbala. Husayn's small force was vastly outnumbered by Yazid's, and he, together with his entire family, was slaughtered. The two sides were so unequal that the slaughter amounted to murder. After the battle, the Sunnis mutilated the bodies of the dead. The mutilation enraged the Shiites against the Sunnis, and those feelings continue to trouble relations between the two Muslim factions to this day.

The word "jihad" occurs twenty-eight times in the Quran. The word literally means "struggle," and today, the argument is made that the word's true meaning refers to a struggle internal to the believer between good and evil urges. However, there can be little doubt that for more than the past 1,300 years, the de facto meaning of jihad has been holy war in a very physical sense. According to the late Ayatollah Khomeini, one of the most revered figures in Shia Islam and an expert in Sharia law, the jihad "means the conquest of non-Muslim territory. The domination of Koranic law from one end of the earth to the other is . . . the final goal . . . of this war of conquest."[12] And it was precisely through this very violent meaning of jihad that Islamic beliefs were spread during Muhammad's life and after his death. It took 1,000 years for Christian popes to come up with the idea of sanctified violence, but in Islam, violence was sanctified right from the start. Jihad is a permanent religious obligation incumbent on all Muslims to expand Muslim territory. The idea is that if new territory (land) is conquered, then, with the proper pressure, the inhabitants of that territory will quickly convert to Islam. Judging by history, the theory has worked very well.

The early Muslims were first and foremost raiders of caravans and merchants, and these activities dictated the essential principles of jihad.

As raiders, the main goal was the acquisition of loot, slaves, and women, and as merchants, the rule was that nothing that could be sold should be discarded (or killed). This means that when territory was acquired through conquest, the proper procedure was to kill the male captives, rape the women, and then sell them, together with any children, into slavery. Any women of comely appearance became wives or sex slaves of the victors (i.e., members of their harem). All of this, of course, was done at the command of Allah. The actions of Muhammad himself served as a procedural model for practicing jihad. There was a Jew living at that time named Kinana who was rumored to have a fortune in gold vessels hidden away in a secret location. When Muhammad heard the rumor, he ordered some of his minions to apprehend Kinana and find out the location of the gold. They brought Kinana back to Muhammad, tied him down to the ground, and lit a fire on his chest. Before he drew his last breath, Muhammad ordered that his head be cut off. That very night, Muhammad took Kinana's seventeen-year-old bride, Safiya, now a widow, into his bed. Later, she became one of his eleven wives.[13] This example differs from the norm for jihad in that usually the heat of battle or the furious pace of executions did not allow sufficient time for torture.

After Muhammad's death, Islam exploded out of Arabia and spread eastward with lightning speed through Syria, Persia, Afghanistan, and Baluchistan and westward through Egypt and all of North Africa and up into Spain. Jerusalem was one of the first large cities to fall. Virtually all of the Christian inhabitants of these lands converted to Islam. Along with these conquests, tens of thousands of lives were lost. But two of the most savage battles were yet to come. The first occurred in 1389 when Christian forces under the king of Serbia tried to oust the Muslim Turks from Bosnia. The Christians numbered between 20,000 and 30,000, and after the battle, which was won by the Turks, the sultan ordered the execution of all the Christian prisoners. After decapitating thousands during a period of many hours, the arms of the executioners were aching so badly that they switched to slashing throats and cutting off hands and feet so that the prisoners would bleed to death. So much blood was spilled that it filled small lakes.[14]

The other slaughter is the one that followed the siege of Constantinople in 1453. For 1,000 years, the city had avoided capture because of its massive thirteen-mile-long wall that surrounded it. But Mahomet II was determined that the city would be his. He had 100,000 Muslim infantrymen and other soldiers at his disposal, so it mattered little how many he had to sacrifice to achieve his goal. Wave after wave threw themselves against the wall until finally it was breached. Then, shouting "Allah is great," they poured into the city like a great flood following the break of a dam. Thousands of defenders, together with their wives and children, took refuge in the huge Santa Sophia cathedral but to no avail. The first to be raped were the nuns, followed by great numbers of female laity. Within a couple of hours, at least 4,000 citizens were beheaded until Mahomet called a halt to the slaughter. If he had allowed his soldiers to kill everyone, there would be nobody left to sell into slavery. As it turned out, 50,000 were sold, which overwhelmed the slave markets of Anatolia. After the frenzied killing had died down, Mahomet obtained from Grand Duke Notaras, who had managed to survive, the names of all the nobles and officials of the city who were still alive, and he had them arrested and decapitated. Finally, after a banquet featuring the best food and wine, Mahomet, who by the end of the evening was thoroughly intoxicated, asked Notaras to bring him his fourteen-year-old boy. Mahomet had a reputation for pederasty, and Notaras refused. The enraged Mahomet retaliated by having Notaras and his entire family decapitated.[15]

The Crusades by the Christians are often considered to be among the most harmful atrocities ever perpetrated by religion, but the Crusades pale in comparison with the jihad. The Crusades lasted less than 200 years (1096–1291), but the jihad, which continues to this day in certain regions, has lasted more than 1,300 years. The Crusades were intended to retake Jerusalem and the Holy Land, but the jihad conquered millions of square miles, and, at least in the minds of some, the intention is to conquer the entire world. Also, the amount of blood shed by the Crusades is vastly less than what has been shed by the jihad. If, at this point, there is any doubt about the connection between religion and power, that doubt should be laid to rest by the jihad, at least as concerns Islam. Islam, for most of its existence, has been all about power and the increase of power. The same is true of other religions, but it may not be as obvious.

## Is God Both Good and Evil?

In the Muslim battles involving Sunnis and Shiites, both sides claimed to have the backing of Allah. In killing their brothers, both sides were following Allah's commands. The writers of Deuteronomy thought that they were acting in accord with the commands of Yahweh when they urged the Jews to kill everything that breathes, but most Jews today would say that Yahweh forbids indiscriminate slaughter. The instigators of the Inquisition thought that their torture and murder of the Jews and the Muslims had the sanction of their God, but Christians today are horrified by these events. Fifteenth- and sixteenth-century religious leaders, both Catholic and Protestant, thought that God permitted the enslavement of Black Africans, but subsequent leaders held that God forbids slavery. What are we to make of these contradictory views? Possible responses are that God is inherently contradictory or that God is both good and evil. Most believers would probably reply that these contradictory views and morally reprehensible actions are the result of *misinterpreting* the voice of God. The Sunni Muslims interpreted the will of God in one way, and the Shiites interpreted it another way. The promoters of the Inquisition interpreted the will of God in one way, but today's Christians interpret it another way. The same is true for the other cases. But if this is so, are we not left with the inescapable conclusion that these conflicting interpretations are none other than God himself as he exists in their minds? God *is* the interpretation, and the interpretation shifts according to the moods and whims of the moment. God is a mere idea that believers have molded and shaped throughout the years to serve their own purposes. It follows that there are even more Gods than there are believers. There are billions of them, each a little different from all the others. Each God is a construct, an object of belief, and each believer thinks that his or her God really exists. But each of these beliefs is an illusion.

What is truly tragic in all these occurrences is that the victims died for an illusion. They did not die because any independently existing deity commanded it. And thousands of them died in ways that are unimaginably horrible. The pain caused by fire is greater than that of being stabbed by a knife or struck by a hurled stone. No one can possibly imagine the pain suffered by someone being burned alive. And then there is the pain, both physical and psychological, of being raped repeatedly by a raging mob, the pain suffered by children whose parents were murdered, the pain of being ripped from one's home and cast into slavery, and the pain of having one's home and livelihood plundered and destroyed. But the atrocities continue even to the present day, all in the name of religion.

Innocent people continue to have their heads cut off by religious fanatics. Young girls continue to be forced into marriage with much older men, their genitals continue to be mutilated, and women continue to be flogged for having committed a minor infraction against some religious norm. Also, thousands of innocent souls continue to be maimed and murdered by crazed individuals sacrificing themselves for a religious cause. The subject matter of illusion is not something real, but the consequences of illusion are terribly real. The pain is excruciatingly real, and the victims who suffer it are more real still.

## Sin

The God of religion has the attributes that it has because it is modeled after human beings. Indeed, many of the early priests were said to be gods themselves, and all the pharaohs of ancient Egypt were gods. So it is no wonder that the God of religion is an anthropomorphic God—a God with human attributes. And now that we are more familiar with these attributes, we can flesh out the religious illusion. Since it is possible to please a God of religion, it is also possible to displease it. Whatever displeases such a God is called a sin. Therefore, since belief in any God of religion is an illusion, belief in the existence of sin is also an illusion. Of course, this does not mean that nothing is morally wrong. An action is morally wrong if it harms other human beings unjustifiably, which is quite different from displeasing God. Since belief in the existence of sin is an illusion, so is belief in the need for forgiveness and salvation. If we have harmed someone by an action considered to be sinful, we should ask forgiveness from the person we have harmed, not from some illusory deity. Demons, devils, and Satan were invented by ancient priests to explain why people sin—namely, because these entities lead them astray. Thus, belief in diabolical entities is also an illusion.

Sin is a product of priestly power, and its intended effect is to create fear in the minds of believers. Sin separates believers from God, and anyone separated from God will never get to heaven. Such a prospect terrifies the devout. Also, the thought that they have sinned generates tremendous guilt. Because God has human attributes, sin is taken to be a form of betrayal. It is betrayal of a friend, which is the worst kind of betrayal. The route back to God's good graces often goes through the priest. Sinners ask

314

the priest what they can do to win forgiveness, and they will do anything the priest says to get it. It is hard to imagine a more effective means for augmenting priestly power.

## Avoiding Illusion: The Call for Evidence

Because illusions are disconnected from reality, religious beliefs produce beneficial results on some occasions and harmful results on others. Religious beliefs are like a loose cannon that can fire haphazardly in any direction. Sometimes the projectile may hit an enemy ship, sometimes it may hit a friendly one. One way of ensuring that a belief is grounded in reality is by requiring that it be supported by evidence. In his essay "The Ethics of Belief," the prominent nineteenth-century mathematician W. K. Clifford made a well-reasoned appeal that all of our beliefs be supported by evidence:

> It is wrong always, everywhere, and for everyone, to believe anything on insufficient evidence.[16]

Not only is it unwise and a bad idea to believe things on insufficient evidence, but it is morally wrong to do so. Clifford cites a hypothetical example involving a shipowner about to send out to sea a ship carrying a great many families to a future home in a new land. The ship was not very well built to start with, and now it was showing definite signs of wear. The shipowner worried that it might not make the voyage. Yet he reasoned that it had made many safe voyages in the past, and it had weathered many storms. Having the ship overhauled and refitted would cost a lot of money. So he put aside his doubts and decided to trust in Providence that the ship would reach its destination safely. Unfortunately, in mid ocean, the ship sank, taking with it the lives of all the passengers. Was the shipowner morally responsible for the loss of life? Of course he was. The owner believed that the ship was safe without sufficient evidence. Before the ship sailed, he had conducted no safety inspection, so he was not justified in believing that the ship would make it to port safely. But even if, by some stroke of luck, the ship had not sunk, the owner would still be responsible for his immoral action because the ship was not safe and the lives of the passengers were endangered.

If we should present Clifford's line of reasoning to a religious believer, will it persuade this person to accept its conclusion and then to abandon all religious belief? Probably not. Many will reply that they already have all the evidence they need. They may say that they feel the presence of God in their lives and feel him interacting with them and that this feeling satisfies any doubt. The problem is that evidence gathering does not produce the same results with everyone. Evidence gathering involves, first of all, perception, and perception is not a merely passive process by which the mind receives information from the outside world and delivers it fully formed. Perception is very much an active process involving the interplay of sensory input with mental frameworks consisting of learning, memories, and expectations. A person gazing at a two-dimensional image of a vase can see now a vase and a moment later two people staring at each other. The different perceptions result from two different mental patterns (gestalts) coming into play: the pattern of a vase and the pattern of a profile face. Once formed, perceptions are then interpreted in terms of additional mental frameworks composed of values, beliefs, intentions, hopes, and fears. Given that all of these components differ from person to person, it is no wonder that people derive different kinds of evidence from experiencing the same event. If two people should survive a car crash, one will attribute the outcome to a caring God, the other to the quantity of steel in the body of the car.

Religious mental frameworks force believers to see events in the lived world in a way that comports with the framework. Suppose you are searching for a lifetime partner, and you pray to God to help you find one. You then happen to meet someone who turns out to be just right. This proves that God is looking out for you and wants you to be happy. Or suppose that you get fired from your job. Obviously, God has a much better job in mind for you, and with God's help, you will find it. Or suppose that your baby daughter is killed in a senseless car accident. Clearly, God has called her home, and you are consoled by the thought that she is with him in heaven. Or you pray for God's help in winning the lottery. When you don't win, this means that God answered your prayer, but he simply said no. Religious mental frameworks serve not only to explain why both good and bad things happen in life but also to prove that God is efficacious in human affairs. Further, each such event serves as a confirming instance of the correctness of the framework. Each is like the outcome of an experiment that serves to confirm a working hypothesis. After count-less numbers of such confirming instances, a person's belief system may become so solidly grounded as to be nearly unshakable.

The purpose of all mental frameworks is to provide stability to our lived experience, and they could not accomplish this purpose if they were fluid or easily replaced. As a result, religious belief systems tend to remain in place until something new happens that forces it out. This something new often involves having certain highly emotional experiences or im-mersive experiences, such as studying abroad. The death of a child or the birth of a child afflicted with a life-threatening illness can cause parents to abandon any belief in a caring God. Going away to college (even if only in a nearby city) exposes a student to all sorts of new people who see the world differently. Having such experiences cannot fail to impact a per-son's outlook. Also, taking mind-expanding courses, such as philosophy, psychology, history, anthropology, poetry, literature, physics, biology, astronomy, and cognitive science, forces the student to see the world in new ways. Taking such courses does not always dispel the illusions that contaminate life, but it may be the most effective way there is.

# EPILOGUE

## Religion and Happiness

It is sometimes said that religion makes people happy, and there are surveys that might appear to support this claim. According to a survey conducted by the Pew Research Center, active churchgoers from twenty-six countries were more likely to describe themselves as "very happy" in comparison with those who were either inactive or unaffiliated with any religion.[1] Yet, it would be a mistake to conclude from this survey that religion causes people to be happy because the survey indicates only a correlation between religion and happiness, not a causal connection. What the survey may indicate is that people who are happy tend to be religious. Under this interpretation, happiness causes people to be religious, not the other way around. Another part of the Pew survey points to a correlation between being actively religious and social involvement. People who are actively religious tend to join nonreligious organizations, such as charities and clubs, at a higher rate than do people who are not actively religious. If we combine the two parts of the survey, a reasonable interpretation is that happy people tend to be socially active and that socially active people tend to be religiously active. In no way can the survey be interpreted to imply that religious *belief* causes people to be happy.

If religious belief, as such, caused people to be happy, this would stand as a good reason to be religious. After all, happiness is what everyone desires in life, and if having religious beliefs is a guaranteed way of securing happiness, no one could be blamed for being religious. But beliefs as such, religious or otherwise, do not cause happiness. Granted, religious beliefs do serve to reduce anxiety, which results from the constant threat of death, fear of eternal punishment, and potential catastrophes, such as the loss of one's job or home or harm to one's spouse or children. But the mere relief of anxiety falls short of happiness. Happiness is more than the absence of something, more than a mere feeling, more than relief of pain or fear, more than contentment or relaxation. Aristotle, whose *Nichomachean Ethics* is devoted mainly to exploring the nature of happiness, argues that happiness is an activity, specifically a mental activity in accord with virtue.[2] This characterization comports with the response of countless individuals who report that they are the happiest when they are actively doing something—writing a novel, preparing a meal, carving a statue, raising children, writing or performing a musical piece, designing a machine, painting a picture, teaching a child how to read, solving a mathematical problem, or designing a scientific experiment. All of these involve mental activity. Also, if they are done in the right way, all are in accord with virtue in that they accomplish something good. After a productive period of creative activity, the poet can look back on how nicely the words fit together to capture the intended insight or evoke the intended feeling. The carpenter can survey the results of a day's work with a feeling of justified satisfaction. This feeling of satisfaction is an essential part of happiness, and it comes as a direct result of mental activity. For Aristotle, the more cerebral the activity, the greater the happiness. Philosophical contemplation brings the greatest happiness, but all of these other activities result in genuine happiness as well.

If happiness is an activity, then it cannot be the case that merely entertaining a belief, whatever the belief might be about, can count as happiness. Beliefs are not activities. Thus, if Aristotle's understanding of happiness is correct, then mere religious belief does not yield happiness. Yet relief of anxiety, even if it does not amount to happiness, is a kind of prelude to happiness. One cannot be happy when incapacitated by constant anxiety. Is this relief of anxiety sufficient to justify having religious beliefs? I think the answer must be negative for the simple reason that the relief is fake. The relief is effected through the creation of illusions. The relief amounts to trickery. Also, the relief has serious negative side effects. One of them is that it blinds the believer to what is really important in life. Imagine a family of campers who pitch their tent on railroad tracks.

They believe that the sturdy fabric surrounding them will afford protection against looming dangers from the world outside. As a result, they pay no attention to the rumbling of the ground that signals the approach of an oncoming train. In the same way, many religious believers discount evidence that the burning of fossil fuels is causing climate change, which, if unchecked, threatens to bring on the sixth great extinction of life on Earth. No need to worry about this, they think, because God will protect us. God has a plan for everything, and even if we do nothing at all, something miraculous will occur that will make the threat magically disappear.

Another side effect of religious belief is that it contaminates and corrupts the thinking process of believers, inducing them to accept the worst kind of reasoning as exemplary and persuasive. Circular reasoning, which is universally recognized as defective, is widely accepted among believers whenever it yields a conclusion that brings comfort and reassurance. Every form of good reasoning, of course, depends on evidence or supporting reasons, but religious belief undercuts this requirement by welcoming conclusions supported by nothing at all. The core belief of every religion is the existence of a god or gods who want to be worshipped and prayed to, but no religion has ever offered a shred of evidence that such an entity actually exists, that is, exists independently of the hopes and wishes of believers. Religious belief also promotes excessive credulity in the minds of its followers, leading them to accept as the final truth whatever comes forth from presumed authorities. Such authorities include anybody from a preacher conducting a revival to a reasonably well educated person who claims expertise in an area where no real expertise is possible. Further, religious believers tend to discount the importance of the laws of nature, and as a result, they accept all sorts of miraculous occurrences without any explanation of how the laws of nature can be temporarily suspended and then restored. The idea that a human being could rise from the dead is met with nonchalance by millions: of course, he rose from the dead; we all know that. Believers even give short shrift to the laws of logic by accepting what appear to be outright contradictions as expressions of great profundity. How something can be both god and man at the same time is strikingly similar to how something can be square and circular at the same time, yet believers are completely comfortable with the idea that there is a Son of God. Also, the idea that a divinity could consist of one entity and three at the same time is seen as unproblematic. What may be the most remarkable thing about religious belief is how, given the mental fog that it generates, its adherents are able to function at all in the real world.

## The Future of Religious Belief

At the end of his *Future of an Illusion*, Freud expresses his guarded expectation (or at least his hope) that modern science, growing stronger every day, will gradually eat away at religious belief until, at some point in the future, religion will be no longer. I take this prediction to be unlikely. Freud, particularly on these pages, seems to view religious belief as similar to a disease such as smallpox that, once eradicated, will be gone for good. But religion is not like smallpox. Religion is more resilient; it has a way of coming back. One way it displays its resiliency is by adapting any scientific discovery it perceives as threatening and by then incorporating it into the body of accepted truth. When Copernicus announced that the Earth was not in the center of the universe, which threatened the orthodox worldview, the Catholic Church condemned it at first, but when it became clear that it faced a losing battle, it accepted the discovery as consistent with Church teaching and went on as if nothing had happened. The same thing occurred with Darwin's theory of natural selection, which was at first thought to challenge the Church's view of creation but which today is considered perfectly consistent with orthodox teaching. I attribute this resiliency to the fact that religion is the product of power, and power always finds a way of working around problems. When a particularly nasty problem inflicts a serious wound, as it did at the time of the Reformation, a new religion pops up to fill the power gap. As a result, I think it likely that religion is here to stay.

In chapter 2, I traced the origin of religion to ambitious tribesmen in the Neolithic period who figured out a way of rising to the top of the tribal power structure. If they could convince their comrades that they had the power to communicate with the spirits of the weather and the spirits of the crops, they would be regarded as very important individuals, and they might even be appointed chief of the tribe. These were the first priests, and by elevating the spirits to a higher level, they created the first gods. But the same conditions that gave rise to the first priests and the earliest religion are very much present in today's society. All aspiring leaders are dominated by the quest for power, and one of the easiest ways of getting it is for them to convince others that they are in touch with the gods, which means they can assist in getting a favorable answer to prayers. Today's televangelists know very well that great wealth and political power are to be had through these means. Being a priest offers so many opportunities for wealth and power that it is unlikely that priests will vanish anytime soon. Also, people today still have their fears, so they are naturally vulnerable to the assurances of the priests. Further, a necessary condition for the practice of religion is secrecy. The thoughts and maneuverings of the priests must be kept secret lest the followers discover what is really going on, and today's priests are just as able to keep secrets as their predecessors were in ancient times. Finally, because the gods are invisible, there is no way of obtaining any positive information as to what they are like. As a result, the followers will never be able to expose the priests for their role in creating them.

One factor that greatly facilitates the role of creating gods is the initial preconditioning of the public mind in favor of things religious. Today, society is literally drenched with religion, and this makes it easier for priests to conduct their business. An example taken from physics may be enlightening. In 1964, the astronomers Arno Penzias and Robert Wilson discovered a phenomenon called cosmic microwave background radiation. It consists of a very faint light that fills all the space between the stars. It came into existence shortly following the big bang, about 14 billion years ago, and it is sometimes called the afterglow of the big bang. Everything in the universe is bathed in this radiation: stars, galaxies, planets, trees, mountains, the furniture in our room, and our own bodies. Religious belief is the cosmic background radiation of human society. It touches and conditions all human thinking, and it has been around for at least the past 10,000 years. Why has the physical phenomenon, the cosmic afterglow, not died out after all these years? One answer is that nothing has absorbed it. The same reasoning may relate to religious belief. Religious belief continues to flourish because nothing has absorbed it. But beliefs are not material things like water molecules, so nothing *can* absorb it. As a result, it could easily be around for another 10,000 years.

All of the philosophers surveyed in chapter 8 viewed power as intrinsic to human existence. Depending on the circumstances, the first offspring of power is either an illusion or some kind of construct, both of which serve to augment the original power. If a construct comes first, then illusion follows in short order. This means that illusion is an inevitable part of the human condition. It will always be with us. The chief manifestations of illusion occur in religion, in politics and government, in marketing and advertising, and in all forms of con artistry. To a lesser degree, illusion infects all human relations. No one is completely honest in his or her dealings with other people, and every breakdown in honesty produces an illusion, at least an insignificant one. So the illusion of religion is just one part of a phenomenon having many manifestations. It differs from the other forms mainly in regard to its objects of belief, all of which are invisible and undetectable by any sense. This makes the religious illusion harder to detect than the other forms, but the difficulty in detecting it should not lead anyone to think that it is not really there.

If religion is destined to be with us for a very long time, what can be done to mitigate its harmful effects both on society and on the minds of believers? Most of the harmful effects come from taking it seriously. The terrorist who plants bombs in public places to please some deity takes religion very seriously, as does the fanatic who murders doctors outside abortion clinics. If believers could somehow be persuaded to tamp down the fervor, much of the harm caused by it could be avoided. Unfortunately, this is no easy task. The reason why these individuals are so fervent in their beliefs is because they take them as being absolutely and eternally true. To persuade them otherwise usually involves appealing to some kind of reasoning process, but religion has so corrupted the thinking of the believer that reason is to no avail. Taking college-level courses related to good reasoning and the meaning of knowledge and truth would help a great deal, but believers often consider such courses to be the work of Satan, so they stay far clear of them. Others cannot afford the luxury of a college education. In the absence of special measures, the gradual materialization of our culture promises to erode religious belief to some extent. Many believers eventually come to see that they can enjoy the best things religion has to offer in the absence of any beliefs. These things include charming and touching stories, such as the good Samaritan, the life of Job, and the birth of Jesus; stories that can enrich life; and festivals that strengthen ties with family and friends. Today, millions of people look forward to Christmas, Purim, and the end of Ramadan as the high point of the year, but they believe nothing about the underlying religion. If this posture ever becomes general through society, religion will not have disappeared entirely, but it will have transitioned from fervent belief to myth. Unlike fervently held beliefs, myths rarely result in any serious harm to anyone.

A similar result can be accomplished by not taking religious expressions as literally true or false. For example, if the expression "The Lord is my shepherd" is taken as a conventional proposition, it is clearly false for anyone who does not have a shepherd, and this includes most of us. But this is largely to miss the point. The meaning of the expression is more complex than that. Many years ago, it was suggested that religious expressions be taken as works of art.[3] This interpretation would, I think, preserve the meaning of these expressions without rendering them vulnerable to falsification. A poem can be full of meaning even though it might contain contradictions. A painting can express a great deal even though what it depicts might violate the laws of nature. And the laws of logic and the laws of nature have no bearing at all on a musical piece. But poetry, painting, and music are never considered to be true or false in the way that conventional propositions are. So if religious expressions are taken to be works of art, they could continue to express a wealth of meaning, even though they would not be considered to be literally true or false. But if they are not considered to be true, they would not be believed, as they are typically are. They would be above belief, so to speak. And, of course, they would not be illusions. So if priests could somehow be persuaded to tell their followers that religious expressions are to be understood as works of art, most or all of the harm caused by religious belief could be avoided, while the good could be preserved. But I doubt that many priests would comply with this suggestion because interpreting religious expressions as not absolutely true would seriously undermine their own power.

An objection to the proposal that we not take religion seriously is that religion is necessary for morality, and if people stop taking religion seriously, they will view morality in the same way, and this will unleash a flood of immoral activity unlike anything the world has ever seen. It is, of course, true that many people are moral because some divine entity, Yahweh, God, or Allah, has allegedly commanded it and those who fail to heed the command will suffer in the afterlife. I would urge that obedience to a command is not a *good* reason for being moral. For people who are incapable of thinking for themselves, following divine commands may be the only reason for leading a moral life, but it is still not a good reason. For a better one, I suggest Aristotle's theory that living a moral life is the only route to happiness. The payoff is immediate. One need not wait for any afterlife. For Aristotle, happiness is the natural goal (final cause) of human life, so we have a natural orientation toward morality, even though many people miss the mark. One way of interpreting this orientation is to see it in terms of empathy. Empathy means feeling with the other person, putting oneself in the place of the other person, and people have a natural disposition toward acting in this way. It can be encouraged in children by bringing pets into the household. Children are quick to see how coarse and domineering behavior is hurtful to the pet, and most learn to avoid it. Behaving empathically toward other people creates happiness. It brings people closer together, and this makes them happy. Behaving in this way naturally gives rise to the golden rule, which urges people to treat others as they themselves would like to be treated, and this is a perfectly good standard of behavior for everyone. So religion is not a necessary condition for moral behavior. Human reason, unassisted by divine guidance, is a fecund source of moral principles.

# NOTES

## Chapter Two

1. Edward Burnet Tylor, *Primitive Culture: Researches into the Development of Mythology, Philosophy, Religion, Language, Art, and Custom* (New York: Henry Holt and Company, 1874), Vol. 1, p. 429.

2. Tylor, *Primitive Culture*, Vol. 2, p. 124.

3. Tylor, *Primitive Culture*, Vol. 2, p. 207.

4. Tylor, *Primitive Culture*, Vol. 2, p. 211.

5. Tylor, *Primitive Culture*, Vol. 2, p. 215.

6. Tylor, *Primitive Culture*, Vol. 2, p. 144.

7. Tylor, *Primitive Culture*, Vol. 2, p. 145. The word "fetish" means something different for Tylor than it does for many people today, where it refers to something having a sexual interest for someone.

8. Tylor, *Primitive Culture*, Vol. 2, p. 147.

9. Tylor, *Primitive Culture*, Vol. 2, pp. 158–59.

10. James George Frazer, *The Golden Bough: A Study of Magic and Religion*, Abridged Edition (London: Macmillan/St. Martin's Street, 1922), p. 291.

11. Frazer, *The Golden Bough*, p. 47.

12. Frazer, *The Golden Bough*, p. 48.

13. Tylor cites evidence that belief in fetishes was common in many parts of Asia, India, Europe, Africa, North America, South America, and islands in the Atlantic, Pacific, and Indian oceans. *Primitive Culture*, Vol. 2, pp. 143–83. Frazer notes that puppet fetishes known as the corn mother, wheat mother, and so on were used to ensure a fertile harvest in Europe, the East Indies, and North and South America. *The Golden Bough*, pp. 290–305.

14. Frazer, *The Golden Bough*, p. 35.

15. Frazer, *The Golden Bough*, p. 35.

16. D. Bruce Dickson, *The Dawn of Belief: Religion in the Upper Paleolithic of Southwestern Europe* (Tucson: University of Arizona Press, 1990), p. 92. See also Edwin O. James, *Prehistoric Religion* (New York: Frederick A. Praeger, 1957), p. 28.

17. To be successful, this reinterpretation of Frazer's theory must be able to explain the uses of puppets and wreathes that Frazer takes to be definitive cases of magic. He observes that certain ancient peoples would throw the corn mother into a river to produce rain, as if this activity engaged some primitive law of nature. *The Golden Bough*, pp. 299–300. However, to be certain of this interpretation, we must have access to the inner workings of the minds of these people, which we do not have. It seems equally possible that throwing the corn mother into a river was simply a forceful way of communicating with it.

## Chapter Three

1. See Serge Sauneron, *The Priests of Ancient Egypt*, new ed. (Ithaca, NY: Cornell University Press, 2000), pp. 52–53.

2. Richard Wilkinson, *The Complete Gods and Goddesses of Ancient Egypt* (London: Thames and Hudson, 2003).

3. A temple was by definition "god's house." Every god of any importance needed a house. See Siegfried Morenz, *Egyptian Religion*, trans. Anne E. Keep (Ithaca, NY: Cornell University Press, 1973), p. 86, and Erik Hornung, *Conceptions of God in Ancient Egypt*, trans. John Baines (Ithaca, NY: Cornell University Press, 1982), p. 229.

4. The priests were needed to perform the daily cult ritual, which was conducted at every temple throughout Egypt; Sauneron, *The Priests of Ancient Egypt*, p. 89.

5. Syncretism resulted in the production of a "new form"—that is, a new god albeit a temporary one; Hornung, *Conceptions of God in Ancient Egypt*, p. 97.

6. Sauneron, *The Priests of Ancient Egypt*, p. 47.

7. Serge Sauneron reports that priests would hollow out a statue of a god and attach an acoustical conduit so that a voice from a hidden speaker would appear to come from the statue. This technique could have been used to convince rank-and-file priests that the statue contained a living god; Sauneron, *The Priests of Ancient Egypt*, p. 100.

8. It should be obvious to the reader that the cult statue perfectly fits E. B. Tylor's definition of "fetish."

9. This account of rituals and processions is taken from Sauneron, *The Priests of Ancient Egypt*, pp. 77–96.

10. Hornung, *Conceptions of God in Ancient Egypt*, p. 18.

11. Hornung, *Conceptions of God in Ancient Egypt*, p. 22.

12. Paul Johnson, *The Civilization of Ancient Egypt* (London: Weidenfeld & Nicolson, 1999), p. 86.

13. Morenz, *Egyptian Religion*, p. 160.

14. Hornung, *Conceptions of God in Ancient Egypt*, p. 189.

15. Hornung, *Conceptions of God in Ancient Egypt*, p. 187.

16. Hornung, *Conceptions of God in Ancient Egypt*, p. 141.

17. Hornung, *Conceptions of God in Ancient Egypt*, p. 141.

18. Johnson, *The Civilization of Ancient Egypt*, p. 44.

19. Siegfried Morenz, *Egyptian Religion*, p. 151.

20. Hornung, *Conceptions of God in Ancient Egypt*, p. 97; Morenz, *Egyptian Religion*, pp. 140–41.

21. See Hornung, *Conceptions of God in Ancient Egypt*, p. 246.

22. Hornung, *Conceptions of God in Ancient Egypt*, p. 248.

23. Quoted from Johnson, *The Civilization of Ancient Egypt*, p. 90.

24. Johnson, *The Civilization of Ancient Egypt*, p. 89.

25. Hornung, *Conceptions of God in Ancient Egypt*, pp. 244–46.

26. See especially the limestone balustrade from el-Armana at the Egyptian Museum, Cairo, and the Boundary stela at Tuna-el-Gebel. Photographic reproductions are generally available.

27. This hypothesis was invented by Hutan Ashrafian, a surgeon at Imperial College London (*New Scientist*, September, 5, 2012). The hypothesis is currently unverifiable because there is not at present a definitive genetic test for epilepsy.

28. Johnson, *The Civilization of Ancient Egypt*, p. 159.

29. Utterance 269, #377.

30. Utterance 304, #470.

31. Utterance 25, #17. The title "Osiris Unas" indicates that Unas is with Osiris, the god of the underworld. The Eye of Horus is a symbol of rejuvenation.

32. Utterance 36, #28.

## Chapter Four

1. Henry Breasted, *The Dawn of Conscience* (New York: Charles Scribner's Sons, 1934), p. 350. Freud cites this point by Breasted in his *Moses and Monotheism*, trans. Katherine Jones (New York: Vintage Books, 1939), p. 5.

2. Freud, *Moses and Monotheism*, p. 4.

3. The setting for the baby in a basket story was probably Thebes, home of the pharaohs. There are no crocodiles in that area today, but in earlier times, they thrived throughout the length of the Nile. Today, they are common in Sudan, on the southern border of Egypt, and parts farther south.

4. Jan Assmann, *Moses the Egyptian* (Cambridge, MA: Harvard University Press, 1997), p. 12.

5. Freud, *Moses and Monotheism*, pp. 17–18.

6. Freud, *Moses and Monotheism*, p. 32, n. 1.

7. Assmann, *Moses the Egyptian*, pp. 30–34.

8. Assmann, *Moses the Egyptian*, pp. 37–38.

9. Assmann, *Moses the Egyptian*, pp. 38–39.

10. So wrote Flavius Josephus (37–100 CE), Roman Jewish historian, in *Antiquities of the Jews*, 2.10.

11. Freud, *Moses and Monotheism*, p. 27.

12. Exodus 3:15.

13. Here and elsewhere, by "rational" I mean standing in relation to other things. A ratio, in mathematics, such as 2:4 as 3:6, is a relation between two numbers. Thus, something is irrational if it bears no such relations to anything else.

14. Freud, *Moses and Monotheism*, p. 22.

15. Arthur E. P. Weigall, *The Life and Times of Akhnaton* (London: Thornton-Butterworth, 1922), p. 121.

16. Freud makes a major point of this. *Moses and Monotheism*, pp. 29–31. The Bible asserts that Abraham was circumcised as a sign of the bond between him and his descendants. But this makes no sense because, as Freud points out (p. 54), circumcision was common throughout Egypt, which was the largest nation in the region with a population that ran in the millions.

17. Freud cites this passage as possible evidence that Moses spoke another language, namely Egyptian. *Moses and Monotheism*, pp. 37–38. Of course, as Freud admits, the passage may mean that Moses had a speech impediment.

18. Richard Friedman credits Scott Noegel with having noticed this connection. But the resemblance is so obvious that hundreds of people before him must have noticed it.

19. As Richard Friedman notes, "Its size, shape, proportions, surrounding courtyard, golden winged accoutrements, Eastern orientation, and arrangements of outer and inner rooms are a match." *The Exodus* (New York: HarperOne, 2017), p. 54. Friedman credits Michael Homan with making this connection: *To Your Tents, O Israel!* (Leiden: Brill, 2002), pp. 111–15.

20. Finkelstein and Silberman observe that scholars have argued that if a historical Exodus did take place, "it must have occurred in the late thirteenth century BCE." Israel Finkelstein and Neil Asher Silberman, *The Bible Unearthed* (New

York: Simon and Schuster, 2001), p. 57. William G. Dever asserts, "The specific time for the Exodus is now confirmed as the middle to late 13th century B.C., not the 15th century B.C. as formerly thought." *Who Were the Early Israelites and Where Did They Come From?* (Grand Rapids, MI: Eerdmans, 2003), p. 8. In saying this, of course, Dever hypothetically assumes that there *was* an Exodus.

21. Assmann, *Moses the Egyptian*, p. 25.

22. Assmann, *Moses the Egyptian*, p. 25.

23. Joseph Blenkinsopp, "The Midianite-Kenite Hypothesis Revisited and the Origins of Judah," *Journal for the Study of the Old Testament* 33.2 (2008), pp. 139–40. See also James S. Anderson, *Monotheism and Yahweh's Appropriation of Baal* (New York: Bloomsbury, 2015), p. 100.

24. Blenkinsopp, "The Midianite-Kenite Hypothesis Revisited and the Origins of Judah," p. 148.

25. Freud, *Moses and Monotheism*, pp. 42–43, 57. There is a rumor to the effect that Sellin later retracted his arguments supporting the claim that Moses was murdered by his own people, but the rumor is arguably false. See the three-part blog by Bruce Miller in the online publication *Contradicciones*, November 4–6, 2009. Freud was attracted to Sellin's argument because, among other things, it agreed with his own psychoanalytic theory about the murder of the primal father.

26. Freud, *Moses and Monotheism*, pp. 57–58.

27. The followers of Moses were supposedly Levites. Friedman cites five biblical sources that support this view. Richard Elliott Friedman, *The Exodus* (New York: HarperCollins, 2017), pp. 72–74. "You do not mess with the Levites. If you do, you find a horse head in your bed" (p. 74).

28. See Dever, *Who Were the Early Israelites and Where Did They Come From?*, pp. 18–19.

29. Pottery is easily broken and the shards tossed out. Also, children's toys were common in ancient Egypt, so they were probably also common in the ancient Jewish community. See Lionel Casson, *Everyday Life in Ancient Egypt* (Baltimore: Johns Hopkins University Press, 2001), p. 18. Children's toys tend to get lost on trips.

30. Friedman, *The Exodus*, p. 17.

31. Finkelstein and Silberman, *The Bible Unearthed*, p. 60.

32. Finkelstein and Silberman, *The Bible Unearthed*, pp. 52–53.

33. Friedman, *The Exodus*, p. 32.

34. Jan Assmann, *The Price of Monotheism*, trans. Robert Savage (Stanford, CA: Stanford University Press, 2010), p. 62.

35. Assmann, *Moses the Egyptian*, p. 35.

36. Assmann, *Moses the Egyptian*, p. 37.

37. Assmann, *Moses the Egyptian*, p. 35.

38. Assmann, *Moses the Egyptian*, p. 44.

39. Dever, *Who Were the Early Israelites and Where Did They Come From?*, p. 28.

40. Dever, *Who Were the Early Israelites and Where Did They Come From?*, pp. 31–32.

41. Finkelstein and Silberman, *The Bible Unearthed*, p. 77.

42. Friedman, *The Exodus*, p. 80.

43. Finkelstein and Silberman, *The Bible Unearthed*, pp. 79–87.

44. Friedman, *The Exodus*, pp. 74–78.

45. Friedman, *The Exodus*, p. 74; Numbers 18:21–24; Deuteronomy 14:28f. This, incidentally, was the same percentage paid the Egyptian priests.

46. Friedman reports that after the Levites arrived in Israel, they collected 10 percent of the produce "in their role as the priests of Israel." Friedman, *The Exodus*, p. 74.

47. Finkelstein and Silberman, *The Bible Unearthed*, pp. 142, 149–50, 155, 158.

48. Finkelstein and Silberman, *The Bible Unearthed*, p. 143. "Until the eighth century the population of the Judahite highlands was about one-tenth that of the highlands of the northern kingdom of Israel," p. 238.

49. Finkelstein and Silberman, *The Bible Unearthed*, pp. 157–59.

50. Finkelstein and Silberman, *The Bible Unearthed*, p. 142.

51. Finkelstein and Silberman, *The Bible Unearthed*, p. 159.

52. "The idolatry of the people of Judah was not a departure from their earlier monotheism. It was instead the way the people of Judah had worshipped for hundreds of years." Finkelstein and Silberman, *The Bible Unearthed*, p. 234.

53. Finkelstein and Silberman, *The Bible Unearthed*, p. 242.

54. The goddess was common to the people of both Israel and Judah, and it was represented by a naked figurine of a fertility goddess. Hundreds of these figurines have been found by archaeologists. See Finkelstein and Silberman, *The Bible Unearthed*, p. 242.

55. See Friedman, *The Exodus*, p. 190.

56. The archaeologist Zev Meshel found inscriptions in the 1970s that refer to "Yahweh of Samaria and his Asherah." Samaria was the capital of the territory of Israel. See William Dever, *Did God Have a Wife? Archaeology and Folk Religion in Ancient Israel* (Grand Rapids, MI: Eerdmans, 2005), 162–63.

57. 1 Kings 18:19 makes reference to the 400 prophets of the Asherah. In Jeremiah 7:18, the people are criticized for worshipping the "Queen of the Heavens." Also, in Jeremiah 44:16–18, the people reply that bad things happen when they fail in their worship of the Queen of Heaven.

58. The phrase is attributed to the historian Morton Smith. See Finkelstein and Silberman, *The Bible Unearthed*, p. 248.

59. Finkelstein and Silberman, *The Bible Unearthed*, pp. 247–48.

60. See Finkelstein and Silberman, *The Bible Unearthed*, p. 247.

61. This description is taken from Finkelstein and Silberman, *The Bible Unearthed*, pp. 261–62. Archaeology has validated the basic details of this description.

62. See Friedman's observations on this likelihood. Richard Elliott Friedman, *Who Wrote the Bible?* (New York: HarperCollins, 1987), pp. 96–97.

63. Friedman, *Who Wrote the Bible?*, p. 97.

64. This report is confirmed by the Babylonian chronicle. See Finkelstein and Silberman, *The Bible Unearthed*, p. 293.

65. Finkelstein and Silberman, *The Bible Unearthed*, p. 293.

66. In *Moses the Egyptian*, Assmann makes many similar observations about the effects of monotheism. He introduces the term "Mosaic distinction" to refer to the barrier that was raised up in the minds of the Jews by the shift to a monotheistic theology. In my view, this term reflects a less-than-perfect choice of words, and I would suggest "monotheistic demarcation" as a replacement. When Moses is considered as a figure of memory as opposed to a figure of history, he is more a product of monotheism than he is the cause of it. Also, the relatively weak term "distinction" fails to convey the idea of a barrier, as does the term "demarcation."

67. Maurice Halbwachs, *On Collective Memory*, trans. Lewis Coser (Chicago: University of Chicago Press, 1992), p. 40.

68. See Friedman, *Who Wrote the Bible?*, pp. 86–87. Friedman dates the so-called E text to between 922 and 722. Finkelstein and Silberman think that the new archaeological evidence supports the view that "the historical core of the Pentateuch and the Deuteronomistic History was substantially shaped in the seventh century B.C.E." *The Bible Unearthed*, p. 14.

69. The list of names that follows is taken from Friedman, *Who Wrote the Bible?*, pp. 18–21.

70. See Finkelstein and Silberman, *The Bible Unearthed*, p. 33.

71. Quoted from Finkelstein and Silberman, *The Bible Unearthed*, p. 34.

72. Thomas L. Thompson, *The Mythic Past: Biblical Archeology and the Myth of Israel* (London: Basic Books, 1999), p. xv.

73. Dever, *What Did the Bible Writers Know and When Did They Know It?*, p. 98.

74. Friedman, *The Exodus*, pp. 109–12.

75. Friedman reiterates both of these stories. *The Exodus*, pp. 72–73.

76. Friedman, *The Exodus*, p. 149.

77. Friedman, *Who Wrote the Bible?*, p. 118.

78. Friedman, *Who Wrote the Bible?*, pp. 91–92.

## Chapter Five

1. James D. G. Dunn, *Jesus Remembered* (Grand Rapids, MI: Eerdmans, 2003), p. 142. As an aside, I note that even though this study is about Jesus remembered, the author has practically nothing on the operation of memory.

2. E. P. Sanders, *The Historical Figure of Jesus* (New York: Penguin Books, 1993), p. 64. For the reasoning behind this conclusion, see E. P. Sanders and Margaret Davies, *Studying the Synoptic Gospels* (London: SCM Press, 1989), pp. 7–15, 21–24.

3. See Bart D. Ehrman, *How Jesus Became God* (New York: HarperCollins, 2014), pp. 90–91.

4. Sanders, *The Historical Figure of Jesus*, p. 66.

5. This pericope along with many others is analyzed by Sanders and Davies, *Studying the Synoptic Gospels*, pp. 58–60.

6. Karl Ludwig Schmidt, *Der Rahmen der Geschichte Jesu, Litterarkritsche Untersuschungen zur ältesten Jesus überlieferung* (Berlin, 1919).

7. Sanders and Davies give a more complete definition in *Studying the Synoptic Gospels*, p. 91.

8. E. P. Sanders and Margaret Davies, *Studying the Synoptic Gospels* (Philadelphia: Trinity Press International, 1989), pp. 67, 112–19. In this book, Sanders, with the collaboration of his wife, addresses the "synoptic problem": explaining how the synoptic Gospels (Matthew, Mark, and Luke) can be so similar in many ways but differ in others.

9. Sanders, *The Historical Figure of Jesus*, pp. 69, 73, 76.

10. Bart Ehrman makes the same point in his *Jesus before the Gospels* (New York: HarperOne, 2016). Unfortunately, this book did not come to my attention until after I had finished this chapter on memories of Jesus. Remarkably, many of the same topics covered in his book are also covered in this chapter.

11. This fact and the quoted passages that follow were taken from Maria Paul, "How Your Memory Rewrites the Past," February 4, 2014 (https://www.north western.edu). Reports of the original research appeared in the *Journal of Neuroscience* 32.35 (2012), pp. 12144–51 and 34.6 (2014), pp. 2203–13.

12. Daniel L. Schacter, *The Seven Sins of Memory* (New York: Mariner Books, 2001), p. 112.

13. Elizabeth F. Loftus, *Eyewitness Testimony* (Cambridge, MA: Harvard University Press, 1979), pp. 61–62.

14. Loftus, *Eyewitness Testimony*, pp. 85–86.

15. Loftus, *Eyewitness Testimony*, pp. 79–80.

16. Schacter, *The Seven Sins of Memory*, pp. 151–52.

17. Loftus, *Eyewitness Testimony*, pp. 86–87.

18. Yael Zerubavel, *Recovered Roots* (Chicago: University of Chicago Press, 1995), pp. 60–76.

19. Constructing this siege ramp was not as difficult or time consuming as it might seem because it was built on top of a natural spur extending from the top of the plateau, so all the Romans had to do was fill in cavities and smooth it out.

20. The chief exponent of this interpretation of Masada is Nachman Ben-Yehuda, professor of sociology and anthropology at the Hebrew University, Jerusalem. See his *The Masada Myth: Collective Memory and Mythmaking in Israel* (Madison: University of Wisconsin Press, 1995); see also his *Sacrificing Truth: Archeology and the Myth of Masada* (Amherst, NY: Humanity Books, 2002). For a shorter account, see "The Masada Myth," http://www.bibleinterp.com/articles /ben-yehuda_masada.shtml. See also Eric H. Cline, *Three Stones Make a Wall: The Story of Archaeology* (Princeton, NJ: Princeton University Press, 2017), chapter 15.

21. Most of this material relating to Lincoln is taken from Barry Schwartz, "The Reconstruction of Abraham Lincoln," in *Collective Remembering*, ed. David Middleton and Derek Edwards (Newbury Park, CA: Sage, 1990), pp. 81–107.

22. Dominic Crossan, *Jesus: A Revolutionary Biography* (San Francisco: HarperOne, 1994), pp. 139–43.

23. Ehrman, *How Jesus Became God*, pp. 156–64. See also Crossan, *Jesus*, pp. 139–43.

24. Toward the end of the first century CE, it became necessary for Christianity to pull itself away from Judaism. This goal was accomplished in part by blaming the Jews for the death of Jesus, and this in turn required that blame be lifted from the shoulders of Pilate. Hence, in the Gospels, Pilate is made to appear ever and ever more innocent. But these accounts mischaracterize the man.

25. See Crossan, *Jesus*, pp. 172–78.

26. Ehrman, *How Jesus Became God*, 159–60.

27. I note that Sanders holds that the term "Son of God," in a Jewish context, does not mean more than human. Since all Jews were considered to be sons of God, when Jesus is spoken of as Son of God, this means that in that respect, he is no different from any other Jew. *The Historical Figure of Jesus*, p. 161. I hold for a different view: when Jesus is said to be Son of God, he is indeed taken to be more than any other Jew and more than any other human.

28. Such as "I and the Father are one" (John 10:30), "Truly I tell you, before Abraham was, I am" (John 8:58), and "The one who has seen me has seen the Father" (John 14:9).

29. Ehrman, *How Jesus Became God*, pp. 124–28.

30. See John (8:58) and John (10:31–33).

31. Sanders, *The Historical Figure of Jesus*, pp. 241–42.

32. Crossan suggests as much. Crossan, *Jesus*, pp. 145–46.

33. Sanders shows definitively that Luke's birth narrative cannot possibly be true. *The Historical Figure of Jesus*, p. 86. The likely conclusion is that the narrative is a complete invention. But a belief's being true is not a condition of its functioning as a component in collective memory.

34. Sanders, *The Historical Figure of Jesus*, pp. 163–64.

# Chapter Six

1. See Alon Goshen-Gottstein, "God the Father in Rabbinic Judaism and Christianity: Transformed Background or Common Ground?," Elijah Interfaith Institute, 2001. "For Judaism, both ancient and later, 'Father' never ceases to be a metaphor," p. 22.

2. Gilles Quispel, *Gnostica, Judaica, Catholica: Collected Essays of Gilles Quispel*, ed. Johannes van Oort (Leiden: Brill, 2008), p. 71.

3. See John Dillon, *The Middle Platonists*, rev. ed. (Ithaca, NY: Cornell University Press, 1977, 1996), p. 128. Eudorus was heavily influenced not only by Plato but also by Aristotle. For Aristotle, the highest metaphysical principle was the Prime Mover, which was pure Mind. Interpreting the Forms as ideas in the mind of God amounts to combining the central concepts of Plato and Aristotle.

4. Birger Pearson, *Gnosticism, Judaism, and Egyptian Christianity* (Minneapolis: Fortress Press, 1990), p. 28.

5. Quispel, *Gnostica, Judaica, Catholica*, pp. 37–38.

6. *Jewish Encyclopedia*, pp. 6–7. The authors continue, quoting Adolph von Harnack: "There is no doubt that a Jewish gnosticism existed before a Christian or Judeo-Christian Gnosticism. As may be seen even in the apocalypses, since the second century B.C. gnostic thought was bound up with Judaism." Adolph von Harnack, *Geschichte der Altchristlichen Litteratur* (Leipzig: J. C. Hinrichs, 1904), p. 144.

7. Quispel, *Gnostica, Judaica, Catholica*, pp. 40, 156.

8. Quispel, *Gnostica, Judaica, Catholica*, p. 40.

9. Quispel, *Gnostica, Judaica, Catholica*, p. 40.

10. Quispel, *Gnostica, Judaica, Catholica*, p. 40.

11. Quispel, *Gnostica, Judaica, Catholica*, p. 160.

12. Tertullian, *Against Marcion*, 3–5.

13. So says Clement of Alexandria. See Elaine Pagels, *The Gnostic Paul* (Harrisburg, PA: Trinity Press International, 1975), p. 2, n. 7.

14. Pagels, *The Gnostic Paul*.

15. It is true that in Romans (1:25), Paul refers to the Creator. He warns against worshipping the creation in place of the creator. In commenting on this

"mysterious passage," Pagels argues that "creation" refers to the Demiurge; Paul is warning against worshipping the Demiurge, which is the "creation" of the higher powers. Pagels, *The Gnostic Paul*, 16. The verse in no way implies that God the Father is identical to the Demiurge, who created the world.

16. See the reference to the work of Hans Bietenhard by C. R. A. Morray-Jones in "Paradise Revisited (2 Cor 12:1–12): The Jewish Mystical Background of Paul's Apostolate; Part 2: Paul's Heavenly Ascent and Its Significance," *Harvard Theological Review* 86.3 (1993), p. 278.

17. Paula R. Gooder, *Only the Third Heaven?* (New York: T & T Clark, 1906), pp. 195–211.

18. Morray-Jones, "Paradise Revisited (2 Cor 12:1–12)," pp. 277–78.

19. Plato, *Timaeus*, 53c–56c.

20. See Dillon, *The Middle Platonists*, pp. 129–30. The line of reasoning leading to the denial of the aether is mine, but I have every reason to think it correct.

21. Dillon, *The Middle Platonists*, pp. 172–73.

22. Gershom Schollem, *Jewish Gnosticism, Merkabah Mysticism, and Talmudic Tradition* (New York: Jewish Theological Seminary of America, 1960), p. 17.

23. This idea of a channel linking the human mind with the divine mind is captured in Augustine's theory of divine illumination. Augustine (354–430 CE) was heavily influenced by Paul.

24. Bart D. Ehrman, *How Jesus Became God* (New York: HarperCollins, 2015), pp. 137–42.

25. Bart Ehrman notes that many scholars think this passage was originally part of an early creed. If so, this might imply that Paul was not the source of the idea that Jesus is the Son of God but that the idea was already widespread in the Christian community. However, in the passage cited earlier from 1 Corinthians (15:3–4), which is also thought to be taken from a creed, there is no mention of Jesus being the Son of God. How should we resolve the inconsistency? Perhaps Paul himself is responsible for the "Son of God" language in the Romans passage, or perhaps the alleged creed in the Romans passage was a later development that reflected Paul's prior influence. Ehrman, *How Jesus Became God*, pp. 218–25.

26. Ehrman gives a good review of these traditions in his *How Jesus Became God*, pp. 11–34.

27. E. P. Sanders, *Paul: A Very Short Introduction* (Oxford: Oxford University Press, 2001), p. 9.

28. Galatians 1:13, 1 Corinthians 15:9, Philippians 3:6.

29. Sanders, *Paul*, p. 10.

30. According to Acts, the Jewish high priest had given Paul license to persecute the Christians. But this story may be apocryphal because the high priest was a Sadducee, Paul was a Pharisee, and the Sadducees and the Pharisees had

little time for each other. Nevertheless, Paul may have had some contact with Jewish priests.

31. In the life to come, the Apostles would sit on twelve thrones judging the twelve tribes of Israel (Matthew 19:28; see also Luke 22:30).

32. When the apostles selected a replacement for Judas, who allegedly committed suicide, they used as a criterion the requirement that the candidate had lived and worked with Jesus (Acts 1:21–26).

33. See Frederick Mansfield Hodges, "The Ideal Prepuce in Ancient Greece and Rome: Male Genital Aesthetics and Their Relation to Lipodermos, Circumcision, Foreskin Restoration, and the Kynodesme," *Bulletin of the History of Medicine* 75.3 (2001), pp. 375–405.

34. The likely answer is that Plato's theory of the afterlife was almost never discussed by the Middle Platonists, so Paul would have had no access to it. See Dillon, *The Middle Platonists*, pp. 96–101. The author discusses the immortality of the soul in connection with Antiochus of Ascalon.

35. After recalling the story in 1 Corinthians 15, where Paul speaks of the resurrection, Ehrman argues that Paul's understanding of post-resurrection existence was very much corporeal while at the same time freed of the deficiencies of ordinary life on earth. Ehrman, *How Jesus Became God*, pp. 176–78.

36. James D. Tabor, *Paul and Jesus* (New York: Simon and Schuster, 2013), pp. 106–7; Albert Schweitzer, *The Mysticism of Paul the Apostle*, trans. William Montgomery (London: A. & C. Black, 1931), pp. 136–37.

## Chapter Seven

1. Tertullian, writing in 200–206 CE, says, "Repeated sickness must have repeated medicine" (*On Penance* 7). He distinguishes two kinds of penance, one as a preparation for baptism, the other to obtain forgiveness of certain grievous sins committed after baptism. Also, see the article on the Sacrament of Penance in the *Catholic Encyclopedia*.

2. This entire course of reasoning is developed by Plato, *Parmenides*, 137c–142b.

3. Tertullian, *De praescriptione haereticorum*, 41. Quoted from Elaine Pagels, *The Gnostic Gospels* (New York: Vintage Books, 1989), pp. 42–43.

4. Heracleon, Fragment 39, in Origen, *Commentarium in Johannes*. Quoted from Pagels, *The Gnostic Gospels*, p. 20.

5. Irenaeus, *Adversus haereses*, 1.14.3. Quoted from Pagels, *The Gnostic Gospels*, p. 20.

6. Pagels, *The Gnostic Gospels*, p. xx.

7. Irenaeus, *Adversus haereses*, 1.13.6. Quoted from Pagels, *The Gnostic Gospels*, p. 21.

8. "The Father must always be a father. He is always father of a Son who is present, on account of whom he is called Father. Only if the Son is always present with him is he always a completed Father, lacking in nothing good. He could not, therefore beget his only Son in time, or in any interval of time." Alexander's Letter to Alexander of Constantinople, 26.

9. Arius, Confession of Faith, 2. See also Arius, Letter to Eusebius of Nicomedia, 4.

10. Perhaps, to extricate himself from this difficulty, Arius claims that the Son was "begotten apart from time." Confession, 4. The father "begat an only-begotten Son before time and the ages." Confession, 2. The Son "was created at the will of God, before time and before the ages." Confession, 3. These statements seem to imply that time began at the instant that the Son was begotten. Yet, Arius says, "Before he [the Son] was begotten, or created, or defined, or established, he did not exist." Letter to Eusebius, 5. Also, "but the Son, begotten apart from time by the Father, and created and founded before the ages, was not in existence before his generation." Confession, 4. But if the act of begetting marks the beginning of time, then there is no "before" when the Son is said not to exist. Arius cannot have it both ways.

11. Alexander's Letter to Alexander of Constantinople, 20.

12. Alexander's Letter to Alexander of Constantinople, 29.

13. The Church historian Eusebius of Caesarea, who was an eyewitness, wrote a detailed description of the emperor's entry into the chamber. *The Life of Constantine*, 3.10, in *A Select Library of Nicene and Post Nicene Fathers of the Christian Church*, ed. P. Schaff and H. Wace (New York, 1890), Series 2, Volume 1, pp. 471–559.

14. If Constantine did not actually introduce the term, the historian Eusibius says in a letter that he supported its use. The letter is quoted by Athanasius, *De Decritis*, 33.17. Taking everything into account, it seems highly plausible that Constantine did indeed introduce the term.

15. Regarding the *ousia* language: "we have thought proper to reject it, as it is not contained even in the sacred writings; and that no mention of it should be made in the future, inasmuch as the holy Scriptures have nowhere mentioned the substance of the Father and of the Son. Nor ought the 'subsistence' of the Father, and of the Son, and of the Holy Spirit, to be even named. But we affirm that the Son is similar to the Father, in such a manner as the sacred Scriptures declare and teach." Creed of Constantinople of 359, Zenos's translated edition of Socrates Scholasticus, *Church History*, Book 2, Chapter 41.

16. This use of the term "hypostasis" occurs mainly in the fifth Enead.

17. Basil of Caesarea, Letter 214.4, taken from "Arianism, Macedonianism, Apollinarianisn and the Cappadocian Fathers" by Marianne Dorman, http://mariannedorman.homestead.com/cappadocianFathers.html. A slightly different translation can be found in the *New Advent Encyclopedia*, https://www.new advent.org/fathers/3202214.htm.

18. Augustine, *The Trinity*, trans. Edmund Hill (Hyde Park, NY: New City Press, 1991), 15.50, final paragraph, p. 435. In support of the belief that we will fully understand the Trinity in the next life, Augustine often cites the words of the apostle Paul in 1 Corinthians 13:12: "We see now through a mirror in an enigma, but then it will be face to face." The word "then" means in the next life, and "face to face" refers to the vision we will have of the triune God. *The Trinity*, 15.14, p. 405, first paragraph. See also 15.44–45 and 14.23; also 9.1: "the certitude of knowledge will not be completed until after this life when we see *face to face*" (1 Corinthians 13:12).

19. Augustine, *The Trinity*, 15.50, p. 434. See Tuggy, *Stanford Encyclopedia of Philosophy*, article on the Trinity, https://plato.stanford.edu/entries/trinity.

20. Thomas Aquinas, *Summa Theologiae*, First Part, Question 32, Article 1, "I answer that."

## Chapter Eight

1. Plato, *Sophist*, 247e.
2. Friedrich Nietzsche, *The Antichrist*, trans. Walter Kaufmann, in *The Portable Nietzsche* (New York: Penguin Books, 1954), p. 570.
3. Friedrich Nietzsche, *Beyond Good and Evil*, trans. Walter Kaufmann (New York: Vintage Books, 1966), p. 203.
4. Nietzsche, *The Antichrist*, p. 572.
5. Friedrich Nietzsche, *On the Genealogy of Morals*, trans. Walter Kaufmann (New York: Vintage Books, 1989), pp. 36–37.
6. Nietzsche, *On the Genealogy of Morals*, p. 121.
7. Nietzsche, *On the Genealogy of Morals*, pp. 125–26.
8. Nietzsche, *The Antichrist*, p. 617.
9. Nietzsche, *The Antichrist*, pp. 617–18.
10. "Truth, Power, Self: An Interview with Michel Foucault," in *Technologies of the Self*, ed. Luther H. Martin et al. (Amherst: University of Massachusetts Press, 1988), p. 13.
11. "The Subject and Power," in *Michel Foucault: Power*, ed. James D. Faubion (New York: New Press, 1994), p. 341.
12. Thomas Aquinas, *Summa Theologiae*, First Part, Question 57, Article 4.

13. The angels are called "kiraman katibin." See the Quran, 50:16–18 and 82:10–12.

## Chapter Nine

1. James Strachey, trans., *The Future of an Illusion* (New York: Norton, 1961), p. 39.

2. See "The Uncanny," in *The Standard Edition of the Complete Psychological Works of Sigmund Freud*, trans. James Strachey (London: Hogarth Press, 1953–1974), vol. 17, pp. 219–53.

3. Brian Clack has explored this idea in "'At Home in the Uncanny': Freud's Account of *das Unheimliche* in the Context of His Theory of Religious Belief," *Religion* 38.3 (2008), pp. 250–58.

4. G. B. Hill and L. F. Powell, eds., *Boswell's Life of Johnson*, 6 vols. (Oxford: Oxford University Press, 1935), vol. 1., p. 471. See also vol. 3, p. 165, and vol. 4, p. 27.

5. See Stephen Prothero, *God Is Not One* (New York: HarperCollins, 2010).

6. A good description of this festival is given by classics scholar Lionel Casson, *Everyday Life in Ancient Egypt* (Baltimore: Johns Hopkins University Press, 2001), pp. 97–99.

7. This account of the Crusades follows Thomas Asbridge, *The First Crusade: A New History* (New York: Oxford University Press, 2004).

8. Asbridge notes that this incongruous final act of devotion almost certainly occurred because all of the eyewitness Latin accounts refer to it. *The First Crusade*, pp. 318–19.

9. The true picture of the Spanish Inquisition has been distorted throughout the years by English propaganda. England became the mortal enemy of Spain at the time of the invasion by the Spanish Armada in 1588. Henry Kamen has tried to set the record straight in *The Spanish Inquisition: A Historical Revision*, 4th ed. (New Haven, CT: Yale University Press, 2014). Kamen's work is widely respected, and the account given here is taken from his work.

10. This account follows Thomas Kaufmann's *Luther's Jews: A Journey into Anti-Semitism* (Oxford: Oxford University Press, 2017).

11. This account of the popes and slavery is taken from Pius Onyemechi Adiele, *The Popes, the Catholic Church and the Transatlantic Enslavement of Black Africans 1418–1893* (New York: Georg Olms Verlag, 2017), pp. 289–365. This 600-page study, written by a Catholic priest, was accepted by the faculty of the University of Tübingen as the author's doctoral dissertation. Adiele refutes Joel Panzer's argument that the Church has always condemned slavery by noting that

the kind of slavery condemned by the Church was the enslavement of Christians by other Christians but not the enslavement of pagan Black Africans (pp. 366–70).

12. Paul Fregosi, *Jihad in the West: Muslim Conquests from the 7th to the 21st Centuries* (Amherst, NY: Prometheus Books, 1998), p. 20.

13. This story about Kinana is taken from Fregosi, *Jihad in the West*, p. 46.

14. For details relating to the Battle of Bosnia, see Fregosi, *Jihad in the West*, pp. 224–30.

15. This account of the siege of Constantinople is taken from Fregosi, *Jihad in the West*, pp. 248–59.

16. W. K. Clifford, *The Ethics of Belief and Other Essays* (Amherst, NY: Prometheus Books, 1999), p. 77. "The Ethics of Belief" was first published in 1877 in the *Contemporary Review*.

## Epilogue

1. Pew Research Center, "Are Religious People Happier, Healthier? Our New Global Study Explores This Question," *FactTank: News in the Numbers*, https://www.pewresearch.org/fact-tank/2019/01/31/are-religious-people-happier-healthier-our-new-global-study-explores-this-question, January 31, 2019.

2. *Nichomachean Ethics*, X, 6–7.

3. Karl Britton, "The Truth of Religious Propositions," *Analysis* 3.1/2 (October 1935), p. 24.

# INDEX

Aaron (brother of Moses), 120

Abraham, 80, 83, 119, 120–21

Abu Bakr, 309–10

Acts of the Apostles, 183–84, 221, 236

adopted versus "begotten" aspect of Jesus, 170–72, 203, 236–40, 243, 251–52, 339n10

afterlife: ancient Egyptian beliefs in, 42–50, 61, 67–68, 77, 87, 96, 102; bishops feeding into hope for, 254; heaven, 176–77, 194–98; Neolithic people's belief in, 32–35

*Against Heresies* (Irenaeus), 229, 230, 234

*Against Marcion* (Justin Martyr), 234

*Against the Valentinians* (Tertullian), 234

agnosticism, 15

Akhenaten: abolishing traditional Egyptian gods, 66–68, 87, 96, 102; Aten and, 19–20, 51, 66–71; competing with other pharaohs, 260; discovery of, 82–83; Moses and, 20, 82–86, 96–97, 102, 113;

as original leper, 113; Osarsiph as alter ego of, 96–97; resistance to, 68, 72, 82; textual evidence of, 82–83, 115–16. *See also* Amarna

Albright, William Foxwell, 100, 118, 119

Alexander (bishop), 238–42

Alexandria (Egypt), 21–22, 185–89, 190–92

Amarna, 67–71, 82, 96–97, 115–16

Amenophis III, 87, 96–97, 115–16

Amenophis IV, 66–71. *See also* Akhenaten

Amon, King, 108–9

Amorite migration, 119

Amun (god), 50, 66–67, 70, 299

anamnesis (recollection), 190

ancient agrarian societies. *See* fetish; Neolithic period

ancient Egypt: about, 41–42; belief in the afterlife, 42–50, 61, 67–68, 77, 87, 96, 102; Book of the Dead, 47–50, 61; burial customs, 34–35, 77; festivals, 298–300; illusions of, 60–61. *See also* Akhenaten; Aten

communication: Moses and God, 184; primacy of, 39; real versus with God, 289; with spirits, 27. *See also* fetish

competition, 259–61

con artists, 284, 285, 289–90

confabulation error, 139

Constantine, 240–45, 253, 255–56

Constantius II, 241, 246

Constantinople siege, 311–12

constructs: about, 9–13; fictive constructs, 13; illusions comparison, 13–14; personal constructs, 11; physical constructs, 9–10, 37–38; power and, 36–38, 178–79, 258–59; social constructs, 10, 36–37, 52, 53–55, 232–33; theoretical constructs, 12–13. *See also* belief constructs

continuity, principle of, 18

converts to Christianity, 234–35, 238

Copeland, Kenneth, 3

Copernicus, 322

Corinthians, 154, 174, 194, 199, 200, 222

*Corpus Hermeticum*, 192–93

corruption, 264

cosmic microwave background radiation, 323

councils, 240–42, 246–47, 253, 255. *See also* Nicene Creed

covenant of Hebrews, 101–2

crop production and ancient gods, 26, 28, 29–30, 36, 42, 327n13

Crossan, John Dominic, 156

crucifixion as terrorism, 156–58

Crusades, 303–5

cult statues, 55, 328n8

culture, 38–39, 60–61

cures. *See* fetish

Darwin, Charles. *See* natural selection

deacons, 222, 225–26, 232

death. *See* afterlife; Jesus' resurrection

death, fear of, 285–86

deism, 15

Demiurge: about, 189, 337n15; as inferior deity, 200–201, 243; Irenaeus on, 229; sin and, 224; Yahweh similar to, 190, 234

Demophilus, 246–47

de Rougé, Emmanuel, 63–64

Descartes, R., 288

determinatives, 71–72

Deuteronomy, 110–11, 122–23, 308–9

Dever, William, 120–21

*Dialogues of the Carmelites* (Poulenc), 285–86

Didache, 219

differential reproduction, 136–37

Diocletian, 242

divine intervention argument, 18

Docetism, 235

documents: Book of the Dead, 47–50; Coffin Texts, 47; funerary documents, 74–76; Gnostic texts burned by bishops, 228–30; as physical constructs, 9–10, 37; Pyramid Texts, 46–47, 76; Quran, 276, 292–93, 301; as reason for beliefs, 292–93. *See also* Bible

Donald Duck analogy, 104

Donation of Pepin, 256

Dunn, James D. G., 127

dynamic monarchianism, 237–38

Edict of Milan, 242, 255–56

Edict of Thessalonica, 255–56

Edom territory, 124

egalitarianism, 228–29, 236

control of people, 269–72; Council of Nicaea outcome as product of, 242; footrace comparison, 259–61; gods invented for, 107, 262; the good and the will to power, 262–69; illusions and, 259; intrinsic to human existence, 323–24; Jesus giving to apostles, 178–79, 217–22; knowledge produced from, 253–54, 272–73, 276–77; passions and, 258, 261–62; performative utterances as manifestations of, 231–33; sources of, 3–5; types of, 2–4, 258–59. *See also* constructs; power, philosophical theories of; priestly power

power, philosophical theories of: Foucault, 23, 269–77, 282; Hobbes, 23, 258–62, 282; as invitations, 282; Nietzsche, 23, 262–69, 282; Plato, 257–58; Whitehead, 23, 257–58, 278–82

prayer, 8, 31, 296

*Prayer of Thanksgiving*, 192

presbytery, 222, 225–26, 232

Price, Robert, 182

priestly power: becoming internalized, 275–76; connected to Yahweh, 125–26; controlling private lives, 32–35; converting Jesus into a God, 179–80; creating omnipotent God, 281–82; creating triune, 22; in crop production, 30–32, 34, 79, 322; flowing from people to gods, 273–77; as illusion, 285–86; as panopticon, 23; *ressentiment* and, 265–69; sin and, 314–15; in today's society, 322–23; Yahweh as construct of, 110–11. *See also*

bishops; Paul the apostle; priests; priests of ancient Egypt

priests: afterlife illusions coming from, 44–45; creating and sustaining gods, 69, 76–77, 79; defined, 30; dishonesty of, 32; as fetish makers, 19; inventing deities, 31–32, 34–35; misrepresentation of, 8–9; organizations growing up around, 37; religion coming into existence with, 17–18. *See also* Levites; Moses; priestly power; priests of ancient Egypt

priests of ancient Egypt: afterlife instructions from, 46–50; creating and sustaining gods, 53, 55, 57–61, 65–66, 69, 79, 328n5; "discovering" gods, 50–53; hierarchy of, 53–55; income, 49–50; physical appearance, 54–55; rituals performed by, 56–57. *See also* gods of ancient Egypt; priestly power

*Primitive Culture* (Tylor), 26

prince analogy, 283–84

principle of temporal continuity, 83

prison design, 272

private lives, control over, 32–35, 274–75, 276

problem of evil, 279

processions, 57

Progressive Era, 150–52

promoters of religion, 4–5. *See also* bishops; Paul the apostle; pharaohs; priests

propaganda, 124–26

prophesies, 236

Protestantism, 2, 12, 277

proto-Gnosticism (Jewish Gnosticism), 22, 190–92, 193–94, 198, 222